The Imperial Experience in Sub-Saharan
Africa since 1870

Europe and the World
in the Age of Expansion

edited by Boyd C. Shafer

THE
IMPERIAL
EXPERIENCE IN
SUB-SAHARAN
AFRICA
SINCE 1870

by

Henry S. Wilson

UNIVERSITY OF MINNESOTA PRESS □ MINNEAPOLIS

Copyright © 1977 by the University of Minnesota. All rights reserved.
Printed in the United States of America at
The North Central Publishing Company, St. Paul.
Published by the University of Minnesota Press, 2037 University
Avenue Southeast, Minneapolis, Minnesota 55455,
and published in Canada by Burns & MacEachern Limited,
Don Mills, Ontario

Library of Congress Catalog Card Number 76-9489

ISBN 0-8166-0854-7

Europe and the World
in the Age of Expansion

SPONSORS

Editor's Foreword

The expansion of Europe since the thirteenth century has had profound influences on peoples throughout the world. Encircling the globe, the expansion changed men's lives and goals and became one of the decisive movements in the history of mankind.

This series of ten volumes explores the nature and impact of the expansion. It attempts not so much to go over once more the familiar themes of "Gold, Glory, and the Gospel," as to describe, on the basis of new questions and interpretations, what appears to have happened insofar as modern historical scholarship can determine.

No work or works on so large a topic can include everything that happened or be definitive. This series, as it proceeds, emphasizes the discoveries, the explorations, and the territorial expansion of Europeans, the relationships between the colonized and the colonizers, the effects of the expansion on Asians, Africans, Americans, Indians, and the various "islanders," the emergence into nationhood and world history of many peoples that Europeans had known little or nothing about, and, to a lesser extent, the effects of the expansion on Europe.

The use of the word *discoveries*, of course, reveals European (and American) provincialism. The "new" lands were undiscovered only in the sense that they were unknown to Europeans. Peoples with developed cultures and civilizations already had long inhabited most of the huge areas to which Europeans sailed and over which they came to exercise their power and influence. Nevertheless, the political, economic, and social expansion that came with and after the discoveries affected the daily lives, the modes of producing and sharing, the ways of governing, the customs, and the values of peoples everywhere. Whatever their state of development, the expansion also brought, as is well known, tensions, conflicts, and much injustice. Perhaps most important in our own times, it led throughout the developing world to the rise of nationalism, to reform and revolt, and to demands (now largely realized) for national self-determination.

The early volumes in the series, naturally, stress the discoveries and explorations. The later emphasize the growing commercial and political involvements, the founding of new or different societies in the "new" worlds, the emergence of different varieties of nations and states in the often old and established societies of Asia, Africa, and the Americas, and the changes in the governmental structures and responsibilities of the European imperial nations.

The practices, ideas, and values the Europeans introduced continue, in differing ways and differing environments, not only to exist but to have consequences. But in the territorial sense the age of European expansion is over. Therefore the sponsors of this undertaking believe this is a propitious time to prepare and publish this multivolumed study. The era now appears in new perspective and new and more objective statements can be made about it. At the same time, its realities are still with us and we may now be able to understand intangibles that in the future could be overlooked.

The works in process, even though they number ten, cover only what the authors (and editors) consider to be important aspects of the expansion. Each of the authors had to confront vast masses of material and make choices in what he should include. Inevitably, subjects and details are omitted that some readers will think should have been covered. Inevitably, too, readers will note some duplication. This arises in large part because each author has been free, within the general themes of the series, to write his own book on the geographical area and chronological period allotted to him. Each author, as might be expected, has believed it necessary to give attention to the background of his topic and has also looked a bit ahead; hence he has touched upon the time periods of the immediately preceding and following volumes. This means that each of the studies can be read independently, without constant reference to the others. The books are being published as they are completed and will not appear in their originally planned order.

The authors have generally followed a pattern for spelling, capitalization, and other details of style set by the University of Minnesota Press in the interests of consistency and clarity. In accordance with the wishes of the Press and current usage, and after prolonged discussion, we have used the word *black* instead of *Negro* (except in quotations). For the most part American usages in spelling have been observed. The last is sometimes difficult for historians who must be concerned with the different spellings, especially of place names and proper nouns, at different times and in different languages. To help readers the authors have, in consequence, at times added the original (or the present) spelling of a name when identification might otherwise be difficult.

The discussions that led to this series began in 1964 during meetings of the Advisory Committee of the James Ford Bell Library at the University of Minnesota, a library particularly interested in exploration and discovery. Members of the university's Department of History and the University of Minnesota Press, and others, including the present editor, joined in the discussions. Then, after the promise of generous subsidies from the Bell Foundation of Minneapolis and the Northwest Area Foundation (formerly the Hill Family Foundation) of St. Paul, the project began to take form under the editorship of the distinguished historian Herbert Heaton. An Advisory Council of six scholars was appointed as the work began. Professor Heaton, who had agreed to serve as editor for three years, did most of the early planning and selected three authors. Professor Boyd C. Shafer of Macalester College (now at the University of Arizona) succeeded him in 1967. He selected eight authors and did further planning. He has been in constant touch with all the authors, doing preliminary editing in consultation with them, reading their drafts, and making suggestions. The Press editors, as is usual at the University of Minnesota Press, have made valuable contributions at all stages. Between Professor Shafer and the authors—from England, Canada, New Zealand, and the United States—there have been voluminous and amicable as well as critical exchanges. But it must be repeated, each author has been free to write his own work within the general scope of the series.

Henry S. Wilson, the author of this book, volume VIII in the series, is a specialist in African history south of the Sahara. He did his undergraduate work at King's College, Newcastle upon Tyne (1946-1949), and his postgraduate work, after service in the Royal Air Force, at Oxford University (1951-1955). He has twice taught in Africa, has done extensive research on Africa in the United States, and has been a visiting fellow at Princeton and Howard universities. Since 1964 he has been in the History Department at the University of

York and, from 1973, in the interdisciplinary Centre of Southern African Studies there. In 1967 he was head of the History Department of the University of Botswana, Lesotho, and Swaziland. He has edited the volume *Origins of West African Nationalism* (1970), which made hitherto inaccessible documents available to students of that vast area.

In the present volume he wishes "to illustrate by exemplary case studies the various modes of the imperial experience in Africa south of the Sahara." What stands out, at this date, he believes, is "the differences between the colonies of settlement—the so-called white man's realm—and the rest."

Boyd C. Shafer

University of Arizona

Preface

This book seeks to analyze the relationships that developed between Europe and sub-Saharan Africa during the period of formal colonial rule. In order to set the imperial episode in historical sequence, the chronological span takes in both the prelude to the partition of Africa and the process of decolonization. The multiplicity of African societies and the variety of European colonizers, as well as the sweep of time, ensure that no such book could be comprehensive in its coverage and that it would be unreadable and superficial if it sought to be so. I have, therefore, selected a number of examples that seem particularly revealing and that, taken as a whole, seem to me to represent significant trends. Wherever possible, I have tried to use case studies, which illuminate the attitudes and assumptions of Africans and Europeans caught up in the imperial experience at specific places and given periods. The availability of such exemplary case studies is, of course, dependent on the insights and hard work of writers, many of whose monographs and articles I have used. Nevertheless, besides the writers whom I have gratefully acknowledged in my notes, many others have influenced my ideas over the two decades I have taught African history, although I have not made direct use of their work in this book. The supplementary bibliography provides the opportunity to acknowledge these intellectual debts.

I am more than glad to express my gratitude to the series editor, Boyd C. Shafer, whose experience and skill have been invaluable. I have learned much in discussion with students and colleagues at universities in Freetown, Sierra Leone; Roma, Lesotho; Aberystwyth, Wales; and, presently York, England, in the Department of History and in the Centre of Southern African Studies.

The librarians from several institutions provided indispensable help: the

University of York, especially the Inter-Library Loan Department; the Royal Commonwealth Society; the School of Oriental and African Studies; the Institute of Commonwealth Studies; and the British Library, all in London. I also thank Sandra Magrath for her careful editorial assistance on the behalf of the University of Minnesota Press. Finally, I am grateful for the unstinted help of my wife Ellen.

H. S. W.

University of York

Contents

List of Maps

The Imperial Experience in Sub-Saharan
Africa since 1870

CHAPTER 1

The Continent and Its Regions

History is grounded in geography and nowhere more so than in Africa. Yet, as geographers regularly remind us, their discipline is not conducive to rigid determinism. Man must come to terms with nature, but ever since the domestication of plants and animals this has been accomplished by asserting some degree of control. (And even hunters and gatherers — though hardly able to control their environments — did, by definition, possess the power to change them.) Moreover, a given environment can be modified or adapted to in a variety of ways.[1]

One of the most powerful symbols evoked by colonial propaganda turned on such ecological issues. The African, pejoratively categorized as the "lazy Negro," was pictured as only too well adjusted to a habitat whose tropical exuberance readily provided his food supply and posed minimal needs, by northern standards, in the way of clothing and shelter. With a plurality of wives completing this spectacle of sloth, near-nudity, and underutilized economic resources, the provocation to European intervention was intense. Improvement could only take place once this too easy equilibrium between man and nature had been disturbed. New appetites for overseas products must be introduced to lure Africans into the dynamic economic processes of the West. Should this prove ineffective, then external patterns of order and discipline — Christianity, political domination, taxes, forced labor — must take charge.

But how closely did the western vision of Africa correspond to the reality?[2]

The Continental Profile

Screened by the desert, sub-Saharan Africa had developed in relative isolation, devoid of any semblance of contact equivalent to that between Europe and Asia or to North Africa's double involvement in the Mediterranean and Islamic worlds. Such waves of migration, invasion, and cultural expansion as did eventually reach that area tended to have lost some of their primal force. Geographical protection from the ferocities of competition as experienced by European and Asian societies also meant lack of stimulus to improvements in production, weaponry, and political organization. Nor, for their part, did Africans launch themselves on the rest of the Old World as invaders, immigrants, and missionaries. When they did eventually emigrate, they went involuntarily to the New World, in chains, as slaves.

Other geographical factors reinforce the role of the Sahara in promoting African isolation. There are few natural harbors and some of these have notably unproductive hinterlands. Africa's coasts are the least indented of any continent's by rivers and estuaries, so that proportionately more territory is located far inland. And because the continent constitutes a vast plateau, Africa's rivers, although often navigable for long stretches inland, usually tumble over the edge toward the coastal plain and the sea, presenting incoming vessels with falls and rapids only a little way inland. The mouths and estuaries of some rivers, such as the Niger, are blocked by sandbars. Add to all this the fact that the prevailing winds made navigating the western littoral especially difficult in the days of sail, and the continent appears uniquely disfavored in terms of water-borne transport.

Africa's geographical location affects the pattern of rainfall with profound results for the continent's history and ecology.[3] The latitudes on either side of the equator are covered by a blanket of low-pressure air that rises from the hot land because of the almost vertical rays of the sun, thus establishing a region of heavy rainfall. Here is located the dense tropical rain forest of the Congo River basin and the Guinea coast of West Africa, able to sustain relatively high population densities. But this exuberant growth does not extend across the continent to East Africa, where highland areas combine with wind and sea conditions to limit precipitation and vegetation.

Precipitation decreases on either side of the equator so that the rain forest quickly gives way to the savannah grasslands, which cover a much greater area of the continent than does the so-called jungle. The effects of the progressive decrease in precipitation are only partly revealed by the figures for average rainfall, which cover wide variations in the amount and timing of the rains from year to year. Such erratic fluctuation occurs because of the unpredict-able behavior of the intertropical front, the line of contact between the hemi-spheric air masses meeting along the equatorial zone. No physical features, such as mountain ranges, control its cyclical drift as it moves north and south with the seasons. Hence, there is marked variation in quantity and timing of the rains year by year. Such violent oscillations are masked by figures of aver-age rainfall, but when it comes to the level of population that can be sus-tained, it is the lower limits, the worst years, that count for any given area.

Tropical soils suffer from a comparative shortage of humus, the vegetable mold formed by the slow decomposition of organic matter in the soil. Where-as in colder climates humus oxidation virtually stops in winter, in the tropics it proceeds more or less unabated throughout the year. Hence while the humus content of farming land in the United States is often 10 to 12 percent of total volume and can be more, tropical soils contain 1.8 percent or less.[4] Also, this land is subject to the violent leaching downpours of the tropics, washing away minerals and other nutrients and leaving the soil thin and sour.

Geography, the most interdisciplinary of disciplines, repays its debts by equipping Africanists with an almost reflex appreciation of the figures for minimal rainfall and humus content. Indeed, a strong ecological awareness constitutes the most obvious interdisciplinary bond in contemporary African studies. Such knowledge has been gained by the cumulative corrective pro-cesses of modern science. Without benefit of western science traditional Af-rican societies had also to come to terms with the facts of their environment, for every society has to behave in a sufficiently adaptive way to survive. An African farmer may not have understood the concept of ecological balance, but he was aware that growing his food crops among various forms of in-digenous flora protected his soil.

Pluming themselves on the regimented monoculture of their transatlantic plantations, as well as on the neat hedgerows and crop rotations of their own agricultural revolution, Europeans dismissed the visible results of the Afri-cans' horticultural pragmatism and condemned African societies for falling far short of the maximum exploitation of their continent. The amount of truth in this verdict varied from case to case, for, although the survival of any society depended on its behaving in a sufficiently businesslike way, the degree to which societies exhibited the optimum adaptation to their environment varied greatly. Such variety needs stressing in view of the tendency of many modern accounts to present a composite picture of "traditional African farm-ing," singling out the lack of the plow and harping on the "wastefulness" of shifting cultivation and slash-and-burn techniques. However, the authoritative postimperial geography of Morgan Pugh noted in West Africa alone seven different systems of cultivation that were in use at least from the sixteenth century: shifting cultivation, rotational bush fallow, rotational planted fallow, mixed farming, permanent cultivation, tree cultivation, and floodland and irrigated farming.[5]

But Europeans for most of our period made no such empirical judgment. Indeed, as hardly any of the work of observation and comparison had been done, how could they? Africa's western coastline has been explored by the fifteenth-century Portuguese navigators, but the easy availability of gold and slaves on the coast, together with the natural obstacles to the exploration of the interior, limited substantial European contact to the periphery till the second half of the nineteenth century. Europe's empirical information about Africa, a by-product of the slave trade, was detailed but specialized and confined to the coast. Thus the judgment on African agriculture represented a blanket indictment based on the complementary notions of tropical exuberance and the "lazy Negro."[6]

In fact, the idea of tropical exuberance was compounded of myth as well as science. The lush tropical foliage was no sure index of potential agricultural wealth, nor did rapid growth relieve the African cultivator of labor. Some tropical soils proved capable of very high yields, whereas others were much less fertile. But at the outset of Europe's colonization of Africa, optimism about agricultural prospects appeared grounded on solid scientific work. European notions of tropical fertility ultimately derived from the amazement of the first white travelers on encountering the spectacular growth of vegetation in the Caribbean and Brazil. Such exuberance was soon converted to profitable account by the plantations.

The eighteenth-century naturalist Henry Smeathman envisaged an equally advantageous relationship between man and nature in West Africa. His own career seemingly exemplified such a happy conjuncture. Arriving in the Banana Islands of Sierra Leone in 1771, he settled there for nearly four years, visiting the nearby Plantain Islands and the mainland and marrying into two West African ruling families. Smeathman built up the first substantial collection of West African plants and insects and interested himself in ethnography. He capitalized on his scientific research by creating his own rice farm and — being the son of a Scarborough distiller and brandy merchant and having traded briefly in wines and brandy in London — by processing brandy from the local grapes. On leaving West Africa, he spent four years in the West

Indies investigating large-scale tropical agriculture, as practiced by Europeans, at firsthand.[7]

Smeathman's own plan for large-scale tropical colonization aimed at countering New World slavery by creating a West African settlement that could emancipate and civilize some thousands of slaves yearly and so dry up the slave trade at its source. In essence his famous "Plan of a Settlement to be made Near Sierra Leone" of 1786 amounted to an ecstatic exposition on the theme of tropical exuberance. He reported that "the woods and plains produce spontaneously great quantities of the most pleasant fruits and spices, from which may be made oils, marmalades, wines, perfumes, and other valuable articles, to supply the markets of Great Britain and Ireland." And he continued in the same idyllic vein, describing the local agriculture in such a way that those less sympathetic to Africans could easily translate the account in terms of the "lazy Negro" myth: "Such are the mildness and fertility of the climate and country that a man possessed of a change of cloathing, a wood axe, a hoe, and a pocket knife, may soon place himself in an easy and comfortable situation. All the cloathing wanted is what decency requires; and it is not necessary to turn up the earth more than two or three inches, with a light hoe, in order to cultivate any kind of grain."[8]

Neither Smeathman's lyricism, so foreign to our contemporary notions of proper scientific exposition, nor the twentieth-century skepticism about tropical exuberance should obscure the point that there was nothing disreputable in his scientific credentials when he set forth his ideas. Eighteenth-century and nineteenth-century scientists embraced the theory of tropical exuberance not only because they wanted it to be true but also because it appeared reasonable to do so. The failure of schemes to introduce new African cash crops prompted a hunt for substitutes rather than a search for fresh theory; thus, half a century after Smeathman, the abolitionist Thomas Fowell Buxton evoked the same dream of tropical plenty, simply altering the promised commodities.[9]

Although the Swedish botanist Adam Afzelius, a pupil of Linnaeus, reported on Sierra Leone from 1792 to 1796, cumulative corrective scientific research did not begin till a century later. The Sierra Leone Agriculture Department was started in 1895, but continuity of scientific information dates from the opening of the research station at Njala in 1911. Since then data on humus and mineral deficiency have been built up there and at other research centers to explain the paradox of tropical exuberance based on infertile soil.

The spectacular tropical rain forests were in fact cruelly deceptive. The trees created their own microenvironment, binding the soil and holding it, providing a constant canopy of leaves to break the otherwise leaching force of the rain, and forming a shield against the fierce heat of the sun. Once this microenvironment was disrupted to harness the supposed fertility for cash crops, then the full force of rain and sun took its toll.[10] Such were the harsh environmental facts to which traditional African science was safely moored by the people's steadying need for subsistence. By contrast, the science of Smeathman and his successors was boldly generalizing, imaginative, and prone to error.

Outside the lush-growing tropical jungle the exuberance myth was irrelevant, and in South Africa a sizable number of Afrikaners did adapt to African agricultural realities. Not being explorers and connoisseurs of the exotic but settlers preoccupied with getting a living, the Afrikaners' approach was essentially pragmatic. The Dutch East India Company had intended that they would settle near the Cape and engage in the kind of intensive farming that would provide its ships with fresh meat and vegetables. Some did and exploited the Mediterranean-type environment in the immediate vicinity of the Cape, using ordinary European agricultural methods but incorporating the indigenous cattle. Many others preferred to try their luck on the vast but arid hinterland plateau. Here, free from the company's close mercantilist control, they were thrown on their own resources. But these resources now included knowledge and animals acquired through contact with the local Khoikhoi (known also as Khoi) population. And African expertise became an Afrikaner resource, quite literally, as contact became domination and the Khoi — or Hottentots, as they were familiarly and insultingly known — were reduced to the status of serf stockmen to the trekkers, or settlers.

By the end of the eighteenth century the Afrikaners had dispossessed the Khoi throughout the Karroo, the arid country to the north of the Cape. "But," states a South African geographer in a classic study of land utilization in the arid region, "the system of land use with which they supplanted that of the Hottentots was not entirely new; on the contrary, it was based not only on the livestock of their predecessors but also upon the experience, knowledge, and co-operation of the countless Hottentot herdsmen, shepherds, wagondrivers, and trainers of draught oxen who had entered the service of the Whites and without whose help the rapid expansion of the colony could not have taken place."[11] Adapting to the vast but arid spaces of the interior, the Afrikaners practiced a system of transhumance, or the seasonal moving of livestock to regions of different climate, and this was the ultimate in extensive land use and the very reverse of Dutch intensiveness.

Not that the Afrikaners were devoid of the white man's capacity for myth where Africa was concerned. Their central myth was race, blending into their religion through their favorite Old Testament texts. Calvinistic Afrikaners found confirmation of their special destiny to prevail over unelect pagans when the Khoi were so badly smitten by the white man's smallpox that the survivors' social system collapsed, and the remaining San — or Bushmen — fled to sanctuaries so barren and remote that pursuit was unprofitable. Outside South Africa mainstream European thought interpreted the Afrikaner triumph in more secular but no less racial terms. The Khoisan — the Khoikhoi and San classed together — peoples seemed yet another batch of aborigines about to follow so many American Indians and South Sea islanders into oblivion when confronted by a more "advanced" and "virile" race.

Only in tropical Africa was the seemingly worldwide phenomenon of vanishing aborigines contradicted. Here, despite the depredations of the slave trade, the aborigines appeared to flourish and especially so in Guinea, "the white man's grave." The Afrikaners had come upon the greatest single area of temperate territory in the most tropical of continents. But in tropical Africa white colonization seemingly contradicted the laws of nature so that "Africa for the Africans" appeared to be a strict biological truth.

The significance attached to the racial factor was crucial to the survival of the notion of tropical exuberance. Despite the failure of schemes to realize the potential of the supposed African eldorado, there was little feedback to promote constructive revision. Racial explanations of such failures, in terms of human inadequacy — the biological inadequacy of the Europeans to survive the tropical climate and diseases and the mental and moral inadequacy of the Africans and their seeming inability to function as responsible economic men — blocked the way to a critical examination of the exuberance myth.[12]

What was the basis for this notion of "Africa for the Africans" as a biological truth? Loss of life among the early European traders and missionaries to Africa was certainly heavy, especially in parts of West Africa, where sometimes as many as four out of five new arrivals were dead within a year of landing on the Guinea coast. The "acclimating fever" seemed to be supplemented by a host of other diseases — plague, smallpox, typhoid, leprosy, pneumonia — but since the researches of Manson and Ross, British pioneers of tropical medicine, at the end of the nineteenth century we know that nearly all such deaths were caused by two mosquito-borne diseases, malaria and yellow fever, rather than by the direct effects of the climate and its "miasma," as was thought at the time. The apparent immunity of the Africans in contrast to the European mortality from "fevers" can equally be explained without resort to racial predestination. Those Africans who survived the very high childhood mortality from malaria acquired a degree of immunity to the effects of the disease in later attacks.

The tsetse fly was second only to the mosquito as an insect scourge, its bite often transmitting a serious, and sometimes fatal, infection of trypanosomiasis, or sleeping sickness, to cattle, horses, and humans.[13] Since horses were especially susceptible to tsetse bites, the tsetse fly added to the isolation of sub-Saharan Africa by checking the penetration of Sudanese horsemen into the forest belt. And the absence of the solid pulling power of the multipurpose workhorse constituted a further constraint on tropical African development. Some breeds of cattle can survive in tsetse country, but they tend to succumb when subjected to the strain of hauling the plow; as a result, when the Dutch introduced the use of oxen as draft animals into the Cape, its diffusion northward was checked at the tsetse belt.[14]

Despite vegetable exuberance, then, Africa was no tropical Garden of Eden. Destructive insects, worn-out soils, uncertain rains, swamps, and unnavigable rivers combined to make it difficult. But so long as the complementary concept of "tropical exuberance" and "race" locked together into a self-sealing explanatory system, Europeans were unable to learn from their errors because they focused on the human factor rather than on such harsh ecological realities.[15]

Regional and Cultural Divisions

The anthropologists George P. Murdock and Jacques Maquet reckon there were about 650 to 700 autonomous societies in precolonial sub-Saharan Africa. Such multiplicity makes the problem of generalizing about Africa on the eve of partition or gauging the impact of European rule thereafter dauntingly complex.[16] In practice Africanists have got around the problem by dividing the continental complexity into more manageable units. In certain cases they have simply utilized categories devised by the European powers; thus the International African Institute's *Ethnographic Survey* uses "Central Africa" to refer to the region that the British Colonial Office designated by that term.[17]

Others have begun their analysis more ambitiously by establishing some correspondence between culture and geography, so that the continent can be split up into a number of culture areas. If this can be done, it has the advan-

Map 1. Herskovits's culture areas of Africa

tage of creating a relatively simple cultural map of traditional Africa upon which the impact of European rule can be plotted. The leading exponent of this approach was the American anthropologist Melville J. Herskovits. On the basis of his cultural area approach, Herskovits argued that precolonial traditions have persisted with far less change in modern Africa than is often supposed. Writing in the mid-1950s, at the end of the colonial era, he summarized this view briefly: "In the back country, all over Africa, life in its basic configurations moves largely as in pre-European days, and where contact has been close and pressures of a social, political, economic and religious nature have been strong, the mechanism of cultural reinterpretation has come into play. As a result, pre-existing values are retained, but given expression in a new outer form." [18]

Herskovits's phrase about "cultural reinterpretation," with its suggestion of a dynamic conservatism, needs constantly to be borne in mind to counteract any notion of stasis or inertia deriving from his chacterization of the cultural areas as "base lines," or fixed locations, from which the direction and velocity of colonial change could be measured. Barrington Moore forcefully makes the point in the epilogue to *Social Origins of Dictatorship and Democracy*: "The assumption of inertia that cultural and social continuity do not require explanation, obliterates the fact that both have to be created anew in each generation, often with great pain and suffering."[19]

In fact, a roster of distinct cultural and political regions has been used quite consciously to enforce consideration of the internal history of Africa and of the African peoples in the modern colonial period by the Nigerian historian J. F. A. Ajayi. Repeatedly, Ajayi stresses that however important the forces of world history are which have impinged upon Africa, there is "no substitute for the history of the African Peoples."[20] Hence the historian must resist the temptation to focus only on those aspects of modern African history such as missionary expansion and colonial rule where Europeans and Africans interact. African societies possessed an internal dynamic of change that persisted through and beyond the colonial period. Africans did not just respond to the European presence: sometimes they took the initiative, oftentimes they were simply reacting to each other. Themes from the precolonial past, submerged under European rule, emerge in the postcolonial present: "Many of the nationalist governments today are finding that on a number of issues they have to pick up the threads of social and political reform from the point where the radical Muslim and Christian reformers of the nineteenth century left off at the coming of colonial rule."[21]

Herskovits's and Ajayi's cultural maps are remarkably similar. On the other hand, Samir Amin, the North African economist and economic historian, thinks the processes by which Europe brought Africa into a state of under-development and dependency have created three macroregions: first, tradi-tional West Africa, the Africa of the colonial trade economy; second, the Africa of the concession-owning companies in the traditional Congo River basin; and, lastly, the Africa of the labor reserves in the eastern and southern parts of the continent. Even in the precolonial period Amin sees the line-aments of a threefold structure of dependence begin to appear through mer-cantilism and the slave trade.[22]

Khoisan Culture

As Herskovits himself observed, the Khoisan peoples of southern Africa con-stituted a glaring exception to his general rule that precolonial patterns sur-vived throughout the colonial period.[23] The Khoikhoi and the San were the first of the present inhabitants of southern Africa to arrive there. But the San were dependent on hunting and gathering and the Khoi on herding, and neither group was able to produce its own iron; because of this they lived in relatively small communities that lacked the resources in manpower and tech-nology to resist African and European advance. By the start of our story on the eve of partition, Herskovits's base line for change, they were broken, dominated peoples or had fled far into the barren interior.

This is not to say that Khoisan culture was erased from southern African history. Just as the Afrikaners were taught how to adapt to the dry interior by their Khoisan stockmen, so were Africans instructed how to use oxen for transportation, agriculture, and warfare by the Khoi and the San. Character-istic Khoisan click sounds were adopted into several African languages, es-pecially Xhosa, and the Khoi permanently influenced the Cape cuisine, intro-ducing, for example, vegetable ingredients into "bredie," a popular South Af-rican stew.[24] Although traditional Khoisan societies were overrun and lost to history, through intermarriage and less formal sexual arrangements a Khoi-san strain was incorporated in both the black and white communities. Indeed, some individuals adapted and prospered so well at the Cape that they pro-moted themselves out of their ethnic identity and passed for white. Some Khoisan groups, together with descendants of Khoisan and white such as the Griqua, utilized European know-how to establish themselves in relatively in-dependent communities in the interior, far from the center of government at the Cape. Thus the Griqua occupied what is now Griqualand West, while a similar group, the Kora, pushed farther into the interior, and still another group, the Nama, settled along the Orange River and in the high country beyond. Such Khoi and mixed-race communities represented the farthest reach of Cape civilization, but by the second half of the nineteenth century they were under pressure from waves of Afrikaners pushing north.[25]

Southern African geography shaped a refuge for the remnant of the San. Rainfall levels decline fairly rapidly inland from the fertile east coast, deteriorating to desert conditions in the west. On the margins of the desert, with a climate too arid for crops and domestic cattle, only a hunting and gathering people could survive. Here, impoverished and devoid of the glorious rock paintings that mark the sites of their old homeland in the Drakensberg Mountains, the San found respite.

East Africa

East Africa, considered both as a geographical and as a cultural region, has special significance in Herskovits's approach to the cartography of traditional Africa. It was with reference to this region that he formulated his archetypal African cultural area, the East African cattle complex, during his doctoral research. Herskovits's cattle complex linked social and economic institutions, politics, and ritual over a vast area stretching from the extreme south to beyond the great lakes, with a western extension into Angola. Subsequently he engaged in a lifelong refinement of his 1926 prototype, searching for similar coherence in culture and ecology in other areas of Africa.[26]

On the basis of his formulation of the huge East African cattle complex Herskovits divided up traditional Africa into basically food-gathering and herding peoples in the east and agricultural peoples in Guinea, the western Sudan, and the Congo basin. In this precolonial cultural division, he believed, lay the key to much of the continent's later economic history. Being mainly agriculturalists, Africans from the west responded with cash crops to the market opportunities presented by the European connection; the easterners, on the other hand, being primarily interested in their prestige cattle economy, and, indeed, regarding the subsistence farming economy as women's work, made no such positive response. The contrast between the agricultural peoples in the west, with their currencies and greater propensity to trade, and the cattle-herding peoples in the east is suggestive though perhaps overdrawn. Herskovits believed that in East Africa there were no traditional trading currencies or markets, so that cattle almost alone represented wealth. When a larger political structure than the local group was built up, some redistribution of goods occurred through the obligation of a chief to provide for his retainers and to entertain strangers.

In certain parts of the area, especially in the north and the south, the ownership of cattle became the prerogative of the rulers. Although there were fewer states, cities, and markets and the population was thinner than in West Africa, there were important exceptions. One was the interlacustrine region between Lake Victoria Nyanza and Lakes Albert and Edward. This was an area of bureaucratically organized kingdoms with a stratified society reflecting waves of conquest. In these kingdoms there was a ruling aristocracy of cattle owners, such as the Hima in Bunyoro and the Tutsi in Ruanda and Burundi. Another important exception was the region south of the Zambezi River, the area of Great Zimbabwe. Here the people used stone for building, imported luxury goods from India and the Far East, and mined gold, iron, copper, and salt. The rich mining culture in what is now Rhodesia stimulated trade and the development of large states in the region.

The East African coastal trade was older than either the empire centering on Great Zimbabwe or the interlacustrine kingdom. It was developed by the Swahili cultures on the coast, which blended Arab and African influences. The Portuguese, who had reached the Indian Ocean by the end of the fifteenth century, were also an influence in this area.

In the south the beginning of the nineteenth century was a time of widespread political changes. Shaka, the Zulu war leader, revolutionized warfare and welded together a state by conscripting all the young men he captured into the relevant age-grades of the Zulu people. The extension of his empire broke down small ethnic groups, leading to far-ranging migration and producing, by reaction, larger kingdoms such as those of the Basuto, the Ndebele, and Tswana.[27] The development of specialist trading groups like the Nyamwezi of what is now Tanzania will be dealt with later. Enough, though, has already been stated to suggest that, however illuminating Herskovits's picture of the East African cattle complex, there were significant political and economic developments in that area that should not be discounted.[28]

Nor should the significance of cattle in East African myth and ritual, stressed by Herskovits, be taken to imply any basic lack of rationality. Harold K. Schneider points out that it is not at all irrational for East Africans to lavish loving care on their cattle, which constitute a kind of mobile bank and are the best defense against famine. Cattle are indeed slaughtered and eaten only on ritual occasions, but such festivities occur frequently enough to prevent overstocking and overgrazing of the local ranges.[29]

Eastern Sudan

To the north of the East African cattle complex lay the area of the eastern Sudan. Whereas for Herskovits the large area to the south represented a remarkably well-integrated cultural complex, the northerly area was very different. A history of invasions and migration had left the eastern Sudan without any coherent cultural shape. The characteristics of the surrounding areas were present in attenuated forms, none being distinct enough to develop sharp cultural configurations.

Hence for Herskovits the cultures of this area were to be thought of as essentially residual, shifting from the Congo type, found among peoples like the Azande to the south, to the almost pure East African cattle complex forms that characterized the Dinka to the east. And away to the north and northwest there were the Berber and Tuareg cultures of the desert. Indeed, confronted by such incoherence and its persistence through the colonial period, Herskovits more or less admitted defeat, there being no scope for the culture area concept as a base line when "questions of cultural continuity and change . . . have only minor relevance for its peoples."[30]

The Congo Basin

The Congo area stretches from the Nile-Congo divide to the Atlantic shore. The forest is thicker than that in West Africa so that the differing ethnic groups developed in greater isolation. In the south where the forest gives way to the savannah belt, there is a history of greater mobility and a political cycle in which a number of states developed and declined. Rich in minerals, notably gold and copper in the Katanga region, the Congo area became a base from which the inhabitants developed trade and kingdoms. In terms of modern polities the Congo basin embraces the peoples of northern Angola, Zaire, Gabon, and the Río Muni, and the eastern section of southern Cameroon and includes parts of the Republic of the Sudan and the Central African Republic, stretching southeast through Katanga to Zambia.

The main groups of the Congo population spoke Bantu languages, but there were also a few pockets of Pygmies, who preceded the Bantu speakers in the region, in the northern and east central parts of the area. The subsistence of the Pygmies was chiefly derived from hunting and gathering. Small animals, deer, wild boar, and even hippopotamus and elephant were hunted by the men while the women collected wild fruits and roots, insects and their larvae, lizards, and shellfish. They kept no domestic animals except hunting dogs and did not farm unless strongly acculturated to the way of life of their Bantu-speaking neighbors. The economically simple life of the Pygmies contrasted sharply with the practices of their negroid neighbors with whom they usually maintained a symbiotic relationship: the negroid Africans farmed the clearings and left the forest to the Pygmies so that each group could engage in a mutually advantageous exchange of crops and hunting trophies. Without chiefs, elders, or priests the Pygmy hunting band was very egalitarian. Ultimate loyalty was to the forest, referred to as "mother" or "father," the provider of all good things: food, shelter, warmth, and affection. And historically the forest provided a variety of foods, which probably nourished them better than did the diet of their agriculturalist neighbors.[31]

The economies of the majority of the Bantu-speaking Africans were essentially agricultural, supplemented by some hunting; they did not raise any large domesticated animals. The peoples were skilled agriculturalists, who practiced shifting cultivation. The dense forest covering much of the area made the work of preparing farms difficult because trees had to be felled and the underbrush had to be cut and burned. The wide ecological knowledge displayed by the Azande in the north has been pointed out. There are more than forty Azande words to denote different kinds of land and the suitability of each for the cultivation of particular crops; in addition, there are six types of eleusine, ten varieties of maize, and ten kinds of cassava distinguished by name, which, as Herskovits observes, points "to a semantic emphasis on agriculture comparable to that made apparent by the number of qualifying words used in East Africa to denote different kinds of cattle."[32] In the west the agricultural technique of the Bakongo of utilizing the savannah vegetation by reducing it through controlled burning to ashes, which were incorporated into the soil and thus built up the humus content, led to high yields and again shows an unusual degree of farming skill.

The cultures of the Congo were marked by craft specialization. Basketry, weaving, pottery, ironworking, and wood carving were widespread in the area. In certain places the craftsmen were organized in guilds represented in the chiefs' council. Specialization extended to the differentiation of tasks within a particular craft. Value was set on time, and there was labor for hire with a developed commercial organization.

Money was used almost everywhere in the area and took many forms. Exchanges were achieved by a system technically called money barter, rather than money exchange, because the money used was often a commodity as well as common denominator of value. Consumer goods used as money included raffia cloths, iron hoes, copper crosses, spear points, iron throwing knives, and bars of salt. And in certain areas imported cowrie shells were utilized. Such money was used in trade. Much of the barter was intertribal, but there was also some within the tribe. In certain cases fixed markets were established at crossroads, though these were not common.

Political authority in the Congo area ranged from stable bureaucratic kingdoms to small groupings where control remained in kinship groups with a minimum of formal organization. Kingdoms were developed in all parts of the area, although the greatest development was in the southern savannah region.

Guinea Coast

The Guinea coast comprises the forested areas of West Africa running along the littoral from the Bight of Biafra to the southern part of the Republic of Guinea. The forested areas, however, are divided by the Sudan, a belt of savannah grasslands that reaches almost to the coast of eastern Ghana and Dahomey.

Herskovits saw, as the distinctive feature of the Guinea coast area, that its successful agriculture allowed a greater density of population than in the Congo. The greater surpluses here produced more specialization and more extensive markets, so that altogether the institutions of the Guinea coast were more structured than those of the Congo.

The most developed economic order lay in the geographical center of the region stretching from Ghana to western Nigeria. Here dense populations and adequate economic support led to the development of a complex cultural superstructure. Money was present in much of the Guinea coast area long before European concepts were introduced. Cowries, copper and brass rods, maps, salt bars, and metal bracelets were all used as currencies in certain areas.[33]

Markets of considerable size, reflecting the specialization in the economy and the use of money, developed especially in the urban areas of the most economically advanced central sector of the region. But such large markets as Kumasi in Ghana or Ibadan in western Nigeria were only the most prominent examples of a network covering the territory of a given people, varying from huge gatherings of thousands of buyers to small groups of wayside stalls, where cooked foods could be bought by travelers.

One significant aspect of the difference between West and East Africa that should be stressed is the differing economic roles of women. In East Africa the men traditionally were preoccupied with hunting and herding, and the women were the principal farmers. But in West Africa the men played the chief role in farming the main subsistence crop, whether rice or cassava, and the women were therefore freer to take part in trade. The women were responsible for vegetable farming, but they still had time for trading; and with their peppers, onions, tomatoes, and okra they would set up shop.[34] Generations of West African women developed commercial expertize, consequently monetizing their society right down to the household level. Whereas in East Africa the Indians achieved commercial domination with relative ease, the Lebanese faced stiff competition from the trading women in West Africa's towns and cities.[35]

Generally the West African forest area was one of small groupings with strong ethnic ties. The village integrated society, and all larger groupings, whether political or social, reflected this. Herskovits points out that the residential unit was the compound, consisting of a cluster of dwellings and storage huts, generally enclosed by a wall, where a man would live with his wife or wives, his children, and his younger brothers with their wives and children. A village was made up of an aggregate of compounds. Several such village conglomerates constituted a ward, which in turn formed part of a township. The township was headed by men who were related and thus formed a distinctive kin grouping. Political, social, and religious power was diffused among the elders, the age-grade associations, and in certain cases, the secret societies. When such societies were extremely powerful and widespread, they integrated large territories.

It was on such a social basis that certain powerful states grew up. The Yoruba, for example, developed an urbanized society and a monarchical government in their towns. There were several Yoruba kingdoms, one of which, Oyo, on the edge of the Sudan belt, had its own cavalry and built an empire of considerable size. However, Oyo could not unite the several Yoruba kingdoms of the forest area into a homogenous state.

With the development of the slave trade the polities of the Guinea coast faced both opportunity and crisis — opportunity in that they were able to purchase ammunition and guns, and crisis in that the peoples were forced to organize themselves to ensure that their villages did not become raiding grounds for slave dealers. A number of polities were formed to control the slave trade. East of the Niger River the Aro organized the trade, and to the west Benin, a state formed by a transplanted Yoruba dynasty, and Old Oyo had the same role. Farther west Dahomey developed on the interior plateau and extended its power to the coast to dominate these slave trading states. In Ghana there arose a number of states — Denkyira and Akim, followed by Akwamu and lastly Ashanti — which dominated the whole of modern Ghana and parts of what are now Ivory Coast and Togo. By the beginning of the nineteenth century Ashanti's power was still expanding so that it threatened to engulf all the nearby coastal states. By contrast, Oyo was declining and collapsed in the nineteenth century.

The Western Sudan Belt

The western Sudan belt, sometimes known as the Sahel, stretches from the Senegal River to Lake Chad. In the north it shades into the desert and in the south into the forested belt. It is a country that varies from open parkland to grassland, thinning toward the north into scrubland on the margin of the desert. The breadth of the Sudan belt has varied with climatic changes in the area; in recent years increasingly dry conditions have tended to push the margin of the Sahara southward, resulting in famine in some parts of the Sudan.

Herskovits sees as the clue to the cultural characteristics of this area the fact that it is a frontier between the Guinea coast to the south and the Islamic and Arab area to the north. As in the eastern Sudan, there is great variety in the cultures, similarly resulting from the long history of conquest and migration.

There is also great diversity in the basic economies of the area, a significant aspect noticed as early as 1912 by Louis Tauxier.[36] He observed the economies of pastoral groups such as the Moors and the so-called cattle Fulani, of agriculturalists and traders like the Mandé-Dyoula, of agriculturalists and herders like the Nankuru, and of pure agriculturalists like the Bobo and the Sankura. Such specialization in the economies of the various groups in the area was possible because they engaged in trade with each other. Herskovits notes that except among the Fulani, cattle in the western Sudan are not special symbols of prestige. Like the rest of the domesticated animals in this area cattle are kept to be eaten and sold.

In this area a trading economy was developed which surpassed even that found in the central portion of the Guinea coast. Kano, Sokoto, and Timbuktu were outstanding for the size and importance of their markets. Such centers are still the termini of the desert caravan routes, bringing them into commercial contact with the Arab north and the Mediterranean. In the modern era many have become important centers for air traffic and railheads.

As in the rest of Africa, the village was the basic unit and was linked by kin affiliation. But the towns, unlike those of the Guinea coast, were not agglomerates made up of village-style groupings. The town dweller was essentially an urbanite, a permanent resident of his community, despite any links leading back to the ancestral village.

The development of trade, which led to the growth of cities, provided opportunities for conquering dynasties and empires in the western Sudan. Along with trade came Islam, which supplied a written language and a class of literate bureaucrats to serve the imperial state. Islam also helped loosen ethnic ties and increasingly provided a bond of union in the new large states.

At first Islam was essentially the religion of the rulers, the bureaucrats, the traders, and the scholars of the main centers. In the countryside the bulk of the population remained attached to traditional religions, laws, and customs. Important areas, like the Mossi kingdoms, resisted the spread of Islam. When the rulers of the Songhai empire were defeated by the Moroccans in 1591, this represented a serious reverse for Islam in the western Sudan. In the eighteenth century there was a growing feeling of frustration among Muslims and a strong desire to revive the great days of the Songhai empire, which was regarded as an Islamic golden age in West Africa. Such feelings of frustration inspired a wave of Islamic revolutions throughout the western Sudan in the nineteenth century.

Herskovits himself stresses that the concept of the culture area constituted a purely analytical tool, a category of convenience permitting him to class together several peoples "in terms of their primary orientation," so that, for example, simply by referring to a group as representative of the Guinea coast area he could indicate that herding was not involved in their economy. Writing in the early 1960s, at a time of general decolonization in Africa, he felt it necessary to warn that culture areas had no geopolitical significance in view of the lack of correlation between their boundaries and the political frontiers that had been imposed on Africa by colonial rule. As the people of an area had no awareness of the cultural unity discerned by the students, it would be a misuse of science to employ this shorthand term as a political instrument.[37]

Herskovits's point can be reformulated, nonpolitically, as an inducement to academic caution in the use of this category of convenience. Mary Douglas has contrasted strikingly the economies of the Lele and the Bushong living on either side of the Kasai River in Zaire. For all their recognition of a common origin, closely related languages, similarity in style of houses, clothing, and crafts the Lele were poor, producing only for subsistence, while the Bushong, who traditionally produced for exchange with an economy distinguished by specialization and the use of money, were comparatively rich. The geographer John I. Clarke has pointed out that separate economic and demographic systems occur within distances of a few miles from each other; for example, in Cameroon there are ethnic groups with rates of population increase varying from 2.8 to 27.8 per thousand.[38] Another geographer, Charles M. Good, Jr., has examined Herskovits's prototype culture area, East Africa, making a detailed correlation of such features as language, mode of livelihood, and staple crops, and has found great diversity in the prototype area, emphasizing "the general problem of delimiting culture 'areas.'"[39] It would indeed be ironic if the object of Ajayi's exercise, a saving sense of the history of the African peoples persisting through the period of imperialism, was jeopardized through the obliteration of such local details by the bold simplifications of the culture area approach. A short course in reading some of the classic anthropological monographs (the Bohannans on the Tiv, Evans-Pritchard on the Nuer, Gluckman on the Barotse, or Douglas on the Lele) should be enough to counter any tendency to obliterate the historic identity of the local African group through the reification of the culture area concept.[40]

Another, more insidious, trap awaits the incautious reader of the anthropological literature in search of a clear picture of precolonial Africa in that the culture area approach and the classic anthropological monograph analyzing the structure and identity of a given people can combine to mislead. Amin suggests that in addition to his three imposed macroregions there were up to two hundred indigenous microregions, of varying size and crossing present frontiers, defined by "the homogenous nature of their social, cultural, economic and even political condition."[41] The development of such indigenous homogeneity tended to be halted and sometimes even reversed by European intrusion. Anthropology came of age as a separate academic discipline, distinguished by intensive fieldwork, during the period of the imperial "pax." The controlling imperial presence influenced the development of anthropology by providing the individual fieldworker with reasonable guarantees of both his personal security and enough general stability to make the perception of recurrent social patterns feasible. And with inter-African diplomacy and fusion movements stalemated by the imperial presence, individual societies could be studied in isolation.

By the close of the colonial epoch a number of anthropologists, as well as the first generation of Africanist historians, approached the study of African societies "not as isolates, or as instances of a continent-wide or world-wide classification of types, but with reference to the immediate regional setting."[42] In 1962 Warren L. d'Azevedo formulated the concept of "emergent regions," illustrated by the example of the Central West Atlantic Region, consisting of what is now Sierra Leone and eastern Liberia.[43] The cultural processes that had created this distinct and expanding regional enclave in the precolonial period were checked by the intervention of Europe. The cartography of such precolonial emergent regions is often extremely difficult to trace, but it is only with some awareness of the shape and the direction of African interaction before domination that the imperial impact can be assessed.

Modern historiography developed inside the framework of the western nation-state; indeed, the search for origins, as well as the celebration of them, was an essential process in shaping separate national identities.[44] No such ready-made framework or focus is given to the historian of empire and Africa; hence there is the need to shift between ethnic group and culture area, between microregion and macroregion, and between metropolitan power structures and a multiplicity of "men on the spot." But the enforced integration of history at such different regional levels is a source of insights as well as problems. Perhaps the variety of perspectives presented on the relationship between the local community and the wider world will be African history's chief contribution to the general development of historiography.

CHAPTER 2

Before Partition

African Empires

Historians and anthropolgists frequently feel impelled to point out that using the term "traditional Africa" as synonymous with "precolonial Africa" is distinctly misleading. Precolonial African societies exhibited great diversity, comprising city-states and self-governing villages alongside sizable nations with distinctive political structures. The concept of "traditional African society" tends to compress such variety into conformity with the user's simplistic preconception of precolonial Africa. The notion also suggests stability, a base line from which modernization or progress can be measured. The idea that African societies maintained a static equilibrium before the coming of the Europeans was fostered by the orthodoxy of functionalist anthropology in the interwar period. But all such societies had their own history, as contemporary anthropologists, no less than historians, agree.[1]

However powerful the currents of world history directed toward precolonial Africa, such as the transatlantic slave trade, so long as African societies retained their identity and independence, they could steer a course for self-defined goals. But the century preceding the scramble for Africa, roughly 1780-1880, was marked by the rise of powerful African-based imperialisms, the so-called "African partition of Africa."[2] Radical changes in the tactics and technology of warfare, as well as revolutionary innovations in religious ideology, were utilized by states or other social groupings to mount successful offensives. Three examples of such African imperialism will be examined: the Zulu empire and the *mfecane*, the trekker republics of the Afrikaners, and the West African jihads.

24

The Zulu Military Kingdom and the *Mfecane*

The turmoil in southern and central Africa in the early nineteenth century is known as the *mfecane*, from a term applied by the Nguni to a series of wars and disturbances, literally meaning "crushing of peoples" (*difaqne* in Sotho languages). At the center of the *mfecane* was the sudden development of a new type of state, the Zulu kingdom, the most thoroughly militarized regime to emerge in precolonial Africa. Several other large centralized kingdoms arose in a chain reaction so that much of the later history of southern and central Africa amounts to the continuation of themes originating in Zululand.[3]

Both the traditions of the peoples in this area and the reports of shipwrecked Portuguese and Dutch sailors show that in the eighteenth century the population was organized in small independent communities. Settlement was dispersed and such polities as existed were subject to fission under the rules governing succession. A chief established a "great house," headed by his "great wife," whose dowry was paid for by his subjects. She thus became the official state bride, and in theory only her children, or those of other wives affiliated to the "great house," could succeed to the chieftainship. As the chief only married his "great wife" after he had succeeded to the chieftainship, he would most probably have older sons by other wives. These sons, who had time to build up a political following of their own, often disputed the succession. This commonly resulted in the division of the chiefdom, with one or more disappointed claimants hiving off to form independent polities, which continued, however, to recognize their common origin and the seniority of whichever group was headed by offspring of the original "great house," but which would in other ways be quite independent and often hostile to each other.

These repeated schisms had economic and military as well as political roots. They were a functional adaptation to an environment consisting of large areas of land that were thinly populated by San hunters and food-gatherers and Khoikhoi pastoralists. The need for rapid retaliation against small cattle raids by San or Khoikhoi dictated political dispersal at a time when there were no large enemy armies to compel consolidation for purposes of defense.

Several reasons have been put forward for the mutation from fission to centralized kingdoms on the Zulu model developed by Dingiswayo and Shaka. One explanation is that the introduction of American maize, which was relatively pest resistant and which produced high yields, upset the ecological equilibrium, leading to such an increase of population that the old political and economic processes of colonization by fission became impossible. A favorite theory of white South Africans of the nineteenth century, flattering to themselves and suggesting that Africans lacked the capacity for innovation, was that Shaka's patron, Dingiswayo, after contact with Europeans, questioned traditional political procedures. It has also been suggested recently that Dingiswayo and Shaka were interested in forming a larger political structure in order to control the developing trade of the area.[4]

Dingiswayo abolished the existing circumcision schools in order to transform the age-grades into age-regiments, the famous Zulu impis. Shaka exploited the potential of such full-time soldiers by creating highly disciplined infantry units, equipped with short stabbing spears in place of javelins. He also made his soldiers discard their sandals and fight barefoot for ease of movement, and he introduced the use of heavy shields. In the classic Zulu battle the wings, or horns, enveloped the enemy while the main body of troops attacked from the front.

In addition to their military function Shaka's regiments had a role in nation building. Soldiers drawn from all over the empire forgot their primordial political loyalties as they developed a regimental morale and an intense devotion to their commander. The Zulu dialect of Nguni and the traditions of the Zulu dynasty were generally adopted. One of the royal herds was attached to each regimental barracks. Shaka himself distributed captured cattle and prisoners from the Zulu wars. He was the ritual head as well as the political and military head of the system, presiding over the annual first-fruits ceremony and the "smelling out of witches" in order to eliminate religious rivals.

Shaka encouraged what amounted to a youth cult.[5] As early as his arrival in 1816 in his dead father's kraal to disinherit his legitimate brother, there is some evidence that he deliberately mocked the elders in this erstwhile gerontocracy by forcing them to wear a uniform of monkey skins modeled upon women's dress. As composer and choreographer — a superb dancer himself — Shaka presided over this youth cult. Yet at the same time as he subverted the gerontocracy, he prolonged the period of youth when his warrior devotees were devoid of political power, so that in some cases men were forty years old before they were allowed to marry. Hence the Zulu could still control population growth when they were threatened by a demographic explosion through the introduction of American maize. Through his command of corresponding female regiments, Shaka kindled in his army an intense but frustrated eroticism that found release in killing. And eventually the finest warriors were rewarded with the most beautiful women.

Yet for all Shaka's drastic restructuring of the social system, a doubt about the solidity of his innovations remains. He was given charge of a small clan in 1816, and thereafter his rise to despotic supremacy was rapid. But by 1828 he was dead, assassinated. By the end of his reign he was dependent on European traders to supply him with Macassar oil to blacken his grizzled hair. He seems to have had no plans for an orderly succession, and he executed any of his wives or concubines who became pregnant. Indeed, he left a curious prophecy that once he was dead the Zulu would be conquered by the white men. For all his fantastic political achievements, a shadow of impermanence — even willful contradiction, as his cult of perpetual youth — hangs over his Zulu kingdom.

The sheer volatility of Shaka's revolution, however, gave it wide impact. Some neighboring groups adopted the Zulu system in order to withstand invasions, and, once Shaka's military innovations were well known, it was better for an ambitious young captain to try his luck farther afield. The thrust of the *mfecane* thus catapulted the Ndebele into what is now Rhodesia, while the Makolo, a Sotho group that adopted Zulu methods, ended up ruling Barotseland in present-day Zambia.

The Afrikaner Trekker Republics

By "crushing of peoples" in so much of the southeastern interior, the *mfecane* opened the way for the Afrikaners' Great Trek out of the British Cape Colony. The movement began in 1836 and lasted a decade, and it led to the establishment of the Orange Free State and the Transvaal.[6] The trekkers amounted to perhaps fourteen thousand people — "the flower of the frontiersmen,"[7] as the British governor Sir Benjamin D'Urban called them — one-sixth of the Cape's total white population. Resentment at British control, especially at what was considered to be its benevolent paternalism toward Africans, combined with land hunger to drive them on.[8] The trekkers outflanked the Xhosa on the eastern frontier and headed for the high veld where the African polities had been pulverized.

The Afrikaners were formidably equipped with European weapons and were well trained. The commando system, which had been developed originally in wars against the San, insured that virtually every male over sixteen years was drilled in musketry and horsemanship and was ready to take the field with his own firearms, ammunition, and rations. The ox wagon — like the covered wagon in the American West — was a useful conveyance for an invading people. The Afrikaners had two methods of fighting, firing either from the saddle or from behind the cover of the laager, a defensive ring of ox wagons lashed together with thornbushes packed beneath the wheels. Their guns and horses gave them a decisive advantage over their opponents, whose only missiles were hurled spears with at best half the range of the Afrikaner smoothbore flintlocks. Short of surprise, the Africans had no chance of victory. But the Afrikaners suffered some setbacks before the decisive battle was fought by Andries Pretorius against the Zulu at Blood River on December 16, 1838. Pretorius and his commando advanced for several days into Zululand and then took up an ideal defensive position on the riverbank where the laager was partially protected by deep water and could be defended by two small cannons. The Afrikaners mowed down waves of disciplined Zulu attackers for two hours and then routed the survivors by a mounted pursuit. Three thousand Zulus were killed at the cost of only three Afrikaners wounded. Plainly, despite Shaka's recent military revolution, the Africans' tactics needed radical revision; above all, they needed guns and horses to stand any chance of successful resistance.[9]

The West African Jihads

The jihads illustrate precolonial partition through the impact of revolutionary religious ideology.[10] At the outset of the nineteenth century Muslim scholars were distressed to find that the Islamic world, which once had led in science, the arts, government, and military power, was threatened by the rising power of Christian Europe. A number of reform movements sought to restore Islam to its preeminence by calling Muslims back to the simple way of live and the purity of faith of their forebears. Such was the origin of the jihads, or holy wars, in the western Sudan.

Islam, in one form or another, had existed in some parts of the West African savannah for nearly a millennium by the nineteenth century. But the collapse of Songhai, the last of the great medieval empires of the western Sudan, at the end of the sixteenth century was a severe setback for the Islamic aristocracies. Henceforth, there were three broad types of Islamic communities in West Africa. Certain states still amounted to political-religious communities ruled by governments that enforced the *shari'a* (the Muslim way of life). Next there were autonomous Muslim communities in certain commercial towns, of which Timbuktu was the most famous, where learned Muslims maintained a high standard of Islamic scholarship and connections with other

Muslim centers. Finally, there were the private, nonpolitical Islamic groups made up of Muslims living in non-Muslim states or under only nominally Muslim rulers who did not enforce the *shari'a*. They suffered many disadvantages. They may have had to fight foreign Muslims and to pay uncanonical tribute to their own rulers. Moreover, as "people of the book," the Koran, Muslims were very conscious of being culturally different from, and in their own eyes much superior to, other Africans. They were likely to know much more about the rest of the world through reading and travel as traders. Muslim jurists divided the world into the "Abode of Islam" and the "Abode of War." Every Muslim had the duty to proselytize. The jihad, or holy war, was a collective religious obligation.

The theory of the jihad seems clear enough, but throughout the history of Islam there have been recurrent disputes about who actually was a Muslim. The Hausa state of Gobir, on which 'Uthman dan Fodio's jihad burst in 1804 exemplified these problems. The Sultan of Gobir and his state were regarded as Muslim; yet he and his subjects were undoubtedly practicing old-fashioned polytheism. Situated in the northern area of Hausa settlement, the Sultan had to deal with raiders from the desert. Gobir therefore developed a formidable army based upon a cavalry able to lunge into neighboring territories in search of slaves and other booty. These campaigns were expensive to finance. Islamic law is precise in matters of justice and taxation, through which the Hausa aristocracy sought to finance the ceremony, even luxury, that traditionally marked high political status. Knowledge of Islam was sufficiently widespread, and the political system sufficiently corrupt, to make puritanical reform welcome. Finally, it had long been prophesied that during the thirteenth Muslim century beginning in 1784 West Africa would be blessed with a great religious reformer who would reign as Caliph, followed by the coming of the Mahdi and the subsequent end of the world.

Dan Fodio came from a Fulani family that had been settled in Hausa country for generations. He was born in 1754 and followed his father's profession of religious teacher, developing qualities of piety and scholarship to the charismatic pitch of holiness that Muslims call *baraka*. He built up a group of followers that included Hausa peasants and Fulani cattlemen until he was strong enough to threaten rulers of Gobir. Dan Fodio belonged to a brotherhood, the Qādiriyya, and at the mystic age of forty he claimed to have had a vision ordering him to "unsheath the sword of truth." By 1795 he was urging that his followers be prepared to use arms. Eventually in 1804 the jihad began.

Dan Fodio left the actual conduct of operations to his brother, Abdullahi, and his son, Muhammad Bello, whose military skill complemented dan Fodio's *baraka*. After fierce fighting the jihad was successful in Gobir by 1808. In the next year Sokoto was founded as the capital of the new, purified Islamic state. Meanwhile, dan Fodio's party had seized power in other Hausa states. Thus was founded the Sokoto caliphate, covering most of what later became Northern Nigeria as well as much of modern Niger and Cameroon. It was the last of the great African states, except for Ethiopia, to fall to the Europeans. It was second only to Ethiopia in geographic extent, and it probably was the equal of that ancient empire in terms of population.

The threat to the European penetration lay in the Muslim leaders' ability to mobilize Africans of differing ethnic groups into a common force. Dan Fodio had Fouta Toro cavalrymen fighting in his jihad, and his descendant, Sultan Atahiru, in his last stand against the British, was joined by the ruler of Djolof, who had been beaten by the French in Senegal and who had moved almost a thousand miles eastward to rally to his Muslim brother against the infidel British.[11]

European Colonies before the Scramble

For most African peoples European rule began during the last two decades of the nineteenth century, in which the European scramble to obtain territory in Africa took place. For some, though, it dated back years, decades, and, in odd cases, centuries. The British colony at the Cape had been carried into the interior by the dynamic pattern of settlement illustrated by the trekker republics.[12] The British might not wish to undertake extensive commitments, but they found it extremely difficult to set limits to the outward movement of the "turbulent frontier."[13] No other European empire thrust any distance inland until Major Louis Faidherbe took control of the French colony of Senegal in 1854.

The British at the Cape

The British occupied the Cape in 1795 to forestall any French attempt to utilize their Dutch ally's base to threaten British control of India. They retained the colony at the 1815 peace settlement of the Congress of Vienna and therefore inherited the problem of recurrent wars between the Afrikaner settlers and the Xhosa peoples of the eastern frontier.[14] In 1820 the British reinforced the European presence by settling five thousand of their own nationals there. The Cape, like the rest of the early-nineteenth-century British Empire, was considered a proper field for philanthropy and missionary activity, with John Philip of the London Missionary Society the most effective practitioner of this work.[15] Largely through Philip, the Khoisan within the colony were given the protection of the law in 1828, and with the abolition of slavery in 1833 Philip sought similar rights for former slaves.

Every Afrikaner considered a six-thousand-acre farm as his birthright, to be claimed on marriage; hence the available land within the colony's boundaries was soon occupied. In 1836 land on the eastern frontier formerly annexed by the colony was returned to its African owners because of the British government's refusal to undertake the costs of administration. This, combined with the liberal racial views of Philip, provoked many Afrikaners into the Great Trek northward across the Orange River. In 1845 the British government annexed the trekker settlement at Natal, forcing those Afrikaners back to the high veld. In 1852 and 1854 it recognized the independence of the Transvaal and the Orange Free State.

By the middle of the nineteenth century modern South Africa had a total white population of little more than 300,000 and an African population of between one and two million. Politically, it comprised the two British colonies of the Cape and Natal, the two Afrikaner republics, and many independent African polities. Nevertheless, many British policy makers, concerned over the staging posts and their hinterlands on the route to India, would have thought that the newfangled term "sphere of influence" aptly described the kind of loose sway they wished to maintain over the whole area.[16]

The mixed racial population at the Cape complicated the problem of proceeding toward representative and responsible government after the approved Canadian model.[17] Articulate Colored opinion feared the surrender of imperial power to a white settler parliament. But in 1853 the Cape gained representative government through a compromise including the comparatively low franchise qualification of property valued at £25. British radicals, Cape Coloreds — still preferring imperial control but seeking the best terms they could get within the framework of representative government — and Dutch farmers were lined up against the substantial merchants who believed that a high property qualification for voting would best serve their interests. The Colored men of Philipton, speaking in the authentic tones of the mid-Victorian "Age of Improvement," talked of their "inexpressible satisfaction" with the £25 requirement, which would allow "a proportionate number of Coloured people" to be enfranchised "so as to preserve the equipoise of political balance between Her Majesty's subjects."[18] In 1872 full internal self-government — responsible government, in contemporary British parlance, with ministers responsible to the Cape parliament — was granted. The low-property nonracial franchise was preserved. The liberal political compromise made at the Cape in 1853 did not obtain elsewhere in South Africa. In the Orange Free State and the Transvaal only whites were recognized as citizens, and only white males had the vote.[19]

Griqualand West: Africa's First Industrial Revolution

In 1867 diamonds were found in land occupied by the Griquas between the Cape Colony and the Orange Free State. Fortune hunters flocked there and two years later a stone worth £25,000, the Star of South Africa, was discovered. The area soon was the world's premier source of diamonds. Suddenly South Africa embarked on a process of industrialization. Diamonds were better fitted than almost any other natural resource to stimulate an industrial revolution: in the beginning they could be mined by quite primitive methods, they were easily transportable, and they were the most valuable of all gems. Outmaneuvering the Afrikaner republics, the British took over the legal claims of the Griqua leader, Nicholas Waterboer, and annexed Griqualand West but forced the Cape Colony to administer it. Within a few years the foreign trade of the Cape Colony and Natal doubled as did their revenues. Money for public works could be more easily borrowed and at lower rates of interest on the London market, and the railroads, hitherto running a mere sixty-six miles, were extended to the diamond fields. Kimberley mushroomed into a town of fifty thousand people, the first truly industrial community on the African continent.

When Anthony Trollope visited Kimberley in the middle 1870s, he regarded it "as one of the most interesting places on the face of the earth." To him there was "no other spot on which the work of civilizing a Savage is being carried on with so signal a success." Missionary activities, education, and political incorporation were all proving doubtful processes, Trollope reported, but

who can doubt but that work is the great civilizer of the world. . . . If there be one who does he should come here to see how those dusky troops of labourers, who ten years since were living in the wildest state of unalloyed savagery, whose only occupation was the slaughter of each other in tribal wars, each of whom was the slave of his Chief, who were subject to the minion of most brutalizing and cruel superstitions, have already put themselves on the path towards civilization. They are thieves, no doubt; — that is they steal diamonds though not often other things. They are not Christians. They do not yet care much about breeches. They do not go to school. But they are orderly. They come to work at six in the morning and go away at six in the evening. . . . The simple teaching of religion has never brought large numbers of Natives to live in European habits; but I have no doubt that European habits will bring about religion. . . . I have not myself seen the model Christian perfected; but when I have looked down into the Kimberley mine and seen three or four thousand of them at work, — although each of them would willingly have stolen a diamond if the occasion came, — I have felt that I was looking at three or four thousand growing Christians.[20]

But Kimberley frustrated Trollope's hopes for the creation of an industrial proletariat along British lines. South Africa's diamond mining began when many African polities were independent; hence many miners were simply warriors in civilian guise, intent on earning the purchase price of the latest available gun.[21] Such limited commitment adversely affected their chances of acquiring technological skills or a good bargaining position. Indeed, their employers developed the theory of a "backward-sloping labor supply": the bigger the wage they paid the individual miner, the more rapidly he would earn the price of the dowry, the gun, the blanket, or whatever target he was aiming at. Hence, as a high wage policy would simply deplete the current available labor force, the prudent mineowner cut wages to the bone.[22] Furthermore, because diamonds were so easily concealed and so well worth stealing, the free and easy labor organization vividly described by Trollope was rapidly replaced by nothing short of imprisonment of the laborers. Lastly, the myth grew among whites in Griqualand West that any well-dressed, apparently affluent black or Colored man had waxed prosperous by illicit diamond dealing. A battery of laws was brought into being to police and repress such manifestations of conspicuous consumption — or aspirations to respectability — on the part of non-Europeans.[23]

The Portuguese Colonies in Angola and Mozambique

By the middle of the nineteenth century Portuguese imperial activity was vastly scaled down from what it had been in its heyday in 1501, when King Manuel I had styled himself "lord of the conquest, navigation and commerce of Ethiopia, India, Arabia and Persia."[24] Portuguese Africa had not been valued for itself but as a supply and staging area for the massive sources of imperial wealth in the East Indies and South America. The Portuguese settlements on the East African coast served as way stations for East Indian shipping, and those on the West Coast functioned as reservoirs of slave labor for Brazil.

When Portugal was forced to surrender the East Indies, its presence on the East African coast virtually collapsed; and when Britain suppressed the slave trade, Portugal's West Coast presence also declined. By the 1850s the

Portuguese empire amounted to little more than the two bankrupt settlements of Angola and Mozambique along with some small trading posts in West Africa and some islands in the eastern Atlantic. Portugal managed to retain its two main African colonies in the presence of more vigorous colonial powers largely because the colonies were considered unprofitable. But as early as 1854 David Livingstone had ominously criticized Portugal's performance in Angola, linking the prevalence of slavery with the general lack of development. Under other rulers the welfare of the Angolans would improve dramatically.[25] By mid-century European standards Portugal itself was considered an underdeveloped and backward territory. Early in the eighteenth century it had chosen to rely on colonial tribute rather than to develop domestic manufacturing industries. In 1703 by the Methuen Treaty Portugal voluntarily dropped out of the European competition in textiles in return for a monopoly of the English wine trade. But it was the textile industry that was to constitute the chief technological base of the European industrial revolution. Thus Portugal was fated to decline to third-rate power status and to suffer in the nineteenth century from foreign invasion, military takeover, revolution, and civil war. During the partition of Africa more powerful states, notably Britain and Germany, would propose contingency plans to divide up Portugal's colonies should the country finally go bankrupt. "Still," as the historian of Europe's role in world banking put it, "financial failures which might have cost a state of more primitive civilization its independence, were permitted Portugal because of its place in the European world."[26]

The British in West Africa

During the centuries of slave trading and subsequent legitimate trade with West Africa, Britain established a series of trading posts along the fringes of the continent. Such small colonies were regarded by Africans as communities of strangers, enjoying certain limited privileges by the favor of their hosts, the African sovereigns, whose overlordship was recognized by a regular system of payments.[27] Designated as *oyinbo* in what is now Nigeria, *oporto* in Sierra Leone, and *toubab* in Senegambia, white men were an accepted part of the trading society. Moreover, the Africans who involved themselves with these strangers were also frequently designated *oyinbo, oporto, toubab*, or white man's *pikin* (child). Such Africans were obviously seen as having cut loose to some extent from their primordial ties.

The trade goods were also available to Africans outside the small prepartition colonies. But the European outposts were increasingly likely during the nineteenth century to lash out at the independent African polities of the hinterland in order to reduce them to some sort of dependent status. Nevertheless, until the scramble in the 1880s the discrepancy in power between these European intruders and their hosts was not so great that the African states were unable to negotiate with them more or less as equals.[28]

Whereas European traders could work from their ships at Sierra Leone and the bights, the surf along the Gold Coast was too dangerous. In this area the Europeans were allowed to build forts but were expected to remain within them.[29] Thus, during the slave trade period the people of the Gold Coast had more opportunity both to learn the white man's skills and to discern his weaknesses. Most European traders had "country wives," and the bigger forts generally made some attempt to educate their mulatto children. Some of the children were sent to school in England or other European countries where their fathers originated, and there quickly developed a group of western-educated Africans. Because the African coastal societies were matrilineal, the mulattoes inherited an established place in African society.

In 1852 Governor S. J. Hill, with the sanguine support of Earl Grey at the Colonial Office, launched an ambitious plan to develop the Gold Coast. The Poll Tax Ordinance, passed by the Assembly of Kings and Chiefs that was convened on British initiative at Cape Coast in April 1852 and ratified by a similar body in Accra, imposed a tax of one shilling per year on every inhabitant in the "protectorate," a vaguely delimited area extending some fifty miles inland. Grey expected that this would achieve nothing less than a political and economic transformation. The Assembly of Kings and Chiefs would draw these "barbarous tribes, possessing nothing which deserves the name of a government, into a nation." Direct taxation would promote economic development by counteracting the "listless mode of life" of the tropics. Grey believed that in temperate climates taxation should bear lightly on the poor, "but the case is very different in tropical climates, where the population is very scanty in proportion to the extent of territory; where the soil . . . readily yields a subsistence in return for very little labor; and where clothing, fuel, and lodging such as are required, are obtained very easily. In such circumstances there can be but little motive to exertion, to men satisfied with an abundant supply of their mere physical wants; and accordingly experience proves that it is the disposition of the races of men by which these countries are generally inhabited, to sink into an easy and listless mode of life, quite incompatible with the attainment of any high degree of civilization."[30] Taxation, therefore, in the tropics should force the poor to work for wages. The revenue would provide for roads, medical services, education, and other essential aspects of development. The Gold Coast African would gradually begin to function as a modern self-improving economic man.

But this bold plan failed. Instead of an estimated annual revenue of £20,000 from the poll tax, only £7,567 was collected in the first year, and even this low yield fell steadily to £1,552 in 1861, when the tax was abandoned.

Africans achieved high rank in the mid-century Gold Coast administration. Governor Sir William Winniett arranged for James Bannerman, a member of a prominent Gold Coast family, to take over when he was out of the country, and when Winniett died in 1851, Bannerman was appointed lieutenant governor. A body of local worthies, including European as well as African merchants and the kings of Cape Coast and Anomabu, petitioned that he be their next governor. But their request was turned down by the Colonial Office, ostensibly because Bannerman's close connections with many merchants would make it difficult for him to function impartially. Bannerman's sons also held high appointments. Unfortunately this early trend toward Africanization was blighted because all the Bannerman brothers were charged with peculation or extortion. They struck back in the columns of the local press, and racial prejudice was inflamed on both sides, with the Colonial Office discounting such educated Africans as "the bane of the West Coast." Later, when a group of intellectuals, merchants, and chiefs organized the Fanti Confederation in 1868, in response to the 1865 Parliamentary Committee's apparent recommendation that West Africans prepare for eventual self-government, they were obstructed by British officials acting on this stereotype.[31]

Sierra Leone, through its philanthropic origins as a refuge for black American Loyalists and Liberated Africans, was markedly different. The Saro — Yoruba term for a Sierra Leonean immigrant — and Creole diaspora affected both the Gambia and Lagos. These colonies will be discussed later along with the Fingo diaspora, which occurred under similar missionary patronage.

The French in Senegal

As early as 1638 French merchants were establishing themselves near the mouth of the Senegal River.[32] In 1659 they found a firmer base on the island of Guet N'Dar within the estuary, building the fort and the settlement that they christened Saint-Louis, after Saint-Louis-sur-Seine. Some two centuries later the settlement was still territorially minute, consisting of Saint-Louis, the island community of Gorée off Cape Verde, and a series of trading posts for which African rulers charged tribute and usually collected a substantial export tax.

Judged purely as a *comptoir*, or trading base, Senegal functioned badly. In what modern historians term the mid-century crisis, the trade of Saint-Louis was almost halved between 1845 and 1850. Nor could Gorée, seemingly crippled since the end of the slave trade and only attaining one fifth of the turnover of Saint-Louis at its worst, provide commercial compensation. The trade depression coincided with a crisis in politics and race relations. The mutable morality of white men, which had prompted the French to withdraw from the transatlantic slave trade and which now, in 1848, banned slavery within their empire, exasperated local African potentates. Freedom was contagious, and France's unilateral abolition of slavery threatened the social order on the mainland. African rulers countered by diverting trade from Senegal, consequently facing the French governors with reduced revenue just when the governors wanted to finance military expeditions to apply pressure on their erstwhile trading partners. Within the colony itself low morale and intense competition for the few jobs available led to a severe crisis in race relations.

And yet, as with contemporary British settlements in West Africa, there was something deceptive about this weakness of the French colonial power. However modest and precarious the French presence might appear, the tricolor flown at Saint-Louis and Gorée signified them to be outposts of what was indubitably a Great Power. Such a status implied ability to mobilize the scientific resources, the wealth, and the firepower to intervene in African affairs both for obvious economic reasons and for what were to Africans more obscure motives of diplomatic and professional prestige deriving from perceptions of the changing European balance of power and notions of military and naval honor, exacerbated by the presence of the traditional rival, the British. The mysterious thought processes of the *toubab*, whereby Africans might suddenly find themselves pitched from a purely local palaver onto the European diplomatic chessboard, meant that even the simplest, most modest European presence could become unpredictably menacing.

The distinction of Senegal was that it had two centuries to shape a specific Afro-European identity in the confined space of the settlement of Saint-Louis before France was committed to mainland expansion. As a venture in mid-century colonial urbanization Saint-Louis was outranked in terms of population by Freetown, nor did it have equivalents to the educational institutions such as Fourah Bay College, which fitted the Sierra Leone Colony for its role in the Protestant evangelization of Africa. But Saint-Louis developed other amenities to cater to the higher proportion of Europeans resident there and its long-established black and mulatto Senegalese elite. Governor George A. K. D'Arcy, from the Gambia, visited in 1860 after Faidherbe's public works program was under way and was impressed by the schools, the four-hundred-bed hospital, the military parade on the Champ de Mars, and "the ball at Government House, numbering at least forty ladies whose toilets might have done credit to a Paris ballroom."[33]

The social structure was strongly hierarchical. At the top were about five hundred Europeans, three hundred of whom were clustered in Saint-Louis. The turnover of top bureaucrats and soldiers tended to be rapid. Among civilians a commercial elite was singling itself out from the ruck of small businessmen and artisans as the "notables of the colony" and the advisers of the administration. They represented the most successful businesses started by the young Frenchmen who had hurried out to Senegal thirty or forty years earlier to take advantage of the boom in the gum trade. Predominantly from southern and southwestern France, they generally began in an established firm and then struck out on their own. When they had a firm foothold, they sent for younger relatives, thus founding the Bordeaux trading companies that dominated the subsequent commercial history of Senegal. With its sub-Canarian climate and moderate winds Senegal's Atlantic strip was a remarkably attractive tropical environment for Europeans. Inland conditions were much harsher, and the French were prepared to leave up-country trade to African and mulatto agents. Moreover, both the gum trade and the peanut monoculture that replaced it were not considered lucrative enough to warrant the effort and investment necessary to establish European plantations. Besides curtailing the size of the white community, Senegal's ecology shaped the rhythm of its year, for the same rain that rendered the parched inland plains verdant brought oppressive tropical humidity to the coastal townships. This humid summer, ironically known as the hivernage, the reverse of the term's connotation in France, prompted an annual cycle of migration by the whites, who abandoned Senegal to the Africans and the mulattoes during part of the year.

The Senegalese Creoles, unlike the group who took the same name in Sierra Leone, were descendants of interracial marriage and concubinage. Frenchmen, like the Portuguese who preceded them, quickly succumbed to the charm of the Wolof women, considered among the most beautiful in Africa. Such women were called signares, after the Portuguese term for "madam," and they were very significant in the development of Senegambia. A few were mistresses, but most contracted marriages according to local custom. Their sons were often educated in France. The daughters stayed behind acquiring freehold property and African captives, whom they usually leased to the government as laborers and artisans. Frequently a newly arrived Frenchman would inherit not only his predecessor's post but his Senegalese family as well. As the prime intermediaries between European and African society, the *signares* were of great importance in the community, frequently organizing trading expeditions to the interior or setting up operations in local commerce. All Creoles tended to accept European culture and Christianity. By the middle of the nineteenth century they were distinguished by their strong opposition to Islam, which they believed must be eradicated if the country were to make progress.

Traditionally the colony's African population was stratified in terms of their status as free Africans or captives. Free Africans set up in trade, worked as craftsmen, or served as interpreters between the colony and the hinterland. Captives were drawn from many different ethnic groups, usually located some distance away, so that they could not easily disappear into Senegal's surrounding African population. Such household slaves were rarely sold overseas, unless as a punishment for a crime or if their masters went bankrupt. In any case, they were freed in 1848, though many elected to remain with their former masters.[34]

Senegal was represented in Paris by a deputy from 1848 on. This link was abolished by Louis Napoleon but was restored under the Third Republic. More important, Senegal was given French-style local government institutions, but in order to be eligible for election a candidate needed to know how to read and write French, a provision that was expected to encourage the assimilation of the African voters.[35] In 1854 a group of Bordeaux merchants requested the appointment of a governor willing to stay long enough to give continuity to French policy in Senegal. They suggested a thirty-six-year-old military engineer, Major Louis Faidherbe, who had been educated at France's elite Ecole Polytechnique. Faidherbe had spent two years in Senegal after service in Guadeloupe and Algeria. Faidherbe's restless curiosity drove him to read everything published and to search archives. He learned the Wolof language, quizzed the local people, traveled widely, and married an African wife. Above all, he had the stamina to stay long enough, from 1854 to 1861 and again from 1863 to 1865, to put some of his ideas into effect.[36]

The transition from the peaceful development of French commerce to war

and annexation must be viewed as a stage in the complicated interaction between the French and the diverse African peoples rather than simply a unilateral decision by Faidherbe. The French had never succeeded in assembling
a durable system of alliances. But in the volatile 1850s, with local traditional
leaders under recurrent attack from militant marabouts, there was great incentive to pursue a pragmatic policy of divide and rule. In 1855 Faidherbe
set up the School for the Sons of Chiefs, also grimly known as the School for
Hostages, which brought potential chiefs and leaders to Saint-Louis to be exposed to western ideas and trained as potential auxiliaries of the French.

While waging a series of sharp local campaigns, Faidherbe utilized his professional expertise to reconstitute Senegal's military strength. He could draw
on his Algerian connections and exploit the obsession of the French army
there with the security of its position in the south to obtain limited French
reinforcements. But his main contribution was to organize what became the
famous Senegalese *tirailleurs* (sharpshooters), a stable, efficient African fighting force under European command. This gave him two advantages over other
European governors in tropical Africa. First, they had been reluctant to use
European troops because of the high death rate from the climate and tropical
diseases, especially malaria and yellow fever. Second, with a disciplined African fighting force under his own command, it was much easier for him to
slip the leash of ministerial control in Paris and to embark on adventurous
campaigns in the interior.

But one battalion of Senegalese *tirailleurs* supplemented by variable numbers in the French rank and file was not strong enough to cope with the much
greater forces organized by Al-Hajj 'Umar, leader of the Tukolor jihad. Moreover, partly owing to increased wealth from peanut crops, the militant
Muslims were relatively well armed with muskets and rifles in addition to
their religious zeal. Hence the French and various traditional African leaders
were driven together by mutual dependence. One such leader was Juku Sambala of Khasso, who was threatened when his brother chose to head 'Umar's
forces in their region. Sambala suggested using the French fort at Medina as a
rallying point for all anti-'Umar forces in Khasso. The French, therefore,
became involved not just in resisting 'Umar but in the dynastic complications
of traditional African states for the next twenty years. In 1857 'Umar turned
against Medina. The Senegalese forces there under the Saint-Louis mulatto,
Paul Holle, resisted stoutly and were lucky in that a sudden rise in the level of
the Senegal River enabled the French to bring supplies to them by water.

The defeat of 'Umar at Medina probably convinced him that further attempts to challenge the French on the lower Senegal would be futile; henceforth he directed his attention eastward to the upper Niger region. But Faidherbe's military success had been purchased at a high cost. Senegalese traders found the 1857-59 wars ruinous and wanted the campaigns stopped. Faidherbe developed a policy of "consolidation" from 1859 onward by strengthening French forts and reaching a modus vivendi with 'Umar.

The net effect of Faidherbe's several campaigns was therefore to assert a general French military supremacy while enforcing low tariffs and freeing France from financial obligations to African rulers. Some new forts were established, but at most of these, as the French authorities carefully pointed out to traders, control was asserted only within cannon range. Direct French rule was confined to areas close to Saint-Louis and Dakar, where Faidherbe appointed the chiefs, generally from traditional allies. This rudimentary administration was financed by a head tax, which also served to push farmers into the cash economy. Faidherbe's administration was modeled on the French practice in Algeria, whereby a subject population was controlled by a few French officers manipulating the traditional leadership.

In outer areas where the French sought to influence African politics without enforcing direct control, they were not always successful; for example, it seems that in the case of Sambala of Khasso, he was manipulating them rather than the reverse, but it took them until 1878 to discover that he was an embarrassment rather than an asset. Their policy in the rich peanut area of Cayor, lying inland between the immediate hinterland of Saint-Louis and Dakar, constituted another territory where their manipulation was counterproductive. Faidherbe tried to install a subservient leader, Madiodio, but chose badly. It was Madiodio's rival, Lat-Dior, who mobilized support for the resistance to the French by embracing Islamic militancy.

Indeed, by the time Faidherbe left Senegal in 1865 the Bordeaux merchants were once more calling for a policy based essentially on commerce rather than on annexation. By 1870 France was seriously considering abandoning Medina, and the disaster of the Franco-Prussian War made any forward policy in Africa impossible. By 1871 Senegal was once more reduced to the status of "an aggregation of colonial trading posts." Yet Faidherbe left behind the geopolitical plans that were developed by his marine officer successor under the Third Republic. Above, all, he created a disciplined, effective, African-based striking force and a tradition of French military imperialism in the Sudan.[37]

The Imperial Diaspora: The Fingo and the Creoles

European outposts in Africa, whether commercial, missionary, or administrative, were part of a worldwide network. Africans who made themselves useful to Europeans could therefore gain information from books, newspapers, missionary magazines, and commercial gazettes about opportunities in that wider world. Both at the Cape and in West Africa important African groups seized such chances with the result that in both areas a western-educated, geographically and socially mobile black elite developed before the scramble took place.

The white presence in South Africa gave novel opportunities to many victims of Shaka's wars. Among the refugees who fled south were some who ended as laborers in the Cape Colony, but many more found refuge in the Xhosa chiefdoms. Border chiefs, eager to increase their followings, accepted them as clients and named them *Mfengu* (beggars) — or Fingo, in the parlance of whites. The Fingo were assigned to tend portions of the royal herds in return for the milk.[38]

The arrangement was welcome enough at first, but because cattle denoted a man's personal standing and were essential to the marriage contract, the Fingo were unwilling to remain mere unpaid herdsmen for long. The Xhosa chiefs claimed that independent Fingo would threaten the security of the royal herds since it would be relatively easy for them to pass off some of the chiefs' beasts as their own. John Ayliff and Joseph Whiteside, white Christian missionary chroniclers of Fingo grievances, describe the "cunning and deception" of their countermeasures: "In order to acquire cattle, the Fingos grew tobacco, and prepared it with great care. They packed it in small rush baskets which they hid in their huts until a favourable opportunity to sell it was found. Under the pretence of visiting a relative living at a distance, where they knew tobacco was in demand, they would form a small party like so many pedlars carrying small baskets of tobacco on their heads. When they arrived at their journey's end, they bartered the tobacco for cattle." The Fingo also acted as middlemen between blacks and whites, exchanging their old cows for beads, cooking pots, spades, and hoes. "These articles they did not use, but reserved them for barter with other tribes for cattle, contenting themselves with earthen pots for cooking and brewing native beer, and with wooden implements for breaking up the soil. Sometimes, they travelled a hundred miles for the purposes of trade."[39]

Close to the Xhosa in custom and language and originally identified in terms of their economic status rather than their ethnic distinctiveness, the Fingo might well have been incorporated into the host culture, which, in fact, happened with considerable numbers who settled among the Pondo. But the presence of white missionaries in the Xhosa chiefdoms offered a choice of patrons. With their traditional culture already weakened by the *mfecane*, the Fingo found Christianity's assertion of the worth of each individual relevant to their sense of being an oppressed minority among the Xhosa, who often expressed their casual contempt by referring to them as dogs.

Delighted by the flow of Fingo converts, the missionaries regarded them as superior to other Africans and eagerly championed their cause. For their part, the Xhosa chiefs frowned on such conversions, seeing clearly their political dimension, and threatened the missionaries with expulsion. The arrival of the newcomers in a border zone where black settlement already was compressed by white expansion increased the tensions between the Xhosa and the Cape Colony. When British troops moved into the Transkei in 1834, the Fingo saw their chance to shake off Xhosa domination, and many fled to the British camp, begging for protection.

Sir Benjamin D'Urban felt it both politic and humanitarian to accept them. Misled by the missionaries who mistook the client role of their Fingo protégés for outright slavery, he claimed to be acting "in the true spirit of the sweeping emancipation so recently made [1834] in the Mother Country" by making them British subjects. Further, as "good herdsmen, good agriculturalists, and useful servants" they should be settled on land taken from the Xhosa, which "they will soon convert . . . into a country abounding with cattle and corn, [and] will furnish the best of all barriers against the entrance of the Kaffirs."[40] Thus, seventeen thousand Fingo were invited across the Kei River at the end of the 1834-35 frontier war, and they arrived driving twenty-two thousand cattle. Little more than a dozen years after their flight from the *mfecane* they were installed with their own herds on their own grazing lands. The reversal of fortune matched that of God's chosen people, with Ayliff, their missionary champion, cast as Moses.

And having chosen the right — white — side, the Fingo continued to prosper. Just as they represented the supreme evangelical success for Ayliff and Whiteside, they functioned as heroes of economic self-help, even when sticking to their traditional religious beliefs. H. M. Robertson in his classic, liberal account of South African economic development, "Economic Contact between Black and White," pointed out that, although the Fingo joined the colony comparatively rich in cattle, from the start "they entered the service of the farmers, and by a combination of regular work, parsimony and acquiring fresh concessions through making themselves agreeable to their protectors, soon became the chief economic power among the Bantu tribes."[41]

Acculturation to white ways now proceeded apace as the Fingo learned to use the plow, to know the value of raising sheep as well as cattle, and to express this general striving for economic improvement within a system of individual land tenure. Fingo women pressed their men to get plows, very conscious that this would give them a much easier life than if they had to continue to do the hoeing. As a by-product of evangelization, the missionaries fostered literacy, the key to western education. And in 1848 "Mr. H. Calderwood, Civil Commissioner for Victoria East, offered money prizes for the most respectably and decently dressed Fingo man and woman throughout the year."[42]

These prosperous, expansive intruders, by increasing the competition for land and arousing jealousy among the Xhosa, contributed to a cycle of frontier warfare of which they were the main black beneficiaries. Whenever fighting broke out, their wagons and cattle sold at a premium, while their loyalty to the whites was rewarded with further lands seized from other Africans as soon as peace was restored. Moreover, because they were pro-British and pro-missionary, they were regarded as unbelievers for whom the shades of the ancestors had no message by the sponsors of the nativistic cattle-killing of 1856-57, who held that if only the Xhosa destroyed all their cattle and provisions, dead heroes, cattle, and food would appear out of the earth on February 18, 1857, and the whites would be driven into the sea. So the Fingo were exempt from the irrational and self-destructive response of their fellow frontier Africans to the white presence.

Fingo history as portrayed by white historians has an unmistakable Samuel Smiles-Horatio Alger ring. Charles Brownlee, commissioner of the Gaika district, records that in 1858 two Fingo families settled there, "both bearing certificates of good and long continued service from their late masters in the Colony. The head of one of the families was named Adonis, and was a thorough heathen. He was possessed of about 100 head of horned cattle and about 1,000 good wooled sheep, and had an annual income of between £200 and £300; he paid his hut tax punctually, but beyond this contributed nothing to the revenue, and his money was either buried or devoted to the increase of his already numerous flocks and herds. Adonis was killed in 1877, and after the conclusion of the rebellion, his son obtained a pass from me to go for his father's hidden money, and brought back £1,400 which his father had buried from time to time."[43] On the strength of such exemplary achievement Robertson commented: "Undoubtedly the Fingoes were comparatively well adapted for the economic struggle.... Members of other tribes did not often make so much of their opportunities."[44]

The Fingo could innovate successfully in many areas because the *mfecane* had unfettered them from custom. It also shattered their political framework so that the traditional leadership had much less power to direct and constrain change. The Cape Colony supplied the peaceful environment within which their enterprise could function, and those who had been chiefs in their homeland, now by no means always the richest, contributed to their political cohesion by providing a focus for loyalty and by dispensing advice on a voluntary basis. Because the Fingo's economic development was self-serving rather than politically directed, they constituted no threat to white supremacy. Participating in the white economy and serving beside the Cape armed forces, they earned the title "the loyal Fingo."

By 1865 they had prospered to such an extent that their locations were becoming overcrowded. Some forty thousand were settled on land from which Sarili, one of the Xhosa chiefs, had been driven, clearly indicating how much their success depended on white patronage. But in the perspective of comparative African history their remarkable success illustrates by contrast the extent to which traditional African governmental structures had controlled and limited the economic development of other African groups. White traders dubbed the Fingo "the Jews of Kaffirland,"[45] and like the Jews — and the Lebanese in West Africa and the Indians in East Africa — they were licensed interlopers, operating by grace and favor of the colonial power while exempted from the political and ritual dimensions of traditional culture.

The Creoles of Sierra Leone had been enslaved, a catastrophe even greater than the *mfecane* that afflicted the Fingo.[46] Like the Fingo they eagerly adopted white men's skills, and many seized on the commercial, missionary, and administrative opportunities provided by the European presence. The Creoles, for example, who settled in the Gambia were important in the development of the peanut trade, and many instituted trading connections with the Sierra Leone hinterland. But the largest Creole group originated in Yorubaland, in what is now western Nigeria, and it was here that the Saros, as they were known when they returned from Sierra Leone to their ancestral homeland, made their most ambitious attempts to act as key intermediaries between Europeans and Africans.

In 1834 the first group of Saros came back to the Egba kingdom of south-western Yorubaland, landing at Badagry on the coast just south of Egba-land.[47] The first European mission in western Nigeria was established at Badagry in 1842, the same year as the missionary Thomas Birch Freeman reached Abeokuta, the Egba captial. The Egba ruler saw the possibility of forging an alliance with the Europeans to operate against his Yoruba rivals and the powerful kingdom of Dahomey to the west. In 1846 the Anglican Church Missionary Society was established at Abeokuta, followed in 1847 by the Wesleyan Mission.

The Egba saw Europeans in terms of the advantages to be derived from their relationship with them but were always suspicious of British inten-tions, a suspicion that increased greatly after the occupation of Lagos in 1851 and its annexation in 1861. The annexation shattered missionary in-fluence in Abeokuta. In 1865 G. W. Johnson, a Saro, organized the United Egba Board of Management to put into operation a program of defensive modernization in order to preserve the Egba's independence from both the Europeans and other Africans. In 1867 the Europeans were expelled from Abeokuta, their mission buildings were sacked, and their printing press was destroyed.

In other Yoruba areas the cycle of Saro involvement as intermediaries was not so dramatic as in Abeokuta. But all Saros faced a basic dilemma: they had to demonstrate that they were "civilized," as indicated by their dress, general demeanor, monogamy, and political allegiance, while proving to their Yoruba kin that their primordial loyalties survived. Frequently the dilemma proved insoluble.[48]

Customhouse Imperialism: Rehearsal for Partition

When a metropolitan power disapproved strongly of any extension of the boundaries of its colonies, it was likely to do so in terms of keeping the costs of imperial administration low. But such instructions would provide a dilemma for the governor to whom they were sent. European and African traders were prone to avoid the ad valorem taxes on foreign trade imposed by the colonies to raise their revenues by concluding their business on some river just outside the colony boundaries. African middlemen situated in the immediate hinterland of the colony also could be bothersome. They naturally sought to maximize the advantages deriving from their location by enforcing tolls on trade goods passing through their territory. Moreover, since much of the trade consisted of arms and ammunition, they occasionally preferred to redirect its flow to their own inland neighbors in order to preserve a balance of power favorable to themselves. In either case the obstructed African inland power was likely to complain to the governor of the European colony that if only the troublesome middlemen could be removed, then trade would flow freely. Often the harrassed governors, seeking to cover their expenses, heeded such advice and annexed the troublemaker only to see the erstwhile inland power become the new middleman and the whole cycle repeated. Similarly, if the governors elongated their colonies by annexing nearby rivers, the offending merchants might simply move out of range to the next suitable trading point.

The dilemma was inescapable. Indeed, it was finally recognized only in 1865 when the Select Committee of the House of Commons adopted the principle of "nonextension" but then, after discussion, added the important qualification that it could not "consent to an absolute prohibition of measures which, in peculiar cases, may be necessary for the more efficient and economical administration of the settlements we already possess."[49]

CHAPTER 3

Background to the Scramble

Recent studies of the period immediately before the scramble have brought into sharp focus the dynamic — and often violent — sequences of the African initiatives just analyzed. Thus, juxtaposed to the European powers with their preference for cut-price informal empire, ideally combining commercial expansion with loose consular control, were the principal African actors in the "African partition of Africa" who proclaimed jihads and mobilized their peoples for less sanctified wars as they sought to reconstruct the political map of Africa. On the European side there were some "men on the spot" who managed to evade the metropolitan controls on expansion as they edged their way along the coasts or farther inland in pursuit of fiscal self-sufficiency for their settlements. And, of course, there was the unique military imperialism of Major Louis Faidherbe in Senegal. But even here the scale was somewhat different from the achievements of Shaka or the Voortrekkers or 'Uthman dan Fodio and Al-Hajj 'Umar.

Such an Afrocentric approach to the preliminaries has prepared the way for a reversal of the old notion of partition. The scramble can no longer be seen as a movement issuing from inside Europe whereby the invaders simply shaped a passive Africa to their will. The Africans, in a succession of local crises, so the argument runs, rejected the informal arrangements preferred by the Europeans: "The spectacular expansion that resulted has often been called imperialism. But at a deeper level it was a reflex to the stirrings of African proto-nationalism."[1] Because the local crises prompted the readjustment of political relationships between Africans and Europeans, the forms of interaction broadly depended on the local type of African society.

Map 2. Africa in 1879, indicating the limited European occupation at that date

The danger to be averted in correcting the distortions of the old Euro-centric viewpoint is that exclusive focus on African initiatives produces a mirror-image distortion by discounting significant elements of European pur-posiveness, premeditation, and aggression. New research on the African factor has illuminated the process of partition in many areas, but the imperial factor cannot be reduced in every case to a subsidiary element caught up in a reflex response to the local situation. The causes of any conquest partly determine its nature and are therefore vital in comprehending its effects on the con-quered. Only when African and imperial history are drawn together as mu-tually complementary factors can a satisfactory historiography of the impe-rial experience in Africa develop.

European Powers in the Scramble

It is necessary first to make some general points before taking a closer look at the policies of the main European states involved in Africa. The economic background against which the partition of Africa was played out was the so-called Great Depression. From 1873 to 1896 prices, profits, and rates of in-terest fell and remained alarmingly low. Modern research and experience of the crash of 1929 has reduced the Great Depression, objectively speaking, to something of a nonevent; yet the twenty-odd years of deflation did reduce the general price level by a third, and in terms of the psychology of govern-ments and businessmen in Europe the effects of the depression were very real, resulting in greater state support for business, sometimes in the form of tariffs, as well as commercial combinations and cartels.[2] Such political effects were heightened by the intensified national rivalries of the time. Germany and Italy achieved national unity in 1870 and could turn their attention to international affairs. France, which had been torn by revolution in 1830, 1848, and 1870, finally stabilized the Third Republic in the mid-1870s. The United States survived the Civil War of 1861 to 1865 and, having absorbed the frontier lands of the Indians and the Mexicans, began a period of remark-able economic expansion. The emergence of a competing group of economi-cally advanced powers in the era of the Great Depression fused political and economic rivalry.

One side effect of increasing state support for private enterprise was the emergence of foreign bondholders, backed by their governments, as a signifi-cant political force in the undeveloped world, undermining Egyptian inde-pendence in 1876 and 1882 and threatening Liberian sovereignty should the republic default on repayment of the £100,000 raised on the London money market by President Edward Roye in 1870.

Southern Africa's great mining bonanzas — Kimberley diamonds from the seventies onward and Rand gold in the eighties and nineties — offered hope to international investors and unemployed miners. Imaginative map reading led to speculation on the possibility of further bonanzas: to the north of the Rand lay the still fabled lands of Prester John, and in the western Sudan men expected to revive the "golden trade" of the Moors. King Leopold II of the Belgians cashed in on the mood with his International African Association in 1876. More innocent, less exalted individuals were caught up in the excitement: in 1883 one Monsieur Caqueraw proclaimed through the press and pamphlets that "in the name of civilization [and] equally in the name of the commercial and industrial interests *de notre beau pays*" he was forming a "Cooperative, Scientific, Industrial, Hospital and Kindergarten Society for Central and Western Africa," which would launch a French colony in the vicinity of Timbo, the capital of Fouta Djallon. Although his committee of patronage boasted such names as General Gustave Borgnis-Desbordes, the conqueror of Timbuktu, Talon, the governor of Senegal, and Victor Hugo, the Ministry of Marine discovered that Caqueraw was only a poor commercial representative with no hope of amassing the capital necessary for his grandiose scheme.[3]

But in order to exploit the resources of Kimberley and the Rand, heavy European capital investment was required. Access routes had to be constructed, a labor force had to be recruited, and mine shafts had to be sunk. The mine shafts were especially expensive in the case of the deep levels of the Rand. All this involved capital expenditure on a scale dwarfing that of traditional European trading interests in Africa. It also required docile, powerful, and efficient government to provide the favorable political climate in which such heavy investment would show a profit. Should the existing African regimes fail to oblige the mining companies, then powerful, broad-based financial interests might well request direct imperial intervention. Moreover, with no systematic geological surveys to supply guidance, the investors pressed their governments to stake out huge preemptive annexations in order to stay in the treasure hunt.

The Great Depression had important economic effects on tropical Africa in that the European demand for oil and fats decreased and the prices of peanuts, palm oil, and palm kernels fell by roughly a third. West African producers, along with American prairie farmers and Irish peasants, suffered as the barter terms of trade moved against them. This had a disturbing effect on the existing "moral community of traders," straining relations among European merchants, African middlemen, and African producers.[4]

Europe's heightened international tension also had unsettling effects in Africa because the arms race between the powers resulted in the rapid obsolescence of guns, which were then dumped on Africa. In tropical Africa small producers of palm products and peanuts were able to purchase guns and therefore to challenge their traditional rulers, leading to what has been termed a "general crisis of the aristocracy" in West Africa at this time. In southern Africa the chiefs directed their warriors to work in the European mines and on farms in order to buy guns with which to resist settler incursions. From the point of view of the overlapping circles of international diplomacy and international business, Africa confronted them with both crises and opportunities in trade and politics.

Some historians have tried to refute economic explanations of partition and have pointed out that the politicians and officials actually responsible for imperialist policies in Britain and Germany tended to be linked with the traditional ruling classes rather than with industry and commerce. It seems wrong, however, to disqualify members of the landed classes from economic motivation in a transaction that regarded Africa as so many blocks of real estate. Title to the real estate could bring with it, after all, the possession of latent natural resources of immense value, as landowners-turned-mineowners well knew. Again, it has been argued that within the lifetime of the first generation of imperialists or even of their successors, the European powers gained scant returns from some of their African possessions. But it is in the nature of a hereditary ruling class to take the long view with regard to its properties. (The historians who draw up the accounts for Europe's dependencies in 1914 or 1939, two favorite dates, do provide "hard," objective data, but our present-day knowledge that the course of formal empire was in most cases more than a third or two-thirds run at these times can easily lead to the application of anachronistic hindsight and the inference that the imperialists of the late nineteenth and early twentieth centuries operated with a similar time scale.)

The sense of Africa as so much real estate was also politically important for Europe. Seventy years before the 1884-85 Berlin Conference on Africa the powers had treated Europeans similarly at the Congress of Vienna, distributing lands and the people living thereon as so much dynastic property in order to reconstruct a balance-of-power equilibrium in the aftermath of the

Napoleonic Wars. But the development of mass nationalism in nineteenth-century Europe made it increasingly difficult for princes to dispose of their lands and subjects in job lots in order to adjust the balance of power. (Even the German empire had some pretext in ethnicity for seizing at least Alsace, if not Lorraine, from France.) One expedient specifically recommended by Bismarck to France, Britain, and Italy was to seek territorial compensation outside of Europe, especially Africa, where the nationality principle was presumed not to operate. The new styles in nationalism exemplified by the Germans, Italians, Poles, Magyars, and Irish, stressing shared literary and historical traditions, gave some semblance of theoretical legitimacy to this viewpoint.

France

In 1876 Colonel Brière de L'Isle, a war hero who had led the French marine infantry at Sedan, became the governor of Senegal. An exponent of "le go-ahead American," he applied himself to this new command with panache, thrusting forward along the upper Niger so that France might dominate the interior of West Africa. At the same time he transformed Senegal's tariff structure with differential duties on foreign shipping and textiles.[5] This double challenge, territorial and fiscal, eventually provoked the British to abandon their policy of informal sway for one of limited expansion.[6]

By contemporary criteria of the national interest, measured in terms of strategy and trade, France was an unlikely candidate to initiate the late-nineteenth-century scramble for empire in Africa. Defeat at the hands of Germany cost France 150,000 men, the industry of Alsace, and the iron of Lorraine — as well as five billion francs in indemnity. For the next half century these losses and Germany's growing power dominated French thinking. Colonial policy therefore had to take second place to the necessities of *haute politique*, turning on the European balance of power.

Politicians seeming to flout this basic rule were swiftly called to account. Any colonial adventure that threatened France's military position in Europe prompted memories of Louis Napoleon squandering men and treasure in Mexico before the bitter reckoning of 1870-71. Premier Jules Ferry learned this when he hazarded forty thousand troops, including many metropolitan conscripts, in a difficult summer campaign in Tunisia in 1881, provoking a crisis that brought down his government. Inside a year Premier Charles de Freycinet suffered similar retribution over the Egyptian crisis of 1882, although in his anxiety to avoid Ferry's fate, he had handled the crisis very cautiously. The radical deputy Georges Périn spelled out the lesson: "France must be economical with the blood of her soldiers; her unhappy past and the present situation in Europe make this a duty. What the English can do with impunity we can only do at our peril." When Ferry returned to office in 1883 and began a considered policy of expansion in Indochina, the retreat from Lang Son, although of not great military significance, brought down his second ministry and ruined his political career.

Nor was the French economy geared to overseas expansion. By the second half of the nineteenth century France's relatively slow industrialization had led to some demand for tropical commodities, but her economy, still geared to luxuries and handicrafts, found it difficult to supply the wants of tropical producers when in competition with those of more industrialized countries like Britain and the United States. The very process of industrialization created a boom in public works, especially in railway building, so that investment in France focused on internal development as investment in Britain had earlier. By the end of the century this was beginning to change. The economic crisis of 1882 and the relatively slack condition of the economy from then until 1894 meant that some Frenchmen found it difficult to secure satisfactory returns for their excess funds at home, which prompted a wave of foreign investment. Yet even in this period French industry and capital sought continental rather than imperial outlets. The leaders of European industry, Britain and Germany, were France's chief trading partners, while Russian industrialization provided the best opportunities for investment. The colonies could not compete; before 1900 they accounted for less than one-tenth of French foreign trade and investment.[7]

There was no history of emigration comparable to that of Britain and Germany to impel French statesmen to consider imperial action to conserve valuable manpower. The combination of a relatively static population with an entrenched peasantry, which had never been uprooted by any equivalent to the English enclosure movement or the Scottish highland clearances, enabled the French to develop and cherish their well-known *casanier* (stay-at-home) spirit as a definitive national characteristic. Even when Algeria was developed as a colony of settlement after 1880, it attracted most of its immigrants from other Mediterranean countries. Hence it was impossible for Frenchmen to preach with conviction in favor of some Gallic equivalent of the global Anglo-Saxon and Teutonic solidarity advocated by Cecil Rhodes and Joseph Chamberlain.

Born in defeat, the Third Republic began by consigning all possible resources to internal reconstruction. The puny finances available for the empire were stretched to cover the increasing cost of the penal colonies as well, and by 1873 more than a third of the colonial budget was spent on the penitentiary service. The metropolitan subvention to Senegal was slashed from 500,000 francs in 1866 to just over 150,000 francs in 1871 and was completely abolished in 1873. The fall in European prices for peanuts and gum cut the value of the colony's trade from 38.3 million francs in 1868 to 28.8 million francs in 1874. Senegal's status as a large colonial trading post, rather than a true colony, appeared to be confirmed when Brière de L'Isle took office as governor in 1876. The economy had slightly improved, but trade languished almost one-fifth below the 1868 level. Politically the outlook was no better, with Sierra Leone threatening France's control over the Southern Rivers (estuaries along the coast of Guinea and Sierra Leone) and the recalcitrant African leaders in the immediate hinterland as well as in the interior. To Paris, peaceful trade seemed the obvious goal of Senegalese policy. Brière de L'Isle was specifically forbidden to make fresh annexations, and he was authorized to resort to military action only when it was essential for the protection of existing commercial interests. On no account must he exceed his budget.[8]

Yet his governorship flouted all such precepts. Political expansion replaced peaceful commercial development as the principle of French policy. New areas of the western Sudan were brought under military control, and in order to do this the fiscal stipulations were completely abandoned. In the process Brière de L'Isle, above all a soldier and intolerant of opposition, systematically replaced civilian officials with soldiers, further enforcing military-style discipline by frequent gubernatorial inspections. By 1881 Senegal's Deputy A. S. Gasconi was complaining: "The colony is not being *administered* but *commanded*."[9]

A prime source of discord between Brière de L'Isle and the Senegalese merchants was his differential tariff, aimed at foreign — in practice usually British — textiles, the famous "blue bafts," or "Guineas," which served as currency or units of account on the upper Senegal. As in all West Africa, trade was organized on a credit basis with European merchants letting goods out on trust to their African agents to be exchanged inland for local produce. Whatever the origin of Guinea cloth, whether from Lancashire or British India, Rouen, or Pondicherry in French India, it was carried and imported exclusively by Bordeaux merchants, who obviously found it in their interest to let out the cheapest cloth available on trust, and this cloth seems to have been predominantly of British make. In 1879 the General Council of Senegal, on which Bordeaux interests were strongly represented, voted against the governor's differential duty. This provoked Brière de L'Isle to elucidate his conception of economic imperialism in his comment to the Ministry of Commerce. The colony, he complained, is being swamped by foreign imports. Free trade was not practicable. It did not make sense, when France was opening up fresh outlets "almost in the heart of Africa, that all this effort should accrue to the profit of foreign industries, while the industries of France were excluded from the markets of Senegal by a few Bordeaux firms."[10] Brière de L'Isle's preaching of imperialism on behalf of national trade in opposition to French traders in Senegal reveals the complex economic background to imperialism.

Brière de L'Isle's subversion of the pacific principles that were intended to guide him was a triumph of persistence. His dispatches shrewdly rationalized his military initiatives in terms of security rather than empire; it was an argument deskbound bureaucrats and metropolitan politicians found morally difficult to resist. At worst, if Paris withheld prior authorization, he could resort to a fait accompli, justified again in terms of military and colonial security. But the most significant aspect of Brière de L'Isle's initiatives was that they became much more than just another series of local ventures by a forceful "man on the spot." His updated version of Faidherbe's expansionism was conceived on such a scale that it required, and eventually received, ministerial backing.

Given the overriding concern with Europe, why was such endorsement possible? Metropolitan political developments provide part of the answer. The years of Brière de L'Isle's initiatives were those in which the Republicans finally took control of the Third Republic by winning the elections of 1877 and 1879, followed by the resignation of Marie MacMahon, the royalist president. A fresh, confident generation of politicians, the "Republicans by birth," grasped the levers of power.

Although France had not shed the humiliation of defeat or escaped from the consequent diplomatic isolation, at least the Congress of Berlin in 1878 allowed her plenipotentiaries to parade once more in the center of the European stage. France's conqueror in 1871, Bismarck, now at the height of his manipulative power, had made it quite clear that French imperial expansion in Africa would gain solid German support. Bismarck's intent was fairly obvious. He aimed to prevent cooperation between France and Britain by encouraging them to embark on colonial expansion in Africa, so opening the way for future imperial rivalry. With the financial crises of Turkey, Egypt, and Tunis after 1875, he persistently encouraged France to take Tunis, Britain to take Egypt, and Italy to take Tripoli — knowing that the partition of North Africa in this way would provoke disputes. For the time being, however, might it not be best to work with the grain of Bismarck's policy, accepting his offer of a safe colonial role from which to initiate some moves worthy of a great power? That, at any rate, was the view of France's professional diplomats in all the major European capitals.[11]

Nationalist and expansionist groups amplified such professional advice. Their main vehicle in the 1870s became the rapidly developing French geographical movement, which began when the Geographical Society of Paris, founded in 1821, announced toward the end of 1871 that it would no longer limit itself to scientific speculation. For, as one of its officials explained, just as the historic civilizations of Phoenicia, Greece, Rome, Venice, Genoa, Portugal, Spain, the Netherlands, and the Islamic world had declined once their overseas enterprises failed, the Paris society could not "forget that our former preponderance was contested from the day we ceased to compete . . . in the conquests of civilization over barbarism."[12] The geographical movement was an international phenomenon but proved much more successful in France than elsewhere; the total French membership of 9,500 in 1881 was nearly twice the membership in Germany and almost triple that in Britain.

This growing group of colonial enthusiasts included articulate and "expert" spokesmen such as railroad engineers, explorers, and geographers as well as some deputies. Prominent among these was the same radical deputy, Georges Périn, who spelled out the basic strategic rule that had been broken in 1881. Périn was a member of the Commission on Missions and Voyages in the Ministry of Public Instruction, and in 1879 the Paris Geographical Society honored him by making him a vice-president. He proposed the first substantial government subsidy for exploration, persuading the deputies to vote 100,000 francs to Abbé Debairze for a journey across Africa from the Indian Ocean to the Atlantic following the trail of Livingstone and Stanley. In advocating this grant Périn complained that France was falling behind in African exploration: "The scientific interest of such a voyage is super-abundantly demonstrated; but aside from the scientific interest, there is a practical economic interest; for, at this moment, one thinks not only of penetrating into the heart of Africa in order to report on its fauna and flora, but with the thought of colonizing this immense continent. . . . Why should not these countries be colonized as America and Australia have been colonized?"

The key to the apparent contradiction in his attitude to expansion lies in the disparate phenomena covered by that term. What Brunschwig has characterized as the "modern French school of colonization" sought to reconcile the humanitarian ideal and the principles of 1789 with colonization.[13] The doctrines of this school, somewhat similar to those propounded by evangelical Englishmen of an earlier generation (such as Henry Venn of the Church Missionary Society), were given their distinctive French stamp by the young economist Paul Leroy-Beaulieu, who played a leading role in publicizing the geographical movement. As against "classical colonization," in which impoverished settlers sought out empty or sparsely populated lands, he recommended a truly modern form of colonization in which rich countries would export capital and technicans to help less economically advanced peoples to develop their resources. It was to be an essentially collaborative process, involving aid, education, and profit sharing, with the inhabitants of the colonized area retaining their individual liberties so that both they and their colonizers would jointly participate in a French civilization regarded by Frenchmen as universalist, positivist, and humanitarian. As Leroy-Beaulieu envisaged it, such colonization would be very different from the militaristic imperialism that had perpetrated atrocities against the civilian population in Algeria. The writings of Paul N. Soleillet, sponsored by the geographical societies dealing with the western Sudan, epitomized for Leroy-Beaulieu this doctrine of "pacific conquest." Soleillet argued that France should regain her glory in Africa, not by feats of arms but by her genius for civilization: "The true conquests of our epoch are not found in the military field, but in that of industry and commerce — De Lesseps had done as much for the glory of his country as Turenne and Bonaparte."[14]

Leroy-Beaulieu focused attention on Africa as "the sole field of expansion remaining open to France." Hopes were pitched high, often unrealistically so. Adolphe Duponchel's *The Trans-Saharan Railway*, published in 1878, created a wave of enthusiasm for developing a huge area of Africa and thus restoring to French technology the prestige won by de Lesseps with the Suez Canal. Similarly optimistic geographers described the small and scarcely known Ogooué River as one of the largest in Africa, leading to an area whose inhabitants lamented the lack of any Europeans to purchase their massive supplies of palm oil, rubber, gum, and wax. However visionary and vague such reports, they served Leroy-Beaulieu's purpose, enabling him to advertise likely future additions to French Africa of great potential value, so long as they were developed by the new-style colonization with its stress on research, investment, and education. Thus Africans would be increasingly caught up in the sweep of human progress that, in Leroy-Beaulieu's vision of modern history, could be measured by objective criteria drawn from science and technology.

The French leader whose ideas on expansion did correspond most closely with Leroy-Beaulieu's was Charles de Freycinet, although his vacillation at the time of the Suez campaign has tended to obscure his significance as an imperialist.[15] (By contrast, Jules Ferry, more famous as an expansionist, seems to have been unaffected by the new ideas.) [16] Freycinet, a graduate of the Ecole Polytechnique, had worked as a mining engineer during the Second Empire and then had found scope in the Third Republic as a kind of political technocrat for his passionate enthusiasm for railways. In 1877 he embarked on a large-scale reorganization of the French railway system. He extended his schemes to include Algeria, and from there the logic of geography led him on to embrace Duponchel's trans-Saharan plan and even Brière de L'Isle's ideas for pushing the Senegal railway farther inland. In 1879 Freycinet became the premier and lost no time in proclaiming his attitude toward imperial affairs: "It is the duty of the Government to look beyond the frontiers and investigate what peaceful conquests it can undertake. . . . Africa, on our doorstep, has a special claim to our attention."[17]

Such expansion would doubly conform to the strict strategic priorities resulting from France's preoccupation with Germany. Further, being pacific in nature, such expansion would not dissipate French military strength; and, by an extension of the logic that assimilated French North Africa to the metropolis, Africa was seen as a continent on France's doorstep. Thus, colonization there did not mean dispersing French resources to the other side of the globe. In a further exposition of the ideas of the new school of colonization Freycinet pointed out: "The Minister of Public Works will have a prime role. . . . Civilization both extends and consolidates itself more surely through communication routes. We should attempt to link up the huge territories served by the Niger and the Congo."[18]

Like the soldier Brière de L'Isle, Freycinet found himself clashing with the French commercial interests in the area. The traders of Saint-Louis believed a Sudanese railway would threaten their monopoly over the commerce of the Senegal River, and therefore they actively conspired against the government projects. Meanwhile, Freycinet had accepted the extravagant notions of

African wealth and population publicized by writers such as Duponchel and, envisaging a population of a hundred million in the Sudan, was intent on securing for France the greatest share in the future development of the area. He was convinced that the race for Africa was about to begin, and he was determined to win. By comparison with this glittering potential prize, existing French economic interests seemed paltry. Thus by the end of 1879 the Ministry of Public Works planned to send a mission to Agadès and then on to Sokoto so that the Fulani empire might be opened up to French trade and influence emanating from Algeria.

This focus on the future, rather than on the promotion of existing commercial interests, was an essential element in the appeal of the new school of colonialism. Louis Napoleon's colonial adventures had profited shady speculators, so that later imperial initiatives that led directly to the advantage of existing vested interests were likely to be denounced as sordid financial machinations. Freycinet's schemes would only reap their profit in a visionary future; for the time being France and Africa could be identified as the beneficiaries in only the most generalized sense. Paradoxically, the new school's sheer lack of touch with existing commercial interests was part of the secret of its appeal.

In February 1879 a former governor of Senegal, Admiral Jean Jauréguiberry, a close friend and political ally of Freycinet, took over as the minister of marine with responsibility for the colonies.[19] A committed expansionist, he provided backing for Brière de L'Isle's plans to advance to the Niger River within weeks of taking office. Proposals for a Senegal-Niger railroad had already been mooted by exponents of the new technological imperialism, including notably the explorer Paul Soleillet. Brière de L'Isle seized on this idea as a way of providing rapid communication for his thrust into the interior. Jauréguiberry agreed, and by July 1879 the Niger railroad was considered part of the proposed trans-Saharan network.[20]

Freycinet and Soleillet's optimistic plans miscarried. Freycinet's high hopes for economic expansion via the trans-Saharan railroad were dashed with the massacre of a survey and prospecting expedition in February of 1881. It was now evident that any attempt to build the railways before the Sahara had been pacified and permanently occupied was out of the question. Moreover, the French army was already committed in Tunisia. Thus in June 1881 a trans-Saharan railway was indefinitely postponed. When Brière de L'Isle made up his mind to aim for the Tukolor capital of Ségou, he decided to employ Soleillet to reconnoiter the route. Soleillet accomplished his "voyage à Ségou," but from there he had to return to Senegal because Ahmadu, the son of Al-Hajj 'Umar, now ruler of the empire, did not wish him to move into areas that the Tukolor found difficult to control, hoping thereby to conceal the weakness of his position from the French. Soleillet returned to Paris, where he enjoyed much publicity and succeeded in obtaining a sizable subvention from the Ministry of Public Works as well as a post on the Trans-Saharan Commission. He attempted a new expedition, leaving this time from Mauritania, but it foundered, giving Brière de L'Isle, by now incensed at the explorer's boastfulness and his attacks on the military, the chance to repatriate him. This direct clash of personalities in the actual theater of operations was paralleled by a basic difference of approach, despite their political and personal friendship, between Freycinet and Jauréguiberry. Freycinet believed in "peaceful conquests" and gave his Saharan missions strict orders that they keep the peace. Although Jauréguiberry assured Freycinet that he only wanted "to take part in the general movement which was bringing the nations of Europe to penetrate to the heart of Africa in order to open up new outlets for their commerce," his intent was strategic rather than economic. He had never been an enthusiast for the trans-Saharan project, and when it collapsed he concentrated his efforts on preserving the Niger railroad scheme. As he saw it, the railroads should extend French rule. Commercial profitability was secondary. As a technocrat, Freycinet believed that rail technology would produce economic development; as a professional warrior, Jauréguiberry was more interested in strategic communications and forts.

In September 1880 Jauréguiberry placed the Sudan under military command, appointing Major Gustave Borgnis-Desbordes as the commander in chief of the upper Niger River. This was the crucial decision endorsing French expansion into the interior and institutionalizing the specifically militaristic character of the transition from informal to formal empire. The timing is significant, for all this happened in 1879-80, two or three years before the scramble began.

Bad planning, financial mismanagement, disaster, and disease soon rendered the building of the Niger railroad a costly farce. By 1882, 16,000,000 francs had been voted for the work, although the preliminary surveys demanded by the French Parliament were not carried out. But the project fitted into the general policy of the thrust to the Niger by generating the finances necessary for military expansion. Only half of the authorized expenditure was actually used on the railway; the rest provided for military fortifications and diplomatic missions. The army's new forts alone cost ten times the original estimate of 200,000 francs. And by now military expansion had developed its own momentum. When Jauréguiberry's successor, Admiral Georges-Charles Cloué, tried to restrain expansion and to recall Brière de L'Isle in March 1881, he merely found that Borgnis-Desbordes was impossible to control now that he was able to assume the role of sole resident expert and therefore could force the hand of the government by pointing to the threat posed by the Tukolor empire and the new African power of Samori.

In 1882 Freycinet and Jauréguiberry returned to office. They continued the policies of formal imperialism they had begun three years before, involving France in the politics of the lower Niger and the Congo in a two-pronged assault aimed at the creation of a huge territorial empire in the interior.[21] This marked France's participation in the actual process of competitive European partition that their activities in 1879-80 did so much to bring about and that will be discussed later.

Because the logic of France's strategic and economic situation in the late nineteenth century runs counter to extra-European involvement, her massive colonial acquisitions have to be explained by a closer examination of the policy-making process than is necessary for the more industrialized states (such as Britain or even Germany) having essential trading links with the undeveloped world. And this policy-making sequence is part of African history as well as European history, for the collapse of the technocrats' grandiose schemes and the incorporation of their wreckage in the vast military empire erected by the marine officers gave French imperialism in the western Sudan its unique character. Both the origins and the nature of the French colonial venture there were crucial for its impact on France's African subjects.

Britain

In the first half of the nineteenth century the economic impulse to further British imperial expansion was relatively weak. Although Britain had lost political control over the United States, its commercial links there were stronger than ever. Unlike its traditional European imperial rivals such as France, Britain had retained the bulk of its archaic imperial possessions. Hence, Britain was comparatively well equipped to meet its needs for tropical foodstuffs and raw materials. Moreover, in this phase of the industrial revolution, the main interest of the British economy was in its own development rather than overseas trade.[22] The conversion of great industries, beginning with cotton, to steam power, the railway and construction booms, and a rapid growth of population focused attention on the domestic market. With the exception of cotton, exports could have no priority so long as the home market absorbed such a large share of total production. Cotton goods alone, because of rapidly falling prices as a result of mechanization, sold in large quantities in remote tropical markets, such as the Oil Rivers (Niger River delta area) in West Africa, beyond the bounds of the empire. Hence, the first half of the nineteenth century constituted a "peculiar interlude" (to use Gerald Graham's phrase)[23] in British imperial and economic history. British paramountcy was characterized during this interval by its industrial lead and commercial supremacy, which were epitomized by the pioneering cotton industry, the navy's command of the seas, and the relative absence of rival powers.

The Great Depression and the intensified national rivalries that accompanied it ended this pleasant and unique combination of circumstances for Britain. Before the depression was over, Britain had been surpassed in some crucial economic aspects, such as steel production, by the United States and Germany. Britain was certainly no longer the unique workshop of the world. Germany and the United States mobilized their economic power through the formation of trusts and cartels and, like France, enjoyed tariff protection for their farming and industrial home markets. All this meant a fierce struggle by Britain to preserve at least the volume, if not the relative position, of its overseas trade and investment.

Britain was unwilling to use some of the weapons employed by its rivals. It was too committed to the decentralized business organization of its own industrial revolution and the ideology of competition to switch wholeheartedly to the new methods of systematic concentration. It was equally disinclined to exchange free trade for tariffs.

This left only one way to deal with the problem. Britain's traditional solution (though one now increasingly adopted by its competitors) was the promotion of economic (and if need be political) primacy in undeveloped areas, i.e., imperialism. The switch from informal economic paramountcy over the undeveloped world to political imperialism was not welcome to Britain's rulers. Foreign Secretary Earl Granville's response to the views of the Manchester Chamber of Commerce on the Congo in 1884 was to query indignantly whether Britain really intended "to take possession of every navigable river all over the world, and every avenue of commerce, for fear somebody else should take possession of it?"[24]

Yet Granville and Prime Minister William Gladstone came to feel they could not stand by while world outlets were closed to British trade. Fear of a French monopoly of the Congo's markets was definitely the reason for concluding the Anglo-Portuguese treaty of February 26, 1884.[25] And anxiety to preserve an open door for international trade in the Congo area was the basis of British policy throughout 1884 and at the Berlin Conference of 1884-85. In fact, as early as November 1883 the aggressive French policy in West Africa had led the British Cabinet to endorse a policy of establishing protectorates for the Niger and Oil rivers, "with a view to the maintenance of an unfettered trade, which unhappily is not favoured by the arrangements of the French in those latitudes."[26]

In 1884 Lord Salisbury, under whose premiership the partition of Africa was largely conducted, criticized Gladstone's opposition to annexation on the grounds that it had allowed France and other states employing discriminatory tariffs to monopolize undeveloped areas. He warned his audience in the Free Trade Hall, Manchester, that as the markets of the developed world were enclosed by tariffs, those of the undeveloped world were threatening to become the only areas in which British commerce might do profitable business.[27]

Harry Johnston was invited in 1889 to spend the weekend at Salisbury's Hatfield House, during which time they discussed British policy in Africa. It was suggested, indirectly, that Johnston might care to expound the government's policy in the press. Johnston's important article in *The Times* on "Great Britain's Policy in Africa" argued that now that the total trade of Africa had reached about £31 million, the British government must play a more positive role: "If free trade were a universal principle, it would matter relatively little to our merchants what particular nation ruled the new markets for our commerce; but in as much as protectionist Powers may, and do, possess themselves of huge tracts of Africa and then proceed to stifle or cramp our trade with differential duties and irritating restrictions (witness the Portuguese everywhere in Africa, and the French in Senegambia and Gaboon) then it becomes a necessity for us to protect ourselves and forestall other European nations in localities we desire to honestly exploit." All Britain wanted, he concluded, was a "fair field and no favour," but "to secure this for our commerce and our civilization . . . we are forced to extend our direct political influence over a large part of Africa."[28]

With British control of the Cape and its advanced mining technology great hopes were placed on the South African mining bonanza. In 1889 the *Economist* reported with satisfaction on the recovery of the metal and engineering industries in response to the "new world of work," which South Africa offered to Britain.[29] By 1892 the same magazine was reporting riotous excitement in "that part of the Stock Exchange" called the "Kaffir Circus."[30]

Now much more dependent on foreign trade to supply food for a vastly expanded population and raw materials for industries, Britain participated in the scramble against the backdrop of the Great Depression and the erection of foreign tariff barriers. In response to the unease of businessmen the Royal Commission on the Depression of Trade and Industry conducted an inquiry into Britain's troubles in 1885-86, showing that German trade was danger-ously competitive in both home and overseas markets. The parliamentary under secretary James Bryce emphasized the diplomatic assistance the government would provide for commerce, "well aware that commerce was the lifeblood of Britain" and that it "could only be maintained, in the face of the fierce competition of today, by turning to account every resource which the government possessed."[31] It was ironic that Britain felt so bound to its free trade principles that it could not provide support of business in the form of tariff retaliation. Hence the pressure for imperial expansion, "the imperialism of free trade" under British auspices, was strengthened. As Salisbury commented retrospectively to the French ambassador in 1897, if France had not been so wholeheartedly protectionist, it would not have found Britain so greedy for territory.[32]

There was a further irony in the British position. Crouzet, the French economic historian, has argued convincingly that the effects of increasing competition, the depression, and tariffs were relatively slight.[33] S. B. Saul has shown that the British Empire only profited Britain insofar as it was integrated into the mainstream of world commerce.[34] Britain's deficits in trade with the developed world of western Europe and the United States were offset by a favorable trading relationship with, above all, India, but also with tropical Africa and Australia, which in their turn sold to the United States and western Europe more than they purchased from them. Britain, therefore, by means of her free trade empire was able to act as the balancer in the dynamic expansion of world trade. Crouzet has further argued that because the effects of the depression and revived protectionism were relatively slight, their influence on British imperialism must have been equally tenuous. But this is to argue after the event in the light of sophisticated analysis, whereas policy was formulated in the light of what contemporaries feared to be the case at the time, however ill-founded such fears might be. The consensus was that the outlook for British overseas trade was bleak. As Britain developed into a rentier nation, the empire, so long as it was an empire of free trade, made sound economic sense and incidentally allowed the British ruling class and bourgeoisie to feel morally superior to those competitors who appeared to obstruct the flow of world trade by tariffs.

Germany

One of the most controversial questions in modern imperial history is why Germany suddenly plunged into African colonization in 1884-85, imposing protectorates on Togo, the Cameroons, and part of Guinea in West Africa, on substantial areas of South-West Africa and East Africa, and on territory in the south Pacific. Bismarck, who directed Germany's grab for African land, frequently went on record to the effect that such imperial ventures were not in the national interest; indeed, "for Germany to acquire colonies would be like a poverty-stricken Polish nobleman providing himself with silks and sables when he needed shirts." Given such statements, both before and after 1884-85, and others in which Bismarck claimed credit for the acquisition of these colonies, the debate has centered on whether Bismarck really did change his mind about the worth of colonies or whether the German empire was acquired for essentially non-African reasons such as the winning of an election in Germany or for its by-products in European diplomacy.[35]

What is not in doubt is that all along Bismarck had been prepared to give solid state support to German business interests in the undeveloped world. Although the chancellor frequently used the old rhetoric of the national interest, he was very well informed about the state of the German economy, receiving detailed fortnightly letters from his banker over a long period of time on the state of the economy.[36] The German version of the Great Depression comprised three industrial depressions (1873-79, 1882-86, and 1890-95) and a structural crisis of agriculture beginning in 1876. Unsteady economic growth and consequent social tensions appeared to threaten the steadiness of the new German empire. Businessmen sought to combine economic development with stability through a "corporate capitalism" characterized by the growth of cartels and mergers. At the same time Bismarck, who was constantly aware that the German empire of 1871 was a very precarious structure threatened by traditional regional divisions as well as by new demands for social and political democracy, began a policy of state intervention designed to damp down protest and ensure the survival of the Reich and its traditional ruling class. Both Bismarck's interventionist state and the new German corporate capitalism hoped that an export offensive in foreign markets would constitute an effective way of coping with the stresses of turbulent industrialization at home. Germany's welfare was therefore made dependent on the success of informal economic expansion in which the state and corporate business sought stability through a pragmatic anticyclical economic policy. Bismarck was impressed by the way Britain had developed an informal economic empire during the period of her industrial lead, and he hoped to solve Germany's problems similarly.

By the period of the Great Depression German traders with Africa, usually operating out of the Hanseatic ports of Hamburg and Bremen, were success-fully challenging the established French and British merchants. By the 1880s Hamburg was estimated to be handling nearly a third of all West Africa's overseas trade through its domination of the recently developed palm kernel market. German farmers were the main buyers of cattle cake, and the Dutch were the largest manufacturers of margarine, both products derived from palm kernels. Both Germans and Dutch were supplied through Hamburg, which was well able to provide Africans with cheap liquor in return.[37]

Hamburg played a leading role in the development of steamship services to West Africa and through the Woermann family firm introduced a new type of European businessman into Africa. The firm was founded by Carl Woer-mann, who entered the Liberian trade in 1849 and who came to dominate it and then to extend his business to Gabon and the Cameroons. He also opened regular steamship services to West Africa. He was succeeded as head of the firm in 1880 by Adolph Woermann, who was elected to the Reichstag in 1884 as a National Liberal deputy and was reputedly a confidant of the chancellor himself. The Woermanns' business success was also responsible for a fanning out of Hamburg enterprise as former agents of the firm struck out on their own, using capital and experience acquired while working for the parent firm, very much in the way that the ambitious young men from Bordeaux used the Victor Régis firm of Marseille to get a foothold in African trade. In the 1880s Adolph Woermann, the vice-president of the Hamburg Chamber of Commerce, was responsible for drawing up its statements of policy on African trade at a time when Bismarck wanted to conciliate the Hanseatic ports that were only then, and with some reluctance, entering the Zollverein, the Prussian-dominated customs union. Hence, although Ger-many's trade with Africa represented only 0.3 percent of her total foreign trade, it was dynamic and not without political influence.[38]

The combination of an industrial depression in 1882 with the structural crisis in East German agriculture, owing to the importation of cheap foreign food, gave fresh impetus to colonial propaganda. Societies that were intent on persuading Bismarck to embark on colonization grew up all over Germany. The most important societies were the Kolonialverein of 1882 and the Gesellschaft für Deutsche Kolonisation founded by Carl Peters in March 1884. The Kolonialverein was the more conservative of the two, representing a powerful alliance of industrial and commercial interests. Peters's society, composed of petty and middle bourgeoisie as well as some Prussian estate owners, was the more radical, pressing for an active expansionist policy and emphasizing the need to provide land for peasant settlers. This ideology of settlement appealed to the anticapitalist attitude of the petty bourgeoisie, but ironically it meant that German colonization could draw on the savings of the lower middle classes for African enterprises that big business was reluctant to back.[39]

German commerce with Africa was still minute, although the achievements of Hamburg and Bremen merchants gave some plausibility to the extravagant propaganda of the colonial societies. The non-European undeveloped world was still the great unknown factor: there was always the possibility that the sanguine forecasts of the colonial societies would eventually come true. So long as the mid-Victorian principle of free trade prevailed, this did not worry Bismarck. Yet in the early 1880s there were signs that the free trade era, which Bismarck himself had undermined in Europe by the protectionist German tariff of 1879, was also under threat in the colonial world. German merchants in Africa complained about the extension of British and French customs posts, protesting that the lack of a German naval presence and German bases and consuls put them at a disadvantage. In March 1883 Woermann sent a memorandum to the German Foreign Office asking for naval support, a base on Fernando Po if this could be bought from Spain, and a full-time German consul, and urging opposition to the proposed Anglo-Portuguese treaty on the Congo, which was confirmed in 1884.

Only a month later Heinrich von Kusserow of the legal-commercial division of the German Foreign Office reported to Bismarck on the secret Anglo-French convention of June 1882, which had been published recently by the French government, observing that the two powers guaranteed each other's nationals immunity from discriminatory customs duties. Actually Kusserow had misconstrued, probably unwittingly, the French text for the convention, in which the parties simply agreed to divide a section of the West Coast in the vicinity of Sierra Leone. It did promise equal treatment of each other's nationals, but only with reference to the protection of life and property and the right to own real estate. Since there were no provisions regarding customs, it was not, as Kusserow stated, an agreement by the two imperialist powers to control the West Coast of Africa by trading mutual privileges to the exclusion of noncolonial powers.[40]

Bismarck responded by asking for the views of the Hanseatic ports. The reply from the Hamburg Chamber of Commerce, with the hand of Woermann evident, suggested a "trade colony" in the Cameroons, a naval station on Fernando Po, treaties with African chiefs giving Germans equal rights with other Europeans, and treaties with Britain and France to ensure that Germans could trade in their territories on an equal footing. The response from Bremen simply asked for naval protection on the coast. The Hamburg merchants wished to preserve their freedom to trade along the coast, but they recognized that under the new conditions of the 1880s they needed adequate naval and consular support in dealing with Africans and other Europeans and also a German base to match Lagos. Like the British traders in the area they did not want their state to adopt a policy of territorial acquisition in Africa.

In 1883 these proposals were still too radical for Bismarck to accept. In December he announced that a naval vessel would be stationed permanently off the West African coast, that a special commissioner would be sent, that eventually a consul would negotiate treaties with Africans, and that he would ask Spain for the right to locate a naval base on Fernando Po. But he absolutely refused to undertake territorial responsibilities in the Cameroons or anywhere else. What had happened, therefore, to lead Bismarck to acquire several protectorates only a year later? The traders had not requested them, and the chancellor had even rejected their request for a limited protectorate in the Cameroons.[41]

There were at least three aspects to the subtle, frequently ambiguous, development of Bismarck's policy. First, there was a growing exasperation with Britain, especially with Prime Minister Gladstone and his foreign secretary, Earl Granville, that led negotiations to become acrimonious on whether the British would provide protection for a newly established Bremen merchant, F. A. E. Lüderitz, in South-West Africa. Bismarck interpreted cumbersome British diplomacy, which had to take account of attitudes of the Cape (where there was a change of government at a crucial time in the negotiations), as malicious. He believed that Britain was intent on maintaining dubious claims to South-West Africa, and ultimately on April 24, 1884, he sent telegrams to the German ambassador in London and the consul at Cape Town informing them, though in somewhat obscure wording, that Lüderitz's claims "were under the protection of the Empire."[42] Second, with elections pending, a positive colonial policy seemed the simplest way to reconstruct the right-wing alliance, bringing the National Liberals back into the Conservative coalition and stigmatizing the parties of the left wing as enemies of the Reich. The government press sharply attacked British policies, labeling the opposition at home as essentially hostile to the Reich and giving support to a foreign power. The exploitation of anglophobia was important in Bismarck's technique of maintaining Conservative control. It allowed him to divert abroad the stresses caused by internal problems. Britain, the powerful rival with an established position in world markets, was an apt target. Anglophobia also externalized anticapitalist feeling by directing it outward against Britain, the capitalist state par excellence, just as anti-Semitism diverted anticapitalist resentment internally.[43]

The third cause of Bismarck's sudden switch to a positive colonialist policy was his belief that he had discovered an administrative device, the protectorate controlled by a chartered company, which would remove the financial and political dangers that he had previously feared. Basically he had opposed colonies because the expense of administering them would "widen the parliamentary parade ground" by increasing the government's financial dependence upon the Reichstag. Hence, an apparently right-wing move would in practice prepare the way for just that parliamentary democratic control over the executive that he was determined to resist. In April 1884 Kusserow suggested that Lüderitz might be given a charter to administer the territory of Angra Pequeña, which he controlled in South-West Africa, on the model of the charter given in 1881 to the British North Borneo Company. In doing so, Bismarck declined to impose German sovereignty on Angra Pequeña but offered protection (*Reichsschutz*). At the same time he declared protectorates over three areas of West Africa — Togo, the Cameroons, and the trading post of Koba Bagas in Guinea.[44]

Thus, like Salisbury, Bismarck reluctantly came around to the view that, provided no large administrative costs were entailed, the state might have to establish a protectorate to prevent the closing of overseas trading areas by a rival power. Again like the British, he found the German state slithering into additional political responsibilities. The arrangement by which chartered companies would take responsibility for administration would only have been viable if Germany had restricted protection to well-capitalized companies. Fearing that Britain might forestall him, Bismarck hurriedly gave protection to a medley of trading establishments along the western coast of Africa, none of which had entered into a previous charter agreement with the government. In the aftermath he found it difficult, indeed in most cases impossible, to persuade the traders to relieve their government of responsibility. He was left presiding over just such an overseas German empire as he had intended to avoid.

Portugal

While northwestern Europe was in the process of turbulent industrialization, Portugal remained a very poor agricultural and maritime country, still economically dominated by Britain.[45] The mid-nineteenth century weakness of the Portuguese in Guinea, Angola, and Mozambique has already been described, and David Livingstone's notion that the Portuguese territories could produce the same amount of cotton as the American South if they were brought under the control of dynamic Anglo-Saxon capitalism was ominous for the future.[46] Some Portuguese were aware of the threat of expansionist industrial capitalism. On August 8, 1877, Mello Gouveia, the minister in charge of the navy and the colonies, argued that the current wave of African exploration should not be "ascribed exclusively to a generous feeling of the human mind." Anticipating the economic theories of John A. Hobson and Vladimir Lenin, he pointed to the connection between industrial overproduction and Europe's civilizing mission: "For several years commercial and industrial crises have been frequently occurring. Today it is cotton goods, tomorrow it is iron, and then another day it is silk; and other articles which are in greater demand for different social uses are successively undergoing a sudden change in their value which disturbs the price of labour as well as the economy of nations. Strenuous efforts are being incessantly made with a view to the opening of new markets for the disposal of this excessive industrial supply, which disturbs the social economy, and is a menace to the political status of the several states."[47]

When Leopold II called an international conference of geographers in Brussels in 1876, he failed to invite the Portuguese. This alerted the Lisbon Geographical Society, formed the year before, and it urged the Portuguese government to take action to maintain its archaic rights in Africa. The society organized a flurry of expeditions to establish Portuguese claims in the hinterland of Angola. For the same reason the estates of the virtually independent Afro-Portuguese plantation owners in Mozambique were brought under the Portuguese crown in 1880.

In these circumstances Portugal called upon its traditional alliance with

Britain. Both felt threatened by the activities of Leopold II and France, which might seal off the whole of Central Africa, especially the Congo basin, from British and Portuguese interests. To check this, Britain, which earlier in the nineteenth century had refused to admit Portuguese claims, sought to recognize Portuguese sovereignty over both banks of the Congo as far as Nóqui in return for freedom of navigation on the river, customs preferences, and a dual Anglo-Portuguese commission to control river traffic.

The treaty of February 26, 1884, involved an alliance of opposites: the most economically developed European power in Africa with the most economically backward. In addition to the weighty diplomatic opposition of Germany and France and the shrewd propaganda protests of Leopold and his henchmen, British domestic opposition soon developed. In April 1883 the draft treaty was fiercely attacked in Parliament; Jacob Bright roundly declared that "the Portuguese have their method of making trade impossible, they have passports, papers, tolls, fines, and fees — fees at every corner."[48] And winding up the debate W. E. Forster stressed that Britain "must first of all make it clear that there shall be no toll-bar, that there will be no dues exacted on the river; that it will be a free highway." But, he added, "if this be done, the motive of the Portuguese will be gone."[49]

Ever since the Reformation religious differences had been a stumbling block for the alliance. Both Bright and Forster regarded themselves as spokesmen for the nonconformist conscience at a time when the nineteenth-century evangelical Protestant revival and the associated crusade against slavery tended to single out Catholic Portugal as especially benighted.

Stanley did much to mobilize commercial and public opinion in Britain against the treaty, arguing that the Portuguese had done absolutely nothing since arriving at the Congo four hundred years before except to ruin trade, whereas Leopold, with unbounded liberalism, was attempting to introduce civilization and commerce among the millions in Central Africa who thirsted for British products. J. F. Hutton, a West African merchant, was another fierce opponent of the Anglo-Portuguese alliance and a supporter of Leopold. British official confidence was further undermined by news of a "trade-crushing Tariff" that was to be applied in Mozambique to destroy British Indian commerce and of differential duties that were already being enforced in Portuguese Angola. On June 26, four months after endorsing the treaty, the British government repudiated it.

Disillusion with the British alliance led the Portuguese increasingly to seek support from Germany and France. But Germany, too, favored free trade colonies in Africa, and Bismarck objected to the Portuguese because their customs would be discriminatory and would be administered by untrustworthy officials. In private he denounced the Portuguese as "worse than the Russians,"[50] so the prospects for effective cooperation of Germany with Portugal were hardly better than with Britain.

Leopold II

Among the powers who scrambled for African territory one was in every sense unique. Leopold II, the constitutional Belgian monarch, was not operating in Africa as the king of Belgium but as a private individual because the Belgian government had refused him support at any stage in his maneuverings for African lands. Leopold was essentially interested in extracting maximum financial profits from Africa, although he intended to use his gains on behalf of the Belgian people.[51]

Leopold had developed his ideas on colonization (years before he actually took control over the Congo) through his study of earlier colonial enterprises in America and recent British and Dutch activity in Asia. Having decided that the economic exploitation of undeveloped lands was more profitable than investment in Belgium's modernized industry, he made recurrent attempts to acquire territory from established imperial powers, especially a Philippine island belonging to Spain, but to no avail. However, the quickening exploration of tropical Africa in the 1870s, especially in the Congo basin, suggested to Leopold that he might find a suitable area of undeveloped real estate there. He had no special interest in the Congo — he never visited the place — and he subsequently considered exchanging it for other territory.

With attitudes of a capitalist promoter Leopold did not at the outset think political domination was necessary to extract profit. Rather he believed that his profits might well be jeopardized if he had to include the costs of political administration in his overheads. Until late in 1882 he intended to establish a purely commercial company, selecting the Congo basin because it appeared to be unclaimed by a European rival and also seemed to be an appropriate place for the establishment of plantations based on his studies of the Dutch in Java. He intended to raise capital for his company through private subscriptions of investors from any country. Leopold's company would establish "stations" for trading and agricultural production and would construct a railroad that would link up with a fleet of river steamers at a point below the rapids of the Congo River.

In 1880 Leopold had Stanley negotiate commercial agreements with African chiefs in the area. But the intervention of the French forced Leopold to send Stanley to renegotiate the treaties to include first the term "suzerainty," and then, realizing that even this would be insufficient, to include the word "sovereignty." Thus Leopold, who considered himself more of a capitalist promoter than a king in Africa and who was happy to act as a constitutional monarch in his own country, was forced to exercise political domination. As the chiefs with whom Stanley negotiated the treaties had no notion what the term "sovereignty" meant, there was no difficulty about this revision.[52]

The idiosyncratic nature of Leopold's imperialism meant that he played a crucial role in transforming relationships between the various powers with regard to Africa. He was essentially a free agent operating behind the philanthropic camouflage of the International Association of the Congo, supposedly dedicated to the substitution of legitimate commerce for the slave trade and unconstrained by considerations of European balance-of-power politics or indeed any traditional concept of the national interest. Also, Leopold and his association represented for all the competing powers a neutral alternative to the annexation of African land by some rival. Paradoxically, his involvement in African affairs accelerated the trend toward political partition by European states.

The Berlin Conference

During the early 1880s the pace of the scramble for Africa quickened. Stanley's activity had led Pierre Savorgnan de Brazza, an agent for French rivals of Leopold, to procure a treaty signed by Makoko, chief of the Bateke country on the northern shores of Stanley Pool, by which he placed his territory under French sovereignty. In summer 1882 Brazza returned to France to a rousing welcome, which induced the government to ratify his treaty with Makoko. A chain reaction of treaty making then ensued, with the British government hastening to acquire territory in the Niger area and Leopold seeking treaties granting him sovereign rights in the lower Congo region.[53]

In 1884 the ninth congress of the International Law Institute, meeting in Munich, called on the world powers to arrange a conference to settle the dangerous disputes that were developing in the Congo basin, citing as a precedent the internationalization of the Danube by earlier European congresses. In view of the Anglo-Portuguese initiative, such a move suited Germany and France. They convened an international conference in Berlin on November 15, 1884.[54] Except for Switzerland, every state in Europe was included as well as the United States. Both the venue and the select roster of participants, exclusively non-African, were significant given the conference's concern with the future of a river basin in Central Africa rather than in central Europe. The powers first discussed the establishment of liberty of commerce in the mouth and basin of the Congo. Next they examined the application of the principle of free navigation to the Congo and Niger rivers. Finally, they determined what formalities should be observed before fresh occupations of territory on the coastlines of Africa would merit international recognition.

Omnipresent at Berlin, though not officially represented at the conference because for the time being it lacked fully recognized sovereign status, was the International Association of the Congo. Leopold ensured, however, that the Belgian party included important association officials. Henry Sanford, a former American consul at Brussels now employed by Leopold, was the most influential American delegate. Stanley acted as a technical adviser to the conference. The processes by which Leopold's self-styled philanthropic association, interested at first in forming an association of several African "free states," managed to transform itself into the Congo Free State, a large territory under Leopold II, illuminate European notions of Africa at this time.

In 1875 the German explorer Georg Schweinfurt suggested in his book, *In the Heart of Africa: 1861-1871*, that the best hope of eliminating the internal slave trade in Central Africa lay in "the formation of large Negro states, to unite the territories most exposed to slave raids, which would be placed under the protectorate of the European Powers." Leopold's association seemed most suitable to exercise such a collective European protectorate. Accordingly he launched his project for a "confederation of Free Negro Republics," but he took care to let those charged with running the proposed state know that they need not take the title too seriously:

It is a question of creating a new State, as big as possible, and of running it . . . [but] there is no question of granting the slightest political power to negroes, that would be absurd. The white men, heads of the stations, retain all power. They are the absolute commanders of stations populated by free and freed negroes. Every station would regard itself as a little republic. Its leader, the white man in charge, would himself be responsible to the Director-General of Stations, who in turn would be responsible to the President of the Confederation . . . The new President will hold his powers from the King, and this President should be resident in Europe.[55]

Such a benign presentation was a superb cloak for Leopold's ambition. There was something in his plans to attract everyone of goodwill. For old-fashioned libertarians — as well as black Americans fired by the "back to

Africa" idea and white Americans concerned to export their race problem —
there was the glittering promise of an eventual "league of negro republics."
For those with a more authoritarian approach Leopold could stress that these
black republics would be ruled by whites. For all humanitarians there was
the intended crusade against slavery. Last, but not least important in legitimizing Leopold's enterprise, such ostensible idealism appealed to western-
educated, articulate Africans who looked to the league of black republics
to uplift less fortunate members of their race and to provide scope for their
own special talents.[56]

The superficial resemblance of the proposed republics to Liberia was not
fortuitous. In November 1883 Sanford arrived in the United States intent on
winning American recognition for Leopold's venture. He explained to Congress that the treaties signed in the Congo were at least the equivalent of
those made by Roger Williams with the Indians of Rhode Island; and after re-
calling for the congressmen the recent foundation of Liberia by private individuals, he entertained them with highly favorable accounts of the free
black republics now being organized in the Congo basin. He won the support
of the influential senator from Alabama, John T. Morgan, of the Senate Foreign Relations Committee, and on February 25, 1884, a joint resolution by
both houses of Congress recommended recognition of the blue flag with the
gold star, the symbol of the "Congo Free States." Secretary of State Frederick Frelinghuysen was more cautious, observing that the "states" did not yet
exist but holding that the United States should assist their creation by recognizing the flag in the meantime. On April 22 the State Department expressed
warm admiration for the benign purposes of the association while betraying
a naive belief that its function was to "wither away" with the emergence of
the Free States of Africa.[57]

On the morrow of this triumph Leopold registered a striking diplomatic
victory in Europe, adroitly ensuring French support through a joint statement in which the association provided "fresh proof of its friendly senti-
ments towards France" and engaged to offer France "the right of first option
if unforseen circumstances should drive the Association one day to realize
its estate." Henceforth France found itself supporting Leopold's pretensions
in order to preserve this right of preemption. In addition, Germany and Britain were forced to maintain the Congo Free State to forestall those "unfore-
seen circumstances" that would permit France to annex the area.[58]

Neither German nor British official circles were naive about Leopold's pretensions. Bismarck disgustedly noted "Schwindel!" beside the pieties about

slavery and "Fantasies!" beside the plan for a council.[59] But it suited neither his European policy nor his stance in German domestic politics to
appease Britain; hence he informed Granville that the Anglo-Portuguese
treaty was unacceptable. A week before the start of the Berlin Conference
Germany recognized the International Association of the Congo, that is, the
Congo Free State, as a friendly state in return for commercial privileges.

Even before this Germany was bringing pressure on Britain to recognize
the association as an international legal entity. On November 15, 1884 Granville held out for the continuation of the existing jurisdiction, arguing that
the United States' declaration meant the recognition of the association as
"Representative of certain native States . . . But until the States under the
care and supervision of the Association have so far developed their institutions as to have acquired a claim to the attributes of sovereignty and to
recognition as an autonomous State, Her Majesty's Government do not
consider that the privilege should be conceded to the Association on behalf
of those States of receiving or accrediting Diplomatic Consular officers, or of
making Treaties with foreign nations, or of exercising jurisdiction over foreigners within the territories which it administers. . . . "[60]

However, in view of the French right of preemption and the continued
pressure from Bismarck and from British merchants in the area, the British
eventually recognized the association. Sir Julian Pauncefote, permanent
undersecretary at the Foreign Office, argued on December 1 that the United
States' declaration was in line with the principles of international law.

The United States' Government do not recognize the Association "as a
State." They recognize the existence of certain "Free States" created by
treaties with "legitimate Sovereigns" in the basin of the Congo and adjacent
territories. These native communities are "under the care and supervision of
the Association." The sovereignty resides in the people who form these communities, and they have chosen the Association as their governing body.

The Association is the mandatory of the Free States and represents their
government. In execution of its mandate the Association "has adopted for
itself and for the said Free States a standard or flag" . . . Nowhere is it pre-
tended that the Association of itself constitutes a "State."

We recognize numerous native communities in Africa and elsewhere as
having a political entity and existence, for we have made Treaties with their
Chiefs.

Why should we not recognize the political existence of the Free States of
the Congo and make a Treaty with their chosen Chief, the Association?"

Pauncefote emphasized his point by adding in the margin, "I see no differerence in point of legal validity between a Treaty with the Association and a Treaty with King JaJa."[61]

A few days earlier Pauncefote had brushed aside the protest of T. V. Lister, the assistant undersecretary at the Foreign Office, that it was "usual in recognising a new state to have a clear idea of its boundaries and even perhaps some proof of the validity of its claims to its territories." Lister thought that "the proper mode of proceeding wd. have been for the Assn. to prove its title, to explain its constitution, to give assurances of its intentions as regards personal, religious and comml. freedom etc. etc. and then to petition the Confce. to recognise its sovereignty." Sir Julian retorted that he agreed with Bismarck that it was not expedient that the status of the association be brought before the conference. "The Association might be recognised not as an actual State, but as a *State in course of formation* . . . on certain defined conditions as to consular jurisdiction, religious liberty, freedom of trade etc. etc. . . . On those conditions it might be provisionally recognised for all practical and necessary purposes as an *inchoate State*. It would be a new feature in the practice of Nations, but I do not see any great objection to it under all circes [circumstances]." As usual Granville simply noted, "I agree" on his forceful permanent official's minute.[62]

Usually this kind of verbal maneuvering around such grand notions as sovereignty and the state can be closely linked with the pursuit of his own conception of the national interest by the politician or bureaucrat involved. But the Berlin Conference has been examined in terms of the history of ideas and the development of international law as well as in terms of great power relationships.[63] Looked at from this angle, it has been taken to be a significant stage in the process whereby the original European state system was transformed into a world system. The common Christian tradition of the European states had inspired the more formal aspects of their mutual relations, and this continued so long as international law was confined to Europe. When the European states extended their influence into other continents, the tendency was to judge the new states that arose in accordance with how far they conformed to the pattern exemplified by the states of Europe. As the European states developed superior military and naval power, they were able to compel the rest of the world to deal with them on their own terms. States that were not made dependencies, pure and simple, of their European masters were expected to adopt the principles of law recognized by the European states in their relations with one another.

Once international law began to be applied outside of Europe, however, the common Christian background that had inspired it was lacking as a source of guidance. The secularized criterion of membership in the expanded system was that each member state must qualify for the general description of being "civilized." A minimum of efficiency in adminstration was required, along with a judiciary that dispensed laws securing the life, liberty, and property of foreigners. Thus what had been originally a Christian law of nations was expanded into an international law applicable to the relations between states throughout the world.

During the 1820s the attempt by the Holy Alliance to restore the rule of the Spanish crown in South America failed against a combination of Britain, the United States, and Latin American nationalism. Europeans filled the breach caused by this rejection of the principle of dynastic legitimism by an instinctive resort to the concept of the sovereign state as a test of international legitimacy. From early in the century Europeans had made the notion of sovereignty, and its implications for international relations, the fundamental principle in their own state system. Now their faith in the utility of their intellectual invention increased with evidence of its success in solving a crisis of legitimacy in the wider world. Henceforth, "these more advanced governments [of Europe] insisted that every political structure must be a state like themselves," as F. H. Hinsley, the historian of sovereignty, put it, citing as an extreme example that "they could not settle the international status of the Holy See without resorting to the device of establishing a Vatican city state."[64] The notion of sovereignty could only emerge within the confines of a centralized, geographically bounded state with an administrative and command framework distinguishable from the social structure of the community. Sovereignty was therefore totally alien to stateless societies based on the lineage system and was even remote from the African proto-states that were encountered by European imperialism when it sought to transform its own political system into one embracing the whole world.[65]

The participants at the Berlin Conference did show a fitful concern that soveignty might prove a deceptive fiction when applied to the Congo basin. Britain, France, and Germany, although believing that their own agents were well-nigh impeccable, were skeptical about the protectorate arrangements made by their rivals. And both the League of Free States and the Congo Free State, which emerged from the league, amounted to attempts at flexibility within the limits set by the European powers' intense commitment to the doctrine of sovereignty.

After having established free trade on the Congo and Niger rivers in the first two bases of its General Act, the delegates at the conference sought in January 1885 to regulate the procedure for acquiring new territory in Africa through its third base. They had therefore to deal formally with the same general concepts of sovereignty and jurisdiction involved in the background discussion of Leopold's "inchoate state." France and Germany, resenting Britain's large territorial acquisitions, urged that protectorates, as well as annexations, should involve administrative and judicial responsibility. Despite this proposal's anti-British aspect, it was a serious attempt to curb the wilder excesses of the scramble. Britain's professional diplomats claimed an equal interest in orderly international procedures and had no wish to be singled out as a dog in the manger by "simply giving Protection for the purpose of keeping other Powers out of certain territories which we cannot use ourselves, but do not like anyone else to use."[66] Nevertheless, even Sir Julian Pauncefote was overborne by the lord chancellor, Earl Selborne, this time.

The whole issue over what the protectorate relationship between Africans and Europeans involved was obscure. Ironically, Selborne, like his opponents, was anxious to curtail European greed. As a "Little Englander," opposed to imperialist expansion, and a most conscientious and learned authority on the constitutional law of the British Empire, he believed British imperial law to be very different from that of the French or the new German colonial empires. Although it very probably made scant difference to the French or Germans whether their territories were considered annexations or protectorates, Selborne believed that the failure to make this distinction in the case of the British Empire would have far reaching consequences. "If we annexed any territory, slavery must at once cease to exist. I am not aware that any other Power is embarrassed with this difficulty."[67]

There is a second irony in the "Little Englander" lord chancellor's fight to maintain the distinction. Ultimately he triumphed when the news reached London that Bismarck had accepted his ideas just after the British government had already decided to give way. It is not certain whether Bismarck yielded because he realized that there would be almost no territories along the coast to which the declaration would apply or because he was convinced by Selborne's reasoning that turning protectorates into annexations was likely to prove burdensome. At any rate it meant that neither Britain nor Germany was to be charged with precise administrative and judicial responsibilities in their new protectorates.[68]

Chartered Companies

Late-nineteenth-century European statesmen, concerned about controlling the costs of empire at a time when intensifying European competition and local African political crises threatened their inflation, returned to the old device of the seventeenth and eighteenth centuries — the chartered company. In the aftermath of Berlin the British, for example, sought to discharge their new responsibilities on the Niger River by devolving them on George Goldie's National African Company.[69] Goldie's firm had successfully swallowed up its British competitors on the Niger by 1876 and furthered its monopoly by bankrupting its French rivals by the eve of the Berlin Conference. At Berlin Goldie acted as adviser to the British delegation, and the British claim to predominance on the Niger was based on the treaties his agents had made with local African rulers. In 1886, therefore, Goldie's company was granted a charter of administration as the Royal Niger Company.

Even at their most successful, as in the case of the Royal Niger Company, the chartered companies proved a transitional form of imperialism, dividing the period of informal expansion in the mid-nineteenth century from formal colonial rule at the end. Although the Royal Niger Company purported to establish an elaborate government, its administration was merely its old system of commercial agents given fresh titles. It did set up its own constabulary, which proved an effective fighting force, but it was not employed on orthodox police duties but rather on punitive expeditions against any Africans who defied the company's commercial monopoly. The chartered companies were essentially unstable regimes, provocative alike to the Africans and to the European competitors, and sooner or later they disappointed the politicians who had grasped at them as a means of imperialism with limited responsibilities. Sometimes, as in the case of Bismarck, disillusion followed very quickly. But whether they made a profit, like Goldie's, or failed badly, like William Mackinnon's in East Africa, in the end they all involved their metropolitan backers in greater formal control.[70]

CHAPTER 4

The European Occupation
of the Interior

The deliberations at Berlin ensured that the European powers could derive their claims to African territory through the extremely vague concept of a protectorate. It was precisely the lack of definition in the notion of what was involved in protectorate administration that constituted its attraction. For only a minimal down payment in terms of personnel and expenditure the European powers could acquire extensive African territory to be developed later at their leisure. Provided that African rulers would come to terms, partition by protectorate treaties seemed altogether more desirable than the expensive and risky process of conquest. There were exceptions. Officers of the French marine infantry, with military reputations and careers to make, usually preferred fighting to treaty making. In Northern Nigeria Frederick Lugard was determined to conquer the emirs, not so much to promote his soldierly reputation as to ensure a free hand unbound by previous treaty obligations. Frequently, though, forceful conquest was merely postponed by the device of protectorate treaties because as the Africans became aware of some of the implications of European rule they frequently rebelled.

Protectorate Treaties

Vagueness among European policy makers about the significance of protectorate agreements was not simply the product of mental laziness and aversion to specific commitments.[1] Disagreement and ambiguity also reflected fundamental changes in both the theory of international law and the theory of sovereignty in the nineteenth century. The classical theory of the law of nations, as propounded by the great Dutch jurist Hugo Grotius and his Portuguese counterpart, Seraphim de Freitas, regarded certain Afro-Asian states as belonging to the family of nations. Their inclusion, which flowed from natural law being regarded as universal, had also been embodied in agreements between European and Afro-Asian states. But increasingly in the nineteenth century international lawyers adopted a Eurocentric outlook, reformulating the history of the family and law of nations. International law was now alleged to have developed from the relationships among the Christian countries of Europe, which were considered the original members of the family of nations. The European founder members now assumed the prerogative of admitting other countries into their club. But even when non-European states such as the Ottoman Empire were admitted, they were regarded as second-class members because they possessed a different — and therefore, by nineteenth-century European standards, lower — civilization. Buttressing this Eurocentrism was the positivist legal theory of the nineteenth century whereby will, not reason, was considered the source of law. Hence, the law of nations was based purely on the consent of the powers, in practice the will of the few western powers, rather than on natural law. But older beliefs still survived to complicate matters for these new legal positivists. Britain's Lord Chancellor Selborne had long opposed the practice of western states treating non-European peoples as if they had no rights. He regarded non-European peoples "almost as if the natives were members of the family of nations," a recent legal historian ironically observed.[2] There were also treaties and other agreements in existence based upon classical notions of the universality of natural law and the inclusivenss of the family of nations.[3]

In Britain, too, the ideas propounded by the jurist John Austin concerning the indivisibility of sovereignty survived to obstruct the development of newfangled continental notions of protectorate jurisdiction. In 1888 the professor of international law at Cambridge, Sir Henry Maine, who had administrative experience in India, cited in his textbook, *International Law*, the German practice whereby the Reichstag actually created protectorates through legislation.[4] Sir Henry Jenkyns, the parliamentary draftsman, took this as his cue to urge that the highly expedient German method be adopted by Britain. When challenged from an Austinian standpoint, he pressed for a free hand in developing international law in "new" protectorates over "uncivilized" states. Eventually Lord Chancellor Halsbury ruled that Jenkyns's approach was unacceptable because it undermined the very idea of a protectorate by practically annihilating "any distinction between the rights and obligations of a protecting power and those of complete sovereignty."[5] When the various British foreign jurisdiction acts were consolidated in 1890, therefore, no major changes were made. However, the Brussels Conference of the same year appeared to increase the obligations of European powers adminstering African territory. To meet these, the British law officers decided in 1891 that the consent of any foreign power could confer jurisdiction over its subjects within a British protectorate — such as American missionaries or German merchants — and that accession to the Berlin and Brussels acts amounted to such consent.[6] Finally in 1895 the law officers held that "the exercise of a protectorate in an uncivilized country imported the right to assume whatever jurisdiction over all persons may be needed for its effectual exercise," bringing Britain into line with France and Germany.[7] Thus in the space of a decade the notion of a protectorate had been drastically and unilaterally revised. The terms of what had originally been reciprocal, even contractual, relationships with Africans had been altered so that there was little check on the will of the imperial master.

The shifting semantics of "protection" puzzled contemporary western jurists, and their complicated evolution is only now being clarified by legal historians. Some African signatories also sought enlightenment. JaJa, king of Opobo, for example, asked for a definition of the term "protection" when Consul Edward Hewett was negotiating treaties in the Oil Rivers. Hewett's reply would have been deemed very proper by the lord chancellor and the legal officers: "With reference to the word 'protection' as used in the proposed Treaty . . . the Queen does not want to take your country or your markets, but at the same time is anxious no other natives should take them. She undertakes to extend her gracious favor and protection, which will leave your country still under your government. She has no wish to curb your rule, although she is anxious to see your country get up."[8] Given such assurances, JaJa agreed to the treaty. But three years later he found the British representative widening protectorate jurisdiction far beyond Hewett's definition. Acting Consul Harry Johnston went so far as to depose and exile JaJa because he opposed British interests, chiefly the wish of British traders to bypass Opobo's "middleman" position and to have direct access to inland markets. Johnston's drastic interference in the internal affairs of Opobo was acceded to, despite some misgivings, by the Foreign Office. When JaJa protested, Lord Rosebery, the foreign secretary, informed him that Opobo was now part of a larger administrative unit and that no single ruler would be allowed to oppose the progress of the whole region, whatever the guarantees in his treaty. Britain, he claimed, aimed at "the promotion of the welfare of the natives of all those territories, taken as a whole, by insuring the peaceful development of trade, and by facilitating their intercourse with Europeans. It is not permitted that any Chief who may happen to occupy a territory on the coast should obstruct this policy in order to benefit himself."[9]

By the end of the century many more Africans would be shocked by the development of protectorate administration. In the Sierra Leone protectorate of 1896, as in the Gambia protectorate of two years earlier, many small polities were declared subject to British sovereignty. Some Sierra Leone chiefs had signed protectorate treaties, but others had not. Most of the treaty chiefs had done nothing more than promise friendship in return for protection.[10] The Protectorate Proclamation of 1896 was never proclaimed up-country. Chiefs resented the district commissioners' courts, where their own subjects might bring them to trial. Above all, they were angry at having to pay and collect the hut tax. At Magbele Pa Suba began collecting in order to pay back his stipend as chief and contract out of the protectorate. In 1898 the British were confronted by a devastating insurrection.[11]

Despite the fact that French jurists adopted jurisdictional imperialism earlier than their British counterparts, in practice French administrators developed an informal theory of indirect rule during the occupation of Africa. Annexations were registered by treaties in which France "recognized X as king of Y," undertaking to respect and enforce the laws and customs of the place provided they were not contrary to humanitarian principles. The constant import of such treaties was that France promised to interfere as little as possible with African rulers. For their part, the chiefs sought protection and accepted the sovereignty of France — whatever that may have meant to them[12] — promising to refrain from acts of barbarism, as judged by French standards, and to facilitate commerce. At this early stage the French colonial officials believed their only concern was with high-level chiefs. The term "king" recurs throughout their treaties, epitomizing the high status they accorded to the Africans with whom they dealt. In practice the person designated "king" was sometimes "only a usurper, a more or less rebel subordinate chief, or even an official in charge of relations with Europeans."[13] But scant resources generally forced the French to keep their intervention within the narrow terms defined by the original treaty.

The comparatively clean slate provided by Germany's lack of a colonial past and the absence of a settled view on colonial relations and administrative decentralization gave remarkable scope to the Germans, some of whom became legendary heroes in the epic traditions of certain African peoples where, indeed, they are often not distinguished from the tribe's own African heroes.[14] Such a man was the young explorer Eugen Zintgraff, who at the age of twenty six was appointed official explorer to the Cameroons.[15] Zintgraff was undoubtedly admired and liked by the African people with whom he was most involved. They regarded him as "Bali nda'ni," that is to say, a true Bali, because of his "energy, humor, approachability, and passionate excitement." On his side, he greatly admired their discipline, loyalty, and rationality, especially evident in their leader Galega, with whom he swore blood friendship in 1889. When Elizabeth Chilver, the historian of the Bali-German relations, visited the area in 1963, she interviewed Zintgraff's mistress, the Princess Fé Ditamina, who "at the age of ninety odd, recalled his fidelity and concern for her, and his attempts to give her the elements of Christian belief."[16]

There was hard calculation, however, as well as sentiment in the initial relations between the Germans and the Bali. When the Germans established themselves in the Cameroons, they forestalled the British, who had developed strong trading and mission ties there. Hence they were faced with the problem of diverting the hinterland trade away from Calabar, which was under British control. Governor J. von Soden felt that the safest policy was to work gradually inland by establishing friendly connections with the nearest African states, but some German traders criticized such caution, hoping that the government would dispatch expeditions that would rapidly open the interior. In 1887 Zintgraff proposed a line of stations running inland along the high plateau behind Mount Cameroon, which he believed would be an excellent caravan route. His scheme was rejected by Bismarck as too expensive, but he was given permission to establish a station in the interior.

He exceeded his instructions by pushing farther inland when he made friendly contact with the Bali in 1889. Germany had in fact been drawn into the complex local politics of the area, which centered around competition between two rival centers of power, the city-state of Mankon and Galega's Bali chiefdom, for the manpower and palm oil of the smaller villages. Galega wanted Zintgraff to establish an administrative and trading post in his area, giving the Bali a decisive advantage in the local rivalry. Zintgraff, with his admiration for the Bali, believed that through them he could ensure German control of trade with the interior. Furthermore, he thought Galega could organize the supply of labor to German firms much more cheaply than was currently the case with workers imported from British-controlled territory or from Liberia.

In August 1891 Zintgraff and Galega signed a treaty bringing Bali under the protection of Germany while simultaneously recognizing Galega's position as the paramount chief of the surrounding tribes. Provision was made to divide such taxes as would be raised from these neighboring tribes as well as the fixed duty that would be paid by caravans passing through the area. Despite the fact that the treaty had to be translated twice — from Coast English into Vai and then from Vai into Bali — there seems little doubt that its import was generally understood by the Bali.

A hundred Mauser breech-loading rifles were distributed to the Bali to enforce this paramountcy. Franz Hutter, a young Bavarian artillery officer, was stationed with Zintgraff. He trained a patrol of fifty warriors to handle the rifles and "blooded" them in October 1891 by attacking and razing three villages that had deserted Bali for their rivals. By the end of the year Hutter had succeeded in tripling the size of the rifle patrol. Small detachments were encouraged to ambush hostile villages, and the warriors were rewarded with a fathom of cloth for each male head taken. Like Zintgraff, Hutter won a distinctive place in Bali oral traditions.[17]

The first lonely white intruders frequently displayed scruples over protocol and tact in personal relationships that smoothed the process of protectorate diplomacy. There were, of course, exceptions. Stanley was responsible for inducing illiterate chiefs to sign highly questionable documents such as his 1889 treaty with Uchunku, the Omugabe of Ankole (in what is now Uganda), which purported "to certify that we, Uchunku, Prince of Ankori and Mpororo, by authority and on behalf of my father, Antari, the King and chief and elders of the tribe of Wanyankori, occuyping and owning the territory of Ankororo and Mpororo, do hereby cede it to Bula Matari [or Henry M. Stanley] our friend, all rights of government of the said districts, and we hereby grant him or his representative, the sovereign right and right of government over our country for ever, and in consideration of value received and the protection he has accorded us and our neighbours against the Kabba Rega." The youth Uchunku was simply a relative of the Ntare ("Antari"), not a son, and it is very doubtful whether he understood the significance of this document, let alone the Ntare who had never even met Stanley. But at least when Stanley handed over the rights he claimed under this and other treaties to the Imperial British East Africa Company, the company took care to replace the treaty with a genuinely negotiated one between Lugard and the Omugabe in 1891.[18]

Lugard's style in treaty making was very different from Stanley's. He believed that he had discovered in the ceremony of blood brotherhood "the nearest equivalent to our idea of a contract (treaty)." He took pains to explain in great detail "the proper procedure followed by responsible and duly accredited [African] diplomats" in reaching treaty agreements.[19]

Whether the treaties resulted from Stanley's sharp practices or were duly negotiated by Lugard, the point is that they did not convey to their African signatories what would be involved under the new imperialism. Throughout Africa the expansion of colonial rule signaled the appearance of a generation of Europeans whose ideas of the proper relationship between white and black were very different from those of the white men who initiated the original treaties. The Herero and Nama of German South-West Africa complained that the ceremonial etiquette that distinguished their relations with the "Old Germans" was being disrupted by new settlers with ruder norms of behavior.[20] West Africa, too, had its "Old Coasters." Thomas Alldridge, who negotiated so many of the treaties with Sierra Leone chiefs in the early 1890s and who was the first white man many inland Sierra Leoneans had set eyes on, had been in Sierra Leone as a trader since 1871. Shortly afterward, the Sierra Leoneans would be able to contrast his concern for protocol with the brusque impatience of the new breed of district commissioners.[21]

Resistance and Conquest

The European invaders of Africa termed their campaigns "small wars," but the size of a war is a relative concept. A campaign that to imperial and industrial Britain, France, or Germany involved mobilizing the merest fraction of their manpower and national income could mean total commitment and, if unsuccessful, total defeat for their African opponents.[22]

The European invaders confronted a dual problem — Africa itself as well as the Africans. Indeed, to one modern European student of such "small wars," their most striking feature, as against those wars fought between regular European armies, was that they were "in the main 'campaigns against nature.'"[23] The hazards and obstacles of African topography and climate were compounded by disease and distance from the metropolitan base, so that the most successful campaigns, such as Sir Robert Napier's in Ethiopia and General Garnet Wolseley's in Ashanti, were astounding logistical and engineering feats. Mountains, deserts, dense forests, swamps, and estuaries presented particular difficulties to the invader because, as Colonel Charles E. Callwell, the authority on "small wars," stressed, they were especially suitable for guerrilla actions. In southern Africa the Basuto skillfully utilized their mountains, and the Pedi used hill defenses in the northern Transvaal to repel their enemies. In West Africa the people of the northern Cameroon Mountains preserved their independence in a hundred years of intermittent warfare with the Fulani of the Adamawa Plateau and proved similarly resistant to subjugation by the whites. The resistance of Nana, the governor of the Benin River, to the British, "clearly the most impressive in all of Southern Nigeria," depended upon clever exploitation of the mangrove swamps.[21] The Baoulé people of the Ivory Coast utilized their coastal forest to fight a twenty-seven-year guerrilla war against the French. But there is no automatic correlation between topography and successful African resistance. The Ethiopians made good use of their terrain to annihilate the invading Italian army at Aduwa in 1896 but took scant advantage of it when resisting the next Italian invasion in 1935, while the Afrikaners and Samori were outstandingly successful guerrilla fighters in the relatively open country of the South African veld and the West African southern savannah.

Rarely did the European generals possess adequate maps. Even in South Africa, where there had long been a British presence, the British commanders fought the second Anglo-Boer war (1899-1902) without them. Some of the worst European defeats were partly the result of ignorance. In the first Anglo-Boer war (1880-81) Sir George Colley lacked a good map of the Majuba Hill, and although he took great pains to gather information before advancing, his ignorance about the amount of "dead ground" on the slopes was an important factor in his defeat.[25] Operating in unfriendly country, the invaders sometimes suspected or misunderstood the intelligence supplied by their local scouts or interpreters. Thus Samori possessed a superb intelligence system while his French opponents suspected their own chief interpreter of treachery, and at Aduwa there is much evidence that the Italians were led into that fatal attack by false information.[26]

The great problem presented to invaders by the Africans themselves was the bewildering variety of their methods of warfare. "In great campaigns the opponent's system is understood; he is guided by like precedents and is governed by the same code. . . . But each small war presents new features," observed Callwell, pointing out that it was "difficult to conceive methods of combat more dissimilar than those employed respectively by the Transkei Kaffirs, by the Zulu, and by the Boers, opponents with whom British troops successively came into conflict within a period of three years and in one single quarter of the African continent." In small wars, therefore, every officer must be his own anthropologist, studying beforehand the habits, the customs, and the mode of action on the battlefield of the enemy. Callwell ascribed the disastrous defeat of the British by the Zulu at Isandhlwana in 1879 "to a total misconception of the tactics of the enemy."[27]

Doubtless Callwell's recommendation was necessary in an age when Europeans tended to refer to all Africans as "natives," "wogs," "fuzzy-wuzzies," or "savages." He himself classified African peoples in terms of their readiness to accept battle. Once this original pragmatic distinction was made, then many further normative judgments followed. The "willingness of the [Ashanti] to accept battle" was filed approvingly in his index. But in general he observed that "happily the war like instincts of races inhabiting bush grown territories almost seem to vary in direct proportion to the thickness of the cover. When the country is fairly open they are enterprising and courageous. When its whole face is clothed in almost impenetrable thickets they are timid and unskilled in war."[28]

Such judgments on the "national character" of African peoples had important effects. The charging Zulu impi perfectly embodied the European stereotype of the noble savage. Africans who did not fit such a picture were regarded as devoid of martial virtues and as generally inferior. In the Langeberg Rebellion of the Thlaping, a group within the Tswana, and the rising in Mashonaland, both in 1896-97, the Europeans paid dearly for such misconceptions because the Africans made good tactical use of firearms. But the Thlaping and Shona also paid a heavy price. The Ndebele, who were an offshoot of the Zulu, conformed to the stereotype and were expected to resist whereas the whites were shocked that "invertebrate tribes" like the Shona and the Tswana should challenge white rule. Cecil Rhodes was willing to negotiate a settlement with the Ndebele to conclude their resistance. But for the Shona and the Tswana defeat meant punishment by despoliation.[29]

The introduction of the machine gun shifted the odds decisively in favor of the Europeans. Wolseley brought the Gatling of the American Civil War to West Africa for the 1874 Ashanti campaign, and his troops made a point of showing off the gun's rapid fire to their hidden but watchful enemies.[30] However, both the Gatling and the later Mitrailleuse, with their multiple crank-rotated barrels, had the disadvantage of being unwieldy and difficult to maneuver on African terrain. They also were likely to jam; hence as late as 1896 Callwell believed that machine guns were unreliable in a crisis and had yet to demonstrate their value.[31] But in 1889 the British army introduced the single-barreled Maxim gun, which used the force of the recoil to load, fire, and eject at the rate of eleven shots a second. It was much lighter than the Gatling and the Mitrailleuse, and the effects of its devastating firepower dominate African accounts of the later stages of the European conquest. Among the Europeans Cecil Rhodes was particularly impressed, arming his Pioneer Column with the new guns for the invasion of Lobengula's realm. Eric Walker reports the results with blood-chilling cheerfulness: "The fighting was soon over. The machine-guns, a novelty in warfare in those days, worked wonders at Shangani and Imbembezi, and the volunteers entered the ruins of Bulawayo to find the king [Lobengula] fled."[32] Nearly a year later, in September 1894, Rhodes annexed the Pondo without a fight, for he "mowed down a mealie field with machine guns before the eyes of the paramount of eastern Pondoland and his councillors and explained that their fate would be similar if they did not submit."[33] Similarly in West Africa after shattering the Ijebu with Maxims and rockets, Governor Gilbert Carter trekked around Yorubaland displaying his Maxim gun.[34] Seemingly, the civil practitioners of empire appreciated the machine gun's coercive effect before the army was absolutely convinced of its purely military usefulness. But in 1906 Callwell, although still cautious, reported that "the place of machine guns in tactics is now fairly well established."[35]

Agricultural states have rarely been able to withstand the superior weaponry of industrialization. In West Africa, Samori came closest to mobilizing his people for total war against the French, but for all the high morale generated by the Muslim-Mandinka revolution and his own organizational ability, the limitations of Samori's essentially agricultural economy were clear. By 1890 he had deployed a regular army of hunters to bring in ivory to buy guns and had massed his blacksmiths into larger, more efficient units. Yet despite requisitioning the gold jewelry of the Mandinka women, he had revenue to keep a mere four thousand soldiers under arms, and only one thousand of them were equipped with modern guns. To divert more manpower from farming would have brought famine. He was forced more and more to resort to exporting slaves to finance the war effort, but ultimately this was self-defeating as it alienated his subjects.[36]

Although no African state was industrialized at the time of its invasion, at least in southern Africa the leaders of the resistance could send their men to the diamond mines in order to earn money to equip themselves with rifles. Following the example of white settlers who had armed themselves with the latest western weapons, the African miners soon became shrewd judges of weapons as well as eager buyers. However much the settlers might be alarmed at the prospect of increasingly well equipped Africans, the demand of the mineowners for labor and of the colonial administration for the revenue derived from the import of arms meant that their protests were overridden. The Basuto were so well supplied that when the Cape authorities ordered them to disarm, they mauled the colonial forces — who claimed they found the Basuto better armed than themselves — so thoroughly that they forced the Cape to withdraw from the Gun War of September 1880 to April 1881. The Cape gave up any pretense of governing the Basuto, who virtually regained their independence when the colony surrendered responsibility to London in 1884.[37]

When the Europeans invaded Africa, they intruded into existing patterns of diplomatic and military competition between African states. At the outset the European presence frequently appeared less menacing to Africans than did their own local enemies. Moreover, the series of dynamic African imperialisms that had erupted in the nineteenth century — the *mfecane* in the south, the jihads in West Africa, the ivory and slave trade empires in East Africa — meant that there was no shortage of aggrieved African peoples to whom the Europeans could turn within the bounds or on the outskirts of the dominant African powers. The British had perfected such divide-and-rule policies in India, and the process of picking off the African polities one by one was systemized for the French by Captain Joseph Gallieni and later in French Equatorial Africa by Governor Martial Merlin in 1909.[38] Eventually an anti-French coalition of African states did emerge in the western Sudan in 1889, but it was extremely difficult to hold together: "For most of the participants, the overriding consideration was the need to preserve their independence not just against the common enemy but also *vis-à-vis* one another."[39] By 1893 the coalition was in disarray. An actual imperial yoke, rather than a general threat of invasion, was needed to transcend particularisms as in the Sierra Leone Hut Tax War of 1898 and the Maji-Maji rebellion in German East Africa in 1905-1906.[40]

Finally, in Northern Nigeria at the outset of the twentieth century "protection" and "conquest" were deliberately blended. Although the home authorities would have preferred peaceful penetration, Lugard was determined to secure a free hand within his protectorate by basing the British title on the right of conquest. The militant Muslims in Northern Nigeria gave him the opportunity. When their leader, the Sultan of Sokoto, eventually replied

MOROCCO
TUNISIA
SPANISH
SAHARA
ALGERIA
LIBYA
EGYPT
0   500
Miles
ERITREA   FRENCH
SOMALILAND
GAMBIA
FRENCH WEST AFRICA
ANGLO-
EGYPTIAN
SUDAN
(condominium)
BRITISH
SOMALILAND
PORTUGUESE
GUINEA
NORTHERN
NIGERIA
FRENCH
EQUATORIAL
AFRICA
EMPIRE
OF
ETHIOPIA
SIERRA LEONE
SOUTHERN
ITALIAN
SOMALILAND
LIBERIA
GOLD
COAST
TOGOLAND
CAMEROONS
UGANDA
BRITISH
EAST
AFRICA
SPANISH
GUINEA
BELGIAN
CONGO
GERMAN
EAST
AFRICA
CABINDA
ANGOLA
NYASALAND
NORTHERN
RHODESIA
Portuguese
SOUTHERN
RHODESIA
MOZAMBIQUE
British
British-occupied
SOUTH-
WEST
AFRICA
French
BECHUANALAND
Belgian
German
UNION
OF
SOUTH
AFRICA
SWAZILAND
Spanish
Italian
BASUTOLAND

Map 3. Africa in 1914, indicating areas controlled by the European powers after partition

to Lugard's messages in May 1902, he made it clear that they would only surrender to force: "From us to you. I do not consent that any one from you should ever dwell with us. I will never agree with you. I will have nothing ever to do with you. Between us and you there are no dealings except as between Mussulmans and Unbelievers, War as God Almighty has enjoined on us. There is no power or strength save in God on high."[41]

Lugard made astute use of his cannons, rockets, and machine guns. On March 14, 1903, the army of Sokoto was defeated; the Sultan fled, and the Sokoto Council of Notables selected Atahiru as his successor. In approving this appointment, Lugard stated plainly that the old Fulani empire was now at an end:

> The old treaties are dead, you have killed them. Now these are the words which I, the High Commissioner, have to say for the future. The Fulani in old times under Dan Fodio conquered this country. They took the right to rule over it, to levy taxes, to depose kings and to create kings. They in turn have by defeat lost their rule which has come into the hands of the British. All these things which I have said the Fulani by conquest took the right to do now pass to the British. Every Sultan and Emir and the principal officers of State will be appointed by the High Commissioner throughout all this country. The High Commissioner will be guided by the usual laws of succession and the wishes of the people and chiefs, but will set them aside if he desires for good cause to do so. The Emirs and Chiefs who are appointed will rule over the people as of old times and take such taxes as are approved by the High Commissioner, but they will obey the laws of the Governor and act in accordance with the advice of the Resident. Buying and selling slaves and enslaving people are forbidden. . . . All men are free to worship God as they please. Mosques and prayer places will be treated with respect by us. . . . It is the earnest desire of the King of England that this country shall prosper and grow rich in peace and in contentment, that the population shall increase and the ruined towns which abound everywhere shall be built up, and that war and troubles shall cease. Henceforth no Emir or Chief shall levy war or fight, but his case will be settled by law and if force is necessary Government will employ it. . . . You need have no fear regarding British rule, it is our wish to learn your customs and fashion, just as you must learn ours. I have little fear that we shall agree, for you have always heard that British rule is just and fair, and people under our King are satisfied. You must not fear to tell the Resident everything and he will help and advise you."[42]

The stage had been cleared for what was to become the most prestigious experiment in early-twentieth-century colonial administration.[43]

CHAPTER 5

Frontiers and Boundaries

The British prime minister, Lord Salisbury, commenting on the 1890 Anglo-French convention at a Mansion House dinner, facetiously remarked that "we have been engaged in drawing lines upon maps where no white man's foot ever trod; we have been giving away mountains and rivers and lakes to each other, only hindered by the small impediment that we never knew exactly where the mountains and rivers and lakes were."[1] Some seventy years afterward the Anglo-French territorial arrangements that occasioned Salisbury's after-dinner joke were transmuted into international boundaries dividing the sovereign states of Nigeria, Dahomey, Niger, and Chad. The changing functions of the political divisions of Africa, as well as the principles and procedures involved in the original imperial map making, affect the significance of colonial boundaries for Africans. But first the pattern and purpose of precolonial territorial divisions must be examined.

Precolonial Divisions

Scholars have developed a helpful distinction between the terms "boundary" and "frontier": "A boundary is a clear divide between sovereignties which can be marked as a line on a map. It has, as it were, length but not area."[2] If the boundary, as set out on the map, is explicitly accepted by the states involved — even if they have not yet set up boundary posts or other markers on the ground — then it is said to have been *delimited*; if it has been laid out on the ground, then it is considered to have been *demarcated*. A frontier, on the other hand, as the term was understood by authorities on imperial

95

cartography, is a zone rather than a line: "It is a tract of territory separating the centres of two sovereignties."[3] A frontier, therefore, had breadth as well as length, so that a dispute over delimiting and demarcating the boundary line through a frontier zone can involve substantial tracts of land.

In 1938 the French geographer Ancel made a brave attempt to formulate a typology of states with an account of the boundaries and frontiers appropriate to each type.[4] His first category, amorphous states, comprises three types of which two — molecular societies (generally known as stateless societies in the anthropologically oriented parlance of Africanists) and nomadic states — were common in precolonial Africa. (Ancel's third type of amorphous state was the maritime empire, which also, of course, established itself in prepartition Africa.) He has been criticized by J. R. V. Prescott, who pointed out that even the small groups living in the Congo forests often clearly distinguished the sovereign limits of the tribe and that "many tribes in Africa clearly marked their limits with fences and ditches and exercised partial control over peripheral zones beyond these defensive lines." Nor, Prescott argued, was it true to generalize that nomadic tribes do not have boundaries: "Sovereignty is vested in the nomads rather than the territories they own, but it is nevertheless a fact that nomadic tribes control the areas which their herds require and which their military strength can maintain. These limits will fluctuate, but at any particular time they would be clearly understood by neighbouring tribes."[5] Such criticisms are valid, but even if Ancel failed to supply a comprehensive typology, his insights into correlations between political structure, economic development, and spatial divides are suggestive.

Certainly most traditional African polities were bordered by frontier zones of varying width rather than by the precise boundary lines associated with modern nation-states. Three characteristics of precolonial Africa contributed to these spatial arrangements: first, the continent was, for the most part, relatively thinly populated; second, harsh environmental conditions often rendered mastery over nature difficult or impossible; third, the comparative flexibility of the African political structures was reflected in border arrangements. In practice, these factors tended to reinforce each other. Africa's relatively sparse population meant that rivalry over land did not attain the intensity associated with the economically developed countries of Europe. Low population density and difficult, often unhealthy, ecological conditions meant that settlement groups were frequently divided by virtually empty areas. Unlike similar areas in Europe and Asia such deserted zones were rarely mountainous — in Africa the mountains were often refuges from politically stronger predatory neighbors — but often were situated in dense forest, swampland, or disease-ridden bush, sometimes marked by the graves of unsuccessful settlers.

Three types of frontier can be identified in precolonial Africa. First, there were the deserted zones just described, the frontier of separation, which usually divided large ethnic groups with distinct cultures. Such a zone separated the kingdom of Bornu and the Hausa cities, and similar zones often separated the polities of the Guinea coast from the savannah states of West Africa. The second type may best be described as a frontier of contact, occurring where clearly defined cultural and political groups lived side by side in relatively heavily populated areas. The Yoruba states and Dahomey in West Africa and Buganda and her neighboring polities in East Africa are examples of such adjacent groups. The third type of traditional frontier existed in mixed zones where there was considerable cultural and ethnic overlap, "where indeed it is easy to talk more intelligibly in terms of enclaves rather than of frontiers."[6] Excellent examples are afforded in West Africa by the Fulani and Hausa peoples and by the region of Masai migrations in East Africa.

The significance of these precolonial frontiers varied with the size and structure of the polities they circumscribed. In traditional Africa these ranged in scale from stateless societies, which were divided into small village units (organized around a lineage, on a simple territorial basis, or sometimes around a mixture of these) and chiefdoms and kingdoms of greater or lesser extent, to imperial structures of varying durability. Through all increases in the scale of the political superstructure the basic units — the village and the chiefdom — persisted, providing the framework within which ordinary Africans lived their everyday lives. At these levels Africans had a precise understanding of their frontier claims. There was no such clarity with regard to the borders of kingdoms and empires, which usually consisted of a closely controlled core, surrounded by marcher zones and areas that were only incorporated to the extent of being raided for tribute.

A frontier's significance partly depends on how far it seals off those dwelling on either side from contact with each other. Therefore it is important to understand that, especially along major trade routes, political and economic arrangements were arrived at that transcended the frontiers of existing polities. Along the great caravan routes of West and East Africa chiefs, traders, and the many individuals who filled both roles developed mutually beneficial arrangements, which they often formalized by alliance, intermarriage, clientage, and, frequently, a common adherence to Islam. Where the societies that developed along such lines of communication and political units were small, new towns and centers of power could be developed. In such areas, with power and authority both decentralized and flexible, the political map could be reorganized to register the effects of the development of commerce in the nineteenth century. A fine example of this adaptation was the ethnically mixed area of the Sierra Leone-Guinea plain.[7]

In prepartition Africa European coastal bases such as Freetown, Saint-Louis, and Lagos sought to coordinate these political and economic lines of communication with the hinterland to their own advantage. Near the inland termini of the caravan routes African powers had similar scope to promote and orient interregional trade. In the case of the Sierra Leone-Guinea plain trade system, Freetown, the Fouta Djallon state with its capital at Timbo, and Samori's kingdom centering on Kankan were the chief sponsors of interregional trade. Freetown, the coastal base of the system, was not simply a British outpost. Within the city there were Mandinka, Fula, and Sarakole communities with recognized political leaders whose family connections stretched back to the inland termini of the caravans up to five hundred miles away. The northern leaders resident in Freetown were crucial to the development of the Sierra Leone-Guinea system that linked the Islamic states of the interior with British power on the coast. Yet Freetown, Fouta, and Samori did not control the system; they merely coordinated and oriented a series of lesser centers.

In a sense, such a flexible system of coordination without control corresponded precisely with the precepts of mid-Victorian free-trade imperialism. In practice this meant that as new centers took advantage of the scope for trade and asserted themselves in the face of the opposition of established authorities, a certain amount of fighting was inevitable. As the 1865 Parliamentary Committee made clear, however, the British were intent on discovering relatively large native states within whose frontiers trade would be secure. Flexible alignments that allowed Africans to adjust their spatial arrangements to the process of becoming part of a European entrepôt's hinterland were generally disliked because they involved some fighting, even if usually on a small scale.

In certain areas of decentralized political power, such as the Sierra Leone-Guinea plain and the Oil Rivers, or the Niger Delta, Africans were highly successful in utilizing the opportunities presented by European commercial footholds. In other areas, notably the Yoruba kingdoms and Senegambia, the replacement of slave trade by legitimate commerce contributed to prolonged, devastating civil wars as successful farmers used their new-found wealth to challenge the old war leaders.[8] Even where there was a dominant power in the immediate hinterland of European colonies — rather than several smaller polities, sometimes cooperating, sometimes competing — relations were rarely peaceful for long. In the case of Senegal ambitious French officers were hardly committed to achieving a stabilized frontier with Al-Hajj 'Umar. But even on the Gold Coast frontier, where in principle both the British and the Ashanti favored good relations, misunderstandings led to recurrent conflict.[9]

In 1878 the Earl of Carnarvon, the colonial secretary, highlighted the general problem of imperial frontiers in the period before the European powers had decided to carve up the underdeveloped world into colonies, protectorates, and spheres of influence. Every great empire, he explained, confronted "similar difficulties of frontier — the same arguments for and against — the same provocations real or supposed — the same questions as to the key of the position — the same temptations of those on the spot to acquire territory."[10] The frontier in tropical Africa, as understood by colonial governors and concerned metropolitan politicians, was a vague zone adjoining territory under imperial sovereignty: "Within this zone a great variety of British activities had developed — missions, trade, treaty relations, military intervention, protection, and even in some cases settlement, administration and jurisdiction."[11] By the early 1870s the metropolitan powers, Britain and France, were convinced that conditions in the adjacent territories threatened the security of their colonies; hence their frontiers must be stabilized. They sought to achieve this in the first instance by "informal control" or "paramountcy," but however they tried to lessen the implication of responsibility they were nonetheless aiming at control rather than the loose coordinating role they had in the past.

In southern Africa imperial frontier problems were complicated by the moving fringe of European settlers pushing beyond the reach of formal political control. Meanwhile, the rise of competing European ports — Cape Town, Port Elizabeth, Lourenço Marques, and Natal — allowed both settlers and Africans some scope to readjust their political and commercial links.

Groups within prepartition Africa, as in medieval Europe, thus tended to live within a plurality of frontiers, the relative importance of which was determined by the relationship involved, none being regarded as supremely significant in comparison with the rest. Moreover, the nineteenth-century African partition of Africa — the *mfecane*, the Fulani revolutions, the empires

of Al-Hajj 'Umar and Samori, the expansion of Buganda – increased the fluidity of the outer frontiers surrounding kingdoms and empires by initiating recurrent processes of attack, conquest, and counterattack. But through all the
flux of conquest and rebellion, the basic local institutions of the village and
chiefdom usually managed to retain something like their traditional shape.
They were shattered by only the most devastating crises, such as the *mfecane*,
which cleared the way for the thrust of white settlement into the hinterland
of southern Africa.

Colonial Boundaries

Complex, diverse, and comparatively flexible political structures shaped Africa's frontiers on the eve of European partition. Her new European rulers
brought their own very different convention that the proper border between
states should be a precise line. This European concern for fixity and exacti-
tude, to be determined on paper and on the ground by the latest techniques
of surveying and cartography, was reinforced at a deep emotional level by the
symbolic significance attaching to boundaries in the age of the nation-state.
Moreover, the Europeans' preoccupation with formulating their claims to
African territory in ways that would avoid conflicts among themselves, manifest at the Berlin Conference of 1884-85, put a premium on strict delimitation and demarcation. The direction of trade through colonial entrepôts to
the metropolitan country involved severing some existing commercial connections by giving Africa's new imperial borders substance with customs
posts, detachments of soldiers, and frontier police. Business interests also
sought precise delineation because they did not wish to risk involvement in
otherwise profitable areas, such as the valuable palm oil producing hinterland
of the Cameroons estuary, in the event that the imperial powers – Germany
and Britain, in this case – transferred the area from one to another for reasons
of general diplomatic expediency without adequate compensation.[12]

The European powers had staked out their claims to Africa's coastline by
1886. In 1890 Britain, France, and Germany concluded a series of treaties
distributing African territory in the hinterland of their coastal possessions in
West and East Africa. This signaled the start of what contemporaries termed
the "steeplechase" or the "scramble" for Africa. After some years of intensive activity the last round of partition treaties – involving Nigeria, the Gold
Coast, Central Africa, and the eastern Sudan – was concluded between 1897
and 1899. However, a large part of these regions was as yet scarcely known,
let alone effectively occupied. Thus there followed a period of delimitation

and demarcation, chiefly completed between 1900 and 1905 but lasting in certain areas until 1911. (Liberia, for example, with no incentive to delimit its extensive claims to the hinterland, and with much to lose from the powerful French and British presence, avoided settling until then.) At last Africa's colonial frontiers had been determined, although they were subsequently sometimes altered in accordance with greater knowledge of local realities.

Treaties with African rulers served as negotiating currency when European diplomats struck the bargains of partition with their imperial rivals. Hence, it has been argued, the Africans were not simply passive victims of the scramble: they participated, albeit only indirectly [13] But the tendency of some African rulers to make optimistic claims about the extent of their territory combined with ignorance and avarice on the part of Europeans to make several such treaties uncertain guides when it came to mapping the boundaries of partition. In the first phase of partition resort was sometimes made to fixed lines following the meridians of longitude and the parallels of latitude or, more frequently, to lines linking astronomic or geodetic points or known places. In the case of German South-West Africa the fact that its frontier zone with Bechuanaland constituted the Kalahari Desert meant that this method of delimitation was not unreasonable. But it was also used in the initial delimitation of the northern frontiers of Nigeria and the Gold Coast. The straight-line boundary between British and German East Africa (Kenya and Tanganyika) divided the land of the Masai, who, not surprisingly, found the arrangement quite incomprehensible.

Greater acquaintance with the interior of Africa allowed the European powers to shift from such obviously arbitrary procedures, which in any case were difficult and expensive to carry out. But they tended to use natural features (watersheds, rivers, lakes, and mountains) rather than the frontiers of traditional Africa. Sometimes the geographical features constituted an ethnic divide, but more often their employment as "natural frontiers" bisected ethnic groups that had previously been united. Thus the attempt to draw frontiers by distinguishing between the basins of the Nile, Congo, and Zambezi arbitrarily divided the Azande and Lunda peoples. Similarly in West Africa the delimitation of the frontier between Sierra Leone and Guinea by reference to the basin of the upper Niger divided the Koranko people.

Occasionally a sparsely populated river valley did divide ethnic groups, as in the case where the Black Volta River formed part of the frontier between the Ivory Coast and the Gold Coast. But in most cases the African river systems had been used to draw people together into commercial and political networks. Hence the adoption of the Congo and Ubangi rivers as the frontiers between the Congo Free State and the adjacent French colonies cut across the existing networks.

Beginning in 1891 the Juba River was the frontier between Kenya and Italian Somaliland, dividing the nomadic Somali in the area. But at least in this case the ethnic division was rectified when in 1924 Britain ceded to Italy the territory known as the "Juba strip." In fact, neither the Italian nor British governments had strictly controlled the boundary, leaving nomadic groups free to cross in search of pastures for their stock. This case is an example of sensible imperial flexibility to set against other instances of insensitivity, but note that it was conditional on the absence of any economic development in the area.[14]

Delimitation by drawing a parallel line or the arc of a circle from a known geographical feature has been stigmatized as the height of arbitrary imperial boundary making. The riverine British colony that intruded some two hundred miles along the Gambia River into the French territory of Senegal is usually cited as a particularly bizarre example.[15] The imperial powers themselves regarded the enclave as anomalous, and between 1866 and 1876 they negotiated to exchange the Gambia for French posts in other parts of West Africa. But the scheme collapsed because of opposition from Creole Gambians backed by the Wesleyan Mission and traders both in the Gambia and in Britain. The Gambia's present boundaries were finally suggested by Governor Jean Bayol at an Anglo-French conference in 1889, which located them ten miles inland from each riverbank. Such a boundary cutting across polities, peoples, and established trade routes inevitably provoked friction and illegality. Warrior chiefs shrewdly exploited the protection afforded by crossing the frontier after their raids, while merchants found their traditional trade transformed into smuggling, which was risky although potentially profitable. In 1898-99 a mixed commission sought to reduce the scope for such outlawry by demarcating the Gambia with boundary posts. In the process they cut through the lands ruled by Moussa Molo and divided the village of Gambissou in two. In 1904-1905 more durable pillars of masonry were erected every 2,600 meters as well as on each track crossing the border.

The meticulous demarcation of such boundaries left five ethnic groups — Wolof, Mandinka, Jola, Fulani, and Sarakole — living on either side. Farms continued to be planted astride the boundary. People crossed over to marry and visit relatives, to trade, and to find work as seasonal laborers. And it is estimated that since independence, when there has been more meticulous

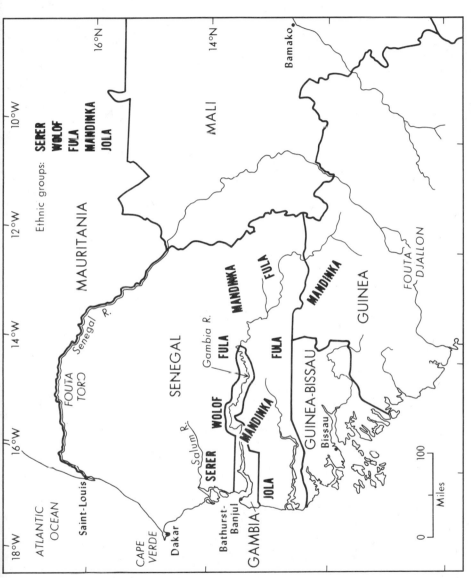

Map 4. Senegambia, indicating the bisection of ethnic groups by colonial boundaries

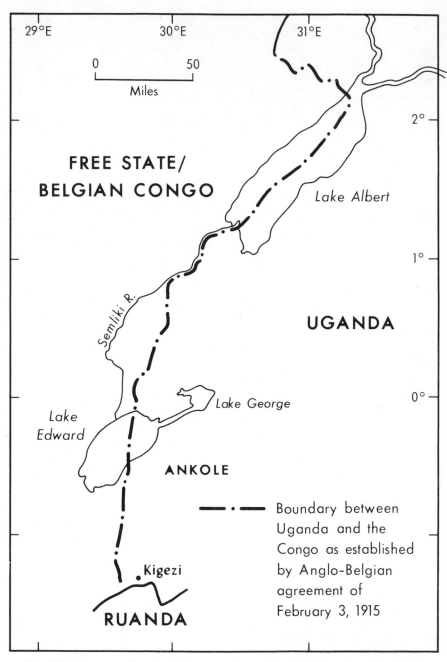

29°E   30°E   31°E

0   50

Miles

FREE STATE/ BELGIAN CONGO

Lake Albert

2°

1°

Semliki R.

UGANDA

Lake George

0°

Lake Edward

ANKOLE

Boundary between Uganda and the Congo as established by Anglo-Belgian agreement of February 3, 1915

• *Kigezi*

RUANDA

Map 5. Southwestern Uganda, indicating the late and complex boundary demarcation

investigating, between 10 and 15 percent of the Gambia's imports are smuggled into Senegal. Plainly, local resourcefulness succeeded in adapting to this unusual frontier situation, however much the overall development of the Senegambia region's total development may have been stunted. The Casamance River area in the southwest of Senegal has been particularly isolated by the peculiar shape of the colonial frontier boundaries where it lies between the Gambia and Portuguese Guinea.[16]

A colonial presence in some ways even more complex than that in Senegambia confronted the peoples of the southwestern sector of Uganda. Here the administrative districts of Ankole and Kigezi, nominally under British rule but at the farthest remove from the center of British power, were bordered by colonies under Belgian and German control. The international border cut across ethnic frontiers and precolonial alignments, so that some of Britain's subjects traditionally owed allegiance to African rulers placed on the Belgian or German side by partition. To compound the confusion, it took the European powers more than three decades of dispute and argument to achieve a settled international boundary. As the provincial commissioner remarked in 1915, it was hardly surprising that the people of Kigezi should be "unsettled" by the war, for part of the district had been in German territory but under Belgian occupation or influence, and "as a result of boundary commissions and of political happenings the natives were exposed to continual doubts and questionings as to what government they would eventually come under."[17]

Given their inability to project a stabilized political future, the best the imperial rulers could expect was a wary acceptance of an overlordship that might well prove temporary. Frequently they found their African subjects taking advantage of the confusion. In August 1914 the district commissioner of Kigezi confessed his failure to bring the people at Chahifi "to their senses": "The people sat on the hilltops by the German border and shouted abuse and refused to come down. Needless to say, their cattle were hidden in German East Africa." Such solidarity effectively countered the 1909 collective punishment ordinance that allowed the authorities to confiscate cattle from all inhabitants whenever an individual absconded.

In 1914 it was reported that nearly half the population in the southern portion of Ankole moved into German territory when the British sought to enforce taxes. Conversely, stricter collection of the cattle tax by the Belgians in Ruanda led to an influx of Tutsi across the British boundary in the early 1930s. The tenuous nature of imperial control in this marginal area meant that the Africans could resist European rule by direct attacks on government patrols — sent to levy taxes, recruit labor, and escort the mail — well into the colonial period. There was also prolonged, widespread violence as the leaders of the Nyabingi, a spirit-possession cult, mobilized resistance to colonial authority throughout northern Ruanda, the western Congo, and southwestern Uganda. In British territory the movement was largely confined to Kigezi, but here the district administration was periodically disrupted, and sometimes immobilized, from 1912 to 1928.[18]

The British themselves were keenly aware of both their own weakness and the unique opportunity afforded their local subjects to study comparative colonial administration. Wherever possible, they therefore pursued a policy of minimal force and conscious appeasement. They deplored manifestations of competitive frontier imperialism and expected collaboration between their district commissioners and their Belgian neighbors "on purely local matters such as erring wives, strayed cows and lost sheep." Sir Harry Johnston set the tone for dealings with their African subjects by insisting in 1900 on "the utmost leniency and discretion" in enforcing tax regulations. He added, "I trust you will do every thing you can in reason to conciliate the Ankole chiefs and to give them no excuse for quitting our territory and going over to the Germans." In this peripheral colonial situation, therefore, the Africans' scope for maneuver and readiness to resort to force led the British to pursue a policy of incorporation by delicate diplomacy rather than straightforward coercion.[19]

Demarcation commissions usually honored the integrity of villages and lesser chiefdoms unless they straddled a river, in which case they might be bisected to achieve a "natural frontier," that dogma of contemporary European political geography. As late as 1917 colonial administrators were still impatiently pressing some Mende villages to decide on which side of the Anglo-Liberian frontier they wished to be.[20] Certain traditional economic rights were also safeguarded by officials concerned to avoid further skirmishes. The Anglo-French agreement of 1906 defined the boundaries between the Gulf of Guinea and the Niger River and stipulated the rights of the villages near them: "The villages situated in proximity to the boundary shall retain the right to arable and pasture lands, springs and watering places, which they have heretofore used, even in cases where such arable and pasture lands, springs and watering places are situated within the territory of one Power and the village within the territory of the other."[21]

Much less concern was displayed for the integrity of such larger unities as traditional kingdoms and ethnic groups. The divisive effects of the frontier in Senegambia and southwestern Uganda have already been examined. In the same area of Mende country where British officials were relatively solicitous toward villages on the Liberian border, they broke up Chief Kailundo's kingdom of Luawa to which those same villages had belonged before partition. The Ewe, split between the Gold Coast, Togo, and Dahomey, and the Nzima people, divided between the Gold Coast and the Ivory Coast, are striking examples of West African groups that were divided by imperial frontiers. Similarly in East Africa the Makonde were divided between the Portuguese in Mozambique and the Germans in Tanganyika, while the Masai were split between the British in Kenya and also the Germans in Tanganyika.

Confronted by such arbitrary boundaries bisecting their domains, Africa's rulers often tried to ignore them in the period before the colonial administrations solidified. The Emir of Yola sought to exercise his traditional functions without taking account of the Nigeria-Cameroons boundary, while the King of Abron similarly ignored the Gold Coast-Ivory Coast boundary.

A remarkable example of the "politics of survival" occurred on the southeastern frontier of Sierra Leone, where, as mentioned earlier, Kailundo's kingdom was partitioned by the Anglo-Liberian boundary. This was first delimited, oddly enough, by the Anglo-French frontier agreement of 1895, illustrating both the European powers' strong wish for clear guidelines in this whole area, understandable enough in the aftermath of the Waima incident of 1892 (when British and French forces disastrously mistook each other for some of Samori's troops) and their cavalier treatment of Liberian sovereignty. In the teeth of these arrangements Fabundeh, Kailundo's successor, determined to maintain his inheritance intact and to bring it under British rule. He showed considerable resource, even collecting the unpopular hut tax from the areas placed under Liberian sovereignty and presenting it to an unsuspecting British district commissioner as a token of both his own jurisdiction and British sovereignty. But although the British in Freetown felt sympathy for the plight of this "friendly Chief," they felt bound by the international settlement.

For some years the Liberians scarcely enforced effective occupation, and Fabundeh was faced by an erosion of loyalty among the Kissi chiefs in the eastern part of his kingdom as they gradually reoriented their loyalties toward ambitious rivals, like Chief Gandi, based in Liberian territory. But the presence of a Liberian military force and the establishment of customs posts in the area in 1907 rapidly reversed this process. In the face of a threatened insurrection against the Liberians, a detachment of the West African Frontier Force forced a Liberian withdrawal. Governor Leslie Probyn, who was inclined to think badly of Liberian rule, endorsed this action. The Liberians decided that their position in Luawa was precarious, and in any case they needed British support for their boundary negotiations with the French, so they agreed to a territorial exchange that brought most of Kailundo's old kingdom within the protectorate of Sierra Leone. But Ndawua, chief of Tengea, was still left under Liberian jurisdiction, protesting his loyalty to Fabundeh. He and his successor, Kanganya, proved so recalcitrant that Liberia eventually relinquished control of Tengea in 1915.[22]

When the imperial powers did seek to follow the frontiers of traditional African kingdoms, they sometimes found these too imprecise. In 1891 Britain and Portugal agreed that their boundaries in central Africa should partly follow the western border of the Barotse kingdom. But the two sides found it impossible to agree about the extent of that kingdom. In 1903 the dispute was submitted to arbitration by the King of Italy. He decided to fix the border along straight lines of longitude and latitude only after concluding that it was impossible to decide the true limits of Barotse authority.[23]

For commoners the situation was less critical. Their casual treatment of the Gambia's boundaries has been described. Similarly, J. R. V. Prescott found while conducting geographical fieldwork on a section of the Lagos-Dahomey boundary that only three of the twenty markers could be found. None of them was complete; each had been used to sharpen cutlasses or axes. Some Nigerian farms straddled the boundary, and the two official crossing points were thirty-two miles apart, so that most borderers crossed by many intermediate, uncontrolled paths. At tax collection time some escaped across the boundary. The Alaketu, a Yoruba chief living in Dahomey and therefore separated from the majority of his people in Nigeria, commented, "We regard the boundary as separating the French and the English, not the Yoruba."[24] The casual, inefficient way so many boundaries were administered therefore minimized the hardship inflicted on divided ethnic groups. Nevertheless, wherever trade had developed, the customs cordon was tightened. Traders, like notables — and the two classes often overlapped — were frequently manifestly disadvantaged by imperial boundary making.

The combination of Portuguese diplomatic tenacity with military and economic weakness at the time of the scramble accounts for the remarkable shape of Mozambique. By clinging to their established stations on the route to Goa, the Portuguese ended with control over a third of the East African coast south of the Horn. But they lacked the means to compete with more industrialized powers, like Britain and Germany, when it came to effective occupation of the interior. Portuguese Mozambique developed as a chain of coastal and river settlements that served as entrepôts to highland hinterlands belonging to other powers. Portugal had not the resources to develop a system of north-south communications to offset such foreign commercial ties. Furthermore, where Mozambique did strike deep inland, it followed the course of the Zambezi River, which itself constituted a massive obstacle to north-south intercourse, virtually cutting the colony in half. Mozambique's elongation also involved great diversity of ethnic ties, stretching from the Makonde and the Swahili in the north with their orientations toward groups in Tanzania, through peoples with affiliations to groups in Malawi and Rhodesia, right down to the Thonga in the south with their strong traditional links to South Africa.[25]

A blending of contemporary geographical theories on the significance of hydrographic systems with the specific practical problems of communication in Africa led to the curious outline of certain other colonies by influencing each imperial power to insist that its territory have access to as many river basins as possible, even where access had to be bought by sacrificing claims elsewhere. To oblige such ambitions Britain extended to the Congo Free State privileges in the district of Lado on the upper Nile and to Germany "Caprivi's Finger," an area linking German South-West Africa to the Zambezi. France transferred to Germany two tonguelike extensions of the German Cameroons, one to Lake Chad and the other to the Ubangi River, a tributary of the Congo. The latter cession divided French Equatorial Africa in two, but it was the price paid for Germany's abandonment of claims to Morocco. The extension of Nyasaland to a navigable outlet on the Shire River accounts for the southern tip of that British colony. In most cases, the existence of falls and rapids made such dearly bought pieces of territory virtually useless for communications.[26]

Once frontiers had been fixed by the partition treaties, the only major alteration during the colonial period resulted from the transformation in the European balance of power owing to World War I. As the defeated party, Germany lost its empire. Nor were its frontiers, then a quarter of a century old, respected: Togo and the Cameroons were partitioned between France and Britain; Ruanda and Burundi were attached to the Belgian Congo after being separated from Tanganyika, which became British. Only South-West Africa was transferred as an entity to South Africa.

The new frontiers of these mandated territories were even more arbitrary than those they replaced. The Ewe people of Togo were freshly partitioned, while the port of Duala in the Cameroons was detached from its previous economic and cultural hinterland. The original boundary between Tanganyika and Ruanda-Burundi was drawn with a view to facilitating the construction of a railway connecting Rhodesia and Uganda through British-controlled territories. This link in the Cape-to-Cairo scheme meant partitioning the kingdom of Ruanda between Britain and Belgium. At least in this case strong protests by the population brought the problem to the attention of the League of Nations Permanent Mandates Commission. The chairman, Marquis Reodoli, reported that the border was "hardly justifiable from the point of view of the well-being, political order, stability and economic development of an African community already well organised." In 1923 Britain and Belgium consequently agreed to adjust the boundary to incorporate all of Ruanda into the Belgian mandate.[27]

The postwar redistribution of German territory provoked opposition from the National Congress of British West Africa. At its inaugural meeting in March 1920 at Accra the National Congress adopted resolutions that were mainly concerned with self-government and the franchise but also included two brief paragraphs about boundaries, in which it condemned "specifically the partitioning of Togoland between the English and the French Governments and the handing over of the Cameroons to the French Government without consulting or regarding the wishes of the peoples in the matter." In addition to its general demand that the local population should be consulted on its allegiance and boundaries, the National Congress also implied that ethnic divisions should be recognized, complaining that sections of the Fanti and Ga peoples and "the ancient capital of the Paramount Chief of Awuna" had been placed in the Togo sphere allocated to France. But the active membership of the National Congress was drawn from the western-educated elite — lawyers, teachers, civil servants, clergymen, and commercial agents — whose career horizons encompassed the total imperial structure. Significantly, therefore, the members of the National Congress sought assurance that the integrity of the four British West African colonies would not be disturbed. The potential contradiction between colonial and ethnic frontiers could be overlooked in the general protest against imperial high-handedness.[28]

In French territories the *evolués* were given even greater encouragement to attach their loyalties to the imperial polity. Although recent research suggests that the European adminstrators' stereotype of the western-educated elite as completely unrepresentative of the traditionalist majority is far from the whole truth, it is obvious that Senegalese *evolués*, Freetown Creoles, and even some Gold Coasters and Lagosians were more detached from ethnic politics than was a later generation of educated men and women, born and bred in the hinterland.

Meantime, Africa's traditional elites were expected to devote themselves to village and chiefdom affairs. The looser, larger networks and alliances they had formed in the precolonial period were ignored by the international and internal boundaries of colonialism. But through marriage and other contacts many families of notables maintained close ties that, although politically submerged in the imperial period, became the basis for party alliances in the 1950s and 1960s. The leading figures in the new nationalist politics were often lineal descendants of individuals prominent in the precolonial networks, illustrating Ajayi's contention that themes from the precolonial past have re-emerged in the modern period.[29]

To conclude, European boundary concepts and procedures proliferated to such an extent that by the early twentieth century they shaped nearly every international boundary in every continent. Hence the pattern of partition imposed upon Africa can be placed in comparative perspective. The contrast between African and Latin American boundary making is striking. Many overlapping territorial claims by the sovereign states of Latin America reached back to the uti possidetis of 1810 and the badly defined Spanish colonial boundary. Moreover, such claims were complicated by the fact that the civil, military, and religious governments of the Spanish did not have identical boundaries, and the actual rule of Spanish colonial officials did not always coincide with their legal domain.[30] Africa's boundaries, on the other hand, were delimited and demarcated when the applied science of boundary making had developed its own principles, procedures, and professionals. Recent students of Africa's boundaries can therefore report that they were well wrought. Europe's own international boundaries are consequent upon factors such as language divisions stemming from Roman rule, survivals of feudal domains, and old armistice lines, which have little relation to the needs of modern, mineral-based, civilization. The fact that Africa's frontiers were imposed by outsiders and the increasing awareness of historians that they distorted, submerged, and ignored significant trends in precolonial history have to be placed in a perspective of world history in which no boundaries are perfect. A boundary's suitability and significance for the peoples it separates depend at least as much on its functions as on its location. That the boundaries of British colonies enclosed what officials hoped would be "open economies" determined their functions and was vitally important to the peoples who lived there, as will be shown later. The internal boundary divisions of European colonies will be dealt with in the next chapter, which is concerned with colonial administration. But, especially in French Africa, administrative divisions sometimes became the international boundaries of separate sovereign states when they later gained independence, providing the most striking illustration of the way that functions determine the significance of boundaries.

CHAPTER 6

The Theory and Practice
of Empire, 1885–1914

In the aftermath of partition the European powers imposed colonial rule upon a multiplicity of African societies that differed enormously among themselves. French, British, Belgians, Germans, Portuguese, and Afrikaners, when pressing their case for African territory, all laid claim to specific qualities that rendered them particularly suitable as rulers. Once having stated that their own national genius gave them "greater insight into the native mind" or made them more conscientious "bearers of the white man's burden," the imperialists differed greatly in how far they were impelled to elucidate the theory and practice of imperial rule in Africa. In 1914, almost three decades after the Berlin Conference, Captain C. H. Stigand presented his seasoned observations and prescriptions for native adminstration: "Ask any official what he is doing in his district, and he will reply that he is administering it. Ask different officials, 'what is administration?' and you will get divergent answers. The general idea will be that it is to hear cases and get revenue for the government, but ideas and ultimate aims will differ with various men."[1] On account of their leniency toward their African subjects, British officials, he believed, were better fitted than their European equivalents for such duties. He compounded class with nationality in characteristically British fashion, holding "that the chief reason for this is that we send of our best, the young man from the varsity or the trained officer, while they send many of a very different stamp."[2]

Stigand drew on his experiences in East Africa, where the colonies were most recent and the European personnel were as yet minimal. In areas of longer European involvement, such as West Africa, the imperialists frequently displayed a more elaborate concern about the correct way to rule their empires, even though their ideas were often confined to bureaucratic reports and memoranda primarily designed for the internal use of the governments themselves. The mass of imperialist writing was policy oriented, and therefore it was deposited in the various national archives or, less frequently, published in government reports. Such national compartmentalization obviously facilitated an analysis of imperialism in terms of different European colonial legacies. Resort to the imperialists' published memoirs, often highly patriotic and romantic, tended to intensify the impression of national distinctiveness.

The view of the imperial experience, however, has been challenged both explicitly and implicitly. Historians, concerned to reveal the reality behind the rhetoric, have attacked notions of distinctive national colonial genius. Some years ago the French historian Hubert Deschamps wittily punctured some of the myths about the distinctively British Indirect Rule.[3] More recently the East African historian Semakula Kiwanuka has challenged "the tendency . . . to seek and to exaggerate differences rather than similarities between colonial policies." He suggests that an Anglo-American interpretation of African colonial history has crystallized that tends to confuse the "aura of liberty and constitutionalism" in such British colonies as Canada and Australia with what happens in Africa.[4] The idea of distinctive national colonial legacies has also been implicitly questioned by social scientists (such as Georges Balandier, the French anthropologist) who have identified an archetypal colonial situation.[5]

In some ways all European colonies in Africa were alike.[6] The administrations in nineteenth-century Europe itself had vastly expanded and in the process had become more complex and professional. During phases of administrative reform each European state adopted bureaucratic structures and improvements in the technology of administration that had originated elsewhere. Hence, by the beginning of the scramble for Africa, the European bureaucracies had many common characteristics, though every country's administration was colored by its own peculiar traditions of command and deference. Such national modifications of the basic pattern of nineteenth-century western bureaucracy were exported, with suitable adaptations, to the colonies. It followed that the patterns of colonial administration were much alike, whatever the specific European government. The chain of command originated in the metropolitan country, where a ministry was responsible for the colonies, and, then, in descending order, ran down to a governor, through one or more levels of provincial administration, finally reaching the local district. Here, at the level Stigand observed, policy had to be converted into practice. Gradually each empire also supplemented this basic command structure with ancillary services, beginning with justice and the army. Later, in part because the scope of the state within Europe itself was expanding, other organs of administration such as health, education, and agriculture would be added.

From the viewpoint of comparative politics, rather than the imperial viewpoint of comparative administration, there are many striking ways in which all colonies differ from other types of societies. A colony is a dependency of a distant metropolitan power. Ultimate authority is exercised by people who are not members of the colonial society. Moreover, few of them are likely ever to have visited that colony or to know very much about it. The policy of the imperial power is therefore determined by metropolitan considerations rather than the realities of the colonial situation. The House of Commons was notoriously thinly attended when colonial issues were brought before it. The Reichstag — ironically, in part because it had less domestic power — proved more assertive in colonial issues, and as a corollary German colonial secretaries did try to acquaint themselves with imperial realities by visiting their colonies.[7] But to most metropolitan politicians most of the time the fate of an African colony was of minor significance. Hence the members of the white minority, both transient and settler, as well as Europe's African subjects, were frequently exasperated because the colony's fate seemed to turn on external and irrelevant metropolitan issues. Indeed the European minority might well appear the more irascible because of its greater awareness of metropolitan ignorance and caprice. In addition, its homeland connections and its familiarity with the formal procedures for registering complaints by constitutional means rendered it formidable out of all proportion to its actual size.

The proverbially low flash point of white minorities was indeed one of their strongest bargaining assets when confronting the metropolitan powers; the African majority sometimes appeared torpid by contrast. This was deceptive. The metropolitan rulers and the African majorities rarely had direct access to each other because normally they could only communicate through the bureaucratic chain of command. In the process the white transient or settler minority, the "men on the spot," deflected opposition. Should a protest message pass beyond the local level, it would ordinarily be smothered or muffled somewhere in the bureaucracy. But not always. The African resistance exemplified by the Sierra Leone Hut Tax War in 1898, the Ashanti

War of 1900, the Zulu War of 1906, and the Maji-Maji rebellion in German East Africa in 1905-1906 represented major imperial disasters. The possibility of such insurrection was always present in colonial Africa. This is strikingly evident if its social and political structure and the flow of communications between rulers and ruled are contrasted with those in a nation-state. Whereas in the nation-state there is a presumption that both the government and the public will not surprise each other unduly because, whatever their differences in class or education, they must to a large extent share the same history and institutions, no such happy assumptions can be made in colonial Africa. With quite different traditions, locked together solely by the colonial situation, the Africans found that their European rulers did not respect all that they held sacred. Nor did the European rulers get automatic obedience to what appeared to them to be rational commands.

The imperialists rarely discussed such critical issues of culture contact, subordination, and domination with theoretical rigor in the period 1885-1914. They tended to see empire in Africa in administrative rather than political terms, focusing on means rather than ends. In earlier periods of history the fact of empire had similarly been taken for granted, but then the imperialist powers had not professed belief in national self-determination and popular government. Africans were believed to be disqualified from the implementation of current European political principles because they were culturally retrograde and racially inferior. The high-water mark of "scientific" racism coincides with the European occupation of Africa. Imperialist talk of this period was thoroughly imbued with the notion that the ruled were permanently inferior to their new European rulers. It was therefore taken for granted that a position of subordination was desirable for Africans, even if some of them were too benighted to appreciate it as yet. Hence, for contemporary imperialists the fact of racial difference constituted a necessary and sufficient explanation of the imperial situation.[8] Of course, in the late nineteenth century Europe's imperialism was locked in a symbiotic relationship with its intense nationalism, so that the rightness of European control over Africans was further enhanced by the fact that the actual rulers were British, French, Belgian, German, Portuguese, and Afrikaner — each claiming to epitomize what was best in western civilization.

The lion's share of Africa's population and resources fell to the British. Their "great debate" on their relations with nonwestern people lasted from around 1760 to about 1860, and it focused upon India. By the time the British moved into the interior of Africa, this discussion of first principles was long decided and replaced by "the settled view," as D. A. Low has made clear.[9]

Even within their metropolitan homelands the Europeans were hardly equipped for major efforts in social engineering. The welfare functions of the state were still rudimentary and largely limited to providing grants-in-aid to voluntary agencies. In Britain, for example, the first act to provide specifically state schools, rather than state-subsidized Church of England and chapel schools, was the Secondary Education Act of 1902. It was the same in the colonies. In Africa the missions first took responsibility for education, usually subsidized by per capita grants from the colonial government. And it was the missionaries who had the most radical programs for reconstructing African society by rooting out such time-honored institutions as the polygynous extended family and traditional African religion. Contemporary discussion of the aims of the missions has a theoretical sweep that is lacking in ideas on colonial administration. Significantly, the black western-educated elite, guided by Edward Blyden, did manage to maintain a "great debate" on fundamental issues but only with the missionaries, not with the adminstrations.[10]

British missionary theory, insofar as it believed that the reconstruction of African society should accompany the spiritual rebirth of individual Africans, represented a religious equivalent of the French imperial theory of assimilation. While the French revolutionaries and British evangelicals seemed diametrically opposed within Europe, both held that the best future for Africa lay in its adoption of a western way of life. Both envisaged conversion to Christianity or some other western world view, responsiveness to market opportunities, western education, western culture, and eventually the adoption of western political institutions. Sometimes these French assimilationists and British evangelicals, whom Philip Curtin has bracketed together as "conversionists," thought that African colonies should develop to the point where they would become politically independent. Others subscribed to the view that they should be incorporated into the metropolitan country as part of "France Overseas" or "Overseas Portugal."[11]

In the second half of the nineteenth century this conversionist viewpoint faced an increasingly powerful double-pronged attack. One assault was launched from the standpoint of pseudoscientific racism, holding that Africans were permanently — that it to say, "racially" — inferior to Europeans; hence they could never successfully adopt western civilization. Europeans therefore had a moral duty to pursue a paternalistic policy that would treat Africans as permanent minors who were incapable of running their own societies properly but were worthy of being governed by those wiser and better than themselves. This doctrine of trusteeship, where superior peoples were seen as guardians, was widely adopted as a moral justification for colonies in the late nineteenth century. But, as Curtin has pointed out, trusteeship and pseudoscientific racism were not necessarily connected in logic. Certainly the origins of trusteeship in European thought go back far earlier than the emergence of the full-fledged doctrine of pseudoscientific racism. The Christian tradition with its emphasis on proselytization was frequently seen in broad cultural terms rather than narrowly religious terms. If Christianity involved an obligation to convert the heathen, European cultural superiority might easily involve an obligation to convert the barbarian to civilization. At this level, therefore, the doctrines of trusteeship and conversionism meet. Some nineteenth-century imperialists indeed developed an interesting composite doctrine whereby the European and the African were seen as siblings with the more developed older brother, the European, having responsibility for the less advanced and younger of God's children, the African. Those racists who believed in permanent trusteeship sometimes resorted to the metaphor of gender, characterizing the Negro "as the lady of the races."[12]

The other prong of the assault on conversionism was based on an increasing appreciation of the strength of tradition in non-European societies, which tended to make them strongly resistant to imperial ventures in social engineering. Such resistance could be extremely violent. This was "the settled view" that emerged from Britain's disasters in India, above all the Mutiny of 1857, and to a lesser extent France's difficulties in Algeria. The viewpoint was forcefully expressed by the Cape Native Laws and Customs Commission of 1883: "The result of the inquiry so prosecuted . . . will be found clearly to demonstrate that many of the existing Kafir laws and customs are so interwoven with the social conditions and ordinary institutions of the native population . . . that any premature or violent attempt to break them down or sweep them away would be mischievious and dangerous to the highest degree. . . . we consider it would, therefore, be most inexpedient wholly to supercede the native system by the application of Colonial Law in its entirety."[13]

Both trusteeship and conversionism had certain common moral overtones in that both justified empire and suggested policy prescriptions. Much less concerned with morality was a third strand of imperial theory, which stressed racial inferiority even more sharply than did the permanent trusteeship school. From this viewpoint the key to the imperial relationship lay in racial domination, though as Curtin has suggested, the Afrikaans word *baasskap*, or domination, better catches its flavor. This view was even more culturally arrogant than that of other contemporary imperialists because it implied that not western civilization or autonomous development but subordination as servants of white men was the best possible future for the Africans. Such a view was by definition ruled out in missionary circles and was not too common among administrators, although both government officials and missionaries could hardly avoid some complicity with the approaches of other whites through their joint membership in the colonial society. Above all, this was the settlers' view of the Africans, prevalent among Europeans in South Africa and Rhodesia, but also making its presence felt in Kenya, in German East Africa and South-West Africa, and in the Belgian Congo. Within Europe itself such cultural arrogance and intense racialism was also common, although it tended to be somewhat muted because it directly challenged so much of the official moral justification for empire. Nevertheless, the charge of "nigger lover" was one that only the braver and more principled politicians responsible for colonial affairs would ignore.

White settlement from the Cape north and east along the highlands of Africa seemed to many late-nineteenth-century Europeans the quickest way to incorporate Africa productively into the world economy. The romance of white settlement as played out in the Americas, Australasia, and South Africa was captured in books like Charles Dilke's *Greater Britain*. Cecil Rhodes capitalized on this with his scheme for a white Rhodesia. Similarly, Carl Peters gained support in Germany from those who were distressed at the flow of good peasant stock to the United States.[14] Sir Charles Eliot, who arrived as commissioner in Kenya in 1901, thought of the country as another New Zealand, "a white man's country in which native questions [would] present but little interest."[15] The Africans in such "white man's countries" were to be an agricultural or industrial proletariat, laboring on behalf of progressive white capitalists. The imperialists were now especially susceptible to transatlantic advice. Their pseudoscientific racism led them to believe that Africans possessed fixed racial characteristics that would be exhibited in whatever social or historical situation they were located; hence Sir Harry Johnston visited the Americas to investigate "the Negro problem." Some white South Africans regarded the contemporary United States as a veritable social laboratory of race relations, equally important for the "failed" experiment of black enfranchisement—the "calamity" of reconstruction—and as a successful model of blacks working for whites in an advanced capitalist country. The way was open for American ideas on race (for instance, southern segregation-ism) to influence imperialist and settler thinking through works like *Black and White in South East Africa* and *Black and White in the Southern States of America*, both written by Maurice Evans, a member of the legislative assembly for Durban who served on the Natal Native Affairs Commission of 1906.[16]

The paternalist preoccupations of the doctrine of trusteeship are exemplified in the General Act of the Brussels Conference of 1890, at which the European powers, along with the United States, Persia, Turkey, and Zanzibar, were represented.[17] In the early summer of 1888 the charismatic French cardinal, Charles M. A. Lavigerie, the founder of the Society of Missionaries of Africa, or the White Fathers, launched a passionate attack on the slave trade with the full support of the Pope. Some of the White Fathers' missions because of this had incurred hostility and had been abandoned, while others were threatened. Determined to mobilize European opinion, Lavigerie claimed that the trade caused four hundred thousand deaths a year. All Christians should press their governments to solve this appalling problem, he urged. The Muslim states should end slavery, and the supply of arms to Arabs in Africa should be stopped. He called for a hundred volunteers, to be sponsored by the Belgian Anti-Slavery Society, who would fight the slave hunters on the Congolese shore of Lake Tanganyika. The response of Catholics in France and Belgium was strong and immediate, and in Germany the first antislavery society was founded.

In some ways the cardinal's crusade was opportune from the point of view of the European powers. In the late 1880s the implications of the occupation of the African continental interior by "paper protectorates" were becoming apparent to Africans and Arabs alike. Some Arab leaders who had previously preferred trade to political domination now organized opposition to the Europeans and aimed at political control themselves in order to safeguard their commercial interests. The Arab counterattack gave some important African leaders a chance to strike back at the Europeans. The Congo Free State was forced to abandon its station at Stanley Falls in 1886, while Leopold resorted to appointing the most powerful Arab leader, Tippu Tip, as governor in order to maintain his claim to sovereignty. In 1889 the British African Lakes Company's post at the northern end of Lake Nyasa was attacked, and sporadic fighting ensued. When the Germans sought to occupy their East African concession from the Sultan of Zanzibar, they met determined Arab and African resistance. In October of the same year Christian missionaries were expelled from Buganda. Moreover, the anti-European forces were suddenly much more formidable because of the high-quality precision rifles that had been thrown on the market when Europe's armies were reequipped with magazine-loading guns in the 1880s. British and German intervention in Zanzibar had weakened the sultan's position so that he no longer controlled his followers. Where previously the Arab slavers had avoided European mission stations, they now displayed no such caution. The increased European presence of explorers and missionaries ensured that the full horrors of the slave caravans were reported in detail.

The response of the European governments to the cardinal's crusade was complex. Britain had led the anti-slave-trade movement and was determined to maintain its preeminence. Prime Minister Salisbury, although skeptical of the enthusiasms of Exeter Hall evangelicalism, was personally deeply committed to the suppression of the slave trade; his daughter regarded this as "perhaps the only purely crusading impulse" he felt.[18] The Foreign Office also was imbued with a strong antislavery tradition. Germany had never been involved in the earlier antislavery movement, and German officials and politicians tended to regard it as hypocritical camouflage for the expansion of British commercial interests. But Bismarck needed the support of the Catholic Center Party, which reflected Lavigerie's views. The French were cautious, believing that Britain was sponsoring the crusade to establish the right of search by her navy in East African waters, thus threatening French trade. More than any other power the French were concerned about keeping the general question of slavery off the international agenda. In French West Africa they were faced by the flight of slaveholding peoples who found their chattels could claim freedom once they set foot on French soil.

The Belgians made the most radical proposals. They suggested that the imperial powers should set up a system of fortified posts in the interior from which flying columns could operate against slave caravans. These posts would also serve as refuges in which liberated slaves and deserters from traditional societies would be educated and taught to defend themselves. A system of inland transport, consisting of roads, railways, and steamboats, should be established, obviating the need for slave porters. A court of law operated jointly by the powers with the cooperation of antislavery societies would try those accused of slaving. Fugitives would be allowed asylum, and rules were to be laid down for their care; wherever possible, they should be returned to their native lands because it was felt that freedom would be meaningless to Africans away from their traditional society. All caravans should be inspected when formed on the coast and again on their return and also should be liable to search in the interior, thus enabling Leopold to supervise the trade in arms and ivory in the eastern Congo.

None of the other powers was prepared to implement the full Belgian plan. Indeed, they combined so effectively to weaken its stipulations that, the Belgians protested, as translated into the final Act of the Brussels Conference, the proposals would be quite ineffective. Yet by enjoining the construction of railways, the introduction of steamboats, and the creation of administrative machinery, the General Act was interpreted to give the powers a mandate to occupy and govern the interior of Africa in order to suppress the slave trade. Britain and Germany found it especially useful in dealing with their parliaments and public opinion. Salisbury supported the application of the Imperial British East Africa Company for government help in building a railway to Uganda on the grounds that Britain was committed to take action against the slave trade. Similarly Germany cited this commitment to build up its presence in East Africa and the Cameroons. Leopold himself was equally disingenuous. He did not wish to encourage the other powers to take control of the interior. The mandate to construct fortified posts would, he hoped, be the basis on which he could defend the Congo Free State against encroachments by powerful neighbors. Throughout the conference Portugal maneuvered to block any changes that threatened its interests.

What had begun, therefore, as a Christian crusade against the slave trade in Africa degenerated into commercial and territorial rivalry among the European powers. Britain had intended to cow the Turks by a show of Christian solidarity, but the Turks left the conference thinking they had little to fear.

Britain also used the conference to attempt to prevent Africans from drinking imported liquor. Sir Percy Anderson of the Foreign Office wrote: "The spirit traffic only promotes the Slave Trade, like cannibalism by demoralising the natives, but if there is a Conference all the English philanthropists who are absolutely illogical, will urge the introduction of the question as they did at Berlin. It is therefore a question of whether it is politic to anticipate them by suggesting its discussion; the suggestion will not be accepted by France and Germany but we might get credit for the effort."[19]

The notion that Europeans were a strong-minded race capable of drinking sensibly, whereas other races were not, was very important to the school of racial trusteeship. Some African mission converts also seemed to have adopted, or at least found it expedient to express, this viewpoint. In September 1872 an anonymous African harangued his rulers in the Lovedale Mission's

Kaffir Express: "Oh ye Britons, be true Britons still, *and kill us not any more with brandy*! Ye know the kaffir mind, merely childlike; *we cannot help ourselves*, put brandy a little further off, as you would anything that you considered not fit food for your child, and which the child was making efforts to grab. . . . Ye are killing us with brandy."[20]

African leaders as varied as Edward Blyden and Khama, the great Tswana leader, also recommended temperance but not on grounds of racial inferiority. In settler-dominated southern Africa certain beverages could only be sold to Europeans. In practice, this meant that Africans were often paid part of their wages in inferior "Cape smoke" brandy — comparable to the notorious "trade" gin and rum of West Africa — just as Cape Coloreds were regularly paid by farmers in tots of wine, contributing to their comparatively high rate of alcoholism.[21]

Petitions from temperance societies bombarded the British Foreign Office and, later, the Brussels Conference. But this temperance initiative met with much opposition. The rapid increase of German trade to Africa out of Hamburg was based on the export of gin, so British support for temperance was naturally seen as self-interested. Portugal and France suggested the temperance proposals be extended to cover South Africa, knowing that this would doubly embarrass Britain because of the importance of alcohol in interracial transactions there and because Britain could not commit the settler governments of the Cape and Natal. In Britain itself those concerned with Africa held differing views. Some British colonies depended for a substantial part of their revenue on a small liquor tax, which if increased would simply drive trade elsewhere, it was feared. In West Africa trade gin functioned both as a medium of exchange in certain areas and a popular consumer import. Should supplies of European liquor be stopped, it was felt, African consumers would drink more palm wine, or spirits distilled from that beverage, with deleterious effects on the palm oil trade.

Again the deliberations of the conference issued in compromise. Regulations on liquor were only to apply to the slave trade zone, which was understood as stretching between twenty degrees north of the equator and twenty-two degrees south — thus the settler area of southern Africa was not included. The powers accepted the principle of prohibition in certain areas, but each territorial power defined such regions for itself. After much discussion it was finally decided to accept a Dutch proposal for a minimum duty of fifteen francs a hectoliter outside the prohibition areas. But it was also proposed that such legislation be periodically reviewed, which gave scope for the temperance lobby to bring further pressure. A significant German temperance movement developed, and higher tariff rates on imported liquor were imposed by subsequent conferences at Brussels in 1899 and 1906.

Negotiations over the control of arms to Africa were equally difficult. Salisbury believed that, because the Arabs were already armed, a general agreement to restrict imports would simply stop their African victims from getting weapons necessary for self-defense. Moreover, the British Colonial Office feared that if arms supplies were restricted by the imperial powers, smuggling from Liberia might divert trade from the European settlements. In southern Africa the British feared that if they undertook to forgo the arms trade, their own African allies would be at a tremendous disadvantage with those of the Afrikaner republics. As with liquor, therefore, the British rejected the French and Portuguese attempts to apply arms restrictions to the whole of the continent. Germany too was somewhat ambivalent toward restrictions on arms sales. Ultimately the powers agreed that territories in contact with the slave trade zone should be exempt from the import of precision weapons.

Salisbury described the Brussels Conference as the first in world history to meet "for the purpose of promoting a matter of pure humanity and good will." But much of the meeting was concerned with commercial and territorial wrangling among the powers. It is problematic how far the Brussels Act contributed to ending the slave trade. Eventually the colonial powers would have acted against it themselves as their administration developed. But while they were still consolidating their control, they often hesitated to interfere lest they antagonized their potential African subjects or destroy the local economy by encouraging slaves to find refuge away from their masters. The provisions for arms control were not effective. For some years the Arabs continued to import weapons through British and German territory, while a thriving trade in gunrunning developed in the Red Sea under the French flag. Nor did the measures taken to control liquor reduce consumption where the trade was already established, but the tax was an important source of income for colonial governments in West Africa. So the powers used the antislavery sentiment very much for their own purposes. Yet, however qualified in practice, the Act did endorse the principle of international imperial trusteeship. It also created at the Brussels Conference a rudimentary international machinery, the "slave trade bureaux," charged with executing the treaty. As already seen with the temperance lobby, the principle of native trusteeship was reasserted, and pressure points through which it could be implemented were established.

CHAPTER 7

The Consolidation of Colonial Rule in West Africa and the Congo Basin

The process of consolidating European control in the massive heterogeneous territories of West Africa and the Congo basin was distinguished, for imperial policy makers and colonial administrators, by the absence of permanent white settlers. Southern Africa was about to be surrendered to settler self-government, except for isolated pockets like Basutoland, where imperial officials could still practice bureaucratic government over Africans, an experience that one of them likened to "drinking a bottle of champagne" after dealing with English-speaking South Africans and Afrikaners, which he compared to "a course of Harrogate [spa] waters."[1] White settlers were also striving to seize control of East Africa. But despite the use of quinine as a prophylactic, the climate and diseases of West Africa and the Congo still appeared capable of keeping substantial numbers of permanent white settlers at bay. Beyond this important negative unifying factor, the huge territories claimed by the imperialists possessed great diversity.

In the last decade and a half meticulous research on the interaction between small- and medium-sized African political and cultural units and their imperial rulers has fundamentally affected the interpretation of colonial history. Historians, seeking to generalize from the resulting plethora of particulars, have suggested that the local ecological and cultural situation had greater effects upon the trend of events in colonial Africa than such grand imperial policy nostrums as assimilation, association, and indirect rule.[2] In this chapter the interaction of imperial history with some of the many African peoples in West Africa and the Congo basin will be examined.

125

The French Colonial System

France organized its vast African empire into two federations, French West Africa and French Equatorial Africa, with capitals at Dakar and Brazzaville.[3] In contrast with the British enclaves French West Africa constituted a solid bloc. In 1895 the adjacent territories developed from the original colony of Senegal were consolidated into the federation of French West Africa in order to muster French military power for a final attack on the resourceful African resistance leader, Samori. The centralization also facilitated control over expenditure. The structure was concentrated further in 1899 and again in 1902, but the crucial reorganization came in 1904, when the new colony of Upper Senegal-Niger was given its own lieutenant governor, thereby freeing the governor-general in Dakar from responsibility for the adminstration of any single colony. The federation was granted its own source of revenue from customs as well as its own personnel.

In contrast, the territories grouped as French Equatorial Africa had no such geographical coherence. Three distinct French initiatives were responsible for this conglomeration: first, the small station established at Gabon in 1843; second, the territories acquired by Pierre Savorgnan de Brazza in the Congo region between 1875 and 1899; third, the area captured by three French thrusts — from Algeria, the Sudan, and the Congo — to Lake Chad in 1900. The result was a territorial monstrosity, five times the size of France, stretching from five degrees south of the equator to twenty-three degrees north and from the savannahs of the south to the Sahara Desert. Such ecological diversity was matched by the variety of France's subjects, who now included Arabs as well as Pygmies and other black Africans. At the turn of the century French administrators, relying on river transport, were forced to make an immense detour to avoid the German Cameroons, which had been delimited in 1894. It took five months to reach Chad from France by way of Libreville and Loango. Faced by the problem of ruling profitably such difficult territory, France in 1899 turned over huge tracts to forty chartered companies, which sought to emulate their equivalents in the Congo Free State with the consequent similar abuses. But in 1908 these concessions were partially brought under control with the creation of the federation of French Equatorial Africa.

The contrast between French West Africa, with its relatively dynamic trading economy, and French Equatorial Africa nevertheless remained. No matter how inept or depraved, administrators were considered good enough for the Congo. One, certified as not being in "full possession of his mental faculties, because of an overdose of certain drugs and alcohol," who had burned down two villages and had amused himself by taking potshots at passersby, was allowed to continue his career of terror and confusion. Indeed, very few officials were dismissed by the French — only five by 1910 — with the Congo generally serving as a human refuse bin for personnel discarded by other colonies in the years before World War I. Administrators dubbed as having "become bizarre" and "neurotic" in Guinea, along with several alcoholics and one dope addict, were all dumped there, which partly accounts for the fact that the Congo was universally regarded by the French as the epitome of colonial misrule.[4]

In 1888 the Ecole Cambodgienne, founded three years earlier to give the sons of Indochinese dignitaries a French education, was renamed the Ecole Coloniale when the King of Porto-Novo's son was enrolled. Training courses for future administrators were set up there, using the Indochinese students as language informants. In 1892 a section to train officials for Africa was set up. The government attempted to confine its recruitment to graduates of the Ecole, but this was sharply attacked by incumbent officials who stressed the importance of practical experience. By 1914 only a fifth of the Corps of Colonial Administrators were graduates of the Ecole Coloniale.[5]

Starting from the 1890s Frenchmen began to formulate the doctrine of association to guide them in ruling their vast new territories as an alternative to assimilation, which they believed had inspired French colonial policy earlier in the century. The kernel of the associationists' doctrine was that culture was hereditable; therefore culture change — as expected by assimilationists — was impossible. It would be much better for France to accept the realities of the colonial situation and to encourage "the native" to develop in his own way. As early as the National Colonial Congress in Paris in 1889-90, the associationist viewpoint had triumphed over rather mild assimilationist resolutions, despite the broadly liberal and republican complexion of the audience. Gustave Le Bon's *The Psychological Laws of the Evolution of Peoples*, published in 1894, provided a theoretical basis upon which Léopold de Saussure formulated associationist doctrine in 1899. But the most influential exponent of association was Jules Harmand, who articulated his ideas in many articles and then codified them in *Domination and Colonization*, published in Paris in 1910. Harmand distinguished between colonies of European settlement, where assimilation to France might well be pursued, and true empire, where Europeans would only be present as rulers. The theoretical similarity between French association and Lugardian Indirect Rule is striking.

Both originated in a time of rapidly increasing racism, and both anticipated an epoch of imperial tutelage that would continue far into the future.[6]

In practice, French officals abandoned the informal indirect rule they had adopted during the occupation of the interior through paper protectorates.[7] They found themselves increasingly involved in conflict with the indigenous rulers once they intervened in the internal affairs of the chiefdoms. This post-conquest period has been characterized as one of triumphant "barrack-room authoritarianism," as many of the first civil administrators came from the marines and military influence permeated the rest. The notorious code of administrative sanctions, the *indigénat*, amounted to the application of the French military code to the colonies, giving administrators precisely the same right to discipline their underlings as commissioned officers had to exercise summary judgment on other ranks. There was also an ideological element in that the officers and ex-officers of the marines were, in general, left-leaning republicans, who were antiroyalist and anticlerical in contrast to those in the metropolitan army and the navy, who were monarchist, and those in the "African" (that is, Algerian) army, who were Bonapartists. Such officials suspected that Africa's traditional rulers, aristocracies, and priests constituted a reactionary force similar to their counterparts in France. In 1894 Colonial Undersecretary Théophile Delcassé declared in the French parliament the need to free the colonial masses "trembling under oppression" by substituting "the beneficial unity of the French genius for the many violent tyrannies of kings or chiefs." In 1914 Governor-General William Ponty, whose attitudes had been formed in the Sudan in the aftermath of Samori's empire, wrote his governors: "My long experience in West Africa among the black popula-tions has permitted me to conclude in the clearest fashion, and you have certainly made the same observation, that the native intermediaries between the mass of the population and the adminstrators of the *cercles* or their subordinates are usually nothing but parasites living on the population and existing without profit to the treasury."[8] During this period a retired sergeant of the Senegalese *tirailleurs* could easily find himself appointed chief of a canton amongst a foreign, even hostile, people. The sacred quality of in-digenous rulers was ignored or was suspect in a system that only took account of their secular functions. The refusal to allow for local diversity led to the attempt to construct a strictly bureaucratic hierarchy from governor-general down to village chief on the model of the army.[9]

The Yoruba kingdom of Ketu in what became the French colony of Dahomey exemplified such changes in policy.[10] The town of Ketu was

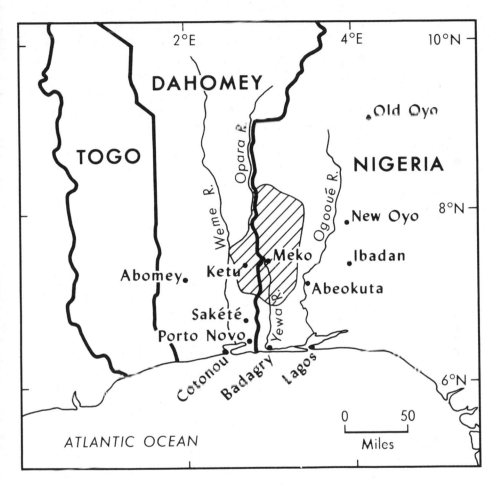

Map 6. Ketu, indicating the bisection of Ketu kingdom by the Nigerian-Dahomey boundary

destroyed in the late nineteenth century in the wars between the Yoruba and Dahomey that troubled the area for a century. The *oba* (or king) of Ketu, known by his title as the Alaketu, and his people then became the prisoners of Dahomey. In 1892, however, the French conquered Abomey and liberated the survivors, many of whom had been treated as slaves by their Dahomean conquerors. These included the Alaketu's senior wife and head of the royal harem, Alaba, who now emerged as the resourceful leader of a pro-French group among her people. She played a leading role in getting them to return to the site of their hometown and also led the successful pro-French faction when the Anglo-French Boundary Commission came to Ketu in 1906 to learn which colonial regime the people preferred. The dynamics of colonial collaboration propelled Alaba into a prominence that flouted traditional Yoruba etiquette, for although titled women could indirectly influence important decisions, traditionally they stayed in the background.

Soon after the people returned to Ketu, the French encouraged them to elect a new king, and afterward the French negotiated a protectorate treaty with the new Alaketu and his chiefs in February 1894. The treaty stipulated that Ketu should be "governed according to the manners and customs of the country whose institutions should be respected."[11] For both king and people it seemed a wonderful turn of fortune. The new Alaketu sought to revive the monarchy and to govern according to the precolonial pattern. The council of chiefs was reconstituted and expected to function as in the old days with the Alaketu himself remaining largely in seclusion. The palace was rebuilt on the same site, and a new set of royal drums was created for use in the traditional fashion. As in other Dahomean protectorates at this time, the Alaketu and his chiefs could claim their customary tributes and dispense justice.

In these first years of French rule the prestige of the Alaketu was high even in towns and villages outside the kingdom as defined in the treaty. In fact, the Franco-British partition had left about half the old territory of the Alaketu under British control. The Yoruba people from across the Nigerian border now traveled to participate in the rebuilding of the palace, thereby expressing their loyalty to the restored kingship. Indeed, in 1897 the British traveling commissioner in the border area felt obliged to warn the Alaketu to refrain from exercising his authority in those parts.

The noninterventionist character of colonial rule in these early years derived from the sheer lack of French personnel and the poor communications with the nearest French residents' stations. In 1905 the French had been faced with a difficult insurrection to the south at Sakété. Henceforth they decided to disturb the rest of the area as little as possible. In 1899 a capitation tax was levied, but because of local conditions in Ketu it was not immediately put into operation. The prime concern of the French was that the traditional authorities maintain law and order, and the Alaketu and his chiefs proved fully equal to this task.

Between 1908 and 1915 this happy restoration of the Ketu kingship with the consequent popularity of the French was changed completely. In 1908 the French carried through an administrative reorganization that defined Ketu as a canton rather than a kingdom, reducing the Alaketu's title in the record from king to *chef de canton*, a mere auxiliary of the European administration. His position and his duties were rigidly circumscribed: he was to transmit orders from the administrator to the village chiefs, recruit young men for military service, conduct a census, and assist in apprehending criminals. His sole judicial function now was to reconcile parties in simple civil disputes. Civil or criminal cases now came before a tribunal presided over by the *commandant de cercle* or one of his French deputies. In his new role the Alaketu received a monthly salary, but he could be disciplined for misbehavior, incapacity, carelessness, or any other civil service offense. He was expected to obey the orders of the commandant, to attend him whenever summoned, and to show him proper respect.

In 1908 the Alaketu went blind, stricken just when the French badly needed his help to recruit more railway laborers. The French therefore appointed Abinbola as *chef de canton*. Though not belonging to a chiefly family, he had impressed the commandant by his strong personality and loyalty to the French. Abinbola attempted to become the Alaketu and his conduct led to the assassination of a French interpreter in 1911, an incident known locally as the "one-gun-shot war."[12] The governor of Dahomey sent a French force of sixty-five soldiers, but the assassin was apprehended and there was no further bloodshed. The people of Ketu, however, suffered considerable maltreatment at the hands of the French troops, whom they also had to feed at their own expense.

The French then pressed ahead with the radical reorganization begun in 1908. A permanent French post headed by an assistant administrator and backed by armed police was established in Ketu. Abinbola was demoted to a subchief in Ketu township. The governor appointed the Alaketu's senior wife, Alaba, as the *chef de canton*. The governor turned to another woman, Ya-segen, the high priestess of the popular Ondo cult, to administer the outlying areas.

After 1911 the collection of taxes that had begun only two or three years before in Ketu was intensified. With the outbreak of World War I the French also raised their demands for laborers and soldiers. In executing these unpopular measures Alaba depended on the wholehearted support of the French forces. She was the uncrowned queen of Ketu from 1911 to 1919, when the Alaketu left the palace because of mental illness. She acquired all the royal apparel except the crown itself, wore the Alaketu's beaded shoes in public, used the royal umbrella, and sat on the carved portable throne. She toured the canton in the Alaketu's hammock. She ordered the royal drums to be beaten daily in her honor and demanded ceremonial obeisance. Both Alaba and Ya-segen, though strong personalities, were very unpopular, for, as the French only discovered a few years later, rule by women was contrary to Yoruba usage.[13]

Whatever their republican commitment, the French were forced by a shortage of resources to be pragmatic in their dealings with kings and aristocracies. They did not depose the Alaketu; they simply appointed Abinbola and Alaba to act in his name. Some African rulers with good traditional title displayed a similar pragmatism. That the Mossi retained their king, the Mogho Naba, and aspects of their system was partly due to the political skill of Mogho Naba Kom, who reigned from 1905 to 1942.[14] Similarly in the Sine area of Senegal the French found chiefs who proved "flexible and adaptable."[15]

The British in West Africa

The British began with certain advantages in ruling their new protectorates. Although their territories were much smaller than those of France and were geographically separated, they contained more than twice the population of the French territories and the discrepancy in wealth was even greater. A long tradition of British civilian overseas service facilitated the recruitment of administrators. Given such assets and some awareness of the African potential for revolt, there was a tendency towards laissez-faire. Colonial Secretary Joseph Chamberlain did make some suggestions toward "constructive imperialism," and his successor, Lord Elgin, proposed a "comprehensive and exhaustive" examination of "native policy" in September 1907, but when Elgin left office six months later this was abandoned. Lady Lugard, the former Flora Shaw, one of the best known contemporary journalists on British West Africa, aptly summed up the general trend as a "go slow" policy.[16]

That the British had no consistent policy for their new protectorates can be seen if their practice in the western district of the Lagos protectorate in Southern Nigeria is set alongside Lugard's policy in Northern Nigeria. This also facilitates comparison of British and French policy because by far the largest part of the old kingdom of Ketu was claimed by the British at partition, although Ketu and the Alaketu were placed in Dahomey.[17] The town of Meko and its dependent villages had been only a small part of Ketu, but they were situated along the key trade routes linking Porto-Novo to Old Oyo. Meko was also boosted demographically by a stream of refugees from the sack of Old Oyo just before the middle of the nineteenth century. Rapid growth in population and economic importance led the ruler of Meko to request greater political status from the Alaketu. His repeated refusal to allow the ruler of Meko, the Onimeko, the right to wear a beaded crown led to conflict between the two towns in the 1860s, with the result that Meko switched its allegiance and began to pay tribute to Oyo in 1868.

Although their territory had not been occupied by force of arms, the people of Meko and their ruler were brought under much more authoritarian militaristic rule by the British in 1895 than were their fellow Yoruba across the French border in Dahomey. There was no prominent Yoruba king in the western district of the Lagos protectorate around whom the British could organize their administration, so they simply chose a number of chiefdoms, more on a basis of geographical convenience than on any notion of seniority, and appointed their chiefs as the salaried heads of administrative districts. Once a chief was appointed headman, then all other chiefs within the district became his subordinates, whatever their position in the Yoruba hierarchy.

The British occupied Meko in the middle 1890s, and late in that decade the Onimeko was appointed headman. His duties were to convey to subordinates the orders of the British traveling commissioner and to supply labor. Justice was administered by the commissioner. Whatever cases could not be tried during his tour were taken to his court at Badagry, more than a hundred miles away. The Onimeko was treated as a paid civil servant; thus it could happen that around the turn of the century an Onimeko was remanded in police custody in Badagry after an incident between some Meko town elders and the police.[18]

At the beginning of the twentieth century the British decided that Meko was too far from Badagry for efficient administration, and they stationed a commissioner there. He presided over a native court at Meko from 1905. A residency, a prison, and some other administrative buildings were built, and the police detachment was enlarged. A British official who later served in the area wrote in retrospect, "Nigerian Police were posted in every town or village . . . which resulted in the power of the local chiefs becoming negligible, whilst the constable became to all intents and purposes, Bale [chief] of the town or village." In 1910 the divisional headquarters was shifted from Badagry to Meko, but in 1914 the headquarters was transferred to Ilaro, along with some of the police and other officials, much to the joy of the people of Meko. Also in 1914 Lugard ordered a new system of administration for the area, which led to a remarkable rise in the power of the Onimeko.[19]

In 1898 the Royal Niger Company surrendered its charter, and in 1900 Lugard was appointed the high commissioner of the protectorate of Northern Nigeria. The company had developed treaty relations with the African rulers, but there was nothing approaching an established colonial regime. As his biographer, Margery Perham, wrote, "a colonial governor can seldom have been appointed to a territory so much of which had never even been viewed by himself or any other European."[20] It was precisely this opportunity to start afresh that led E. D. Morel to contrast Northern Nigeria's "priceless advantage" of beginning anew with Southern Nigeria's plight of being "a thing of shreds and patches."[21] The journalist, Flora Shaw, who married Lugard in 1902, evoked the British myth of superior African races dwelling in the healthy uplands: "Here in these far inland States, remote from touch with European civilization is all the light and leading of the country." For the Southern Nigerians she reserved her vituperation: "The nearer to the coast the worse was the native type. . . . Sorcerers, idolaters, robbers and drunkards, they were indeed no better than their country."[22]

Lugard's occupation of Northern Nigeria by military conquest, rather than by peaceful penetration through protectorate treaties, was expressly designed to secure a free hand.[23] The oath he required from individual Muslim rulers utilized religious sanctions to strengthen British sovereignty further: "I swear, in the name of Allah and Muhammad his prophet, to serve well and truly His Majesty King Edward VII, and his representative, the High Commissioner of Northern Nigeria, to obey the laws of the Protectorate and the lawful commands of the High Commissioner and of the Resident, provided they are not contrary to my religion. And if they are so contrary, I will at once inform the Resident for the information of the High Commissioner. I will cherish in my heart no treachery or disloyalty, and I will rule my people with justice, and without partiality. And as I carry this out so may Allah judge me." For non-Muslims this oath was adjusted to their religious beliefs.[24]

Lugard rejected arguments that the Fulani empire should be dismantled, and he incorporated those emirs he chose to employ into the unified command structure. Britain's new subjects were not to be presented with alternative rulers. "The prestige and influence of the Chiefs can be best upheld by letting the peasantry see that . . . there are not two set of Rulers — the British and the natives — working either separately or in cooperation, but a single Government in which Native Chiefs have clearly defined duties."[25]

Lugard also codified the etiquette for meetings between administrators and chiefs: "When a Resident interviews a Chief of the first grade he will offer him a carpet or mat to sit upon. . . . The Resident should also rise to meet him. . . . Chiefs of the second grade should be given a small carpet or mat, and of lower grades a native mat . . . whenever a Resident visits a chief he should take a chair with him. . . . A government official should never sit on the ground in the presence of a chief. . . . The Governor will only shake hands with chiefs of the first grade."[26] Despite Lugard's directives, however, dignified relationships sometimes broke down. When Sir Hugh Clifford was governor-general, he was provoked into criticizing a certain staff member as a "hectoring bully" and a "mannerless oaf" and was required to point out, what should have been obvious, that a district officer should not take his dogs along when calling on a Muslim chief.[27] Nevertheless, British formality seems to have prevented excesses of the sort that occurred in the context of French republicanism where chiefs were sometimes made to wait for hours outside the administrator's office, only to be received eventually by a brusque subordinate, and in a number of cases chiefs were publicly slapped by French officials.[28]

There was greater loss of life in the Anglo-Fulani suppression of the Mahdist rising at Satiru, only fourteen miles from Sokoto, in 1906 than in Lugard's initial conquest and occupation. With British forces dispersed, primarily to cope with rioting among the Tiv, the situation became hazardous for imperial power when a small British force was destroyed by the Mahdists. In the event, however, only two emirs were inclined to join the Mahdist rebels. The prompt support of the Sultan of Sokoto, who must have been aware that a successful revolt by a radical religious leader would threaten his own preeminence, was decisive. On March 9, 1906, Lugard wrote to his wife, the leading publicist for the Northern Nigerian regime: "I fear the slaughter of these poor wretches has been terrible — but in the face of the death of three British officers I could hardly order them to treat them with mercy and had to leave it to those on the spot. They fought very bravely indeed. The execution which our weapons can do will have a great moral effect." Next day he told her that his figure of 1,500 killed out of the rebel force of 2,000 had been low and that the enemy had been exterminated.[29] The defeat of the Mahdist rising marked the blending of the British and Fulani systems into a solid fabric of domination.

In the same year Lugard left Northern Nigeria. His successors as high commssioner — Sir Percy Girouard from 1906 to 1909 and Sir Hesketh Bell from 1909 to 1912 — admired the Anglo-Fulani system of Indirect Rule but lacked the expertise to supervise it closely. With control relaxed, Lugard's developing administration evolved into what became the classic Indirect Rule system. His replacements were forced to rely on the experienced residents in the emirates. Pointing to the Satiru revolt, the residents stressed the need to conserve the prestige and the capacity for initiative of the emirs — incidentally, of course, making the case for their own freedom from central control.[30]

Sir Richmond Palmer, at this time resident in Katsina, developed what was to be the key financial institution of the Northern Nigerian system of Indirect Rule, the native treasury. Following the Satiru rising, he had faced much passive resistance when he asked the emir and other dignitaries to supply labor to build the fort speedily. One by one these leading men excused themselves. A certain district headman volunteered to produce enough men to do the work and he fulfilled his promise; when asked to name his reward, he suggested the emirate. Shortly thereafter the reigning emir was deposed for incompetence. Not being of the traditional ruling line, the new emir was exceptionally dependent upon the British. Palmer persuaded him to provide an itemized budget. Such public exposure of how the revenue was spent would, Palmer argued, popularize the parvenu but progressive regime. Under Bell this native treasury scheme was adopted for all Northern Nigeria. It devolved further authority on the residents by making them responsible for the assessment. The residents also exerted a powerful influence on how the money actually was spent by the emirs.[31]

Charles Temple, who became the lieutenant govenor in 1914, was the prime exponent of classic Indirect Rule. He had been a resident from 1901 to 1910 and subsequently had been promoted to chief secretary. The son of Sir Richard Temple, the governor of Bombay, he was imbued with the wisdom acquired by the British in India after the mutiny in 1857 showed them the danger of disrupting the fabric of native society. Imperial trusteeship meant preserving the aristocratic life of the north from the solvents of capitalism, democracy, and individualism introduced from the south.[32] Most of the northern residents accepted that they ruled a colony with a superior social system to that in the south. This reflected their own social origins, for the proportion of northern residents drawn from the gentry appeared to be significantly higher than that of the southern residents. (The fact that Northern Nigeria was mostly north of the tsetse belt, permitting the expensive sport of polo, may have contributed to this.)

Paradoxically, as Northern Nigeria shifted from the original Lugardian model of administration, the formidable Lugard husband and wife publicity team was promoting his personal reputation and the superiority of the Northern Nigerian system. It was highly successful. Accordingly, when Britain decided to amalgamate Northern and Southern Nigeria, Colonial Secretary Lewis Harcourt announced on June 27, 1912, that he had secured "the one man marked out for this great work, Sir Frederick Lugard." He continued, "Northern Nigeria is in the true sense the product of his foresight and genius. He reclaimed it from the unknown; he gave it a legal code, differing only in its civilisation from the essential lines of native custom. . . . He now returns to the field of his early and brilliant labours to complete and consolidate what has proved, I think, to be the greatest tropical province of the British Crown."[33] Temple immediately became apprehensive that the importance Lugard attached to unified administration would subvert the relative autonomy he had won for the residents and the emirs.

The southerners — especially the shrewd, resourceful, and articulate politicos of Lagos — soon feared that Lugard was a threat to their limited, but nonetheless real, constitutional liberties. As early as August 1913 the *Lagos Weekly Record* was asking southerners how welcome would be the proposed imposition of the northern system of a district officer with wide judicial powers and the consequent abolition of the supreme court appeals so dear to the Yoruba.[34] This had been an isolated attack, but a series of judicial incidents in the north were reported in detail by the Lagos press, reinforcing the idea of the "high-handed and tyrannous" justice administered by the district officers. By March 1914 the *Times of Nigeria* caricatured Temple riding through Kano behind a herald flying a banner reading "Behold the Emir of all Emirs" and published a prayer:

> Good Lord, deliver us
> From a prancing pro-consul who must have his own way,
> From a born-and-bred-in-the-law Chief Justice who mercilessly
> drafts out oppressive Ordinances;

> From a Colonial Secretary who, having been influenced by the
> man on the spot, deliberately deafens his ears and shuts his eyes
> to the moans and groans of an oppressed people.

By mid-1914 the *Times* was roundly denouncing "The Hidden Meaning" of
unification, "broadly speaking, the conquest and subjugation of Southern
Nigeria by Northern Nigeria."[35]

Lugard, in fact, found it impossible to reverse the process of devolution,
but the extension of the northern system did not lead to an automatic increase in British sensitivity to traditional institutions. Lugard quickly got rid
of the first British government anthropologist, Northcote Thomas, who had
been appointed to elucidate traditional institutions, by transferring him to
Sierra Leone in 1914. Lugard was "generally speaking, inclined to think that
researches into native law and custom are best conducted by Political
Officers." Thomas had been regarded by some officials as "a recognized
maniac in many ways. He wore sandals . . . lived on vegetables and was
generally a rum person." Some residents did not want "an object like that
going about . . . partly because he was calculated to bring a certain amount
of discredit upon the white man's prestige."[36] But with Lugard's concern for
a single structure of command, any anthropologist, however carefully he conformed to colonial standards of dress and diet, must have been suspect. He
might gather grassroots information that would endanger the carefully
wrought chain of command.

Throughout this section Nigeria, north and south, has been used to ex-
emplify the complex, even contradictory, nature of the British colonial
impact on West Africa.[37] In the Gold Coast, Sierra Leone, and the Gambia,
with their longer involvement with Britain, there were other complexities and
contradictions. These will be discussed in the final section of this chapter.

The Germans in West Africa

Chancellor Otto von Bismarck, it will be remembered, long sought to avoid
imperial commitments because the need to obtain funds would give the
Reichstag a lever with which to control the executive. Indeed he only dabbled
in imperial ventures when assured that they might be administered as protectorates by chartered companies that would bear the cost. But German
business did not oblige; therefore Germany's first expedient solution to the
problem of colonial rule in Africa was aborted.

Bismarck's gloomy prediction of Reichstag intervention proved true, although by that time he himself had left office. The imperial German constitution, drawn up in 1871 when Germany had no colonies, was federal and inflexible. It soon was obvious that any serious attempt to amend it would threaten the breakup of the Reich, so that the administration of the overseas empire had to be fitted into the existing arrangments, with less of a view toward efficiency than toward minimizing the dislocation of Germany's internal structure. Within the federal state the imperial government controlled foreign relations while the constituent state governments directed internal affairs. The imperial government bore the responsibility for administrative functions acquired after 1871, and the Reichstag gained control over the corresponding financial matters. By a law enacted in 1892 each colony's revenue and expenditure and all its local taxation became subject to annual scrutiny in the Reichstag, especially in the Budget Commission. The Reichstag, unlike the British Parliament, had relatively few such responsibilities and therefore could examine a governor's budget in remarkable detail. In Britain there was only the most cursory debate on the revenue and expenditure of each colony. These matters were controlled by the governor with the supervision of the Colonial Office and the Treasury. But all German colonial decisions involving finance had to be taken in consultation with the Reichstag. As a result, paradoxically, German colonial governors had less time to supervise their underlings, and officials at the district level had perhaps more scope than their counterparts in the Gold Coast or Northern Nigeria.[38]

The changing terms of the bargain struck between Chief Galega and Eugen Zintgraff in the Cameroons illustrate the consequences of such initiative.[39] Neither Zintgraff nor Galega was able to capitalize on the Bali-German protectorate and paramountcy arrangements of 1891 as he wished. The Bali and the Liberian Vai servants of Zintgraff's expedition, equipped with breechloading rifles, dispersed on slave-raiding forays; they now considered portering a task fit only for slaves or subject people. One of the main aims of German involvement, therefore, a supply of disciplined Bali labor, was frustrated. German criticism of Zintgraff's choice of the Bali ranged from a suspicion that their pretensions to a traditional paramountcy were fictitious, for they seemed to depend heavily on German support in their dealings with their neighbors, to the notion that their depredations were caused by failure to establish themselves successfully as middlemen. Governor Eugen von Zimmerer and Bismarck's successor, Chancellor Leo von Caprivi, were not persuaded by Zintgraff's and Franz Hutter's sanguine account of their expedition. In 1892 Zintgraff resigned, and the link between the Bali and the Germans became tenuous.

On his return to Germany Zintgraff persuaded Max Esser, one of the principals of a consortium supported by major banks for the purpose of acquiring plantation lands in Angola, to visit the Cameroons with a view to a similar development there. Zimmerer was by now succeeded as governor by Jesco von Puttkamer, who immediately welcomed Zintgraff's and Esser's project. Plantation labor in the Cameroons up to then had been supplied largely, and at considerable cost, from Liberia. Zintgraff's idea was to seek Galega's help in recruitment. When this was first put to the Bali leader, he appears to have been reluctant, but eventually he found the lure of wealth for himself and his people persuasive. Several hundred Bali reached Esser's coastal plantations in June 1897. A second batch arrived in December, a week after Zintgraff's death at Tenerife.

By the turn of the century German official reports showed that the pattern of recoil from involvement with the Bali, started by Governor Zimmerer a decade earlier, was being repeated. The Germans complained about the independent initiatives of the Bali, especially their entry into long-distance trade — which was somewhat ironic, considering that Zintgraff had established the "Bali road" precisely for this purpose.

Two developments brought the Bali back into favor. First, in 1903 the Swiss-based Basel Mission reached an agreement with Fonyonga, Galega's successor, to establish a missionary community. The Bali leader hoped that in addition to providing general benefits the mission would bring significant influence to bear on German colonial policy. Next, Bali auxiliaries served in the German punitive expeditions sent against the restive peoples of the northern forest, close to the Nigerian border, in 1904. Fonyonga was rewarded. In 1905 Zintgraff's paramountcy and protection treaty of 1891 was finally given substance. The Bali chief was issued a new letter of protection that listed some thirty-one villages under his control. This public proclamation was preceded by sharp German campaigns against Fonyonga's rivals. The crystallization of the Bali paramountcy was based apparently on general instructions that do not survive, although they are frequently cited; the instructions, dating from 1903, favored the preservation of larger chiefdoms and, if necessary, the amalgamation of culturally similar small groups. At last, therefore, German local initiative and control policy were brought into line.[40]

By 1908 the cycle of Bali-German relations was once more coming full circle. The local commander began to question the wisdom of placing "a whole string of new subjected tribes . . . under the authority of the Bali." The Bali had used their German connection to build up their armaments, and their freebooting use of their breechloaders disrupted the peace of the area. The commander argued that every effort should be made to recover the guns. Governor Theodor Seitz suggested that Fonyonga should be given a suitably impressive tent through the Basel Mission in return for handing back five hundred rifles and ten thousand rounds of ammunition. The commander, Captain Menzel, did not bother to conceal his contempt for this suggestion: "The Bali is too good a businessman to exchange 500 rifles and 10,000 rounds of ammunition for a tent . . . the Bali [ruler] knows to perfection how to use the Mission, which on its side has not the slightest influence on bringing about decisions the effects of which are not yet clear to him."[41] Menzel's tactlessness meant that any reappraisal of the paramountcy was shelved while he and the governor remained in office.

In 1911 a new station commander, Lieutenant von Adametz, hinted that the sheer size of the district made government difficult, and by 1912 he was questioning the whole basis of the paramountcy. Adametz saw Fonyonga as the evil genius who misled Menzel's predecessor as commandant: "Bali's policy is clearly defined. Fonyonga, with false evidence, which Hptm. Glauning was unable to check at the time, demanded control of these [surrounding] areas. At first the chiefs did not object because Fonyonga sugared the pill by telling them through his interpreters that there was no question of subjection in the true negro sense; he was only being appointed by Glauning as a sort of mediator for the Grassfields tribes. The chiefs only began to oppose him when he asked for slaves." Adametz pointed out that Fonyonga was now asking him to intervene against recalcitrant "subjects." The German officer felt that "it would be a very disagreeable task to shoot at good-natured but brave tribesmen only because they refused to be under the control of a tribe which had never defeated them in war and whose warlike qualities are much despised." He suggested that these tribes should be freed from Bali paramountcy in return for giving a single cash payment, or a percentage of their tax, to Bali.[42]

German policy did not change at once, and Adametz found himself criticized for acting as an instrument of the Bali. But immediately before the outbreak of World War I his plans were accepted. The Bali were given compensation for subjects transferred out of the district while those chiefs who remained vassals collected taxes and presented them directly to the German

station, which deducted a small proportion for Fonyonga. He was still regarded as the titular overlord of most of the thirty-one villages that formed
his paramountcy at the height of his power. But now that the collection of
tax or tax-labor was taken out of his hands and given to his erstwhile subjects,
the former subjects regarded themselves as freed from what had been the
traditional obligations of conquered chiefs. The resident Basel missionary
accurately reported that "the old Bali Kingdom . . . dissolved without a
blow."[43]

Adametz was determined to dismantle the Bali paramountcy because of
his disregard for Fonyonga and his chiefs, who had failed to protect their
people from the abuses of private labor recruitment. He dismissed the Bali
elite as motivated purely by greed. Similarly his superior, Governor Karl
Ebermaier, regarded them as unreliable mediators between the Germans
and the other Grassfields peoples. But the situation was more complex
than that. The private German employers had established links with the
Bali before the advent of the military station. The role of the Bali as labor
recruiters conflicted with their role as political mediators. Furthermore,
their activities progressively irritated the commanders of the station, who
wished to keep decisive political influence in their own hands and to retain manpower for local economic development. The contradictions involved
in their relationships with the Germans were partly the result of the Bali
admiration for everything German. Both the 1905 paramountcy and the
attempt to reform labor recruitment were connected with German efforts
to formulate a general imperial policy.

Reacting to major wars in Tanganyika and South-West Africa and to
scandals concerning labor recruiting and brutal floggings in the West African
colonies of Togo and the Cameroons, the Germans sought to institute stronger imperial control in 1907. They began by establishing an independent
Colonial Office under Bernhard Dernburg, a dynamic investment banker with
considerable political skill. Some earlier writers have seen the "Dernburg era
of reform" (1907-1908) as marking a decisive assertion of imperial control
over the concessionary companies and settlers and stricter regulation of the
treatment of Africans. Certainly Dernburg's reforms seem to have checked a
recurrence of such atrocities as the flogging to death of a Togolese chief on
one governor's orders. However, Elizabeth Chilver's research on the Cameroons shows little evidence of a general change in administration at the level of
relations between Africans, plantation owners, and administrators.[44]

The German administration was based as far as possible on the grouping

together of peoples of similar culture into single units, as in the Bali paramountcy. Where these peoples already possessed chiefs, the chiefs were made
German agents. Where there were no chiefs, the Germans appointed village
headmen or loyal servants to act as chiefs. Justice in Togo and the Cameroons
was partly the responsibility of the chiefs and partly, in theory at least, the
responsibility of the German administrators, who were supposed to deal with
more serious cases with the help of African assessors.[45] In practice, as Chilver
points out, the effectiveness of these German courts was very limited. Away
from the local German stations, traditional ordeals were still administered,
witches were still disposed of, and people were still sold into slavery.[46]

Wilhelm Solf, the colonial secretary between 1912 and 1918, made a
further attempt to transform German policy immediately before World War
I. Writers such as the German Islamic scholar Carl Becker and the explorer
Passarge encouraged German admiration for Muslim societies as hierarchical
and disciplined, qualities that could be turned to imperial advantage. They
believed that Christian missions should be restricted to non-Muslim territories
and that Islam should be directly sponsored by the German state. Solf was
influenced by these ideas. He also was one of the most enthusiastic students
of comparative colonial administration. In 1912 he toured South Africa,
German South-West Africa, German East Africa, and Kenya. The following
year he visited the Cameroons and Togo and also, significantly, Nigeria. He
expressed his warm admiration for British administration there, "more especially so with regard to the northern protectorate," and begged Lugard for
a copy of his Political Memoranda. It is clear from Solf's diary that he intended to introduce a system of administration similar to Indirect Rule into
the Fulani area of Adamawa because he felt strongly that a similar style of
administration should be practiced on both sides of the Nigeria-Cameroons
border.

World War I intervened before Solf had formulated his plans for reform.
He hoped to focus attention in Germany on West Africa rather than on the
settler territories of East Africa. In practice, this involved taking Togo, with
its indigenous cash crop farmers, as the model colony rather than the Cameroons where the establishment of European-owned plantations threatened
to disrupt traditional societies. He hoped that the peanut production that had
developed recently in Northern Nigeria would constitute a norm for economic development. He had as little time as Lugard for those whom he called
"trousered niggers," but he believed that they represented little threat to "the
preservation of native law and custom." He had, in fact, encountered opposi-

tion from Manga Bell, the western-educated leader of the Duala people, who bitterly contested the expropriation of some of the land around Duala town. Solf's focus on the north, like Lugard's, meant that coastal centers of economic development and political protest were neglected.[47]

The Congo Free State and the Belgian Congo

Leopold II was the absolute ruler of the Congo Free State, which comprised territory eighty times the size of Belgium.[48] Decision making within the administrative hierarchy, from the lowliest *chef de poste* upward, was expected to be referred to higher authority, ultimately to Leopold himself. The administration was aptly characterized as "an arrangement ideally contrived to multiply correspondence and to paralyze effective action."[49] By 1885 the king had spent ten million gold francs, and by 1890 the Congo Free State had consumed his personal fortune. He regarded himself not only as the absolute ruler but also, as he put it in 1909, as possessing "absolute ownership, uncontested, of the Congo and its riches," just as any contemporary captain of industry might speak of his concerns.[50]

Leopold believed that a colony existed for the sake of the profits it could provide its owner. As early as 1885 the Congo Free State claimed all "vacant land" within its boundaries, while Africans were given title only to the land they occupied. This in itself was not unusual colonial procedure; it often was used to prevent speculation and to maintain a reserve of territory for future African occupation. But in 1891 Leopold decided that the state should reap the profit from such "vacant land" by securing a monopoly of all ivory and rubber gathered on it. This was to be the essence of Leopold's regime: the exploitation of the state's territory, either directly by a state monopoly or by monopolistic concessionary companies. Before 1890 officials who were badly paid had been allowed a commission on ivory, and this had prompted the English Baptist missionary George Grenfell's comment that it seemed to be "a great mistake to give officers who possess almost absolute power a pecuniary interest in the collection of the principal product of the country."[51] Leopold's economic policy resulted in a remarkable improvement in the finances of the Congo Free State from 1892 onward. He also reserved a large private domain. It financed the extensive program of public building at home, through which Leopold indulged his patriotism and kept himself and his mistresses in luxury.

The 1884-85 Berlin Conference and its successor of 1890 in Brussels inspired legislation intended to safeguard the personal and property rights of

Africans. Slave trading was declared illegal along with ritual murder and ordeal by poison. Africans could, in theory, bring their complaints in civil matters either to their own chiefs or to European courts. But as an investigation in the Congo in 1906 showed, the only court authorized to deal with civil and commercial cases was the Tribunal of First Instance at Boma, the capital, consisting of a single judge, so that the right of a European-style trial was theoretical. In criminal cases the European tribunals theoretically dealt with Africans, but it was also correct for officials to allow chiefs to handle such offenses. Any European official could assume power of imprisonment and flogging or, although this was illegal, could delegate them to an African underling. In many cases formality and due process were replaced by summary punishments.

A decree in 1891 recognized African customary groupings through the investiture of the chiefs, who were made responsible for carrying out certain officially imposed tasks. By 1906 more than four hundred chiefs had been invested. But in practice Leopold's administration was too preoccupied with immediate results to work patiently with traditional authorities. Hence, Africans distinguished only for their obedience to orders, such as ex-soldiers and personal servants, were appointed more often than indigenous chiefs. Where chiefs did collaborate with authorities in the rubber areas, they might well face a flight of their subjects, as happened with many Basengele, who resettled on Batende land with the permission of the Batende chiefs. In other cases the legitimate chiefs themselves would put forward dummy chiefs to avoid compromising themselves.[52]

In 1906, under international pressure, a new decree defined more closely the rights and duties of chiefs, and it was laid down that they should receive salaries and have limited control over the movements of their people. Africans now expected the dummy chiefs to hand over a substantial portion of their stipends to the legitimate rulers.

A rather halfhearted attempt was made to copy the French policy of assimilation for western-educated Africans. Provision was made for the registration, or immatriculation, of Africans who were prepared to accept the Belgian civil code. But the decree on immatriculation never had practical force since no qualifications or conditions were laid down for its operation. Furthermore, the officials of the Congo Free State feared that in practice the result of allowing any African who requested such status to be removed from the authority of his chief would be to produce chaos. Behind the failure of the immatriculation policy lay a significant difference in race relations in the Congo Free State, where something of a settlers' *baasskap* approach was developing, from attitudes on the French side of the river. A French bishop who was about to travel fourth class with African passengers on the railway was hurriedly offered a seat on a special train by the Congo Free State administration. Africans from the French Congo, who came to work on the railway, insisted on flying the French tricolor, provoking a Belgian observer to note that "they say they are French, these Negroes! they even claim with pride that they are electors."[53]

The military Force Publique was a distinctive institution of the Congo Free State. At first Leopold had recruited soldiers from other parts of Africa since it was difficult to find Congolese volunteers, but from 1885 onward there was a steady increase in Congolese recruitment. In 1895 there were 6,000 Africans in the force, 4,000 of them from the Congo. By 1905 this paramilitary body numbered 16,000 men, led by nearly 360 white officers. Recruitment in the lower Congo was carried on by agreement with the local chiefs, who were obliged to supply a certain number of men each year. In the east freed slaves from the Arab-Swahili zone provided recruits, although they never were very successful soldiers. The period of service was at first fixed at five years, but it was raised to seven years in 1900. At the end of their service the soldiers were repatriated at state expense or were settled in special villages. These ex-soldiers' villages were strongly marked by Belgian influence; their standard of living was generally higher than that of their neighbors, who tended to imitate and envy them.

Throughout the 1890s international criticism of Leopold's harsh treatment of his African subjects mounted. In September 1896 the king sought to head this off by creating a Commission for the Protection of Natives, consisting of three Roman Catholic and three Protestant missionaries, but the members chosen came from areas far distant from the places where the atrocity stories were originating. They were separated from each other by as much as a thousand miles, and no provision was made for traveling expenses or for giving them the power to take evidence. In April 1897 Sir Charles Dilke, backed by the British Aborigines Protection Society, brought the question of Congo atrocities before the House of Commons. There also were revelations from British and American Protestant missionaries. In February 1904 the report of Roger Casement, a British consul in the Congo, corroborated the evidence produced by the missionaries. In March E. D. Morel formed the Congo Reform Association in London. Leopold that year created a commission of inquiry, but it only confirmed Casement's account.

Every colonial regime produced some instances of brutality; the Congo Free State's "red rubber" regime provided many of the worst. In 1899 an official described to a British consul his method of rubber collection in the Ubangi region. It was

to arrive in canoes at a village, the inhabitants of which invariably bolted on their arrival; the soldiers were then landed, and commenced looting taking all the chickens, grain, etc., out of the houses; after this they attacked the natives until able to seize their women; these women were kept as hostages until the Chiefs of the district brought in the required number of kilogrammes of rubber.

The rubber having been brought, the women were sold back to their owners for a couple of goats a-piece, and so he continued from village to village until the requisite amount of rubber had been collected.[54]

Alfred Parminter, an Englishman who had worked in the Congo Free State, recounted one incident to Reuters: "On one occasion, at Bopoto, having dined with Lieutenant Blochter . . . I was smoking with him on the bank. It was late in the evening when suddenly a force of his troops returned from an expedition on which he had sent them in the morning. The sergeant held up triumphantly a number of ears fastened on a string . . . The soldiers were praised for their success, and ordered to return next day and capture the chief."[55]

Mutilation constituted a "macabre system of accounting," in Anstey's biting phrase. In 1899 an official of the crown domain in the Momboyo River region told an American missionary how it worked: "Each time the corporal goes out to get rubber cartridges are given to him. He must bring back all not used; and for every one used, he must bring back a right hand! . . . As to the extent to which this is carried on, he informed me that in six months they, the State, on the Momboyo River had used 6,000 cartridges, which means that 6,000 people are killed or mutilated. It means more than 6,000, for the people have told me repeatedly that soldiers killed children with the butt of their guns."[56] African soldiers known as the Zappo-Zaps (from the Basonge, a cannibalistic tribe) were used to raise a heavy food tax in the Luluabourg area. Missionaries reported that the Zappo-Zaps were slave raiding with the backing of the state, practicing cannibalism, and generally committing atrocities upon other Africans.

The British Baptist missionary A. E. Scrivener exposed the outrages of the notorious Malu Malu, the local name of the European official who was stationed in the Lake Leopold II region from 1898 to 1900. (More than half a century later Anstey found a nearly universal folk memory of Malu Malu's atrocities in this region.) On a number of occasions men who failed to produce their rubber quota for him were shot dead on the spot. He was also known to have lined up a group of such men so that he could slaughter them all with one bullet. Anstey records that "though Malu Malu lacked the technical equipment of a Heydrich or an Eichmann, he was precisely in the same category of bestiality."[57]

Not all Leopold's employes were Malu Malus, and Casement's African informants insisted that he must make this distinction in his reports on individuals. Nevertheless, the system put a premium on skimming off the Congo's rubber and ivory without regard to the methods used. As Leopold's own commission of inquiry put it, "a good number of agents only thought of obtaining the maximum possible in the minimum possible time, and their demands were often excessive."[58] Leopold had great difficulty in recruiting suitable officials in a country that had no tradition of imperial service. He turned to the Belgian army, but it could not always supply enough men. He then resorted to civilians and foreigners to make good the deficiency. Belgians frequently asked about anyone who served in the Congo, "Why? What has he done?" suggesting that many of the king's servants may have been fugitives escaping from the law.

The Africans enthusiastically welcomed Leopold's commisson of inquiry. They dubbed the three commissioners the "Great Judge," the "Elegant Judge," and "Pole Pole" ("he who walks slowly").[59] The rumor spread that the commissioners were more powerful than Bula Matari, their name for the Congo Free State (and originally the sobriquet given to Henry M. Stanley, the "breaker of rocks"). When the commission report confirming foreign atrocity stories was published, Leopold appointed another commission to implement reforms, and a series of corrective measures were announced in June 1906. These showed a trend toward indirect rule, exemplified by the chieftaincy regulations already examined. Economic reforms were to include some measures against the concessionary monopolies and a new land policy that reserved for Africans three times the amount of land they actually occupied. This at least was better than the 1885 ruling, but in view of African methods of cultivation as well as their traditional hunting and fishing rights, a much greater increase would have been appropriate. In any case, neither Leopold's British nor American critics were mollified. The British government had proposed reconvening the Berlin Conference to consider the Congo Free State atrocities. But a more feasible solution emerged whereby Belgium would annex Leopold's private state. In November 1908 the Belgians responded dutifully, if rather reluctantly, and assumed sovereignty over what now became the Belgian Congo.

They faced the harsh prospect of administering a very thinly peopled country, vastly greater than their own, with no prepared theory of colonial administration. Indeed, they took a stolid pride in their "practical" approach to politics and administration. The law effecting the annexation, popularly known as the Colonial Charter, reflected their reaction to the scandals associated with the earlier regime. Wide powers were accorded to the king but only in his constitutional capacity, as Article 9 made explicit: "No act of the King can be effective if it is not counter-signed by a minister, who by that action alone makes himself responsible for it."[60] The charter also sought to reproduce in the colony the fundamental law of human rights embodied in the Belgian constitution. The liberty of the individual, the rights of property, and freedom of worship were guaranteed. However, specifically political rights, such as freedom of association and of the press, were not accorded. The crown's right to delegate authority was severely restricted to prevent repetitions of the summary proceedings of officials and concessionaires under Leopold. The king, in fact, died only a year after annexation, removing the immediate threat of personal royal autocracy that so conditioned the terms of the charter.

The charter established a colonial council of fourteen members; eight were nominated by the king, three were elected by the senate, and three were elected by the lower house. The council proved to be an independent body, but one that focused on the detail rather than the substance of the draft decrees submitted to it. Policy became the responsibility of the minster of the colonies, Jules Renkin, and his officials.

Renkin decided to cope with the great size of the Congo and the previous overcentralization by administrative devolution. Late in July 1914, on the eve of World War I, he established a policy of decentralization centered on the capital of Boma and extending to four constituent provinces — Congo-Kasai, Equatur, Orientale, and Katanga. The change was timely. Soon Belgium was overrun by German invaders, and the Belgian government, in exile in France, was preoccupied with sheer survival.

For his African policy Renkin built on the 1891 and 1906 decrees. His own order of May 1910 divided the Congo into *chefferies* (chiefdoms) and in some cases *sous-chefferies*. Large traditional groupings fell into the former category, while chiefs previously recognized by the Congo Free State were given the latter status. Each chief was paid according to the size of his chiefdom and was to have administrative and police powers and expanded criminal jurisdiction.

Nowhere did Renkin or the colonial council stipulate how traditional authorities should proceed. Many had been irreparably weakened by the slave trade and Leopold's methods. Belgium kept in being the independent Commission for the Protection of Natives, and its 1911 report on the working of the 1910 decree was not encouraging. The commission reported that some chiefs were abusing their power, while others were unable to carry out their duties. "In short, we believe that the existing chiefs are, on the whole, incapable of executing the civilizing program contained in the decree," said the commissioners, adding that they saw no practical alternative to supporting the chiefs.[61]

The same commission found that under the new regime tax apportionment was more equitable. In July 1914 African taxation was placed on an even more definitive basis when a head tax was levied on virtually all able-bodied adult Africans, with a supplementary tax in the case of polygynists. (The Belgians generally held polygyny, along with such diseases as sleeping sickness, responsible for depopulation in the Congo; foreign critics, on the other hand, blamed the brutality of the Congo Free State administration.) The amount of the head tax was to be determined annually. Belgian officials were responsible for collecting it but could delegate the task to chiefs. Cash payments were envisaged to avoid the abuses of taxation in kind that had occurred in the Congo Free State.

The new Belgian administration tended to divide into a two-class system with administrators and district commissioners generally having a university education, whereas the *chefs de poste*, carrying out policy at the grassroots level, had only secondary education. On a visit to Katanga in 1911 Henri Rolin, a judge and a university teacher, was informed by an eminent missionary that of ten or twelve *chefs de poste* in the area only two were gentlemen. "All witnesses," he reported, "agreed that the *chefs de poste* are generally of the N.C.O. type." Rolin had talked with some new arrivals. One, "twenty-one years old and about to be sent into the interior, assured us that he did not know the native language. He had been to a Belgian athénée [secondary school] and in the matter of how to treat Africans, professed 'strong arm' views. 'Why does one come to the Congo,' he said to us, 'unless to make money quickly and get out?' . . . 'Here,' we sadly said to ourselves, 'are the men to whom we entrust the supremely delicate task of governing Africans!'"[62] The quality of such local officials caused Belgium, as Rolin also reported, to be reluctant to decentralize by granting initiative to the "men on the spot." Even Renkin's devolution measures meant in practice that provincial capitals exercised close supervision over local officers.

The international pressures that had toppled Leopold's Free State did not end with the creation of the new Belgian Congo. As early as 1910 British consular and missionary observers noticed real improvement in the treatment of the Congolese, but British recognition of Belgian annexation was withheld until June 1913 after a House of Commons debate. The next month the Congo Reform Association held a self-congratulatory final meeting in London.

Marvin Miracle, the historian of agriculture in the Congo basin, confirms the impression of rapid improvement under Belgian rule. The new administration was "charged with bringing the Belgian system of justice . . . to the subjected Africans whether or not there was immediate economic gain."[63] In fact, there was a notable increase in exports almost entirely produced by Africans in the first years of the Belgian administration. The futility of Leopold's harsh rule was seen in the fact that exports of rubber, "the commodity for which the most bloody forms of coercion" were used had been falling in the Congo Free State's final years.[64]

Like most European colonial administrators the Belgians were selective, partly owing to ignorance, in their recognition of traditional authorities. Some strongly urged that the roles of the clan and the tribal elders in African society be explicitly recognized. Van Wing, an administrator with particular experience in the lower Congo, stressed the usurpation of indigenous authority by obedient parvenus or the practice of the chiefs themselves of putting forward men of straw to serve in the colonial hierarchy. But these early anthropological exercises were somewhat foreign to the spirit of the administration, as is shown by a statement in the Congo Annual Report for 1917: "In measure as civilization progresses, the former power of the chiefs will pass into the realm of memory and they will become civil servants applying the laws and regulations of the State."[65]

Old Colonies and New Protectorates

Although for most Africans European rule arrived in the guise of paper protectorates or outright conquest toward the end of the nineteenth century, some of them had belonged to European colonies much earlier. Several generations had elapsed since Senegal, the Gambia, and the Gold Coast had come under European control, while Sierra Leone's colonial history went back a hundred years; even Lagos, although only occupied in 1851 and made a crown colony ten years later, had been subjected to a variety of cosmopolitan influences through its involvement in the Creole diaspora.[66] Within such colonies the Africans had developed a multiplicity of institutions in order to claim limited but nonetheless real constitutional rights. The western-educated elite discovered both benefits and disadvantages in the new imperialism. Within their own colonies they suffered from the turn-of-the-century Europeanization of top posts in government, the churches, and business as more Europeans, emboldened by improvements in tropical medicine, claimed careers in West Africa.[67] On the other hand, the extension of the bounds of empire brought a multitude of new opportunities for Africans who were willing to travel. "All along the West Coast," declared the *Sierra Leone Weekly News* on November 15, 1890, "the influence of this colony is felt and recognized. The man from Sierra Leone, bent on improving his condition, adventures wherever he has reasons to believe that his labour, intellectual or manual, his intelligence and enterprising spirit, may meet with encouraging remunerations. He has left his footprints in the Sands of Senegal. He dips his hands into the waters of the Congo. He followed in the train . . . to the conquest of Ashantiland. He colonises Lagos and makes it a prosperous settlement. He was present at all the explorations of the Niger from the earliest. He has largely contributed to the development of the Niger trade. The Niger mission — its conquests . . . its conversions, are mainly his work."

On August 5, 1905, an article in the same paper adapted the vocabulary of contemporary British imperialism to West Africa. "Little Freetonians" were scorned as "the pigmy-souled, little-minded, stay-at-home, conservative folks" in contrast to "Greater Sierra Leoneans," who crossed the seas to build up the reputation of Sierra Leone and who shouldered "the noble task of assisting the Westerner in his grand work of reformation and civilization" as "the principal agents in the transformation from wildness and savagery to civilization and religion [of] such large areas as the Gambia down to Sokoto." But the terms in which inhabitants of the old colonies proclaimed their suitability for transmitting western values were used by the Europeans to disqualify them. Boasting of their cultural superiority, the educated elite unwittingly had reinforced a favorite European rationalization of "de-Africanization," which focused on the difference between such detribalized and literate persons and the silent majority of "pure and simple" African peasants who would grow the agricultural produce Europe required.

The degree of self-deception involved in this key colonial rationalization has been exposed sharply by recent research. The Gold Coast Aborigines' Rights Protection Society proclaimed the natural alliance of the educated elite and the chiefs to defeat British legislation concerning land.[68] In Lagos politicians, journalists, and barristers sought to protect the interests of their fellow Yoruba in the hinterland.[69] In Sierra Leone the Creoles transmitted Temne protests against the hut tax and other objectionable aspects of the new protectorate.[70]

In Senegal the period between 1900 and the outbreak of World War I has been characterized as the "African political awakening."[71] Galandou Diouf became a spokesman for African interests after the 1909 general council election, and Blaise Diagne was elected deputy in 1914 in defiance of the old French-Senegalese Creole entente. The basic issue was the protection of the legal status of French citizens against administrative despotism involving their freedom from forced labor and the *indigénat*. Such freedoms had more than local effect because Senegalese citizens traveled throughout the new French Africa. Furthermore, the Africans in the hinterland understood the close connection between the citizens' privileges and their own defense against arbitrary rule. From the turn of the century the rural Africans of the Senegalese protectorate had been politicized by the sudden emergence of the public letter writer (*écrivain publique*), who was usually an urban African, sometimes a citizen, with some education and a good deal of political wit, and who served as a "rural notary, an embryonic lawyer, and a public tribune."[72] The most celebrated of them was Mody M'Baye, who succeeded in organizing an extensive intelligence network. M'Baye's backing proved crucial to Diagne's election victory and ensured that he became the popular spokesman of the countryside as well as the city. Earlier the rapid spread of Amadou Bamba's Mourides, a new Islamic brotherhood, had rescued the countryside from apathy in the aftermath of the French conquest in the 1880s.[73] Bamba also bankrolled Diagne, who therefore represented much more than the old four communes of the Senegal colony. The dynamism of his subsequent political career expanded this informal constituency until he was regarded as representing Africans throughout French West Africa and French Equatorial Africa, even though only the citizens of the communes could vote.

CHAPTER 8

Establishing the White Man's Realm

Imperial administrators .had to decide whether white settlers were necessary to develop their colonies. In the traditional area of European trade, West Africa, a negative answer was simple because the African peasants were already successfully exporting such crops as palm oil and peanuts, to which they soon added cocoa, and at the same time it was believed that the climate ruled out large-scale European settlement. In South Africa the method again seemed obvious. White settlers had developed capitalist agriculture and were in the process of directing Africa's first industrial revolution based on diamond and gold mining. But South Africa was linked by what General Jan Smuts called a "broad backbone" of mountainous plateau to equatorial regions in the northeast. Hence the question of where precisely to draw the frontier of white settlement preoccupied imperial politicians.[1] Cecil Rhodes directed whites from the Cape to claim their "inheritance in the interior" by extending their settlements to the Zambezi River or even to Lake Tanganyika. Expansionists in the Transvaal had hoped for an "Africa for the Afrikaner," a United States of South Africa from the Zambezi to Simon's Bay.[2] Rhodes welcomed individual Afrikaner settlers to the territory of the British South Africa Company but forcefully broke up the Adendorff trek into what became Rhodesia in case it might constitute a foothold for Afrikaner nationalism. Ironically, the defeat of the Afrikaners in the Anglo-Boer War contributed to the expansion of their range of settlement. The first white settlers to reach the Arusha area of German East Africa in 1902 were Boer diehards fleeing postwar depression in South Africa. By 1908, eighty Afrikaner families

154

were among the roving adventurers settling in Kenya. With the formation of the Union of South Africa, Smuts, the arch-expansionist, welded together the goals of both the early settlers of the Transvaal and Rhodes with the vision of a South Africa extending from "Simonstown to the Equator."[3]

European administrators who were responsible for the territories Smuts coveted tended to consider development in terms of either a "West Coast policy" of African peasant agriculture or a "South African policy" of European settlement. A third alternative, a "South East Asia policy" of large-scale plantation agriculture, which had been adopted by the Belgians in the Congo, also was sometimes considered.[4]

A balanced combination of all three solutions was often thought best, although in practice the methods generally proved incompatible. But administrators seldom decided by strict cost benefit analysis or outright political fiat. Frequently events appeared to determine which alternative prevailed. In Kenya the British found themselves drifting toward a South African solution through the pressure of the European residents and their governors. In Uganda they discussed the merits of both European plantations and African agriculture, but the long-drawn-out debate was only resolved when the economic success of the peasants in the 1920s contrasted strikingly with the failure of the European plantations. After the revolts of 1904-1907 in South-West Africa the Germans did make a clear-cut choice in favor of European settlement with the surviving African population constituting a laboring class. In German East Africa the process of decision making was highly complex. In the aftermath of the Maji-Maji rebellion Governor Albrecht von Rechenberg opted for African peasant agriculture, but his program was reversed by local settler opposition backed by politically powerful right-wing groups in Germany. German East Africa serves admirably, therefore, as an exemplary study, not least because the historiography for this area is of particularly high quality. (In the Portuguese colonies of Angola and Mozambique European settlement was encouraged but more with a view to securing "effective occupation," without maintaining a bureaucracy comparable to that employed by other imperial powers, than as a sustained program of economic development and is thus dealt with elsewhere.)

German East Africa

Whether or not German East Africa should become a "white man's country" was a question that remained open for much of the period of German rule.[5] From 1885 until 1891 the administration of Tanganyika was nominally the responsibility of Carl Peters's German East African Company. The company was an offspring of his Gesellschaft für Deutsche Kolonisation, which stressed the desirability of diverting to German colonies some of the stream of good Teutonic peasants who were currently emigrating to the United States. The German government itself sought to turn the problem of its rural overpopulation to political advantage and committed itself to a massive expenditure of over a billion marks to settle German peasants among the emperor's dissident Polish subjects. The strong body of right-wing opinion that supported imperialism believed that similar policies should certainly be pursued in Tanganyika and South-West Africa and possibly even in the West African colonies of the Cameroons and Togoland. "One settler holds a hundred blacks in check," boasted an imperial enthusiast in the aftermath of the Maji-Maji rebellion in Tanganyika, which had been concentrated in the south and east where there were very few settlers, while the settled northern areas tended to escape.[6] Amateur strategists of *weltpolitik* also believed that German settlement should be built up as a means of preparing for any future war with Britain in Africa — the professional strategists employed by the German government not having revealed to them that these colonies were already written off in the event of such a war. German colonial enthusiasts also deployed the arguments of social imperialism, in which colonies were regarded as safety valves for social unrest. "Fewer proletarians, more colonists!" was the message of the colonial propagandists in the 1907 election.

The right-wing supporters of colonization achieved no unanimity on the proper type of settlement. The Conservatives wanted to follow the Polish model of small peasant settlers, dubbed the "radish policy." The National Liberals, backed by much expert opinion, thought that settlers must have access to capital, and they favored the recruitment of ex-officers, the younger sons of the commercial and industrial bourgeoisie, and, above all, the Prussian lower nobility. Outside the right-wing coalition, the members of the Catholic Center, with their mission connections, and some powerful Liberals believed that white settlement was not in the interest of the Africans, and the Social Democrats viewed settlement schemes as defrauding the German working class.[7]

Even among right-wingers there were old Prussian Conservatives who saw Germany's future in terms of eastern consolidation and expansion rather than in the sea power and colonial enterprise favored by *weltpolitik*. Rechenberg, Tanganyika's most distinguished German governor, was an easterner who believed that German settlement should concentrate on Eastern Europe.

With the money settlers needed to establish themselves in East Africa, he believed, they "could easily acquire a small holding in the Polish-speaking areas, where they are sure of support and are of quite as much value to Germanity [Deutschtum] as they are in Africa."[8] In the face of such divided counsels the government chose to regard European settlement as a desirable experiment but not one to be subsidized from public funds. With no clear-cut decision "the progress of German East Africa towards a white man's country was not marked by grand initiatives but by the terms of legal contracts and municipal rating provisions." Such progress was nonetheless real.[9]

The first important impact of German rule on Africans, especially inland, was likely to be in the form not of settlers but of army officers such as those in the force that came to the rescue of Carl Peters's beleaguered company. This force was transformed in 1891 into a regular arm of government with responsibility for the administration of the interior. On two counts it is difficult to generalize about the interaction of African societies and this German administration. First, German East Africa was made up of many small-scale societies; by contrast, Uganda's colonial history focuses on the kingdom of Buganda, while in Rhodesia there are two major tribes, and even in Kenya there are only five major tribes. Second, German administration was very decentralized with the individual district officer having enormous responsibility. The only limit to his authority over the Africans in his district was an order defining the punishment he could impose. The offenses he might punish were not stipulated. The Germans spoke, only half humorously, of an officer's district as his "Reich" and talked of making a border agreement with him.[10]

Although the Africans were legally, as Governor Rechenberg once wrote, "totally in the power of the administration,"[11] this was usually mitigated in practice by a strong awareness among German officers of the great numerical superiority of their African subjects. Lieutenant Carl Herrmann, when he set out for the Lake Victoria area in 1891, was warned to model himself on his predecessor and to maintain a "diplomatic-mediating rather than a dictatorial-military role."[12] The method used by the man he succeeded, Lieutenant Wilhelm Langheld, to obtain the obedience of the chiefs was, in his own words, to "play one off against another."[13] Herrmann paid closer attention to traditional political institutions, advancing beyond Langheld's simple policy of divide and rule to an equally manipulative notion of ruling indirectly. "Indeed, the still prevailing principle 'nothing without the permission of the chiefs' is, after all, quite comfortable for us — one gives orders to the chief, he commands his people to work, and there are no expenses.''[14]

At this early stage German administration made a somewhat limited impact on African society, merely requiring the chiefs to recognize German sovereignty and to provide certain quantities of labor and building materials. The advantages proffered by the German administration at this time were similarly limited, usually being restricted to diplomatic and military support for collaborating Africans. African polities were therefore able to accommodate their German rulers without seriously revising their traditional political structures. Even those African leaders who had a very sharp eye for the advantages of accommodation saw them in terms of existing political patterns. German power was understood as a new factor that could be manipulated within the framework of traditional political and social conflicts. It was not yet seen as transforming traditional patterns and therefore giving scope for new roles. Hence the most significant change caused by German control at this stage was often a shift in the balance of power between or within African polities as the African allies of the Germans exercised "subimperialism" over those who had failed to come to terms. By the end of the nineteenth century colonial rule rested on a series of such local compromises.

Opportunist African chiefs skillfully utilized the German presence. Among the Chagga of Kilimanjaro, Marealle, chief of the previously insignificant Marangu, emerged as the leading ally of the Germans on the mountain. Marealle's subimperialism was based on his friendship with the local German commander, his willingness to provide auxiliaries for the German campaigns, and a series of brilliant intrigues against his rivals, culminating in a plot that linked two rival chiefs with unrest among the Arusha and Masai peoples so that the Germans hung them, along with seventeen other leading men from several chiefdoms. In return for his collaboration Marealle achieved virtual hegemony over the southeastern slopes of Kilimanjaro, with special privileges related to land rights and economic opportunities, including license to plunder women and cattle from the outlying eastern area of Rombo.[15]

The German policy of divide and rule involved dismantling some promising African attempts to enlarge the scale of traditional politics. The proliferation of chiefdoms in the Kimbu tribe had been checked between 1870 and 1880 by the establishment of the "empire of the Ruga-Ruga" (warrior bands) under Nyungu, a successful warrior of chiefly descent.[16] Nyungu posted his own officials among the conquered chiefdoms. Chiefs who had indicated their submission were allowed to remain, but those who resisted were seldom replaced when defeated. The real local rulers now were Nyungu's officials, known as *Vatwale*. The *Vatwale* themselves remained mere administrators, not chiefs. Only at the center of the empire, in Nyungu himself through his ancestry, was ritual power combined with political authority. When Nyungu died in 1884, he left a durable realm, unlike several other empires constructed at this time. He was succeeded by his daughter, Mgalula, who repulsed an attack by the powerful Hehe ruler, Mkwawa, in 1892-93. Around 1894 she was succeeded by a much younger woman chief, Msavila, who welcomed the Germans as allies against the Hehe. The new chief and her councillors were persuaded by the Germans to withdraw all the *Vatwale* from the areas Nyungu had conquered, while all the chiefs he had exiled were ordered to return to their homeland. In a very real sense, therefore, the advent of the Germans amounted to a restoration of the old order, and a Kimbu Swahili history refers to the German-inspired removal of the *Vatwale* as the dismissal of the spies and the coming of peace. From a different perspective, though, the German dismantling of Nyungu's empire has been described by the modern historian of the Kimbu, Father Alyward Shorter, as destroying "the only realistic attempt ever made to reform the Kimbu tribe and halt the process of proliferation and decline."[17]

In any case the grand German restoration of Kimbu chiefs gave ample scope for opportunism. Mutitimia, a chief who had fought alongside Nyungu but was exiled in about 1882 after an unsuccessful rebellion, chose to return to part of another chiefdom rather than his own. In 1899 he was denounced to the new German official in the area, Heinrich Fonck, by the legitimate chief and another neighboring chief. But Mutitimia adroitly turned the tables by charging his accusers with failing to comply conscientiously with a German request for food supplies — probably instead of tax. This accusation was equally true and was more significant to the Germans than the dispute about Mutitimia's title. In the end he was confirmed in office while his two accusers were carried off to jail in chains on Fonck's orders.

Mutitimia's triumph was short-lived. He was destroyed by the enmity of his half-sister, Muyela, who thereby avenged his murder of her full brother, Mpaje. According to oral tradition, she poisoned Mutitimia's son, who thereafter went mad and shot himself. His father held a general trial by ordeal and two or ten — the accounts vary — suspected witches died shortly afterward, either by the ordeal poison or by subsequent execution in the forest. The oral tradition collected by Father Shorter, which is generally favorable to Muyela, recounts that when she heard this she said, "'Thank you, my brother. They [the executioners] killed them. Thank you. They [the suspects] killed my nephew who was so handsome.' In her belly, she said: 'I have got him now.'" She denounced Mutitimia as a murderer to a detachment of soldiers, who arrested him. The oral tradition comments with satisfaction, "His trickery was at an end." The soldiers set off on the long journey back to the district office with their prisoner. But near the end of their travels, Mutitimia, fearing torture, committed suicide — though some accounts say he was murdered. Fonck, who had once confirmed him in office, resolved the matter this way: "Enough, if he has hanged himself, that shows that he really did murder the people. The case is finished. Now, who is going to rule? His kinswoman, Muyela. She is here." Muyela became chief in 1903 and retained the title throughout the period of German rule.[18]

By the beginning of the twentieth century German administrative costs were rising more rapidly than revenue. Both plantations and smaller European settlements had been tried with only limited success, so a fresh initiative was necessary. Count Adolf von Götzen, the governor from 1901 to 1906, decided that cotton should be grown as a peasant crop in the south. He was advised that the notion of a cash crop would be completely foreign to the local cultivators and that forced communal labor would be necessary. He ordered each headman to establish a cotton plot where all of his people would come to work. When the crop was sold, the headman, the workers, and the marketing organization would each receive a third of the profits. The scheme was begun in the Dar es Salaam district in 1903 and was extended over the southern coast and inland in the next two years.

The project constituted a radical interference with traditional peasant subsistence farming and might well have provoked a serious opposition even if it had operated as Götzen had intended. But it did not work: in the Dar es Salaam district, for example, it was said that many peasants received no payment whatsoever during three years. There was great hardship throughout the area, for the land selected was unsuitable and the crops were poor. The organization of forced labor was inefficient and frequently brutal.

The farmers rebelled in July and August 1905, just before the cotton harvest.[19] The rebels were aided by their traditional spiritual leaders, who supplied a water medicine thought to guarantee immunity from European bullets. The Swahili word for "water" is "maji," hence the rebel war cry from which the Maji-Maji rebellion was named. Beginning in the hinterland of Kilwa, the insurrection swept through the southeastern part of Tanganyika.

For three months the Germans lost control, and the rebels killed the few Europeans available and all their non-European agents, burned cotton crops, and sacked government posts and mission stations. Then, using scorched earth tactics themselves, the Germans gradually restored control. In the war and the subsequent famine seventy-five thousand Africans are thought to have died.

For both Africans and Germans the rebellion became central to their intepretations of the imperial experience. In itself, Maji-Maji represented an attempt to transcend the tribal divisions with a religious ideology. The water medicine was distributed by priests of Kolelo, a spirit who lived in the Uluguru Mountains. But later Maji-Maji became millennial, linked to a vision of a new world to come, a world without evil — especially without the two unfathomable evils, European rule and sorcery — ruled by a new god. Such a millennial movement represented a threat to all established authority, African as well as European, for a chief who refused to commit himself might be swept away. When a Vidunda chief opposed Maji-Maji, the Hongo (spirit priest) appointed himself chief of the district.[20] Kiwanga, the powerful Bena chief in the Kilombero River valley, obviously saw the movement as dangerous. He killed all the Hongo he could lay hands on and then fought against the rebels and finally was killed by them.[21]

Yet the Maji-Maji rebellion failed to regain independence for the Africans. It rammed home the lesson of African technological inferiority and clarified the nature of German power. Earlier the Africans either had accommodated to the imperial presence by traditional techniques of opportunist diplomacy or had resorted to resistance. Maji-Maji was, Iliffe suggests, something of a watershed; henceforth resistance and diplomacy "were widely superceded by techniques of improvement."[22] He cites as evidence of the new appreciation of the German presence the comments of Martin Ganisya, a freed slave who had risen to the position of senior African teacher with the Lutheran mission in Dar es Salaam, on the occasion of the emperor's birthday in 1910:

For what reason do the people celebrate this festival? . . . The Lord God gives the Kaiser strength and power to accomplish all that happens in the land, and to govern and to order all things so that they continue in peace. . . . As an example I take this land of German East Africa, our land, the land of the black people. Formerly its condition was one of injustice. The man with power treated unjustly the man who had none . . . but now there is peace everywhere. There is none who terrorizes, for all are under the Kaiser's rule . . . If anyone will not keep the peace and live peacefully in his land — if he seeks to disturb the country — that man will be severely punished, for the Kaiser lacks nothing, he has many soldiers. His strength and power are great. You have seen how those rebels, the Maji-Maji or Hongo-Hongo people, were defeated in the years 1905 and 1906![23]

The rebellion profoundly affected the Germans as well. From then on they could no longer take African loyalty for granted. Two opposing views of the rebellion emerged. One focused on the magic water cult that had given the rebels their cohesion and fanatical courage. This opinion held that the rebellion had been secretly plotted by witch doctors and dispossessed headmen, using magic to mobilize support. The opposing view saw the rebellion as a popular protest against specific grievances, especially economic ones, into which the religious leaders had quite naturally been drawn. This "protest against abuse" theory was adopted by left-wing politicians in Germany, most missionaries, and a minority of administrators in East Africa. The "witchcraft" theory was endorsed by Governor Götzen, backed by most of the settlers and soldiers and the right-wing politicians.

Believing that both the motivation and the mechanics of Maji-Maji were irrational, the members of the right wing thought that insurrection was endemic and could only be repressed by constant military readiness, stern administration, and a larger settler population. This viewpoint was expressed in the instructions issued to every German officer after 1911: "The negro does not love us, but only fears our power. Any sign of weakness which he thinks he sees in us will be a temptation to him to take up arms and to drive us from his country. Cruel by nature, the negro does not understand devotion, gratitude, or loyalty in our sense. He will, therefore, support those whom he fears or who offer him the greatest material advantage. This material instinct is influenced by superstition and . . . racial hatred . . . There are no tribes whatever on whose loyalty we can with certainty depend."[24]

Those who endorsed the "protest against abuses" theory sought the remedy in eliminating grievances and ending compulsion on the peasant producer. Götzen resigned early in 1906 after his troops had regained control. He was succeeded by Rechenberg, whose reconstruction policy was designed in the light of his own analysis of the Maji-Maji rebellion. He was haunted by the fear of further insurrection and determined to avoid it. Drawing on his experience of rural unrest in Eastern Europe, he was certain that the only solution was to offer obvious economic benefits to subject peoples. "From what I have seen so far," he wrote in 1907, "I have not the slightest doubt that the recent rising was due to economic causes, and this of course with experience gained in other lands. I have repeatedly had opportunity to observe popular movements more or less closely, and wherever heterogeneous elements united in a general rising, as was the case with the various tribes here, economic questions have been the root cause, to which other factors have been joined only subsequently."[25]

Götzen's scheme to raise cotton with forced labor had failed, Rechenberg believed, because it did not treat the peasant as an economic man who would respond to market forces. Far from being irrational, rebellion was the only means of protest available to a subject people who were badly ruled. "Apart from a rising, the natives have no means available against an ordered government which takes no account of their economic conditions and existence . . . in an uncivilised land which, for example, is exposed to raiding, the condition of a native is indeed afflicted, but not hopeless. He can always hope to beat off the raiders, to bar their way, to win the protection of another powerful tribe to avoid these intermittent raids, and so on. But under an established administration which is based on false economic principles, the native lacks any means of escaping oppression. It deprives him of even the hope of improvement, and leaves him no choice save either to perish or to eliminate it through a rising. He naturally chooses the latter."[26]

Rechenberg did not see European settlers as a solution. Indeed the existing settlement schemes and plantations were failing; furthermore, their mere presence was likely to provoke insurrection. He concluded that a "West Coast policy," with the diversion of resources to the African sector of the economy, was the best way to promote economic development and to avoid future rebellion. But, as the debacle of Götzen's cotton experiment showed, a delicate touch was needed. Direct compulsion was ruled out from the start. Rechenberg similarly doubted the effectiveness of technological solutions. Many European experts believed that African farming should be revolutionized by replacing the hoe with the plow. Rechenberg was skeptical. Hoes were still used in intensive peasant farming in Eastern Europe. Plows required animals to draw them, and the peasant, whether East European or African, could not afford these, even where cattle disease was not present. When it was suggested that the answer lay in increasing the number of veterinary officers, he asked, "Are the vets to pull the ploughs?" He despised agricultural experts, believing that they knew far less about peasant farming than the peasants they sought to instruct.[27]

Rechenberg worked for a gradual expansion of indigenous agriculture. The effect of the British-built Uganda Railway on German East Africa south and west of Lake Victoria, which it reached in 1901, suggested the proper means of encouragement. European observers were startled to find that as soon as the peoples in this area were linked to a market they began to expand their agricultural output. Rechenberg decided that the German railway should strike out as quickly as possible for the territory of the Nyamwezi, who had already demonstrated their response to economic opportunity. Once connected to a market, Rechenberg thought, the Nyamwezi would increase their production of peanuts for sale to Indian or coastal traders. The Nyamwezi would have money then to pay their taxes and the customs duty on imported consumer goods. The resulting boost to revenue and economic development would be achieved without compulsion and with a minimal European presence.

Rechenberg's policy has been characterized accurately by an opponent as "Nyamwezi and peanuts" and equally correctly by a modern historian as "economy and quietude."[28] But he provoked a settler reaction that won strong right-wing support in Germany, so that ultimately policy shifted in the direction of making Tanganyika a "white man's country." The European community that finally succeeded in reversing the "Nyamwezi and peanuts" policy was quite small. There were 2,772 Europeans in Tanganyika at the end of 1907, but this total included 319 officials, 168 soldiers, and 303 missionaries. The effective settler element was thus reduced to 1,982, including 479 male settlers and planters, of whom some 70 percent were German. This small European community was afraid both for its security and its economic interests. Such fear was quite reasonable. Those who had suffered in the Maji-Maji rebellion were paid only 30 percent compensation — after a delay of four years. They asked pointed questions about the absence of military preparedness revealed by the rebellion, and they demanded with little success that a European volunteer force be raised and trained to use machine guns. Rechenberg, intent on economy, created panic by reducing the number of Europeans in the defense force.

The real measure of settler strength was in the extent of their support at home, however, rather than in their numbers. The settlers were a right-wing cause between 1907 and 1912, a time when the right was stronger than it would be at any point until 1933. "Black, white, red — true till death."[29] Such patriotic extravagance had tremendous appeal in Wilhelmine Germany.

Like all settlers, they sought to determine their own affairs. In the German constitutional idiom, this meant asking for *Selbstverwaltung*, or local self-government. During the long centuries of particularism this concept had come to be accepted as good by Germans of all political persuasions, although it was capable of a variety of interpretations. In Germany the antithesis of self-government was usually understood to be the centralized authoritarianism of the old Prussian bureaucratic state. Rechenberg, who opposed self-government in East Africa, because he believed in putting African interests first, was condemned by Germans as a reactionary. In the colony the demand for local self-government was made not so much against the bureaucracy as against the Riechstag. In this three-party controversy — settlers, bureaucracy, and Reichstag — the settlers were able to exploit successfully the disagreement between the other two parties.

Rechenberg's reconstruction policy had been accepted early in 1908. It was gradually reversed, at first in administrative detail but later in principle, until by 1914 the German government was strongly pro-settler. When Rechenberg planned German East Africa's future, he had no notion of the coming boom in rubber and sisal that was to bring prosperity to the European settlers and smaller planters. Even the peasants preferred to grow export crops rather than indigenous crops. Poor communication, great distances, and the decentralization of German government meant that district officers were able to practice compulsion quite against the spirit of Rechenberg's recommendations. Gradually the German administration began to switch expenditure to the settler and plantation sector, financing this by increased taxation on the Africans.

Iliffe has identified two major reasons for this change. First, the settler view of the Maji-Maji rebellion as a consequence of "savage superstition" gained increased support while Rechenberg's explanation of it as a protest against bad government lost ground. Götzen published the first and only substantial account of the rebellion in 1909, a lively and competent book but one which contained no reference to his cotton scheme. His narrative of a superstitious conspiracy reinforced the notion that the Africans were incapable of progress; hence the government should concentrate on the European sector while holding the Africans down through military vigilance.

Second, the political situation within Germany was crucial. The government was preoccupied with matters it considered more important than German East Africa. The right wing was exceptionally strong, and its support was vital to the government's attempt to deal with such matters as the reform of the imperial finances and the construction of a navy. The colonial secretary, Bernhard Dernburg, who was forced under the German constitution to be a political administrator, reflected the change. When he came to office in 1906, he had favored colonial retrenchment. In 1907, when selling the idea of the colony in an election campaign, he was for European settlement and investment. In 1908, influenced by Rechenberg, he supported "quietude and economy" through concentration on the peasant economy. But by 1910 he had come full circle to his original position in deference to right-wing pressure. He was succeeded by Friedrich von Lindequist, whose South-West African experience made him the leading advocate of European settlement on the South African model. On the eve of World War I there were significantly more Europeans in German East African than in British Kenya. Furthermore, the German settlers had an elected majority of twelve to four on an advisory council, whereas the Kenya settlers had only two nominated settlers on the legislative council. The German settlers also did not have to take into political consideration an Indian community, backed by the Indian Office, which significantly weakened the British settler position in Kenya. The strength of the settler community should not be exaggerated, however, because the colony was not self-sufficient and depended upon imperial protection — how dependent was shown with the outbreak of the war in 1914.

German South-West Africa

In March 1893 Chancellor Leo von Caprivi dismissed all talk of withdrawing from South-West Africa because of its poverty. He criticized the imperial commissioner who had embarked on a preventive war against the Nama: "We do not intend to make war, we wish to become masters of the country and to consolidate our sovereignty without bloodshed. We possess South West Africa once and for all; it is German territory and must be preserved as such."[30] The official who implemented this policy was Theodor Leutwein, who was the first territorial commander of South-West Africa from 1894 to 1898 and then the first governor of it from 1898 to 1905.

Leutwein was determined to guide South-West Africa toward the procedures of a modern western territorial state, a province of Germany. He drew upon the works of German historians for a model of the process of European state development from medieval tribal origins, which would be comparable to the societies he observed in Africa. Like the medieval German emperors Leutwein refused to call insurrections "wars" because this would threaten the image of absolute state sovereignty. But the Nama and the Herero were organized in large tribal groupings and were armed with modern breech-loading rifles. Hence the consolidation of German sovereignty involved endless compromise and negotiation, similar in style to the policies of successful medieval German emperors.

Leutwein's economic aim was to develop South-West Africa to produce

cattle for export. This meant the reorganization of the economy and the
social structure through free enterprise. European settlers who were able
to make large capital investments would set the pattern of efficient commercial management. The impact of capitalism would inevitably result in the
collapse of African tribal societies. But Leutwein believed that in the meantime several decades of skillful rule would facilitate African adaptation. The
chiefs would obviously be crucial to the success of his plans, so Leutwein
took care to establish good personal relationships with them. He made them
salaried officials of the emperor and expected the most successful of them to
develop into efficient bureaucrats and wealthy cattle ranchers. For all his
romantic medievalism, he had little notion of the tremendous difference
between the sacred authority of a chief and the subordinate and secular role
he was creating for them as "prominent natives" within a colonial territory
dominated by Europeans. The African rulers had no such illusions about the
drastic nature of the German impact. As early as 1894 one of the most astute
Herero chiefs, Manasse of Omaruru, commenting on the German style of
government as exhibited in their courts, said that the Herero "could not
tolerate justice practiced with such vehemence."[31] German justice might be
fair according to their code, but an African chief would be primarily concerned with the conciliation of disputes through protracted discussion.
Africans were discovering that equality before the law, of which Leutwein
was so proud, regularly worked to the advantage of the rich, the powerful,
and the well informed — the Germans, in the context of South-West Africa.
Nor were the German courts always impartial, as Leutwein himself noted.
Settler magistrates tended to favor their own kind over African supplicants.

In 1897 the rinderpest epidemic in cattle that was sweeping over South
and Central Africa struck the Herero, bringing a death rate for their uninocu-
lated cattle of 90 percent or more. In its wake came malaria epidemics among
the people. The Herero lost much of their stock, which, because of the ritual
significance of cattle, shook the religious as well as the economic foundations
of the Herero nation. But the rinderpest epidemic proved to be the turning
point for the European economic sector. Cattle raising where inoculation
was practiced became highly profitable, and new European settlers swept
into tribal territory. Such new arrivals had no idea of the fighting resistance
shown by the tribes just a few years earlier. Political, social, and legal discrimination increased. The Herero paramount chief, Samuel Maharero,
charged Leutwein with allowing cases of the manslaughter and murder of
Herero to go unpunished in the German colonial courts and with deaths in

the colonial prisons. All this, he said, could only be construed as a declaration of war upon his people. He called on the Nama chiefs to unite with him in a general rising. As he put it, " . . . it is my wish that we weak nations should rise up against the Germans. Either we destroy them or they all will live in our country. There is nothing else for it." He challenged Hendrik Witbooi, the Nama paramount chief: "Let us rather die together, and not by German cruelty, in prison."[32]

In January 1904 the Herero rose, catching officials, settlers, and even missionaries off guard. In October the Nama rebellion also took the Germans by surprise. Leutwein was in the far south with most of the German forces settling a local revolt when the Herero struck. Over a hundred Germans were killed at the outset, and it cost them over two thousand more lives, including deaths by typhus, and 600 million marks before the armistice. Women, children, Boers, British, and a few German men particularly noted for their exemplary behavior were spared by the Herero.

The Herero paid dearly. With Leutwein temporarily out of touch and to some extent discredited by having been caught unawares, Berlin snatched control. The emperor placed Alfred von Schlieffen, the chief of the general staff, in charge of operations, which were thereby regarded as measures in a full-scale war rather than in the suppression of a local colonial revolt. Leutwein, with the agreement of the colonial authorities, would have conducted an essentially political campaign, negotiating while fighting. But the emperor and Schlieffen insisted that the governor should surrender military control to their own nominee, the former German commander in East Africa, General Lothar von Trotha. When Trotha arrived, Leutwein requested him to conduct the war in such a way as to preserve the Herero nation. Trotha peremptorily refused.[33]

At the battle of Waterberg on August 11, 1904, the Germans intended to encircle their enemy in the expectation of taking prisoner the majority of the Herero army. Prison camps were in readiness for over eight thousand men. The Herero were decisively beaten, but the battle did not achieve the intended total destruction of their political structure. About a thousand Herero, including the family of the paramount chief, Maharero broke out to the east. Ruthless German pursuit through the waterless desert killed many of them and further shattered the tribal structure. Somewhat disappointed that world attention was focused on the contemporary Russo-Japanese War rather than on this first war of the Wilhelmine empire, the Germans nevertheless made the most of their victory in their official report: "This bold enterprise shows up in the most brilliant light the ruthless energy of the German command in pursuing their beaten enemy. No pains, no sacrifices were spared in eliminating the last remnants of enemy resistance. Like a wounded beast the enemy was tracked down from one water-hole to the next until finally he became the victim of his own environment. The arid Omaheke (*sandveld*) was to complete what the German army had begun: extermination of the Herero nation."[34]

Some Herero, including the paramount chief, after crossing the desert, stayed in Bechuanaland, but most survivors began drifting back to their homeland. Trotha was merciless. He believed that "the Negro is not bound by any treaty, but only by brute force." He referred to his own reports from East Africa in 1896, when he had claimed that a local revolt he had suppressed was the begining of a race war that the Africans would fight as soon as they were properly armed. In view of such danger he felt it was immaterial whether the Germans treated them well or ill in peacetime.[35]

On October 2, 1904, Trotha made a proclamation: "The Herero are no longer German subjects. They have murdered and plundered. They have hacked off ears, nose [sic], and other organs from wounded soldiers. Now, out of cowardice, they want to give up the fight. . . . The Herero nation must leave the country. If it will not do so I shall condemn it by force. Inside German territory every Herero tribesman, armed or unarmed, with or without cattle, will be shot. No women or children will be allowed in the territory: they will be driven back to their people or fired on. These are the last words to the Herero nation from me, the great General of the mighty German Emperor."[36]

Chancellor Bernhard von Bülow, as well as Leutwein, the missionaries, and even the settlers, objected to Trotha's proclamation. Extermination, Bülow insisted, was a "denial of all Christian and humane principles" and would be "detrimental to Germany's place among the civilized nations and would add fuel to the violent campaign being waged against Germany." He also used an argument put forward by many settlers in the press — that the Africans were "essential both for farming and stock-breeding and for mining"; further, Germany had sacrificed "blood and money" but was now losing productive forces by expelling part of her labor supply to British Bechuanaland — an argument directed at the emperor's animosity toward Britain.[37] Eventually the chancellor prevailed over military opinion, and an order countermanding Trotha's proclamation was ratified by the emperor on December 8, 1904. It declared that the emperor would exercise clemency toward those Herero who surrendered voluntarily, provided they had not been directly responsible for killing or for war policy. It also accepted the mediation of the Rhenish Mission, which Trotha had rejected. Trotha, however, still had unlimited executive power and fought hard for his policies until his recall in November 1905, construing his orders in a way that allowed him great latitude.[38]

Only a quarter or a fifth of the Herero survived, some sixteen thousand out of between sixty and eighty thousand. The Nama, by fighting a guerrilla war, did slightly better, losing between a third and a half of their population of between fifteen and twenty thousand. The Herero lost their cattle, and the land of both groups was appropriated by an ordinance in 1907. Such tribal structure as remained was destroyed, and tribal insignia were forbidden. Bülow's economic case for clemency proved sound: without material resources or the support of their traditional tribal organization the surviving Herero and Nama were forced to labor in the mines and on the farms of Europeans.

The British Presence in East Africa

On April 1, 1902, what had been until then the Eastern Province of Uganda was transferred to the East Africa Protectorate, as Kenya was then known, in order to bring the Uganda Railway under a single administration.[39] Much of the area appeared empty of African inhabitants or was thinly peopled by the nomadic, pastoral Masai. The commissioner, Sir Charles Eliot, was charged with insuring development so that the railway would pay. Sir Harry Johnston already had reported that these East African highlands were potentially "white man's country," and, because he believed that Africa could be developed through racial cooperation, he also spoke of the same land as a future "America of the Hindu."[40] Proposals were made to settle Finns in the protectorate. Colonial Secretary Joseph Chamberlain, after a visit to East Africa in 1902, suggested to the Zionist Congress that they might find a temporary Jewish National Home there, but after some deliberation the Zionists refused. Johnston's idea that Indian settlers be invited was also taken up. In 1902 Eliot supported land grants, the distribution of free seed, and agricultural loans to Indians who would settle in the highlands. An official mission went to the Punjab as late as 1906 to recruit settlers, but it failed, mainly because the Indians would only accept the offer if whole villages could emigrate, which the British authorities considered would be too expensive.

Eliot himself had decided that the protectorate must concentrate on white settlers. In 1902 the few European settlers present founded the Society to Promote European Immigration. Fearing Indian competition, they successfully appealed to Eliot to stop sponsoring Indian settlers officially. As an alternative Eliot sent a mission to recruit white South Africans. Many responded, and from 1904 until 1912 South African settlers outnumbered those from Britain.

Eliot had no doubt that the area now known as Kenya should become a white settler colony. Shocked by what he considered the savagery, as well as the nudity, of the Africans, he regarded the formation of British East Africa as a whole as "the greatest philanthropic achievement of the later nineteenth century" because British control had ended slave raids and famine. When he eventually resigned in 1904, partly because he thought the Foreign Office was tending to take advice from underlings more favorable to the Masai than to the settlers who wanted their land, he made his view plain: "We should face the undoubted issue — viz., that white mates black in a very few moves. . . . There can be no doubt that the Masai and many other tribes must go under. It is a prospect which I view with equanimity and a clear conscience . . . [Masaidom] is a beastly, bloody system founded on raiding and immorality."[41]

Eliot's ideas had grown increasingly close to those of Hugh Cholmondeley, the third Lord Delamere, who had first visited the East African highlands on a shooting expedition in 1898. He returned in January 1903, followed by his brother-in-law, the son of the Earl of Enniskillen. Kenya began to attract other members of the English and Anglo-Irish nobility and gentry. "Sun and space, mountain scenery and lions were and long remained Kenya's most important assets."[42] Such "resident tourists" made it possible for the colony to survive a huge adverse balance of trade throughout the years of British rule.

As the farthest frontier of European settlement, Kenya attracted plain adventurers as well as aristocrats. Captain Ewart S. Grogan, famous for being the first to make the journey from the Cape to Cairo in 1898 and 1899, was the spokesman for these, reveling in his self-description as "the baddest and the boldest of a bold bad gang."[43] Settler politics tended to be highly individualistic, as Winston Churchill noted when he visited Kenya in 1907: "Every white man in Nairobi is a politician; and most of them are leaders of parties."[44] Grogan, Delamere, and others thrust themselves forward, but eventually, in September 1910, the rival groups united and formed the Convention of Associations under Grogan's chairmanship.

When Eliot, an authoritarian though one sympathetic to the settlers, resigned as commssioner in 1904, he was replaced by Sir Donald Stewart, who died a year later. Sir James Sadler, who succeeded Stewart, later became Kenya's first governor after the protectorate was transferred from the Foreign Office to the Colonial Office. An amiable but weak man, dubbed "Flannel-foot" by the settlers, he had to cope with some of the worst instances yet of bullying and brutality by the settlers. In March 1907 Grogan, who had been elected president of the Colonists' Association, played the leading role in the public flogging of three Kikuyu servants in front of the Nairobi court-house. The settler press and the evidence at the subsequent trial clearly showed that this was a deliberate challenge to British administration, especially to the courts: "The frontier was seeking to assert itself in a main street of Nairobi."[45] For the settlers much of the attraction of Colonial Office rule was the proposed legislative council, which was to include nominated unofficial members. Because of the flogging scandal officials in Nairobi and London urged that the legislative council should be abandoned, but Sadler recommended that, because only a small South African group was responsible for the flogging incident, preparations for the council's first meeting should go on, provided that Grogan himself was not nominated in his capacity as president of the Colonists' Association. Sadler was considered by the British administration as well as by the settlers to be ineffective and weak, so in 1909 he was transferred to the governorship of the Windward Islands. Sir Percy Girouard, Lugard's successor in Northern Nigeria, was appointed in his place; Girouard was thought to be both firm and competent.

When Kenya was transferred from the Foreign Office in 1905, Major Humphrey Leggatt, who had served on the Poor White Commission in South Africa, was sent to report on the protectorate's economic prospects. Leggatt's South African experience had left him deeply skeptical about the viability of small-scale settler farming; hence his 1906 report forcefully recommended the alternatives of highly capitalized plantations and African peasant farming. Both peasants and planters should concentrate on cotton, which was highly priced at this time. In 1902 the British Cotton Growing Association had been established to reduce dependence on American supplies. In 1906 it provided most of the money for the British East Africa Corporation, with Leggatt himself in charge of operations, which included the distribution of cotton seed to African farmers and the erection of a gin at Kisumu. With most of Kenya's white settlers on the verge of bankruptcy and the Colonial Office exasperated by their bullying, Leggatt's experiment, had it suceeded, might have altered the direction of development. Cotton was introduced into both the Nyanza Province of Kenya and the adjoining Eastern Province of Uganda in 1907, but by the 1912-13 season the Uganda province was producing roughly 6,000 tons of seed cotton annually, and the Kenya province a mere 166 tons. Plainly the Kenya experiment had failed.

The contrast between the Kenyan and Ugandan response has led to close analysis and some debate by economic historians.[46] Some importance must be attached to the presence of powerful Buganda chiefs in Uganda, with ideas similar to those of westerners about the virtues of industry. This is indicated by the success of the cotton legislation of 1908, which sought to improve the quality of Uganda cotton, in view of alarming reports from the British Cotton Growing Association in 1907. Drastic legislation directing that only one type of seed be planted and that all hand gins be withdrawn and destroyed was obeyed, because as Governor Hesketh Bell admitted, the authority of the chiefs was such that their "bare orders" were sufficient to ensure effective execution. The Church Missionary Society, in its attempt to make the country of the Buganda people a showpiece black Christian community, also deserves some credit. Missionaries began propaganda work for cotton growing even before the British East Africa Corporation and the missionary society had pioneered technical education. The contrast between the Buganda's easily grown food crop, plantain, and the relatively more demanding crops, such as maize, grown by the Luo, was also very important. In Buganda complete failure of the subsistence crop was highly unlikely; hence the risk of devoting time to growing cotton was considerably less than in Kenya. Further, because plantain growing was women's work in Buganda, with the men traditionally engaged in fighting and court politics, the imposition of the Pax Britannica left the male population with considerable unemployed energies that could be devoted to the new cash crop. Finally, the greater European presence in Kenya in 1908 made it possible for Africans to hire out their labor rather than to cultivate an unfamiliar, risky, and inedible crop.

The failure of Kenya cotton was offset by developments in other sectors of the economy. After a long depression the price of coffee rose sharply in 1910, coinciding with an unprecedented boom in British overseas investments. Coffee began to shape the country's economic and social structure as prospective European immigrants saw a way to render the pleasures of East African settler life profitable. The coffee planter "combines the economic role of a substantial capitalist and employer of labour with the social outlook of a farming settler, and this combination is the key to a great part of Kenya's subsequent history."[47]

The high price of maize attracted the settlers to another profitable crop. The protectorate government, following South Africa's lead in this as in many other matters, lowered railway rates to make the export of corn profitable.[48] But the growth of maize farming registered the general expansion of the economy, especially in the plantation sector, for the growers who supplied the African labor force realized the most profit in the market. Economic advance by the settlers was matched by political progress. Girouard had served in South Africa as well as in Nigeria and had married into Transvaal society. Far from being a strong governor who would restrain the settlers, he proved to be very sympathetic to them.

Some of the benefits of economic growth reached the nonwhite population. The Indian community obviously benefited as its members became traders and government employees in response to the opportunities opened up by the railway and the administration. By 1914 this community surpassed the whites in number and probably in aggregate wealth as well. The Africans benefited to some degree also. New crops and new methods of production combined with substantial reductions in the cost of transport to make it possible for most of them to earn cash incomes in excess of the taxes imposed on them. The purchasing power of this money income was, however, somewhat dubious: "A very large part of it was converted into livestock, which was desired both for its own sake and as a means to earlier and more frequent marriage; and since the supply of livestock was not very elastic and the supply of women was completely inelastic, the new wealth was largely dissipated in inflation."[49] But at least there was a steady rise in wages from 1909 to 1912. Nor were Africans limited to wage labor as a source of cash. There were recurrent angry complaints from employers that Africans could earn cash too easily as independent small farmers. The railway carried nearly fourteen thousand tons of maize in 1913-14, of which nearly nine thousand tons were produced almost entirely by African farmers in Kavirondo, who also grew the whole of the important sesame (benne) crop. Until 1914 African farmers were still contributing much more than their settler counterparts to the country's wealth. The rapid development of European coffee and sisal plantations made it clear that this would soon change, but it was by no means obvious that Kenya's colonial future pointed toward the exclusive development of agriculture by Europeans more than the continued expansion of both the African and the European sectors.

European observers of Uganda were enthusiastic about the African response to economic opportunity. The Buganda were singled out in this
respect: "Wherever prospects of trade open up, the Baganda will go," wrote
a missionary.[50] Their eagerness to earn money was explained by Sir Charles
Eliot on the grounds that Uganda "presents a feature totally lacking in East
Africa [Kenya], namely a large native population which is assimilating
European ideas and is anxious to purchase European goods." As a settled
agricultural people the Buganda could appreciate the furnishings that only
cash could buy for their permanent dwellings. Moreover, they were encouraged by the missionaries and their chiefs to live a Christian family life, with
all the specific expenditure that entailed: a house with two rooms instead
of one, if the children were to sleep at home, and with windows to admit the
light so the convert could read his Bible; money to pay for school fees so that
his children might be educated — money that must be earned while he did
without their services on the farm — and to pay his church tithes. Increasing
imports of superior textiles, books, stationery, and bicycles indicate the
rising level of prosperity in Uganda before 1914. Despite such African
achievements in Uganda, too, the decision about whether the protectorate
was to follow the West Coast model, the South African model, or the plantation model — or some combination of them — was by no means certain. A
white Planters' Association was formed in 1910, and by 1912 the settlers
had their own press, the *Uganda Herald*. Through such institutions they could
bring pressure on the home government to develop Uganda in their interests.

The intrusion of European settlers, claiming freeholds in perpetuity for
themselves and their progeny, immeasurably sharpened every possibility of
conflict within a colonial situation. Once Europeans claimed slices of African territory as their birthright, then whatever the rationale of empire in
terms of trusteeship and the "white man's burden," Africans were bound to
reflect on why they had been collectively cast in the role of the disinherited.
The development of racially stratified economies and societies, in which the
"uniform of colour"[51] determined who would perform manual work for
whom, rammed home the message. Some imperial administrators, like
Rechenberg, were committed to promoting development through African
farming. Others, like Sir Charles Eliot, were equally committed to fostering
settlement. But several, as we have seen, attempted balanced development —
some would say they "muddled along" — with a combination of settlers,
planters, and African farmers.

In such divided societies, held together much more by naked political power and shared economic transactions than by common culture and history, it is doubtful if there was any voice to articulate general, as against sectional, interests. When the societies of western Europe had been divided into distinctive estates, the medieval church had traditionally claimed to speak in universal terms. Now the missionaries, confronted by an even more fragmented society, sought to do the same. But they could only operate within the margin of discretion allowed them by those with political power. Hence they were often reduced to providing cultural enclaves, or refuges, from both the traditional African tribal society and the new settler-dominated sector. Here they were tolerated, especially as they produced a steady flow of those who in southern Africa are called "school people," who could be employed in the imperial administration and in European-owned economic organizations or could serve the chiefs as advisers.[52]

Ultimately, only the governor had power enough even to contemplate acting for the good of all, when faced by such sharply divergent interests. Partly because the Germans came to imperialism late and therefore did not inherit "a settled view" from somewhere else as the British did from India and partly because of a tradition of speculation encouraged by contemporary theorizing on the nature of the state, they pondered the principles of colonial administration when confronted by a settler situation much more exhaustively than their English counterparts had. Nor, with massive recurrent revolts in both German East Africa and South-West Africa, could they ever assume that the Africans were simply pawns to be manipulated on the imperial chess board, as did Eliot, for example.

Leutwein focused most closely on this problem. His key concept was government, but government that would not simply serve the interests of the Europeans. Indeed, he rebuked a trader who once referred to the administration of South-West Africa as "his" government. Leutwein believed that he was the only person in a position to "plan for 'the general good,' hemmed in as he was by the conflicting demands of the Colonial Department, the Reichstag, the settlers, the Africans and the concession companies."[53] Yet he was forced to recognize the contradictions inherent in such a stance. In July 1896 a Reichstag resolution demanded that the Geneva Convention be extended to colonial wars. Many members of the political center and the left were highly critical of the fact that no prisoners were taken during the recent fighting in South-West Africa. Prisoners were invariably shot because, it was claimed, they could not be successfully guarded on long marches and once they had escaped they would join the guerrillas to continue the war.

Leutwein was against extending the Geneva Convention because he believed the lives of European settlers on isolated farms would be endangered by fugitive rebels. The convention's humanitarianism was, he pointed out, "in conflict with our humanitarian concern for our own countrymen."[54] Characteristically he pushed the argument further:

A consequential colonial policy would no doubt require the execution of all prisoners capable of bearing arms. I myself would not like to adopt this practice, but I would not reproach any one who did. Colonization is always inhumane. It must ultimately amount to an encroachment on the rights of the original inhabitants in favor of the intruders. If that is unacceptable then one must oppose all colonization, which at least would be a logical attitude. What is impossible is on one hand to take land from the natives on the basis of questionable treaties and risk the life and health of one's countrymen to this end, and on the other hand to enthuse about humanitarian principles in the Reichstag. Yet this is precisely what many delegates have done.[55]

Such was the moral dilemma of colonization in a settler context that Leutwein never resolved.

CHAPTER 9

The First World War

Africa's new rulers considered themselves true heirs of Rome, bringing imperial peace to backward, warring peoples. But the Pax Romana and western Christendom had long since collapsed into separate, competitive states, captured in the late nineteenth century by an intensified nationalism that was itself an important ingredient in the scramble for Africa. The cartographers' colors by which the national territories of Europe were usually identified, such as red for Britain and blue for Germany, were replicated in crazy-quilt fashion on the map of Africa. But such structures as the Pax Britannica and the Pax Germanica, though they might suppress Africa's localized, so-called tribal wars, also involved her peoples in the world war of 1914 that originated in Europe. The irony did not escape certain radical thinkers, such as the great black American theorist of Pan-Africanism, W. E. B. Du Bois, and in Africa it drove John Chilembwe to revolt in Nyasaland in 1915.[1]

The European general staffs prepared for a short, sharp war of movement, a repetition of the blitzkrieg demonstrated by the Germans against Austria in 1866 and against France in 1870. The Germans regarded their colonies as expendable. They designed their navy for battle with the British grand fleet in the North Sea rather than for the defense of imperial bases that could be used to launch attacks on Allied seaways. When war broke out, they therefore suggested that Africa be considered neutral, in line with the Berlin and Brussels agreements; in any case, if the Allies refused this diplomatic ploy — which they did — then victory in the decisive European theater was expected so swiftly that captured German colonists would soon be released.[2]

178

The European war was fought in four areas of sub-Saharan Africa, and many Africans fought and died abroad as well. Brushing aside a special appeal from the acting governor of Togo that it be treated as neutral in order that Africans might not witness white men fighting each other, the British and French swiftly occupied that colony in the first months of the war. The other German possessions proved much more difficult to capture. The Cameroons campaign went on for nineteen months before the German commander, Colonel Zimmerman, who had made such resourceful use of the forests and mountains, fled to Spanish Guinea at the end of 1915. German South-West Africa was occupied by the forces of the new Union of South Africa by July 1915, after they also had suppressed an Afrikaner nationalist rebellion at the turn of the year. In German East Africa Colonel Paul von Lettow-Vorbeck brilliantly eluded capture, only surrendering after the European armistice on November 23, 1918, in Northern Rodesia, although the main operation in Tanganyika had been concluded in 1917.

The Black Army of France

France, having pioneered the use of tropical African troops — Major Louis Faidherbe's famous Senegalese *tirailleurs* — during partition, now formulated plans to use them to redress the demographic balance with its neighbor, Germany.[3] Colonel (later General) Charles Mangin was the chief exponent of a black army. He argued in 1909 that the drop in the French birthrate would lead to the loss of four army corps in ten years' time. The shortage could partly be rectified by conscripting Algerian Arabs, but European settlers feared insurrection once Arabs had been trained in modern military methods. The settlers would be reassured, however, "if they felt themselves protected by regiments of Senegalese infantry, most of them fetishists," Mangin pointed out.[4] Mangin formed part of a five-man mission to French West Africa in 1910 to study the possibilities for recruitment, and the commission reported in favor of his scheme for reinforcing the metropolitan army with Algerian infantry while defending the empire with a black army, "which might even, should the need arise, fight by the side of the other two" in Europe.[5] A 1912 decree permitted the conscription of men between twenty and twenty-eight years of age for four years' service should there be a shortage of volunteers for this African army.[6]

The prognostication of the European general staffs that it would be a short war was rapidly proved wrong. The slaughter on the western front led France to call upon perhaps as many as 181,000 soldiers from French West and Equatorial Africa, while estimates of Africans killed varied from 35,000 to 65,000.[7] By 1917 seventeen Senegalese battalions were engaged on the Somme River. French propaganda dwelt on the terror they would arouse in the Germans and on their personal bravery, which made it possible to use them as "sacrificial" troops in places where the French were beginning to refuse to attack. Many Africans died in the mud of Flanders, far from the burial ground of their ancestors. Others returned home mutilated or shell-shocked, destroying the warrior myth of glorious struggle.

As the war dragged on, wild estimates were made of calling upon a million men from Africa. (The total population of French territories has been reckoned at a mere twelve million.) Yet even when the war broke out, the established French military system in Africa was under strain. The Senegalese *tirailleurs* had been a professional force recruited from the warriors of Senegal and the Sudan. The soldiers had claimed traditional warrior privileges, and their extortions of women and booty from defeated enemies had been approved by their French officers. But to meet the new French demands recruitment was extended to the coastal areas. Here there was no ready-made professional warrior class, and even before the legal establishment of conscription in 1912 recruitment operated much like a press-gang.[8] Many potential soldiers fled across the borders into British West Africa or Liberia. The French suspected that their British allies were halfhearted in response to their requests for the return of such refugees, and some British administrators in thinly populated regions do seem to have welcomed the tax potential that the newcomers represented.[9]

Large-scale rebellions against the voracious French appetite for manpower broke out in several areas.[10] By 1917 Governor-General Joost Van Vollenhoven, who had been sent especially to organize the war effort, begged the minister of colonies to end his demands for more men, or otherwise French West Africa would end in "blood, fire and ruin."[11] By 1918 France's calls for help were becoming counterproductive because the danger of insurrection that resulted forced the West African administrators to deploy more and more troops at home.

The imperial crisis in most of French Africa was in marked contrast to the political situation in the original four communes of Senegal. In 1911 Senegalese citizens serving in the metropolitan units of the army under the same conditions as Frenchmen were discharged in what appeared to the Senegalese to be a new policy against a racially mixed army. In his 1914 election campaign, therefore, Blaise Diagne insisted that all native-born inhabitants of the communes, whatever their race, should be subject to the same kind of conscription as any other French citizens.[12] By September 1916 the French, now desperate for manpower, acceded to his demand and enacted a law of compulsory military service that was taken as confirming their rights of citizenship. The law was popular, for it seemed to clear the way for full-scale assimilation.[13]

In January 1918 Diagne was offered the post of "High Commissioner for the Recruitment of Troops in Black Africa," with status equal to that of the governor-general himself. He accepted, in return for pledges of reforms at the end of the war including easier access to French citizenship, relaxation of the indigénat, better medical services, and job reservations for ex-servicemen, as well as general programs of welfare and economic development. Governor-General Van Vollenhoven, who earlier had vehemently warned that further heavy recruitment would provoke even wider revolt and would interfere with the increased food production France required, now resigned; he was not prepared to share power with Diagne. But Diagne proved highly effective, recruiting 63,378 men, 23,378 more than had been stipulated.[14]

Diagne traveled in a style appropriate to the governor-general, insisting upon full courtesies from both Africans and Europeans. His staff included three African officers as well as bemedaled noncommissioned officers, demonstrating that Africans were in line for promotion at the front. Europeans were distressed by the style of his tour, denouncing his ready welcome for "petitions of the natives against their European masters" as well as the "offhand manner with which he treated certain Europeans, the pomp with which he surrounded his mission. . . . the natives are raising their heads, they display on all occasions a detestable attitude towards Europeans."[15]

The East African Campaign

Outside of Europe the Africans' worst wartime experiences were in East Africa. Casualties frequently were high. As the Germans moved south out of Tanganyika, the British lost 2,700 out of 4,900 infantrymen in the four-day battle of Mahina in October 1917; altogether they lost 967 officers and 17,650 troops of other ranks.[16] Lack of communications led to the employment by both sides of considerable numbers of porters, many of whom suffered substantial hardships. The Germans recruited 20,000 extra porters in 1916 to cope with a food shortage on the Kilimanjaro front. About 2,000 of these died for lack of blankets. On New Year's Day, 1917, the British general, Sir Edward Northey, reported, "All this time the supply difficulties have been getting greater; many carriers desert on the road over the Livingstone Range and many die of the cold."[17] The grievances of the British Carrier Corps, particularly those members from Kenya and Nyasaland, were an important factor in the emergence of East African nationalism.[18]

The long campaign seriously and lastingly damaged the economy of German East Africa. Seven years after the armistice the British government's East African Commission reported that "the task of restoring the wreckage of war has now been largely completed but in such matters as education, medical work and scientific research the pre-war standard has not yet been reached."[19]

Western education and welfare had been largely the responsibility of the missions, and these were badly hit as the Germans and the British interned each other's missionaries. A great amount of mission property was destroyed in the fighting. Furthermore, the Christian converts of British missions located in German East Africa were treated as disloyal by the Germans, and when the British occupied areas of the country the Africans converted by German missions were similarly suspect, for British officials were much influenced by John Chilembwe's rising in Nyasaland.[20] Such missionary setbacks provided scope for Islam; indeed, the greatest Muslim expansion in Tanganyika occurred during and just after the war.[21]

The war discredited other Europeans as well as the missionaries. It taught the natives, wrote a German missionary, "to see the white man from a point of view from which he never knew him before. The native has seen him in his hatred, his hypocrisy, brutality, dishonesty and immorality. He often could justly say 'The blacks are better men.'"[22]

The uprooting caused by war also had positive results. The same witness reported the "great mixing of the most various peoples and tribes — various Indian races, West Africans, West Indians, Manyena, Cape Boys, Japanese etc."[23] Such contact led to a further spread of Swahili, already the lingua franca of the German army and increasingly of the British African forces. Another positive result was the Mbeni dance societies, which had originated among young men employed by the German administration at the coast. The participants wore European-style uniforms, took European titles, and adapted military band music. Their songs provided a shrewd commentary on urban life. As an expression of what Iliffe has called "the age of improvement," the Mbeni societies proved remarkably popular in other colonial milieus. Soldiers and porters who served in the East African campaign carried the Mbeni idea as far afield as the Rhodesias, Katanga, Mozambique, and even Angola.[24]

It is difficult to assess the spread of less tangible ideas attributable to the war. The colonial authorities certainly feared the spread of subversive notions. In October 1917 the Kenya secretariat warned the provincial administration that Kenyans who had served in the East African campaign were likely to have met fellow Africans "acquainted with the pan-African ideal of the Ethiopian Church . . . and for the first time in the history of this Protectorate, a conception may have arisen in the native mind of the possibility of a black Africa. It is in conjunction with a native conception of the idea of 'Africa for the Africans' that any conjunction of Islamic propaganda is to be regarded as a real danger. Islam would provide a cementing factor."[25] More work on the roots of East African independence movements must be done before the substance of such white fears can be judged.

The Kenya adminstration's African subjects had good reason to be suspicious of their governors. The European settlers had shrewdly exploited their established political position to wring concessions from a British government weakened by war, much as Blaise Diagne and the Senegalese citizens had forced concessions from the French in similar circumstances. But in Kenya surrender to the settlers meant progress toward their goal of a "white man's country" at the expense of African and Asian rights. In 1915 the Colonial Office accepted the settlers' demand for greater security of land tenure by extending their leases from 99 to 999 years. After the war the new governor, General Northey, who had led the Allied forces against the Germans from Nyasaland, further consolidated the power of the settlers. He issued the notorious Northey circulars on labor recruitment in line with the settlers' wishes, nominated two Europeans to his executive council, introduced a settlement scheme for British ex-officers to double the white population, and alienated a further 4,560 square miles of land in the highlands. When the protectorate was formally annexed, declared a crown colony, and renamed Kenya, there appeared a distinct possibility that it might after all become another South Africa.[26]

Before the war German East Africa had boasted more white settlers than the East African Protectorate.[27] But the German settlers left their plantations, many of which fell into decay, to serve in the defense force. Those who survived the campaign became prisoners of war and were eventually expelled. The British had originally intended that East Africa would be returned to Germany as part of a general negotiated settlement under which Germany would gain territory outside Europe and return Alsace and Lorraine to France. But as the campaign dragged on, its sheer costliness swung opinion around — it was difficult to consider surrendering what had been so hard won. Moreover, as German geopoliticians had suggested a vast German territory stretching right across the continent as one of their war aims, all the old fears for the safety of the route to India gained fresh strength, compounded by a realization of just how dangerous the German empire would have been if utilized for submarine warfare against British mercantile shipping.[28] British policy makers decided, therefore, to hold on to the territory. This assured that the German attempt to develop Tanganyika as a "white man's country" was doomed, but the form of the successor regime was undetermined.

The Postwar Settlement

During the war Allied opinion hardened in favor of annexing conquered Germany's colonies. Partly it was because the Allies began to believe their own propaganda about Germany's "black record" in colonial administration. This had been tailored for American consumption, for American friendship and even direct military aid were needed increasingly in view of the prolonged and costly stalemate on the western front. The British even had suggested that the United States should take over one of Germany's colonies and share the "white man's burden." President Woodrow Wilson made it clear that this was out of the question, but he did favor some internationalization of the regimes that succeeded Germany in Africa, as had been suggested in earlier Allied propaganda which had stressed the altruism of British and French colonialism. General Jan Smuts had already proposed that in order to obviate great power rivalry in the Middle East, Britain and France should hold the Arab territories conquered from Turkey under a mandate from the proposed postwar League of Nations. Somewhat to Smut's chagrin, because he regarded control over South-West Africa as part of his own country's "manifest destiny," he now found his proposal for a League mandate suggested as the proper means of dealing with the German colonies in Africa. Instead of being free to annex it outright, he was given South-West Africa only under a mandate.[29]

There were to be three types of mandate — A, B, and C, — but only in the A mandates of the Middle East was it envisaged that the League's proclamation of national self-determination would quickly apply. In the B and C mandates Article 22 of the League of Nations Covenant declared that the colonized peoples were not capable of governing themselves "under the strenuous conditions of the modern world." The mandatory power would therefore act as trustee for its new African subjects, reporting to the Permanent Mandates Commission of the League of Nations. The trusteeship provisions of the Berlin and Brussels acts concerning such matters as slavery and traffic in arms and liquor would be the concern of the new international civil service. The essential difference between B and C mandates was that the C mandates could be incorporated, for purposes of administration, in the territory of the mandatory power. South-West Africa, unlike the other German territories, became a C mandate, allowing the Union of South Africa to treat it as an integral part of its own territory. South Africa's administration was to incur international criticism but not international control.[30]

The redistribution of Germany's colonies carried the British, French, and Belgian empires to their greatest physical extent. But the territorial expansion of northwestern Europe's empires masked a profound decline in Europe's relative power in the world. Only the United States' intervention in April 1917 had ended the stalemate of imperial Europe's civil war. By 1918 Britain, France, Germany, and Belgium were exhausted, drained of treasure and manpower, while General John J. Pershing, the United States commander, could still anticipate fighting if need be until 1920 or 1921.[31] The revolution in the balance of world power, with the decline of Europe manifest in the closing stages of the war, would eventually be registered in African liberation and decolonization.

Meanwhile, the bankruptcy of statesmanship and generalship, evident in the outbreak and conduct of the war, inspired disillusion over national aims and pessimism about the future everywhere in Europe. As self-doubt replaced the old hubris, Europeans acquired greater sensitivity to the achievements of other civilizations. The new mood of cultural relativism found expression in the development of anthropology and the appreciation of "primitive" art. The claims of Europe's subjects, newly optimistic in the postwar mood of internationalism, reinforced this trend. In February 1919 the first of a series of interwar Pan-African congresses was launched in Paris to coincide with the deliberations of the peacemakers at Versailles. In the same year territorial committees in the British West African colonies began to organize the National Congress of British West Africa, which met in the Gold Coast in March 1920. The congress formulated proposals for orderly progress toward self-government within the British Empire and deplored the redistribution of Germany's colonies without reference to the wishes of their peoples as "tantamount to a species of slavery."[32]

CHAPTER 10

Changes in Government
between World Wars

After 1918 the colonies were one theater in which Europeans could seek the illusion of their prewar supremacy. The United States' retreat into isolation and Soviet Russia's complementary preoccupation with "socialism in one country" prolonged the failure of the European powers to grasp the changed geopolitical realities. Meantime, in Britain much attention was directed to preserving imperial strength during the transformation from the old empire into the new commonwealth. France demonstrated a further practical use of its black army by deploying some of the African soldiers in the occupation of the Ruhr — thereby provoking an outburst of racial prejudice in some quarters at "the militant enforcement of coloured soldiers on an unarmed and conquered population."[1]

The chronology of Europe's wars provides a useful periodization for the imperial epoch in African history, but our awareness of the outcome should not trick us into assuming that contemporaries knew what would happen in 1939. In hindsight, the administrative interlude of 1918-39, lying between the establishment of imperial control and postwar decolonization, seems brief enough, but both Margery Perham on the British side and Hubert Deschamps on the French side remind us that imperial administrators generally believed they had plenty of time.[2]

The Dual Mandate and Indirect Rule

Lord Lugard retired as governor of Nigeria in 1918. In 1922 he published *The Dual Mandate in British Tropical Africa* and began fifteen years of service as the principal British representative on the Permanent Mandates Commission of the League of Nations. His book enunciated ideas that, with some modifications by later practitioners and theorists such as Sir Donald Cameron and Margery Perham, provided guidelines for British policy. Lugard and the subsequent writers believed that an imperial power had a double responsibility — to the African peoples it ruled, on the one hand, and to the outside world, on the other. The colonial power should guide its African subjects toward material and moral "progress" leading ultimately to self-government. To the rest of the world it had the obligation to see that the natural resources of the colonies were exploited for the world's markets.[3]

In administration, the Lugard school recommended the general adoption of the principles of Indirect Rule, first implemented by Lugard and his successors in Northern Nigeria. Perham, who had studied the system in both Tanganyika and Nigeria, described it in 1934 as "a system by which the tutelary power recognizes existing African societies, and assists them to adapt themselves to the function of local government. . . . It is the great merit of the system that while it gives to native institutions the fixity and status that only detailed statutory recognition can give, it yet allows that wide variety both in the forms and in the degree of authority delegated which is absolutely necessary under present conditions."[4] By the mid-1930s sensitive and well-informed exponents of the theory were careful to avoid unqualified use of the word "chief," realizing that "chief-in-council" more aptly indicated the precolonial situation where real power was generally shared. Africans, insofar as they were involved in the discussion of policy, stressed the same point.[5] But Perham's recommendation that British officials recognize the complex balance of traditional institutions was a counsel of perfection that came relatively late in the game. In practice, she admitted, the colonial administrators frequently simplified matters by co-opting the chief but not the rest of the indigenous political system.[6] Yoruba kings, for example, became much more powerful under the British: "They could only be deposed by the British administration which often tended to protect them against their own people." [7]

Lugard thought, though not all his avowed followers agreed, that the traditional local government should be progressively modernized. By the time he wrote *The Dual Mandate*, he believed that native treasuries were essential to a proper system of Indirect Rule.[8] Traditional rulers — chiefs or chiefs-in-council — should keep a proportion of the taxes they collected for these native treasuries, spending the money, largely at their own discretion, for the salaries of such employees as clerks, messengers, and police-men, as well as on public works such as courthouses, markets, dispensaries, and footpaths. Perham, at least, was aware of the consequences:

Even the best-informed and most sympathetic government cannot ask the co-operation of an African chief without modifying his position. It wishes him to act, and to act quickly, in collecting tax, producing labour and clearing roads. It wants him to be constantly accessible, and not to keep disappearing in order to make rain, to visit ancestral graves, or to consult diviners. In the native adminstration ordinances we can read a list of the duties which native authorities have to perform. If you run your eye down the list you will see mention of sanitation, noxious weeds, the regulation of gambling, prohibiting the cutting of trees, restricting the carrying of arms, exterminating tsetse fly, with many other duties which the chief at first either does not understand or of which he cannot approve. In order to induce him to use his authority we tend to rely, more or less consciously, upon the hold we have over him through his dependence upon us for his position and salary. He, on his part, must endeavour not to strain an authority which at that very moment is being undermined as a result of our influence. The old authority of the chieftain-ship, in fact, tends to drain away from below while we pour in our new authority from above. By the standards of indirect rule native administration might be judged by the degree to which a process, inevitable up to some point, has gone.[9]

By 1936 Perham was claiming that trusteeship for Britain meant in large part the training of subject peoples in self-government.[10] Lugard, too, had progressed from his crude assertion in 1922 that "the African Negro lacks power of organization and is conspicuously deficient in the management and control alike of men or of business."[11] Lugard's years of service with the League's Permanent Mandates Commission and as first chairman of the International African Institute (founded in 1926; publishers of *Africa* from 1928) at a time when African studies, especially anthropology, were consciously being cleansed of the kind of racist assumptions and theory that riddle *The Dual Mandate* led him by the mid-1930s to a more benevolent, certainly more tactful, paternalism, even if he still spoke of "educated natives."[12]

Although some administrators deeply imbued with the basic assumptions of the British colonial service about the all-around practical competence of the "man on the spot" disliked the idea of intervention by specialist academ-ics from outside, the gist of the articles in *Africa* looked forward to a happy blending of practical anthropology and scholarly administration.[13] Malin-owski, the key figure in all of this, taught in his highly influential seminar at the London School of Economics that "there are few subjects in applied anthropology which are as interesting to the ethnologist as Indirect Rule, for in this policy we have a practical recognition that Native institutions work."[14] The next generation of anthropologists, several of whom were taught by Malinowski, tended to analyze situations of "culture contact" rather than to delineate examples of "traditional African society" uncontaminated by European domination. Research by Audrey Richards, Lucy Mair, Monica Hunter, and Isaac Schapera led Perham to see "Africans as no passive sufferers under our influence . . . but as showing considerable initiative in taking what they want from us and keeping what they want from their own."[15]

The economic corollary of Indirect Rule was opposition to the establishment of plantations by outside enterprise and support for African cash crop farmers. On this point, at least, the western-educated African political elite agreed with the indirect rulers. In 1926 the National Congress of British West Africa expressed this in a resolution: "Experience having shown that production by peasant-proprietors working on their own land is more advantageous than the plantation system, the Congress deprecates any attempt to introduce the latter into British West Africa. . . . The Congress affirms that the lands of British West Africa are the lands of the people."[16]

The Dual Policy in Settler Africa

The whites who had been encouraged to settle the uplands of Central and East Africa demanded self-governing institutions, without waiting until, in the words of their leader, Lord Delamere, "two thousand years of evolution are enacted."[17] This was the area of tropical Africa where the dual policy recommended by Lugard ran into the most difficulties. In Rhodesia the process of settler self-government was already far advanced. In 1923, when the British South Africa Company asked to be relieved of its governmental responsibilities, effective power was surrendered to thirty-three thousand white settlers. Henceforth, although Southern Rhodesia refused incorporation within the Union of South Africa and its European leaders frequently banded with others from the north to assert a joint settler viewpoint, it was effectively part of the white south and will be considered in that context.[18] But north of the Zambezi the situation and British government policy were more ambiguous.

When the European settlers in Kenya pressed for greater political power in 1922-23, at the same time as internal self-government was granted to the white Southern Rhodesians, they were resisted. Thus, in July 1923 the British government issued a white paper that stated: "Primarily Kenya is an African territory and His Majesty's Government think it necessary definitely to record their considered opinion that the interests of the African natives must be paramount, and that if and when these interests and the interests of the immigrant races should conflict, the former should prevail. As in the Uganda Protectorate, so in the Kenya Colony, the principle of Trusteeship for the Natives, no less than in the Mandated Territory of Tanganyika, is unassailable." But the declaration of "native paramountcy" was politically expedient. It was, after all, contained in a white paper significantly titled *Memorandum on Indians in Kenya*, and it represented a victory of a sort for the European settlers on the issue of Indian immigration.[19]

The means by which the settlers thwarted Indian aspirations to equality were also highly significant. The Europeans had been ready to use force and had even plotted to kidnap the governor. The British government did not feel able to mount effective countermeasures, perhaps because it felt that British troops would not prove loyal if called on to fight European settlers. The colonial secretary, the Duke of Devonshire, told the Cabinet that to use native troops would destroy British prestige and threaten European lives throughout Africa. As George Bennett observed, "The incident, in fact, established a precedent whereby European settlers in British Africa could hold British governments to ransom."[20]

The governor, Sir Robert Coryndon, persuaded the settlers that they should refrain from violence and trust him during the negotiations on the white paper by pointing out, "Gentlemen, you may remember that I am South African born." Coryndon also produced a dual policy, which he defined as "the complementary development of non-native and native production"; it was significantly different from Lugard's dual policy and more in line with the notions of "two pyramids" and "parallel development" of Sir Godfrey Huggins in Southern Rhodesia.[21] The British Parliamentary Commission on the Future of East Africa, chaired by William Ormsby-Gore (later Lord Harlech), reported in 1925 in favor of Coryndon's ideas. It stressed that there need be no conflict between the interests of the settlers and those of the indigenous inhabitants. European settlement should not restrict the agricultural training of the Africans or their general education. Indeed, the settlers feared that Coryndon's dual policy, especially as interpreted by the Ormsby-Gore commission, would lead to a decline in their labor supply through its encouragement of African small-scale farming. But with a South African director of agriculture, Alex Holm, making European agriculture his prime concern, their fears of the dual policy were groundless. The ambiguity regarding British policy toward what Smuts termed "the broad backbone of Eastern Africa"[22] persisted, with recurrent debates and commissions focusing on "contentious Kenya" for the rest of the colonial period.[23]

Kenya was not simply a local or even regional problem — at this time it was very much an imperial problem. As the farthest frontier of South African expansion its settlers lobbied in Pretoria and Cape Town as well as in London, while South Africans, notably Smuts in his 1929 Rhodes Memorial Lectures at Oxford, were among the most effective spokesmen for white settlement. Britain sought to build up a body of support in India, especially in the business community, against the demands of Indian nationalists for independence from the British Empire. But even those "moderates" tended to make equality of treatment for their fellow Indians in Kenya the test of imperial sincerity.

French Policies

The harsh demands for manpower by France in World War I and the series of insurrections they provoked led Governor-General Joost Van Vollenhoven to insist in 1917 that his subordinates in French West Africa make every effort to deal with Africans through the agency of their traditional chiefs.[24] But a gloomy warning by his successor, Gabriel Angoulvant, in May 1918 suggested that the traditional order might already be too damaged for such tactics to prove effective; "the indigenous populations must inevitably develop towards a more advanced political and social situation. . . . The war unquestionably accelerated the speed [of change] and has set aside all our previous plans. . . . There is no doubt but that one could have wished a less speedy evolution."[25]

Lugard's French counterpart in giving guidelines for interwar colonial policy was Albert Sarraut, the minister of colonies in 1920-24 and 1932-33. Before the war, Sarraut argued, France had been preoccupied with expansion, followed by administrative consolidation. Now, after the second partition of Africa through the redistribution of Germany's colonies by the mandate system, the period for territorial aggrandizement was over. France should therefore concentrate on economic development. The newly acquired Cameroons, with its high level of development by the Germans and with Duala as one of the few good harbors on a surf-beaten coast, should "become the pivot of French policy in tropical Africa." Sarraut's classic exposition of his view, *La Mise en valeur* (untranslatable, but the dictionary suggests "development" or "improvement"), consists of a series of chapters listing the potential of each colony and schemes for its realization, with an especially long section devoted to the Cameroons.[26]

Sarraut's economic ideas had political implications. "Our colonies," he wrote, "must be centers of production and no longer museums for specimens." In line with Angoulvant's diagnosis, he proposed that representative assemblies be established in recognition of the extent to which the colonies already had evolved and to guide their future progress. Such assemblies should at first be based upon a limited franchise and gradually should be made fully representative. They would, he argued, knit the empire together rather than disrupt it by producing demands for independence. Sarraut's ideas for representative colonial assemblies were taken up by a group of parliamentarians in 1922 in a scheme which provided that only a third of the members be indigenous, the rest colonial officials, while all governors-general would have veto powers. Nevertheless, this project for limited self-government was not acceptable to the French parliament or to even the most liberal of colonial officials.[27]

Sarraut's emphasis on production dominated French policy, although his development plan was stunted because the necessary imperial investment that he stipulated was not forthcoming. Some of the most influential teachers at the Ecole Coloniale, such as Henri Labouret and Robert Delavignette, urged their pupils to take account of social results as well as export statistics. Labouret complained there was too much talk by Frenchmen about economic exploitation of the colonies and too little concern for their human resources, the African populations.[28] Delavignette's semiautobiographical novel, *Black Peasants*, transferred to Africa the French mystique about their own peasantry. The title itself gave Africans an identity beyond the general term "indigène," which, like its English equivalent, "native," was often used in a way that connoted African inferiority. *Black Peasants* also projected a sympathetic image in France, influencing many young men to join the colonial service.[29] Many of the administrators in Africa came to identify profoundly with their *cercles*, or districts. Their pride in the progress of their protégés could be somewhat ridiculous, as Hubert Deschamps observed, for many officials "had the feeling that the country was their possession, their work, and this feeling gave to some of them an extraordinary possessive language; we all used to say 'my cercle,' 'my road,' 'my buildings.' Some even said 'my natives,' 'my river,' 'my rain,' "[30] Exponents of such localism turned to British writings on Indirect Rule for an ideology of devolution.

Margery Perham found an item in the budget of the French Cameroons for translating *The Dual Mandate*,[31] while Deschamps himself, as a young Socialist administrator, found *"Lugardisme"* so rife among his colleagues – and so antipathetic to the French revolutionary tradition of assimilation – that he launched a blistering attack on it in 1930.[32]

Belgian Policy

In the Congo Louis Franck, who succeeded Jules Renkin as colonial minister in 1918, adopted many of the ideas put forward by anthropological critics like Van der Kerken, suggesting that chiefs be given a more formal place in the structure of administration. Franck's concern for Flemish linguistic integrity within the Belgian state may have inspired in him a similar respect for African traditions, which he attempted to transmit to his subordinates.[33] Defining his policy by contrasting it with what he took for French assimilationism, he claimed the Belgians wished to produce better Africans; they had no desire to make copies of Europeans, who will never be more than "humans of a third category."[34] But in the aftermath of depression the trend toward indirect rule was sharply curtailed. As a result of the administrative economies instituted in 1933 the process of building up the authority of certain important chiefs was virtually abandoned.[35]

Contrasts: Myth or Reality?

What difference did it make to Africans what colonial regime they lived under? Was the theory – Indirect Rule or *"Lugardisme"* – more important than the nationality of the ruler? Perham thought not. For all the French investment to translate Lugard's book, she doubted that "for reasons which lie deep in race and history" the Africans would appreciate British African policy.[36] But were the subtle yet profound differences discerned by European academics and administrators less significant to Africans than the basic, all-embracing fact of subjugation?[37]

Perham herself found one criterion for judgment when she pointed to the striking financial advantages the chiefs derived from Indirect Rule. With his salary calculated on the basis of traditional tribute, the Emir of Kano was paid as much as the governor of Nigeria and lived in suitable pomp. By contrast, she remembered, "the meagre household of an emir across the [French Cameroons] border, once the peer of Nigerian rulers, into which the interpreter who was my guide entered unannounced and unceremoniously, making no secret of his own greater importance."[38] Similarly, whereas the Onimeko

of Meko owned two cars at the time of Nigerian independence, the Alaketu
of Ketu, to whom the Onimeko owed fealty in the precolonial Yoruba
system, could not afford a bicycle in French Dahomey.[39]

The Nigerian historian, A. E. Afigbo, on the other hand, using very different criteria, thinks the very fact of colonial rule was so revolutionary that it
negated the avowedly conservative aims of Indirect Rule: "The colonial
powers were accursed with something akin to the Midas touch; but instead
of turning every indigenous institution they touched into gold, they debased
it into an alien machinery of control."[40] Concluding a model survey of the
period of British control over Tanganyika, that other showpiece of Indirect
Rule, Ralph Austen states flatly, "To the extent that chiefs were able to
assimilate bureaucratic norms established by the central government, they
became alienated from their subjects."[41]

Afigbo's and Austen's views are borne out in the eloquent memoirs of
Matungi, a chief from Orientale Province in the Belgian Congo, collected by
the anthropologist Colin Turnbull. The memoirs deserve quotation at length
because they crystallize so much that is crucial in the imperial experience
and bear witness from a quarter that through the accidents of record accumu-
lation has had scant hearing:

> You white people had not come to live here when I was a child, and your
> teachers did not set up their schools until they needed to make use of us.
> Then I was a man. So I was thought of, conceived and born in the manner
> of my ancestors, and I became a man in the manner of my ancestors. . . .
> My father was a good man. He was young when Bulamatadi (H. M.
> Stanley) came through our country three times, making war on everyone,
> but he fought back. . . . he had to run away with many others to the country
> of the BaLese, and there . . . he married my mother. . . .
> Not long after I finished drinking my mother's milk my father returned
> here. His own father had been killed by Bulamatadi. He had heard that the
> white men were . . . ill for shortage of food. He thought he would bring some
> bananas and make peace, for the camp was on the edge of his old plantation.
> But he and all the others with him were killed as they approached. . . .
> When the other white men came later we were afraid, because we thought
> that they too had come to kill us. For a long time they left us alone. They
> built their villages and we used to give them food. They called the chiefs
> together and said they came in friendship and wanted to help us, and particu-
> larly they wanted to stop us from fighting among ourselves. This was a good
> thing, because for too long we had been fighting. . . . In those days we could
> trust nobody except our own family, and sometimes even they were be-
> witched.
> I was chief in my father's place then, and even though I remembered what
> had happened to my father I offered to help the white man. . . . for many

months they ate my food. Then more and more white men came, and their villages grew. They brought some of their own food with them, yet they needed more of ours than we could spare. They . . . asked us to supply men and women to do their work for them. I refused, because our people had work enough to do to keep their own fields cultivated and their own roofs thatched. . . . The white men said that in that case we would have to supply them with more food. They . . . demanded, as though it was their land. I told them that . . . if they wanted to stay as my guests they were welcome to . . . make their own plantations . . . but they would have to do their cutting and planting themselves. . . . when their men with guns started forcing us to work it was a bad thing. I took my family and my village and we all moved away deep into the forest and lived like savages until we could build another plantation.

The BaNgwana were the only people who helped the white man then. . . . And it was the BaNgwana who told the white man exactly where we were living . . . so even there we were not free from their guns. If we had had guns we would have driven them out . . . they had come to make us slaves on our own land. But we had no guns.

After some years the white men were so many that they were able to send parties of soldiers into the forest. Their soldiers were . . . black like us, but they came from tribes to the north who were our enemies. . . . We were forced to move back to where the white men were building the big road that now runs from Kisanganyi (Stanleyville). It took many years to build, and they demanded that we supply men . . . as well as food for all their soldiers. . . . The white men did not always carry guns themselves, often they carried whips and they beat us like animals.

I remembered my father, and I said I would not let my people work for them. Because of the guns . . . I said that we would supply whatever food we could spare, and for a time the white men accepted that. . . . Then they . . . told us we had to plant cotton and other things we did not want to plant. . . . I explained that if we planted cotton we would have to grow less food. They said we could buy food with the money we got for the cotton and I told them this was like the play of children, because we could easily grow our own food without money, and have enough left over to give them.

It was then that they told me that I was not a man, that I was evil . . . that I only wanted to make trouble. . . . Masoudi was to be chief in my place. Masoudi was a weak young man who had been to one of the first schools set up by the white men. . . . He was . . . an empty shell filled with the words and thoughts of foreigners. . . . He was a Christian as well, and that meant he could not lead the people as the representative of their ancestors, and he could not initiate men into manhood. Nobody would follow him.

The white men simply said that . . . they [the people] would obey him because if they didn't the police would be sent in with their guns. . . . tribal initiation was thoroughly evil and a wasteful thing. . . . all the time the boys were doing nothing in the initiation camp . . . they could be working on the plantations or on the road gangs. . . . I tried to explain that initiation was necessary for us [to] fit ourselves to join the ancestors when we die. . . . But they would not listen. . . .

The chief of the white men came to our village himself and . . . told them that I was no longer chief, that Masoudi was. People were astounded . . . and they expected the white man to be struck dead. But I stepped forward and said . . . I gladly gave up being chief in the eyes of the white man, but to them, my people, I would remain as I had always been.

This pleased the village, and I think it even pleased Masoudi. . . . But the white men caught me and told one of their soldiers, an Azande, to beat me. For this I have never forgiven them. . . . to have me beaten by one of those savages from the north is a shame I shall never forget. . . . But . . . now that I know the white man better I do not feel hot; because he will kill himself as surely as he kills others. In trying to destroy the pride of others he loses his own, and becomes a worm. . . . They lie so much to others, they cheat and they steal from each other and they sleep with each other's wives. They may be more powerful than we, but we are greater. . . . Masoudi saw to it that cotton was planted, and that there were extra plantains to feed the road gangs, and . . . men to work on the roads. . . . Masoudi was the white men's chief. . . .

Even then I did not realize just how evil the white man was. I thought he was merely stealing our land, and sometimes our lives. . . . But they were not content with this — they wanted to steal our souls as well.

It is our custom to come to the head of the family whenever there is any dispute we cannot settle, and if the head . . . cannot deal with it, he takes it to the chief. If the chief cannot settle it, he takes it to the paramount chief. . . . we discuss our grievances, and all members of the family take a part because blame is seldom on one side alone. . . . many disputes were brought to me because I was the senior member of our village. . . .

But Masoudi . . . complained to the white man. The white man came and told me I was to hear no more cases . . . Masoudi was to hear them, and record them in a special book, or send the disputants to the tribunal at Matadi. . . . I told [Masoudi] that I would not interfere with his work, but that he was not to interfere with mine. If anyone brought a case to him he could enter it in his book . . . but that he was not to let his eyes see what I was doing. He understood, and so I continued to be what I was, the real chief. . . . In time [the white man] came to collect taxes from all of us, out of the money he paid us for the cotton and plantains. The rest of the money he took back by fining us for various things. . . . then the white man began to say we were not to have more than one wife, and that we were to stop exchanging gifts of wealth at times of marriage. . . . he made many men and women lose their self-respect. . . . the white man began to try to prevent our . . . initiation ceremonies. . . . They said . . . we should send [the boys] to a mission school. . . . They said that our initiation schools were savage, and . . . for no other purpose than to stir up discontent. If it were not so, why did we not allow the white man to watch and supervise?

I told the white man that we did not let him watch because he would defile our youth with his filth; that his eyes were evil, and he could only bring evil to our souls; that his body was unclean and he would desecrate the holy ground of the ancestors; that his mind was twisted and he would only see and tell untruths; that his heart was stone and he would not understand and respect, and so he could only bring unhappiness to us and to our ancestors. . . . He told me that people like myself should be locked away in a box for ever. . . . I walked away and left him talking to himself.

Every three years . . . we held initiations . . . and every three years the white men went around trying to persuade mothers not to let their sons enter. But I told the mothers that this was because the white men did not want the children to become men . . . in this way white men would gradually win all the land, and we would just die out, with a home neither in this life nor in the afterlife. And so the women always entered their children . . . and we still survive and we are still worthy of our ancestors. . . .

I have tried hard to understand the white man . . . but I can only see harm. . . . They have given us a road we did not need, a road that brings more and more foreigners and enemies into our midst, causing trouble, making our women unclean, forcing us to a way of life that is not ours, planting crops we do not want, doing slave's work. . . . He sends us missions to destroy our belief. . . .

The white man talks of law where we talk of the way of our ancestors. . . . It is better to do something because one believes in the ancestors than because one is afraid of being beaten or put in a box. . . .

I have tried to keep my dignity. I have tried to remain a man in the eyes of my father. Whatever I may have done with my body, I have never betrayed my beliefs with my mind. But for my children it is different. . . . the white man fills their heads with different ideas and they doubt. I circumcise my sons, but I cannot circumcise their minds and their hearts. I can make their bodies acceptable, but they have to make their souls fit for the afterlife. . . . until I die, which cannot be long, I shall keep trying, for myself and my people. After I am dead there will be no one left, unless somewhere I have planted a seed that has yet to grow and provide nourishment for those who live on. If I have done this, then maybe I too shall be thought fit to be given life at the side of my fathers.[42]

In French Gabon conflicting notions of jurisprudence on the part of the Fang, the dominant ethnic group in the hinterland, and their European rulers bear out Matungi's overall indictment. Although the Fang had no formal courts, *palabras* — "palavers" in African parlance — were a constant feature of village life. The parties to a dispute would put their cases before several of the village elders, who would act as judges. Cross-examination was allowed, with the judges themselves taking little part in this; afterward, each side might feel obliged to make a restatement of its case. After some consultation among themselves, the elders would return their verdict, provided tempers were not running too high. Throughout the dispute and the judgment, proverbs and similar cases would be cited, generally without drawing direct parallels: "Finally the judge, after subtly steering his way through a sea of diversities, came to the head of the matter and announced a verdict. Thus was the palabra carefully disentangled and neatly sliced."[43]

The local administrator who acted as the judge in the colonial district courts operated very differently. His cross-examination and analysis were intended to elicit the general category into which a particular case fitted, so that it might be judged by reference to the colonial lawbooks. To the Fang such procedures appeared hasty and arbitrary; instead of untangling the palaver and slicing it they broke it, producing "two jagged ends very difficult to rejoin." Unlike the official, the Fang judges and protagonists conducted cases in such a way that the disputants were brought together, not forced apart. What to the white official appeared barely relevant recollections represented to the villagers the continuity of their community, stretching far beyond the immediate dispute.

Is it correct, then, that apart from the actual arrival of European settlers the colonial regimes were much the same in their impact? Largely, but not entirely. I. A. Aswiaju's research on Ketu and Meko (see chapter 7) demonstrates that there were more than just differential material rewards to the contrasting approach of the British and French to traditional leaders on either side of the Nigerian-Dahomey border. By the British the Onimeko was given much higher status than his traditional overlord, the Alaketu, received from the French. Similarly, contrasting Senegal and the Gambia, two Americans, Martin Klein and Clement Cottingham, find a greater "tendency of the British to explain what they wanted people to do and why" — suggesting that Perham's judgment that the French failed to understand Indirect Rule because of profound differences in national character may have been right after all.[44]

But each European official enjoyed so much discretionary power that his personality defined much of the reality of the imperial situation as perceived by his African subjects. A clerk from the Cameroons who served the French administration in the interwar years and became his country's ambassador to the United States after independence portrays the variety of temperament displayed by successive administrators in the district where he was employed:

The first [French administrator] was in 1916, a military officer. . . . [He was] impetuous, authoritarian, rowdy, and severe, but not spiteful. . . . more of a passing horseman than a stationary administrator. . . . He did not remain a long time. He celebrated the event of November 1918, danced with the villagers on the public place, and left. . . .

M. le Commandant B. [was] silent, timorous, afraid of everything, intimidated by everything, exaggerated everything. Of a wisp of hay, he would make a haystack. . . .

Then there was Commandant C., a small old twisted man who rarely came to the office, or came rather when the clerk was gone, searched in the latter's writing pad and read the scraps of paper in the wastepaper basket. . . .

The writer still remembers Commandant E., a very conscientious, humane, honest, just, understanding, and Christian man. When he returned to France, he wrote the clerk a friendly postcard. . . .

The clerk also got to know M. le Commandant F. Alas, this one was mad. . . . The very day of his arrival he had asked the clerk what the "going rate" was for the local wenches. When the clerk answered him . . . he pulled out his wallet and exclaimed, "I only have enough for six sessions." His whole stay was marked by this weakness. He had a deficit in his treasury. . . . He also left and was subject to public ridicule. . . .

The clerk had known M. le Commandant H., a hard worker and a married man. His wife had small get-togethers with the wives of the functionaries in the region. Both learned the local language. The population was very happy, they had a child during their stay to whom they gave a name from the country. They were well liked in the region.[45]

By the end of the period the best European minds applying themselves to policies of colonial administration were aware of a bankruptcy of ideas. Writing of Tanganyika, which since Cameron's time had been regarded as a model of Indirect Rule, Lord Hailey noted that "the progress of the Territory as far as native affairs are concerned seems to have come to a standstill. Improvements continue to be made in the machinery, but as a whole, the machine does not seem to move forward."[46] Deschamps described the period of 1919-39 as decisive but lost years: "We fell asleep somewhat from a political point of view . . . when it would have been wise slowly and resolutely to lead an evolution." Because France failed to take any initiative in these interwar years, according to Deschamps, "from then on we could do nothing more than follow developments without being able to guide them."[47] By the end of the 1930s Africans increasingly were bursting out of the imposed framework in new and challenging political movements.[48]

CHAPTER 11

The Colonial Economy

The economic impact of colonialism has provoked more discussion than any other aspect. Much of the debate has been theoretical and, quite frequently, very polemical.[1] The strategy in this chapter is to postpone consideration of theoretical issues, such as the relative importance of political and economic factors, until a more straightforward historical examination of the topic has been completed, although even purely narrative history — let alone the topical and comparative treatment attempted here — is obviously grounded in assumption and theory.

Mining

Many of the dreams of future Rands, which lured Europeans into the late nineteenth-century scramble, never materialized; others, like the Nigerian oil fields, were only discovered and appropriated on the eve of independence. But some mineral prizes were located early. By the mid-1930s gold, which had actually risen in price during the depression as many countries abandoned the gold standard, amounted to nearly half of the total domestic exports of Africa. The pioneer historian of Africa's involvement with the capitalist world, S. H. Frankel, commenting on this and other export statistics, proclaimed mining to be the touchstone of economic development in most of Africa.[2]

The first significant mineral find was located by the Belgians in Katanga, where the Union Minière began to produce copper in 1912, smelting the ore before shipping the metal to Germany for refining. In 1910 a railway from the south reached Elisabethville, giving the mines an outlet at Beira in Mozambique and allowing them to import Southern Rhodesian coal and mining equipment from South Africa. In response to the sharp increase in demand caused by World War I, the company boosted production to twenty thousand tons by 1918. In the immediate postwar depression the company decided to maintain and even increase production, while the more established copper companies elsewhere were closing down their mines. Such expansion required the introduction of sophisticated equipment and the use, from 1930, of hydroelectric power. Tin, cobalt, radium, and zinc also were produced, and the company created ancillary industries for its minerals in both Belgium and Katanga.[3]

In Northern Rhodesia surface copper also had been found, but as it was of a much lower grade than that in Katanga, it was thought to be impossible to work at a profit. In 1924, however, when the Colonial Office took over direct administration from the British South Africa Company, American experience in working such low-grade sulphide deposits was utilized rapidly, and the industry made spectacular progress. The British South Africa Company kept possession of the mineral rights — which normally in British Africa were vested in the crown — and so retained full power to grant and regulate prospecting and mining. Private British, United States, and South African capital, mobilized by Selection Trust and the Anglo-American Corporation, was therefore quite remarkably free from the interference of the colonial administration and responded with a multimillion-pound investment in the copper belt.[4]

The Belgian government, by contrast, was much more directly involved in the development of copper mining in Katanga. Both the Belgian and Congo governments had substantial interests in the Union Minière as well as other companies operating in Katanga. The Belgian administration was imbued with a paternalist approach that assumed that private enterprise should be subordinate to government policies. An all-Congolese freight route was therefore constructed and was favored by the administration, even though it was more economical to export copper by the Rhodesian Railways or the Benguela Railway to Lobito Bay.

Nor would Belgian paternalism defer to its white employees, who were not permitted during the interwar period to organize trade unions. In 1920 white South African miners in Katanga were sacked, because they had struck, and were replaced by Belgians on three-year contracts, subject to dismissal at any time. At the end of the first three-year period they had to return to

Belgium before they could be reengaged or allowed to settle. The Union Minière could therefore replace whites with Africans without encountering fierce European trade union opposition as was the case across the border in Northern Rhodesia. In 1922 it opened a school to train African employees in carpentry, metalwork, engineering, and locomotive repair, following the example of the Bas-Congo-Katanga Railway, which had established four such technical schools a year earlier.[5]

The training and promotion of Africans to replace skilled Europeans flowed from the "stabilization" policy regarding African labor adopted by the Union Minière and other big companies in the mid-1920s. The companies decided that the labor shortages and the low productivity that crippled their efforts to expand production in these boom years were chronic accompaniments of the hitherto unquestioned policy of recruiting miners as short-term migrant laborers. Judged in terms of pure economics this led to reduced productivity because of poor health and other problems as the miner rarely had his wife living with him to cook proper meals and to keep his quarters clean. In addition, there was a high incidence of venereal disease caused by resort to prostitutes. In general, efficiency was low because the rapid turnover gave the individual worker no opportunity to acquire technical skills. The stabilization policy involved a three-year renewable contract. Strong encouragement was given to the workers to bring their wives, whose fares were paid, and a concern was shown for the welfare of the worker and his family.[6] Bachelor recruits of the Union Minière were offered a contribution to the bride-price provided that their fiancées passed a medical examination.[7] Maternity and infant welfare clinics were established and primary education was provided. Rations were supplied for the wives and children of the workers. Roman Catholic priests and nuns were closely involved in employee welfare work and also were allowed to conduct their religious activities within the workers' community. Supervision of the community was entrusted to a *chef de camp*, who was supplied with a dossier for each worker as well as comprehensive instructions from the employer. He was expected to give sympathetic consideration to complaints and to settle disputes.[8]

Stabilization was never intended to produce a permanent urban proletariat. Belgian planning sought to ensure that the worker's home village survived as a viable community to which he could return. In 1924 a commission of enquiry estimated that no more than 5 percent of the able-bodied men could be employed on long contracts at substantial distances from their homes without serious damage to the village economy. Throughout the worker's three-year tour of duty requests for home leave were freely granted. At the end of each contract, and even if he signed for another term, the worker was expected to go home to restore old ties. Finally, the long-term migrant was expected to retire to his native village.[9]

Belgian paternalism was never monolithic. In particular, there was sharp Catholic critcism to the effect that the percentage of men stipulated as available for labor recruitment was much too high for the good of the home village — and as the president of the 1924 inquiry was also the general secretary of Forminière (International Society of Forestry and Mining of the Congo), one of the largest of the concessionary companies, such strictures were at least plausible.[10] Nevertheless, the combination of religious and industrial paternalism produced striking statistics. The mortality rate in the mining communities had been as high as 117.7 per thousand in 1917. In the period 1925-29 it dropped to 39.1 per thousand, and by 1935-39 it was down to 7.1 per thousand; between these quinquenniums infant mortality was cut from 161 per thousand to 43.1 per thousand. In 1925-29 the percentage of women living there was only 26 percent of that of men but by 1935-39 it had more than doubled. Although the *chef de camp* was ordered to put no pressure on a worker to reengage after his three-year contract, in the belief that only a true volunteer would perform well, by 1940 nearly 78 percent of the workers were willing to reengage. Whereas between 1921 and 1929 the Union Minière had recruited an average of ten thousand men a year, during the period 1935-42 the average fell to eighteen hundred, despite the fact that this period included the rapid wartime expansion. By 1934, 5 percent of the African employees were working at jobs previously held by Europeans, and 60 percent of the African workers on the railways were holding such jobs. It is clear that in its own terms stabilization, unlike many other equally ambitious colonial policies, was no mere rhetoric: it worked.[11]

The various European groups in Northern Rhodesia never achieved, or even sought to achieve, coherent policies to match the unified approach of church, state, and concessionary company in Katanga. The district commissioner was "tolerated, but not welcomed" by the companies in the mine townships, which tried "to keep him out of the picture as much as possible."[12] Effective government intervention in labor matters was virtually confined to suppressing the African riots of 1935 in the mine townships. The white miners feared, and with good reason, that the government and the mineowners wanted to replace them with cheap African labor. When Major

Granville St. J. Orde-Browne, the Colonial Office expert on African labor, visited the Rhodesian copper belt in 1938, he was appalled by the "menacing situation." He reported confidentially that the copper belt was close to insurrection. The European miners were alienated from the administration and inflicted their own unlawful "discipline" on African workers. He reported that there was "insulting and disgusting treatment of the natives; spitting at a servant is not uncommon, incredible as this may sound."[13] The control of such unruly Europeans presented grave difficulties. In 1939 there were only some forty European and two hundred African policemen on the copper belt, and they were not trained to deal with the civil commotions that Orde-Browne feared. There was a company of African troops, officered by whites and stationed nearby, but, Orde-Browne stated, the use of Africans against whites "cannot be advocated."[14] By 1939 the Northern Rhodesian government seemed to have no solution to such problems, and anyway it appeared likely to be soon replaced by a settler regime through amalgamation with Southern Rhodesia.

The very name "Gold Coast" encouraged the idea that a new Rand would be found in British West Africa. The influx of capital in the early 1900s was carefully, and indeed often dishonestly, engineered and the boom soon burst.[15] The gold-bearing strata was insufficiently rich, and Gold Coast Africans were too well organized and astute to surrender their land. Some companies did make headway, but the British administration refused to allow them to institute the compound and pass law system that they had developed already in South Africa, as, in the words of Governor Sir John Rodger in 1909, "excepting from a mine owner's point of view . . . indefensible."[16] Nevertheless, in the immediate postwar period, when the mining companies had to compete for labor against successful African cocoa farmers and the government itself, which under Governor Gordon Guggisberg was embarking on an ambitious program of public works, both much less dangerous and generally more congenial than mining, they were assisted by the administration in what amounted to forced labor on behalf of private commercial companies. In the Northern Territories recruitment for the mines became associated with the government's own recruitment for public works, which was itself "on the shadowy borderline between 'communal' and 'forced' labor."[17] The system was scarcely satisfactory, however. Hard-pressed northern chiefs safeguarded the agricultural viability of their own villages by forwarding the halt and the lame: for example, one group of twenty-five Dagarti laborers included one elderly man, one who suffered from an ulcer on the left ankle, one who had both arms deformed from fractures, and one who suffered from a hernia. Other gangs included youngsters, old men with conjunctivitis and several who were blind in one eye, together with several suffering from ulcers and hernias. The system was finally abandoned in November 1927.[18] In the 1920s the government also located its deep-water port at Takoradi and shaped its railroad system in deference to the wishes of representatives of British mining capital, especially those associated with the new manganese mines, and to the detriment of African capital invested in cocoa farming.[19] On balance, this seems to have retarded the long-term economic development of the Gold Coast. But, like the marginal gold mines in South Africa, the Gold Coast mines benefited briefly from the abandonment of the gold standard so that in the middle of the depression about 40 percent of the country's exports consisted of minerals, mainly gold and diamonds.[20]

Agriculture

Although mining dominated the export statistics of sub-Saharan Africa in the early twentieth century, agricultural exports also began to rise sharply. Agricultural development could take three forms. First, there was cultivation by African peasant farmers, who organized themselves in the economic unit of the household; second, there was farming by European settlers, for whom Africans worked for wages; third, there were some large-scale plantations run by big concessionary companies. The problems of the settler economy are considered elsewhere in the present volume. In this section the issue of whether African agriculture would be developed by self-employed African peasants or by European-owned plantations will be studied.

Anthony Hopkins has recently reopened discussion of the reasons why the official colonial policy in West Africa eventually favored African rather than expatriate enterprise in agriculture.[21] He points out that neither the climatic factor nor the trusteeship factor was conclusive. Tropical disease and discomfort did not prevent European plantations from being established in the Congo basin or in Asia, nor did they stop attempts at plantation agriculture in West Africa. The notion of trusteeship was sufficiently elastic to permit colonial officials to favor European agriculture elsewhere in Africa, as the views of Sir Robert Coryndon show.[22] Furthermore, European-owned plantations were being established in West Africa before World War I. By 1913 there were fifty-eight plantations in the German colony of the Cameroons, employing eighteen thousand African workers. Expatriate plantations also had been developed by the Germans on a lesser scale in Togo and by the French in the Ivory Coast and Dahomey. In British West Africa a few plantations had been established on the Gold Coast and in southern Nigeria at the start of the century. W. H. Lever, the Liverpool soap and margarine magnate, campaigned strenuously for plantations in West Africa from 1906. After the war he pressed his campaign further, winning some sympathy from policy makers, including Lord Lugard.[23]

Expatriate plantations failed in the long run to develop on any substantial scale in West Africa, with the significant exception of politically independent Liberia. There were four reasons for this failure. First, African farmers already had developed an export economy through their own enterprise by the time the expatriate capitalists applied for concessions. Second, the existing trading interests, both European and African, had already established links with the African producers and feared the intrusion of rivals with direct control of production. Anxious Manchester and Liverpool traders organized a powerful campaign to stop Lever in 1906 and again in 1920. Similarly, the great French trading combine, the Compagnie Française de l'Afrique Occidentale, opposed plantations in French West Africa as did German traders in Togo. Third, of those few European plantations that were established almost all failed. Lastly, the preoccupation of West African colonial administrations with security led officials to fear the disruption of the existing social order if African labor were to be diverted away from the household unit into a full-fledged capitalist agricultural system.[24] The failures of such expatriate plantations as were created and the successes of African agricultural enterprise both merit further discussion.

Expatriate plantations frequently failed to establish themselves because their managers were ignorant of tropical agriculture and were also undercapitalized. Further problems awaited such plantations even after they were successfully established. As potential African employees were already members of household farming units, there was a shortage of labor, which meant that wages had to be comparatively high in order to attract workers. Plantations also, unlike the African household units, were highly specialized and therefore were particularly vulnerable to shifts in world demand. The French plantations on the Ivory Coast were beset by such problems and only survived through government assistance in the form of forced labor and tariff preference. The poor record of these expatriate ventures tended to discourage further requests for such concessions as well as the government's commitment to the plantation solution.[25]

Whereas European plantations in West Africa were either unproven or failures, the peasants already had demonstrated their ability to grow the tropical products the rest of the world needed. The export market for palm kernels and oil recovered from its troubles of the late nineteenth century and expanded in the twentieth century. Peanuts were established as a main export staple of Senegambia from the middle of the nineteenth century. Exports tripled within five years of the building of the Dakar-Saint-Louis railroad in 1885, opening up Cayor to production. By 1914 peasant-produced peanuts had also become very important in Northern Nigeria. Unlike palm trees, peanuts were not suitable for plantation cultivation. But costs for plantation palm products could be high, as noted earlier in the general discussion of labor and capital problems. Where plantations did succeed in cutting costs and providing higher quality palm products than their peasant competitors, their advantage might be cancelled by political difficulties, as in the Congo and Indonesia.[26]

The most striking success in African-produced agricultural exports was the Gold Coast cocoa industry, which had become the world's biggest by 1910.[27] This position has been maintained, and today Ghana exports around 400,000 tons of cocoa a year and the industry employs several million people. The rapid development by African enterprise is all the more impressive in view of the fact that the cocoa tree is not native to West Africa, takes several years to begin to yield, and does not reach maturity for about fifteen years. "Cocoa farming was a thoroughly capitalist enterprise from the outset: it involved taking risks with an unfamiliar product; substantial investments of time and money; an ability to plan ahead; and a willingness to defer present consumption for the sake of future return."[28] The local kinship systems and other traditional social institutions, so often denounced by theorists of "development," helped rather than hindered such African entrepreneurs by providing group support. Success was achieved despite erroneous advice proffered by the colonial agricultural department, which mistakenly criticized the quality of Gold Coast cocoa after having noticed that it appeared to be different from its own laboratory specimens — understandably so since the laboratory specimens were acquired from the West Indies and represented a different type of cocoa.[29] The administration also favored expatriate mining enterprise over African cocoa producers in its transportation policy. Indeed, such was the success of these indigenous agricultural capitalists that District Commissioner Allan Cardinall feared their disruptive effects on the social order, much as Governor Hugh Clifford of Nigeria had objected to the establishment of expatriate plantations:

The development of the [cocoa] industry has been practically spontaneous on the part of the inhabitants. The inevitable result of the rapid increase of the people's wealth has been to bring about what almost amounts to a revolution. The communal ownership of land is being largely repudiated for individual ownership; the sale of land, an almost unheard of practice, has become a matter of everyday life; a tendency for the maker of a cocoa plantation to leave his property to his son rather than his sister's son has almost brought a change from matrilineal to patrilineal descent; the industrious planter has been forced to hire labor in order to cope with the fruits of his industry and is gradually ceasing to be a working farmer with the inevitable result that in course of time he will be a non-working landlord; an influx of strangers drawn as it were to El Dorado has opened up the country to an extent no man could have forseen as possible within so short a period; fresh problems of the gravest nature, such as preservation of forests, slum conditions, unemployed, spread of disease, transport and shipment, and a people which has learned to gallop before it could crawl have been set for Government to solve.[30]

Only in Liberia, ironically the one independent state in West Africa, did expatriate plantations become important. Failing to develop any continuously successful export crop equivalent to Senegambian peanuts or Gold Coast cocoa, Liberia drifted into external debt. Eventually in 1926 the government, desperate for foreign capital, leased one million acres for ninety-nine years to the giant Firestone Tire and Rubber Company in the United States. By 1950 rubber accounted for 90 percent of the value of Liberia's exports.[31] It has been suggested that the ruling political oligarchy of the True Whig party preferred to have economic enteprise in the hands of expatriates rather than risk an indigenous challenge based upon economic power outside the political system.[32]

The Congo basin in the aftermath of the slave trade constituted a vast refugee zone, many of whose peoples had sought protection from coastal raiders in remote areas of difficult terrain and ecology.[33] The development of "legitimate commerce" to replace the slave trade was never as successful as in West Africa because of the low density and comparative inaccessibility of the area's population and the pulverization of traditional hierarchies, which elsewhere in Africa frequently demonstrated the capacity to organize long-distance trade as well as a keen appetite for its products. The occupying powers, France and the Congo Free State, were saddled with huge territories devoid of any prosperous network of legitimate trade in tropical agricultural products. They turned over the area to concessionary companies that operated what amounted to an economy of pillage, looting the territory of wild rubber and ivory, with minimal capital investment.[34]

The logical successor to the economy of pillage — which was in the nature of things self-liquidating — was the expatriate capitalist plantation, again functioning through the mechanism of the concessionary company. Lever Brothers, which had been rebuffed in British West Africa through the combined hostility of established European and African traders and some administrators, was granted large concessions in the Belgian Congo in 1911.

The Depression

The world economic crisis, beginning with the Wall Street crash of 1929, reached Africa in the middle of 1930. The trade depression hit the colonial governments through their heavy dependence on customs receipts. The French West African Federation's customs dues fell by 47 percent between 1930 and 1931.[35] Sierra Leone, which Hopkins judges to be typical of the British West African colonies, lost a third of its customs receipts between 1928 and 1934.[36] Such losses produced budgetary crises because the colonial governments were committed to much larger fixed charges (salaries, pensions, loan repayments) than in the past when their administrations were more rudimentary.[37]

In order to raise revenue the colonial governments first increased the customs duties, but this was offset by the decline in trade; and the main effect was to increase the price Africans paid for imports. Next they followed the orthodox economic policy of retrenchment pursued by the metropolitan governments of Europe. European officials were retired early, and Africans were discharged. The Nigerian railways dismissed two thousand indigenous workers, who then had to compete for jobs with others dropped from the civil service.[38] In Sierra Leone about a fifth of the European employees on the railway were dispensed with, and the daily-wage African employees were put on short time.[39] Expenditure on public works in both French and British West Africa failed to reach the level of the 1920s until the eve of World War II, by which time it was heavily influenced by military concerns such as the development of Freetown as a key base in Britain's imperial defense system.[40]

The third method used to cope with the depression was for the metropolitan government to make money available in the form of grants and loans to the colonies, thus abandoning the traditional doctrine of colonial self-sufficiency, although out of necessity rather than principle. In France the Great Colonial Loan was authorized in 1931 to finance the Maginot Plan of the same year. The plan sought to revive Sarraut's postwar schemes for economic development, which had been abandoned when the massive German reparations that were to finance them failed to materialize. Although some useful improvements in transport were carried through, the showpiece project, the Niger irrigation scheme, foundered badly. An American expert was recruited in Sarraut's time to choose the most suitable types of cotton to grow in the area: "Beginning his work in 1922, he had 'almost' finished by 1940."[41] No proper study of soils and their reaction to irrigation was made. Later, bitter experience would show that irrigation, "after producing less than average yields, sterilized the soil by washing it out."[42] The Popular Front government of 1936 drew up a further economic plan for the colonies, but the government fell in July 1937 before the plan was put into effect.[43]

The British government's Colonial Development Act of 1929 established a fund for "aiding and developing agriculture and industry in the colony or territory and thereby promoting commerce with an industry in the United Kingdom." The colonial secretary of the new Labour government, Lord Passfield, better known as Sidney Webb, stressed that "the principal motive for the introduction of this measure is connected with the lamentable conditions of unemployment in this country, and this is an attempt to stimulate export trade."[44] In British West Africa by 1936 a total of £836,000 had been disbursed under the act, comprising £171,000 for Nigeria, £100,000 for the Gold Coast, £25,000 for the Gambia, and well over half — £540,000 — for hitherto neglected Sierra Leone.[45] Sierra Leone's massive share consisted of £500,000 to assist iron ore mining and £40,000 for such assorted projects as street drainage, a passenger jetty for Freetown, and the expansion of rice farming.[46]

The bulk of this assistance was channeled through the colonial government to the Sierra Leone Development Company (Delco), an expatriate firm formed in 1930. Governor Sir Joseph Byrne at first found the idea highly unorthodox, and on October 1, 1929, he wrote that on principle he was opposed to the government becoming involved in supplying capital to commercial ventures. Six weeks later he was afraid that if his administration hesitated over the principle or even the details of its dealings with the expatriate mining concern, Sierra Leone would be forestalled by other colonies seeking and getting the funds. An agreement was reached on March 5, 1930, by which Sierra Leone loaned the company £500,000 for twenty years at 5.5 percent interest.[47]

Despite the depression production once begun rapidly increased in response to the armaments race in Europe. Indeed, the producers of iron ore in Sierra Leone found it difficult to break into the British market and sent their ore along a route via the Netherlands and Belgium — the route already taken by some of the country's palm kernels — to Germany; thus, ironically, the British Colonial Development Fund seems to have subsidized German war preparations.[48] Exports began in September 1933 and for 1938 were 861,955 tons.[49] Between three and four thousand Sierra Leoneans were employed by the Sierra Leone Development Company during the depression. Yet W. M. Macmillan, on a visit to the company's mine at Marampa, noted that "the supply of labour was obviously in excess of real demand. . . . many hundreds [were] clamouring for thirty or forty vacancies," despite wage rates that were "by any reasonable measure extremely low."[50]

Although Macmillan was one of the most forthright exponents of West African development through industrialization with British capital investment, he reported to the British Colonial Office that the company's procedures at Marampa were "thoroughly unsatisfactory examples of the use of African labour by industrial enterprise."[51] At Marampa African miners "faced the pit for wages ranging from 4d a day to a maximum of 1/-a day. Living conditions in the mining compound were terrible — congested, squalid, unsanitary with practically no medical services available." The company took advantage of the abundance of cheap labor to introduce only minimal mechanization. The Sierra Leoneans, for their part, habitually sought work at the mines for only two or three months in the year. The general acceptance of a very low grade of efficiency drove Macmillan to suggest that to break the vicious circle the mines "might . . . be encouraged or compelled, to resort to mechanical aid rather than calculate entirely on the use of African sinew."[52] Meantime the results of company policy reinforced European managerial stereotypes of African incompetence. The district commissioner at nearby Port Loko found attitudes of "hatred with which certain Europeans regard the native labourer" similar to those on the contemporary copper belt. "Young engineers are taught on their arrival that all Africans are lazy, dishonest and thoroughly bad and above all, that they are devoid of human feeling and self-respect. Ruthlessness and strict discipline are regarded as the essential qualities for handling native labour and any form of sympathy or consideration is condemned as the most culpable weakness."[53] At the end of December 1937, when the workers at Pepel (the company's own port for the Marampa mine) struck, he reported "that there was a strong school of thought which suggested that the best method of dealing with the strike would be to arrest a number of strikers and have them tied up and severely flogged."[54]

The Sierra Leone Development Company's transport policy was in marked contrast to such inefficient employment practices. The company decided to build its own port and railway rather than to hook onto the country's existing rail and road facilities. As an exercise in swift extraction from an unindustrialized milieu — with minimum contamination from that milieu — it was faultless commercial logic. But it meant the quite conscious adoption of what was later dubbed "enclave development," which proceeded without reference to the progress of the country as a whole.

The depression moved Britain, France, and Belgium some way toward accepting the idea of a managed economy. In Britain itself the Macmillan Committee on Finance and Industry in 1931 provided guidelines for the conduct of future policy, suggesting that "we may well have reached the stage when an era of conscious and deliberate management must succeed an era of undirected natural evolution."[55] In 1936 John M. Keynes published his *The General Theory of Employment, Interest and Money*, attacking orthodox laissez-faire economic theory and leading well within a decade to a successful "Keynesian revolution" in both economic theory and policy. In specifically imperial affairs the new currents of thought favoring social welfare rather than laissez-faire appear in the International Missionary Council's *Modern Industry and the African* of 1933. The author of the economic section in that work, Austin Robinson, went on to help Lord Hailey to prepare his book *An African Survey*. Later he pointed out that in the survey "we assumed the paramountcy of African native welfare as one of the axioms of all our work."[56] The Moyne Commission to the West Indies late in 1938, in the aftermath of strikes and unrest, found a pressing need for "large expenditure on social services and development" in view of the appalling economic and social conditions that it brought to light.[57] The findings of the commission, which were published in a white paper in February 1940, provided guidelines for the new Colonial Development and Welfare Act of that year.

Robinson and Hailey found "similar streams of thought, sometimes by hindsight over-paternalistic but none-the-less sincere, in the minds of the best French and Belgian administrators" they encountered while preparing the book.[58] Léon Blum's Popular Front government launched a very powerful team of a dozen – including a trio of former administrators, Delavignette, Deschamps, and Labouret, who were known for their reform views, the famous ethnologist Lévy-Bruhl, and André Gide – to prepare a plan for the development of black Africa. The commission was ineffective, however; Lévy-Bruhl, charged with reporting on African "aspirations," was one of the few members to make a final report, which proved to be an investigation of the causes of the continuation of cannibalism in certain remote areas – hardly a triumphant demonstration of the utility of applied anthropology. In any case, the Blum government fell in 1937, and in 1938 the Senate Finance Committee forced the study group's disbandment by refusing to vote the funds necessary to continue the work.[59]

Such responses to the depression were still portents rather than practical policies in the 1930s. But though they pointed the way to postwar colonial development policies, they also pointed to a parallel change in the imperial countries' thinking about their own national development. The domestic stagnation that permitted the high level of overseas investment by the most developed countries, especially Great Britain, in the period 1900-1914 would in these mid-century times of Keynesian economics and collectivism "bring governments crashing."[60] The same currents of thought that produced "colonial welfare" led simultaneously to the "welfare state," and postwar European governments were of course much more vulnerable to the criticism of their domestic voters than to that of their colonial subjects; hence paradoxically the amount of the gross national product available for overseas development was sharply cut back just when it was accepted that "colonial development and welfare" was a good thing.[61]

Development, Underdevelopment, and Welfare

A quarter of a century ago Sir Keith Hancock scathingly condemned the confusion caused by muddleheaded use of the word "imperialism."[62] Since then the terms "colonialism" and "neocolonialism" have entered everyday language, providing greater resources for the excesses of vituperation or elegant variation without discrimination of meaning that Hancock deplored. Honed down, though, such concepts are beginning to serve the purposes of serious historical analysis.[63] K. O. Diké's pioneering study of *Trade and Politics in the Niger Delta* made the point that five hundred years of trading activities led in the nineteenth century to the political domination of West Africa by Europe.[64] A hundred years ago West Africa and the settler society at the Cape exemplified the alternative futures facing the rest of Africa. Since then the remainder of Africa has been brought, with varying degrees of discomfort, within the framework of a worldwide economy. Formal political control was hardly necessary for such economic integration, as the case of the Liberian plantations illustrates. Both the neo-Marxist historians, who make "the development of underdevelopment" their central theme, and the historians like Hopkins, who stress the continuing importance of Africa's domestic economy, make actual political control simply an episode, however significant, in Africa's economic history. Certainly the economic transformations wrought by colonialism need to be assessed in the context of postcolonial as well as precolonial development. Furthermore, if the terms of trade are acceptable as an index of African economic welfare, as Hopkins argues, then for large areas of tropical Africa conditions were worsening at least from 1930 to 1945, and possibly from 1914 to 1945.[65] The discontent caused by such economic changes had important political consequences, all of which served to hasten the end of formal colonial control.

CHAPTER 12

Religion and Imperialism

During the 1970s historians have reacted sharply, but constructively, to the contention — or the assumption — that, whereas Christianity and Islam are proper subjects for historical study, "traditional" African religious ideas and institutions must be left to anthropologists, forever marooned in a timeless ethnographic present.[1] The historical approach to African religion has already produced some stimulating revisionist history of the impact of Christian missions and Islam.[2] Meanwhile, from the area of anthropology has come Robin Horton's influential article on African conversion, which also forces reconsideration of the interaction of African religion with the two "world" faiths.[3] A fruitful discussion has developed around Horton's model of African religious change and the researches of new historians.[4]

Horton boldly — he says, brashly — postulates a "typical traditional religious cosmology."[5] African religions possessed the idea of a supreme being, a High God or Creator God; they also possessed the idea of a range of lesser spirits, including the ancestors, natural forces, and alien beings. In what Horton terms the "microcosmic situation" — small-scale, relatively self-sufficient societies — Africans naturally emphasized the agency of the various spirits, and the concept of the High God remained undeveloped. Ancestor spirits or nature spirits dominated the cosmology because Africans were preoccupied with their relations with their relatives and neighbors or the local environment. But once they had to deal with other people, along trade routes or in cities, their ancestor spirits and local nature spirits were no longer effective. Even those Africans who stayed at home, inside the micro-

215

cosmic society, felt its boundaries weakening through contact with the wider world. It was at this stage in African history that students of comparative religion, as well as theorists of missions, also discerned a crisis in the old order, because they believed African religions had not the resources to adapt to this new macrocosmic situation. The only recourse left, it was suggested, lay in conversion to a "world" faith like Christianity or Islam.

Horton, though, insists that African religions had the potential, in the shape of the as yet undeveloped notion of the High God, to cope with the wider world. The High God could formulate moral rules for dealings with the new macrocosmic world. African religions could meet the continuing need for spiritual sources of healing, prophecy, and protection against witches by developing the concept of God as the source of spiritual power. In order to maintain morale in the face of European conquest and general technical supremacy, African religions could stress ideas of the divine intervention of an African God.

Horton postulates this independent African religious revolution as taking place just when Christianity started to penetrate Africa. The Christian missionaries, insofar as they were successful, identified the Christian God with the indigenous African supreme being. Olorun, the Yoruba High God, for example, was identified by the missionaries, who then informed the people of his "true" nature according to their own definition of the personal nature of God and suggested their own worked-out ways of access to him.[6] The indigenous African religious revolution was often led by the traditional religious leaders, as these were the people most aware of the need for a religion to cope with the problems of society and most conscious that the traditional religious forms were not meeting such needs. Frequently these same leaders welcomed Christian ideas about God and about the means of access to him because these corresponded closely with their own efforts to reformulate African cosmology.

Horton, having suggested Christianity's attractions for many Africans, then argues that the correspondence between what it offered and what Africans needed was by no means exact. Africans could borrow ideas about God as a person to fill out their notion of a supreme being, but western institutional Christianity could not meet their needs for prophecy, spiritual healing, and protection against evil because of its "renunciation of the functions of explanation, prediction, and control."[7] Missionaries were modern western men who compartmentalized their own cosmology by combining the

idea of a personal God with the assumption that he abstained from interference with the scientific laws that governed everyday events.

Such a dichotomy bred mystification. Hilda Kuper, the anthropologist,
tells of the missionary hospital in Swaziland that functioned in accordance
with the prescriptions of modern medical science but was adorned with a
picture of Jesus, the miracle worker.[8] Missionaries, however much they
aspired to bear other-worldly tidings, were also bearers of modern western
culture, and their reports "are full of accounts of African *emerveillement*
before some gadget or another of European daily life: matches, collapsible
drinking cups, bicycles," reports another anthropologist, James Fernandez,
who worked with the Fang. Many missionaries, Fernandez tells us, "succumbed to the temptation to credit these marvels of material culture to the
Christian way of life, the *bonnes nouvelles* they were preaching."[9] In 1910
one Monsieur Cadier wrote enthusiastically of the voracious appetite of the
young Fang for knowledge of the Word of God, "an astonishing zeal, always
eager to penetrate further this mysterious science that gives this power to
the white man" and a little later told of a woman who while bringing him
water and bananas "piously asked if it was God himself who gave me my
beautiful machine . . . my bicycle."[10]

The mystification eventually led to disillusion as many Fang became
convinced that the "good tidings" the missionaries preached must be fraudu-
lent because they had provided no tangible material benefits. Still, they
persisted in their search for the secret of the white man's mysterious
"science." At the end of the 1950s Fernandez found many adherents of the
Bwiti cult, founded before World War I, who described their religion as the
science of hidden things. "It was futile to try to convince them that there
was no such thing as a science of hidden things. I began to wish that instead
of the Bible the missionaries had brought the collected papers of Michael
Faraday as their *bonnes nouvelles*."[11]

Horton's article starts from a sympathetic summary and critique of John
Peel's study of the Aladura churches in Yorubaland.[12] He argues that the
movement of theological reinterpretation that had begun outside Christianity
could not be permanently accommodated within the mission churches. The
independent spirit churches such as Aladura pressed beyond what the missions could offer to adapt fresh combinations of ideas stressing the power of
God's spirit to heal the sick, to inspire prophecy, and to eradicate witches.
Aladura, like Bwiti, dates back to before World War I, but when the terrible
visitation of the influenza epidemic from 1919-21 gave grim confirmation to

the prophecies of its leaders, support for the church mushroomed. In 1924-26 another terrible epidemic, the bubonic plague, ravaged Yorubaland. It was followed by depression, famine, and disruptive social change through the late 1920s and 1930s. The leaders of Aladura developed a stark rationale for such misfortunes, explaining them as the result of God's wrath at the people's sins.[13] In the Zionist churches of southern Africa the great African movement of theological reinterpretation gave a similar explanation for even greater distress and dislocative social change.[14]

Many Africans, of course, stayed within their mission churches, and Horton sees the African reinterpretation working within this context as well. Certainly his ideas provide a basis for interpreting both the millennial ferment and the return to traditional faiths in John Chilembwe's Nyasaland and suggest a closer focus on the interaction between them. And they are equally relevant to present-day Malawi, where "leading officials of rain shrines do not disguise their allegiance to the major churches of the country."[15] By focusing on African creativity rather than passivity, Horton and the group of historians connected with *African Religious Research* point to the need for a revision of the whole missionary encounter with Africa.

Missionaries and Government

Christian missionaries were drawn into relationships with governments in Africa that sometimes troubled their consciences and compromised them in the eyes of potential converts. Almost all African rulers were invested with spiritual power, so the sheer presence of a mission, unless it could take on the attributes of a state church, constituted a threat. Relationships between the Tswana, living in what is now Botswana and in the Republic of South Africa, and the missions strikingly illustrate the complexity and variety of possible responses.

The Tswana

The first Tswana encountered by European missionaries were the Thlaping in 1816, who proved quite discriminating in their approach to European culture.[16] They allowed James Read of the London Missionary Society to settle among them on the condition that he would not preach or teach. They rejected any attempt to change the old customs as had happened among their Griqua neighbors, "who once wore a corrass [skin apron], but now wear clothes, once had two wives, now one, this . . . the Boochuannas will never submit to." The London Missionary Society had arrived on the scene in response to the Thlaping Chief Mothibi's request for instructors. But the day after this invitation, Chief Mothibi "asked for what seemed all along to have been in his heart, *viz.* for a gun." To the Tswana missionary contact meant trade and trade meant firearms. The missionaries had no practical alternative but to accept this situation. In Tswana society, therefore, the missionary found himself operating as gunsmith, commercial and diplomatic agent, and irrigation expert. But he had little reward in converts for these secular gifts.[17]

Frustrated, the missionaries sought British intervention to free them from their limited role. John Mackenzie, who became the arch-exponent of missionary imperialism in Bechuanaland, reflected in 1876: "On the whole, the old feudal power of the native chiefs is opposed to Christianity; and the people who are living under English law are in a far more advantageous position as to the reception of the Gospel than when they were living in their own heathen towns surrounded by all its thralls and sanctions."[18] As he acknowledged two years later, missionary interests demanded British rule, for missionary success was "the work of conquerors."

To the missionary imperialists European conquest had to be undertaken by the British, not by settlers from the Afrikaner republics. The missionaries urged the Tswana, who lived in large townships clustered about springs, to fan out, finding new sources of water and thus bringing more land under effective occupation. The clarion call of the missionaries to the British government was that the Bechuanaland mission stations constituted a road to the north that must be kept from falling into the hands of the Afrikaner republicans in order to safeguard Cape Dutch and English loyalty to the empire. When gold was discovered in northern Tswana territory in 1868, the missionaries hoped that economic attractions would supplement the strategic function of the road to the north. Mackenzie invited "John [Bull]'s attention to this delicious morsel of a gold field; let him spread it like jelly over Transvaal and Free State and Bechuana countries and swallow the lot."[19]

Missionary frustration was matched by the chiefs' exasperation. The missionaries were well aware that if they successfully encouraged Tswana dispersal they would undermine the close control of the chiefs in the *kgotla* — traditional council place where the chief listened to news, petitions, and complaints and settled disputes — and would also forestall prospective Afrikaner colonization. Both as secular modernizers who set themselves up as irrigation experts and exponents of economic individualism, especially the private ownership of land, and as clergymen who denounced the initiation ceremonies to the age-regiments as licentious paganism, they were challenging indigenous institutions. Lecturing to Tswana students, Mackenzie said that "the feudal and tribal system could be superseded by a general government, without loss of personal property, the unoccupied lands and the supremacy of the chiefs being the only things taken away." He even suggested that chiefs adjust their attitudes to be "the chief of today and not of the olden times"; thus they might recognize the new appeal of economic individualism by granting their subjects private titles to land.

Conflict between missionaries and chiefs came to a head in 1878, when sections of the southern Tswana rebelled against white domination, whether Boer or British. The Thlaping around Kuruman complained, "We accepted the Word of God in our youth . . . but we did not know all that was coming behind it." Angry traditionalists attacked manifestations of the new order, especially the missionaries who "were to be killed . . . especially those connected with the new school at Kuruman, which was stealing the hearts of the young people." The Tswana rising was not a race war, although most of the people seem to have rallied behind the outraged traditionalists against the leaders who had discredited themselves by association with whites. But some Tswana had benefited from missionary reforms in agriculture and commerce. Farmers, hunters, and traders, following the missionary gospel of individual enterprise and pursuing personal prosperity above the well-being of the community, resented traditional restraints and observances. Indeed, they supported the missionaries, looking toward further change and a shift to a new basis of authority.[20]

The British missionaries were far from discomfited by the rising. They resisted it, of course, but also argued that it constituted a crisis of the old order that should be exploited. They anticipated great good from it in the establishment of a better government in the country and the removal of the power of its innumerable chiefs. They welcomed the British expedition sent to quell the disorder, and the Kuruman missionary station became a military headquarters, with the mission press printing notices calling on the Tswana to surrender. John Mackenzie played a key role in the resettlement, encouraging private leasehold and individual land tenure. Many rebels surrendered to him personally and were dispatched to farms and villages to begin plowing. He also induced the southern Tswana leaders to petition for British rule, putting it to them that their conduct during the rebellion could bear only two interpretations: they had been either unwilling or unable to restrain their subjects. Faced by this and by examples of deposition, the chiefs asked for British government.[21]

The missionaries advocated that the power of the Tswana elite be destroyed by legislating that not more than six or eight huts should be built on one farm. The inevitable desire of all natives to collect power (and vassals) had to be made impracticable and unlawful. The traditional order was too restrictive of individual enterprise and should be replaced by a system of individual title to land to promote a class of "native yeoman."[22]

Mackenzie's missionary imperialism appeared to be on the brink of success. British officials in South Africa and in the Colonial Office seemed to accept the gist of his argument. But in 1879 war broke out again in Zululand and in 1880 in the Transvaal. The Conservative government was replaced by a Liberal one, and the confederation scheme in South Africa collapsed. Gladstone's Liberal government refused to undertake territorial responsibility in Bechuanaland. The British government now adopted a policy of informal control that depended on the successful survival of traditional Tswana government. Suddenly, missionary imperialism seemed to have collapsed. But the missionaries would not admit defeat. Instead, they pressed their campaign in Britain, bringing influence to bear on the "official mind" through the churches and allied pressure groups. However, the founding of the South Africa Committee in 1883 by Mackenzie and his supporters properly belonged to the era of the scramble and the new imperialism.[23]

The most northerly Tswana group, the Ngwato, was also the largest. Here Chief Khama achieved a quite different accommodation with the mission, making the London Missionary Society into nothing less than his own state church. Being located farther into the interior, remote from the Kimberley diamond fields, the Ngwato had some breathing space. They were, however, faced with difficult African neighbors in the militarized Ndebele monarchy to the northwest, who systematically conducted raids for tribute, and in 1866 reports of the discovery of gold in their area carried the danger of Boer and British incursions. Then in 1873-74 a large band of Afrikaners trekked through Ngwato territory en route to South-West Africa.[24]

Khama's very able father, Segoma I, pursued a policy of pragmatic modernization comparable to that of the southern Tswana chiefs. Indeed, he went further, allowing his sons to become Christians in the process of acquiring some western education from the missionaries. But he subsequently bitterly resented their refusal to assist at the initiation ceremonies for a new age-regiment in 1865. The rift between father and sons ultimately resulted in civil war, and Khama, who had acquired a considerable reputation as a warrior fighting against the Ndebele, succeeded in ousting his father in 1875.

Nearly forty years old when he usurped the chieftainship, Khama ruled the Ngwato for almost half a century. He was a convinced, indeed fervent, Christian, but the adoption of the new faith was a matter of state as well as religion. As a usurper he was vulnerable to censure from traditionalists, but he made the new religion the public faith. Even in 1872, before he had finally ousted his father, he had begun the practice of substituting Christian services for the old seedtime and harvest ceremonies. He succeeded in transforming the Christian services into essentially tribal rites, jointly organized by the chief and his missionary, attended by heathens as well as Christians, and often held in the *kgotla* rather than in the church. Moreover, Khama was almost always among those who led in prayer, and he sometimes conducted the Sunday service in church when his missionary was away. Similarly, the ceremonies for initiating a new age-set were Christianized by abolishing the practice of circumcision and traditional sex instruction. Khama also sought to control Christian teaching by enforcing a missionary monopoly. In 1879 he refused to admit the Jesuits because the London Missionary Society was already established, questioning the Catholic supplicants searchingly before rejecting them on the grounds that "if the two religions, the Catholic and Protestant, are the same, we clearly need only one of these two. If they are different, there will be constant conflict between them and they will cause division among my subjects."[25]

Khama's missionary policy was the most important facet of his general approach to European intrusion: he collaborated in order to control and limit its effects. Boer hunters were to be banned because they "destroyed the game in a most wasteful manner, [but] . . . Khama is happy on personal application to grant permission to any gentleman hunting for sport."[26] Likewise, rather than allow settlers to stop where they wished, he deliberately set aside limited areas of Ngwato territory for them. One of the main reasons for his desire to control contact between the Ngwato and the whites was his fear that his people's health would be undermined by European alcohol. Undoubtedly his fierce opposition to drinking contributed to his remarkable reputation among European missionaries. But Khama's fame stretched far beyond missionary circles. James Bryce, for example, regarded him as eminently statesmanlike.[27]

The Northern Rhodesian Copper Belt

The missionary churches were inextricably implicated in the conflicts and contradictions of the imperial experience. Some missionaries, like Mackenzie in Bechuanaland, courted involvement in order to breach the defenses of independent African societies. In Barotseland François Coillard of the Paris Evangelical Missionary Society played a crucial role in helping Frank Lochner, Cecil Rhodes's agent, to secure a protectorate treaty with the Lozi. Once the Lozi learned that their land and its subsoil had been seized by the British South Africa Company under the pretext of protection from Queen Victoria, they turned on Coillard "as a traitor, and members of his society suffered indignities and occasional physical harm as a result of their role in helping to secure the treaty."[28]

When colonial rule was firmly established, the dilemma was somewhat changed. Particularly when Africans were expropriated by white settlers and mining companies, missionaries found themselves simultaneously protecting their converts from the harsher forms of exploitation while at the same time, by their educational work, preparing them for it. In such societies, split along the seam of race but held tightly together by economic and political bonds, the church was challenged to adopt its medieval role of the only estate of the realm that could transcend sectional interests and speak out on behalf of the community as a whole. At the 1928 International Missionary Council in Jerusalem, R. H. Tawney, the Christian socialist and historian of the disruption of the communal basis of medieval European society under the impact of capitalism, and Harold Grimshaw, the director of the native labor section of the International Labor Office, called upon the international missionary movement to pay special attention to the economic and social transformation of hitherto unindustrialized areas of the world. In response, Joseph H. Oldham, the secretary of the International Missionary Council, proposed that its new department of social and industrial research "undertake a thorough field study of the effect of modern industry, and particularly that of the great copper mines of the Belgian Congo and Northern Rhodesia, upon African tribal society." A powerful commission of inquiry into conditions on the copper belt was established under the chairmanship of John Merle Davis, an American with experience in the international work of the Young Men's Christian Association and in race relations on the west coast of the United States. The commission published *Modern Industry and the African: An Enquiry into the Effect of the Copper*

Mines of Central Africa upon Native Society and the Work of the Christian Missions in 1933.[29]

Davis was immediately impressed by the failure of the existing institutions in the copper belt to act in terms of the professed religious and ethical ideals of Christian society. The mining companies seemed generally unconcerned, while the missions concentrated on rural areas and government "seemed out of touch with events it was expected to direct."[30] Confronted by such a vacuum of moral interest, Davis responded eagerly, "I have been profoundly impressed from the day I landed in South Africa with the tremendous responsibilities and opportunity of Christian missions in Southern Africa. I have experienced nothing to compare with it in any other part of the world. While in some parts of Asia missions have been wondering just what their job might be, in Africa they have placed in their hands the greater task of recreating the life of the race, of rebuilding the Black Man's world and adjusting him to his new surroundings. It is a staggering task, literally dumped upon missions by the government concerned. The leaders ... frankly say were it not for the missionary program of educational, industrial and religious work they would find themselves in an untenable position."[31]

The contributors to *Modern Industry and the African* formulated both a program for Christian action and, by the standards of the early 1930s, an essentially liberal program for the general development of the copper belt. In the mission field they suggested that the Protestant churches should combine their efforts in the interests of efficiency and in order to avoid the stimulation to African church separatism provided by missionary competition.[32] Furthermore, the churches should offer Africans greater scope for responsibility and leadership, especially those returning from the mines with a new self-confidence and sense of their own capacity.[33]

Austin Robinson, the economist in Davis's team, supplied an especially penetrating section of the report, dealing with the consequences of industrialization. Among his several specific recommendations were two – that the government should provide a coin smaller than the threepenny piece and that it should establish produce markets – which when implemented facilitated African participation in the cash economy.[34] In contrast, the sociologist Charles W. Coulter criticized Africans when they complained that the white management's response to the depression was both racially biased and commercially absurd. They persisted, despite his theoretical arguments, in believing that blacks were discharged and replaced by whites at higher wages.

"He ["the Native," in Coulter's parlance] seems oblivious to the fact that if the white community does not look after its unemployed it must support them, and the Native, despite the inconvenience, has a home and a tribal right to share the last pot of mealies with his kin."[35] The rationale behind the policy of low wages and early dismissal for migrant indigenous labor, and the converse for whites, as patented by the Nationalist-Labor government in contemporary South Africa, could hardly have been put more succinctly or self-confidently. Significantly, Coulter, a professor at Ohio Wesleyan University as well as a participant in a Chicago race relations survey, also had been a member of the South African Poor White Commission of 1930. In the settler societies of southern Africa the interests of white and black were so far apart that it was difficult for a representative of one race, even when placed in the relatively detached role of church layman and visiting academic, to do justice to the logic of the opposite side.

The commission report, *Modern Industry and the African*, despite Coulter's ethnocentrism, adequately spotlighted the problems of Africans on the copper belt, so that the administration, the church, and soon anthropologists as well paid it special attention. Leo Marquard, in the section on government, pointed out the lack of regular institutions by which urbanized Africans could draw attention to their grievances. The copper belt riots of 1935 underline his prescience but make it difficult to assess the precise effects of the book: "If Davis and his colleagues," writes Rotberg, "provided the intellectual framework within which sympathetic administrators could understand the riots, the disturbances themselves engendered the necessary sense of immediacy."[36]

Despite the solid research and the generally liberal trend of the analysis and policy proposals embodied in *Modern Industry and the African*, it failed to transcend the contradictions of the missionary situation within a settler society. Coulter established the social framework within which reform should take place, a copper belt sociology that accepted the logic of white capital and management's employment and wage policies toward Africans. In a racially divided society like Northern Rhodesia, accepting the white race's rationalizations meant dismissing the black race's perception of its interests as "childish."[37]

African Initiatives

Many Africans found that their religious needs were best met by new organizations operating outside the orthodox European missionary churches.[38]

African-led religious bodies did not react in a stereotyped manner to the pressures and opportunities provided by the European presence. The variety of response is illustrated by John Chilembwe's revolt in Nyasaland and the modernizing Muslim brotherhood, the Mourides, in Senegal.

John Chilembwe

John Chilembwe was born in Nyasaland in the 1860s, the son of a Yao father and a Chewa mother.[39] He was educated at a Church of Scotland mission and later was associated with the radical fundamentalist preacher, Joseph Booth, who, because of his strong support for African aspirations, was deported in turn from Tanganyika, South Africa, and East Africa. Booth and Chilembwe went to the United States, where Chilembwe attended a black Baptist seminary in Virginia. Here he learned about revolutionary American leaders such as John Brown, whose career was eloquently summarized in the message "strike a blow and die." In 1900 Chilembwe returned to Nyasaland and established his own Providence Industrial Mission with the support of black American Baptists. From his mission station he organized independent African schools while his followers grew cash crops. He attracted backing from some of the "new men," including Duncan Njilima, the most prosperous African businessman in the country, who owned an estate, three stores, and a timber business. Chilembwe himself organized a kind of chamber of commerce to facilitate further African enterprise.[40]

At first the British administration approved of the Providence Industrial Mission as a center for black self-help and modernization. But the period 1900-1914 was one of increasing distress for many Africans. The government tended to favor white planters and traders, while Africans worked on European estates under harsh conditions. The hut tax was increased in a period of famine in 1912, forcing massive labor migration as well as the burning of homes to avoid assessment. The Ngoni people lamented the increase in divorce caused by such disturbances.[41] Attendance at orthodox western churches dropped away as Africans sought relief from such distress in indigenous faiths or the millennial vision preached in the many semiindependent churches. In 1910 the passage of Halley's comet sent hundreds of villagers in a remote area fleeing into the bush to confess their sins and to prepare for the end of the world.[42]

The general distress was compounded in Chilembwe's case by personal misfortune. By 1914 he had known bereavement, debilitating asthma, heavy debt, and government surveillance with the likelihood of deportation. The outbreak of World War I, which was to drag Africans to their deaths in a European quarrel, prompted him to protest in public that Africans were "imposed upon more than any other nationality under the sun"; he hoped that "in the mercy of Almighty God . . . some day . . . Government will recognize our indispensability and that justice will prevail."[43] At the beginning of 1915 he launched his insurrection with a few hundred supporters. Three white men were killed, including William J. Livingstone, the manager of the European-owned estates that bordered the Providence Industrial Mission, whose head was cut off to adorn Chilembwe's church. The rebels obeyed Chilembwe's strict orders against looting and molesting white women. There was no attempt to win mass support, and on February 3 Chilembwe was killed. By the end of March forty rebels had been hung or shot by firing squads and about three hundred were in jail.

Despite its limited impact in terms of sheer numbers, Chilembwe's rising made a profound impact on both whites and blacks. On the day of Chilembwe's death Governor George Smith wrote that there was "a wide and well-organized movement to attack and massacre the whites"; and when he contributed to the five-volume official history, *The Empire at War*, in the mid-twenties, he still believed that "however ill conceived . . . the rising was full of potentiality."[44] Clements Kadalie, the Nyasaland leader of the Industrial and Commercial Workers Union (ICU), wrote home from South Africa in 1921, describing his pride in his fellow countryman: "It was a few days ago that I was relating his activities to my staff at the office and they were indeed inspired. Further particulars about him will be much appreciated as I would like to obtain this information for [the] future history of Africa as I believe that white men will not preserve the genuine history of the black men."[45]

Despite the preoccupation of Malawian historiography (some of it of very high quality) with Chilembwe, his real nature remains curiously elusive, especially during the period of the rising. For some, like Kadalie, he was an "African patriot," to be viewed in the perspective of African protonationalism; for others, his actions and his ideology derived directly from the revolutionary chiliasm of his contemporaries. To George Simeon Mwase, writing in 1931-32, Chilembwe, like John Brown, aimed at a sacrificial demonstration, calling on his followers to "strike a first and last blow, and then all die by the heavy storm of the white men's army," forcing the white men to recognize that colonial rule was morally untenable.[46]

Historians have recently contrasted the small scale of Chilembwe's rising with the Maji-Maji rebellion in the German colony of Tanganyika, where traditional religion supplied a unifying ideology.[47] The adherence of Africans to competing missions fragmented Chilembwe's potential Christian support; in particular, none of the Catholics seemed to have joined the rising, which indeed took a strikingly anti-Catholic direction. Nor could a specifically Christian revolt, based on the more militant passages in the Bible, rally Muslims, although it is known that the Yao Muslims — and Chilembwe was half Yao and was interested in Islam — had many grievances and also thought in millennial terms.[48]

The Mourides

In the immediate aftermath of the defeat and death of the Wolof leader, Lat-Dior, at the hands of the French in Senegal in 1886, a distinctive Muslim brotherhood developed. The leader of the Mourides, Ahmadou Bamba, was born in 1850. He provided a simple, comprehensive, and flexible interpretation of Islam, which facilitated its synthesis with traditional Wolof society and culture. The two most distinct characteristics of the brotherhood were the importance Bamba attached to the submission of the disciples to a *shaikh* and the emphasis he placed on work rather than on study and prayer. The Mourides developed a widespread organization — which today numbers half a million people — in which individual disciples participated through their physical and spiritual submission to those superior to them in the religious hierarchy. Each follower pledged himself to his *shaikh* with the words "I submit to you my body and my soul" and demonstrated this allegiance by carrying out the founder's directive to "go and work" on behalf of his *shaikh*.[49]

The French were at first very apprehensive that Bamba would mount a holy war against them and exiled him to Gabon. But between 1902 and 1912 they gradually reversed their policy, concluding that they could utilize the brotherhood as an apparatus for indirect rule. Bamba returned from his second exile in Mauritania in 1907. In the same year his disciples began to expand their settlements for peanut cultivation along the Thiès-Kayes railroad.[50] Hitherto uncultivated lands had acquired new value with the development of the peanut cash crop, but these were difficult to settle by individual landless Wolofs, not least because of the presence of tough Fulani pastoralists. The corporate discipline of the Mourides aided them both in the expulsion of the Fulani and the difficult work of colonizing new land. After about eight years of agricultural labor for his *shaikh*, a disciple was usually granted a farm of his own.

The Bay Fall branch of the Mourides represented the extreme adaptation of Islam to traditional Wolof society. It was founded by *Shaikh* Ibra Fall, one of Bamba's first and most celebrated disciples as well as a brillant propagandist in his own right. The Bay Fall believed that the acts of submission and hard labor were substitutes for the traditional obligations of Islam. They did not pray, study, or keep the fast of Ramadan. Recruited mainly from the slave-warrior class of the old Wolof kingdoms, the *Tyéddo*, the Bay Fall preserved the dress and style of those warriors, including their inclination to heavy drinking. Through their feats of physical strength and endurance and their rather showy presence as bodyguards of the *shaikhs*, the Bay Fall maintained an acceptable equivalent of their traditional role in Wolof society in the modern world of capitalist agriculture and Islam.[51]

The leadership of the Mourides was hereditary, following normal Sufi practice. Hence the charisma (baraka) inevitably became routinized, as recognized in the Mourides' proverb, "The child of a saint is a king." The leaders were expected to spend lavishly in a conspicuous display of their wealth and generosity. They "must have large cars, expensive clothes and the best French perfume — the odor of sanctity in the Mouride leaders' compound very often comes with a whiff of Lanvin or Chanel No. 5."[52] This ostentation set limits on their capitalist investment; on the other hand, the development of electoral politics in the postwar era of decolonization and independence gave the leaders great power as the controllers of a huge, highly disciplined patronage machine. And in this epoch of state capitalism, political — rather than strictly entrepreneurial — capacity has constituted the appropriate talent for getting rich.[53]

CHAPTER 13

Theory and Practice of
Colonial Education

Europeans charged with the drafting of educational policy for Africa in the colonial period commonly claimed that traditional African cultures were disqualified, in one way or another, from functioning as proper bases for progress. Lord Lugard observed that whereas "Islam carries with it its own religious sanctions . . . the Animism and Fetish of the pagan represents no system of ethics, and no principles of conduct."[1] Even A. Victor Murray, one of the most liberal-minded of the interwar educationists, made a similar assertion: "A fact of primary importance in African education is that outside Egypt there is nowhere any indigenous history. . . . This . . . has had two effects. It has prevented the growth of a self-conscious culture, and it has lowered the status of the African in the eyes of the outside world."[2]

From such a viewpoint, education meant "schooling," the subculture of the schoolhouse within the total colonial situation. At a time when African aspirations to a liberal education were being blocked by development of "Bantu" education in South Africa and the diffusion of Booker T. Washington's Tuskegee philosophy with its emphasis on manual training to the rest of British Africa by the Phelps-Stokes commissions, Murray was eloquent on this score. He noted that although "there is no 'African culture,'—as yet[—t]here is this universal heritage waiting to be taken up by them." Unfortunately, he continued, the image of European civilization presented "in the person of the trader, the labour recruiter, the Government demand for taxes, missionaries of every sort of view, and administrators of every sort of policy" confused the African. Thus Murray arrived at "the real function of the school . . .

[and] the rationale of African education. . . . [It] should present this alien civilization *as it really is.*"[3]

An alternative tradition, deriving on the Anglophone side from Mary Kingsley and Edward Blyden and on the French side from Maurice Delafosse, was founded on the belief that African culture should not be excluded from the schools' curricula. In Sierra Leone in 1906 the Bo School for the sons of chiefs was opened, with a prospectus stressing that "special care will be taken to strengthen the tribal patriotism natural to the pupils. . . . Especially, the boys will be taught to honour and respect their parents, or the aged, and those in authority in the towns of their country; that Book knowledge is not the same thing as Wisdom; and that many who possess the former are sadly lacking in the latter."[4] The Advisory Committee on Native Education in the British Tropical African Dependencies worded its proposal in 1925 somewhat less pithily: "Education should be adapted to the mentality, aptitudes, occupations and traditions of the various peoples, conserving as far as possible all sound and healthy elements in the fabric of their social life; adapting them where necessary to changed circumstances and progressive ideas, as an agent of natural growth and evolution."[5]

To Africans, any deviation from the European pattern was suspect. The Reverend Metcalfe Sunter, who had resigned as the principal of Fourah Bay College to become the first inspector to the Sierra Leone Board of Education in 1882, was regularly criticized for displaying prejudice against everything African. But when he asked questions about ancient African civilizations or about the impact of Islam, he was accused of being "unreasonable" by an indignant correspondent in the *Methodist Herald*, who demanded to know what such matters had to do with English history.[6] The Reverend Samuel Spain, addressing the Grammar and High School, complained he had heard too much about "Afric's Universal sway"; instead of such talk and dreams, let the students get down to serious work. He believed the proposal to establish science scholarships at Fourah Bay was a move in the right direction, because science had made England great.[7] But the cultural nationalism advocated by Blyden was winning support. At the same time as Spain, then the senior tutor at the high school, advocated the English ideal, the senior resident master, who had just completed his bachelor's degree at London University, announced that he had changed his name from W. J. Davis to Orishatukeh Faduma.[8]

The history of education takes us directly to issues of cultural domination and the life-chances of individual Africans under colonial rule—issues that are at the center of the imperial experience. Early twentieth-century educationists responded eagerly to this challenge and were much given to statements about what African education should accomplish. The historian has to be on guard against taking such policy statements and normative opinions as descriptions of what actually happened. Government reports generally function at some remove from schoolhouse realities. Nevertheless, such writers as Foster on the Gold Coast, Abernethy and Koehl on Nigeria, Clignet on Francophone Africa, and Yates on the Congo Free State have succeeded in producing a social history of education in Africa rather than simply describing the development of educational administration.[9] By shifting attention to the responses and initiatives of the colonized Africans, these writers have given us a much more realistic picture.

Several milieus, which did not always overlap, constituted the total educational culture in colonial Africa. Education was generally identified with literacy and schooling in the European manner, but it must be remembered that Africans had trained their children through the centuries in other ways. Often the child received instruction by watching a parent and then helping to perform a task until proficiency in it was acquired. At other times, the child listened to the elders telling stories that expounded the workings of the universe and the values by which people lived. But traditional education was not restricted to such informal techniques. Ironworkers and ivory carvers learned their crafts through apprenticeship systems. Initiation rites involved education in conduct, morals, military arts, and ways of getting a living as well as in the traditions and myths of the people. These educational institutions existed in most parts of the continent and have attracted the attention of anthropologists. Thus in southern Africa the Venda had what amounted to a puberty school, and in Sierra Leone and Liberia the Poro and Sande secret societies had complicated and sophisticated modes of initiation into adult life.[10] Another educational milieu was that of Islam. Just as much as Christians, African Muslims were people of "the book," the Koran, which all pious Muslims aspired to read in Arabic. Islamic institutions did not necessarily drive out older forms of education, however; the Nupe of Nigeria, for example, had both Koran schools and age-grade associations.[11]

Neither the societies of traditional Africa nor Muslim Africa were detached from history in a static past, however much this might seem so to western observers. Because culture is dynamic, incorporating and rejecting tools and values, developing and digesting alien items, "that part of a people's culture

which enables them to prepare their children to live on when the older generation is gone is no less likely to be dynamic and self-modifying."[12] Within
many precolonial African societies there was scope for the innovator, particularly the mediator between two or more cultures. Chief Bosun, the founder of
the Bosun Confederacy in what is now Liberia, is a good example. As a Mandinka immigrant who had worked on European ships, he brought knowledge
of both Islamic and western cultures to the Gola peoples.[13] Such mediators
between the people and the outside world might be a king or a prince in one
society, a loyal slave in another, and perhaps most frequently, traders. Certainly there was a battery of roles within traditional Muslim and African
societies that could interpret the European impact. The educated Africans
who were deplored by so many officials because they sought to manipulate
the colonial situation in order to acquire high status as go-betweens were not
acting in unprecedented ways.

The colonizers also belonged to several partly intersecting milieus: missions, colonial officialdom, the semiscientific educational and other behavioral
disciplines of nineteenth- and twentieth-century Europe and America, and,
lastly, the specific colonial educational environment, such as the Bo School in
Sierra Leone and the Malangali School in Tanganyika. It was never simply
that Europeans acted as donors and Africans as recipients. In using the new
educational systems, Africans transformed them by exercising selective preferences. And in their role as mediators, the Africans enlightened their more
receptive European teachers with a stream of insights into the meaning of
their cultural heritage and the total colonial situation.

The French

French educational policy generated one of the most powerful colonial
myths: the notion that African schoolchildren were instructed that "en
autre fois notre pays s'appellait la Gaule" ("in olden times, our country
was called Gaul"), just like their contemporaries in Brittany and Toulouse.
For Anglo-Saxons and Anglophone Africans, this epitomized what they
took to be the distinctive French goal for remodeling Africa in the metropolitan image. Despite recurrent efforts, now spanning forty-odd years,
to pin down specific classroom situations in which this cameo of acculturation allegedly occurred, it defies localization. Free-floating, it eludes
routine historical criticism. Ultimately, because it continues to shape consciousness, it must be measured in its own terms, as myth: an imaginative

evocation, symbolizing crucial aspects of the Francophone experience.[14]

The search for the substance of education under the French has to begin with a chronology derived from France's general imperial aims, and the apparatus available to implement them, because these modified any specifically educational ideas. Briefly, there were three phases in French involvement, beginning with nineteenth-century protocolonialism. During the first stage, imperial influence was confined largely to trading posts on the coast, missions, and (in West Africa especially) an increasingly vigorous military presence. This stage was followed by a watershed decade, bounded by the Berlin Conference in 1884-85 and the establishment of the Ministry of Colonies in 1894, which inaugurated the phase of formal colonialism when distinct administrative and educational structures were set up. This period of consolidation of colonial rule lasted until 1945, when the formal apparatus of government began to be modified in ways that led to political independence by 1960 (although this outcome was not apparent to Frenchmen at the beginning of the process). In analyzing French colonial education these three phases — protocolonialism, formal colonialism, and decolonization — must be kept chronologically distinct.[15]

At the outset the French developed strongly assimilationist ideas grounded in the logic of the situation of informal empire. Precisely because the imperial presence was minimal, it was hoped that the psychological programming of individual Africans for absolute cooperation would be perfect. In this early phase assimilation was conceived by the French as a relatively passive process. Confident of the triple allure of commerce, Catholicism, and the French language — which was believed to encapsulate all that was best in western civilization — the French expected that enough recruits would attach themselves to the missions, commercial establishments, and government agencies to fill their needs for "Black Frenchmen."

As aggressive imperial rivalry developed, cultural chauvinist groups within France rallied behind the cause of colonial education. In 1868 the Alliance Française was founded by government officials and members of colonial and missionary societies to create support for overseas education. During the quickening military and economic expansion of the late 1880s and 1890s the Alliance kept pace with a specific program of cultural imperialism and in the western Sudan began to supply annual subventions to schools. Such private intervention was very welcome to colonial regimes beset by official parsimony. Soon the Alliance and the Catholic societies were providing the bulk of education funds with the government only stepping in with occasional subsidies in cases of urgent need.[16]

For all the enthusiastic employment of the term by French officials, it is misleading to think of anything so formal as a policy of assimilation in these years. Lacking an organized body of teachers to command or a supervisory staff to enforce standards, and devoid of even a regular budget for education, the French authorities perforce relied on the voluntary bodies and much high-flown talk about assimilation as a surrogate for a properly articulated government educational policy.

With the establishment of the Ministry of Colonies in 1894 France acquired the machinery to formulate and carry through such a policy. By now the need was urgent. Huge areas of Africa recently had been conquered, and France required African officials in the lower echelons of the new imperial apparatus. One mode of expansion would have been to encourage the voluntary organizations to increase their work, relying on inspection and subvention to control standards. But this was ruled out by the sharp break between church and state in metropolitan France. The anticlericals within the First Republic succeeded in the 1880s in establishing lay primary schools in spite of Roman Catholic opposition. But even the doctrinaire anticlericals like Jules Ferry applied a dual standard to Asia and Africa, proclaiming that "anticlericalism was not for export" and encouraging the church to keep its schools in the colonies. The Dreyfus affair, in which the church was implicated in the mistrial of a Jewish army officer for allegedly spying for Germany, ended colonial cooperation when the French parliament on January 22, 1903, passed a resolution calling for the secularization of church schools in West Africa.

In two ordinances of November 24, 1903, Governor Ernest-Nestor Roume formulated the basis of French policy for the colonial period. All instruction was to be in French. This, on the face of it, was pure assimilationism. But there was a pragmatic element as well. Finding no single dominant language throughout their territories, the French turned to their own language to facilitate communication.[17] The new schooling was to be completely free and secular. It was also to be geared to the need for administrative personnel. The students from the écoles de villages would serve the local administrators as interpreters, those from the écoles regionales could act as subordinate clerks in each territory, and those who went on to the federal schools in Dakar could serve as teachers or as commis d'administration available for service throughout the federation.[18] These educational ordinances were to be implemented in line with the new vogue for "association."[19] Education would sustain rather than undermine native society as the Africans by a slow, controlled process acquired skills permitting a gradual improvement in their traditional patterns of living, as the French saw it.

In September 1912 Georges Hardy, an academician by temperament and training, was appointed inspector general of education for West Africa. He brought to his task a passionate desire for system, vigorous administration, and a coherent view of empire.[20] A prolific, lucid writer, he set forth his ideas with power and precision. After half a century his brief *Vue générale de l'histoire d'Afrique* of 1922 still exhilarates the reader, despite its dated, racist assumptions, by its bold imaginative sweep. A crisis in the colonial system, owing to the shortage of French officials after the outbreak of World War I, gave Hardy the chance to press for a rapid increase in the supply of trained African personnel from the schools in Dakar. He linked increased enrollment to a much more systematic stress on practicality and adaptation, seeking to imbue his corps of teachers with his own pedagogical principles and techniques through a journal, *Le Bulletin de l'enseignement de l'Afrique Occidentale*, and a stream of textbooks and teachers' manuals.

Hardy was forced to sharpen and refine his thoughts on educational imperialism because of the opposition of many of his fellow administrators who believed that the schools would become seedbeds of African rebellion. In 1917, in the depths of the war, he published his patriotic testament, *Une Conquête morale: L'Enseignement en Afrique Occidentale Française*, a 356-page refutation of such views. In his opinion colonial education must be precisely that, a moral conquest, designed to complete the process of physical conquest by capturing the minds of France's African subjects.

To be effective, teaching had to be carefully adapted to the colonial context, he held. Africans would not study the geography of France as such but rather the development of French power viewed from a geographical standpoint. Geopolitical imperial geography would be matched by a similar approach to history. There would be no more parroting "our ancestors the Gauls" or learning long lists of French government officials. Instead, history would be the history of French power with specific reference to West Africa. Moreover, the colonial school would attack "the tendentious, often-anti-French history purveyed by the Marabouts [Muslim holy men] and above all by the griots [the traditional oral historians of Senegal]." Such history would be vivid since the children would be learning more about figures they already had been taught to hate or venerate. To Hardy, the committed, culture-bound

French imperialist, a clear theme ran through recent African history: the liberation of the mass of the people from the oppressive native slave dealers and booty hunters exemplified by Samori: "The grandfathers of all these children have either made history or been its victims . . . a fresh victory will be won when the generosity that marks French imperial history has been understood."[21]

Hardy's stress on curricular adaptation reinforced an informal binary system of education. The urban schools for Europeans and a small elite of mulattoes and blacks were very different from what was offered to the majority of Africans. Although racial criteria for selection were not formally admitted, it became increasingly obvious that Europeans were automatically put in the urban schools whereas Africans were pushed toward "adapted" rural education. The African political elite of the four communes strongly opposed this trend, denouncing Hardy for sabotaging their schools. Eventually the administration brought him home for "convalescent leave," after which he was appointed director of education for Morocco, where he served from 1919 to 1926, and then was given the key post of director of the Ecole Coloniale in Paris.

Hardy's policies, designed for the inhabitants of the extensive new territories occupied by France at the end of the nineteenth century, ran counter to the quite different expectations of the Africans in a prepartition colony like Senegal. The limited constitutionalism of such prepartition colonies gave the Senegalese scope to mobilize formidable resistance. There was an inherent contradiction in the policy of adaptation that failed to take account of such important local realities. Systemized adaptation, given French centralization and uniformity, became a contradiction in terms.[22]

By a further irony, Hardy, the apostle of accommodation, contributed to the legend that French policy continued to advocate assimilation during the high noon of empire. During World War I Frenchmen were afraid that African Muslims would rally to the side of the Ottoman Turks. Hardy sought to prevent this by writing songs that would solidify allegiance to the French. But the songs, when read out of their historic context, have been taken to mean that the French sought to turn Africans into Frenchmen:

> . . . O France,
> Des maintenant [bis] tu peux compter sur nous,
> Enfants du Dahomey, de la brousse ou des villes.
> Souvenons-nous toujours que nous sommes Français.
> Quel que soit l'avenir, confiants et tranquilles.
> Nous resterons Français, toujours Français.

O France,
From now on you can count on us,
Children of Dahomey, from the bush or from the towns.
Let us always remember that we are French.
Thus our future will be confident and peaceful.
We will always remain French, always French.

From Hardy's limited perspective, the key phrase was "you can count on us," not "we are French."[23]

One last point about the gap between policy and reality should be made. By the 1930s, despite Hardy's best efforts and his successors' attempts to continue his programs, it was clear that actual pedagogic practice was increasingly based on the metropolitan model. Hence in 1931 there was a fresh burst of reform aiming at systemized adaptation or "readaptation."[24] Formal policy consistently pressed the teacher to diverge from metropolitan practice. But in any given situation subconscious models supervened so that French teachers fell back on metropolitan practices "through sheer economy of effort and conditions of uncertainty."[25]

The Belgians

State, church, and industry combined to set their stamp, at once paternalistic and utilitarian, on the educational policy of Belgium.[26] King Leopold II had strongly favored Roman Catholic missions as educational agencies, once he had arranged with the Vatican for the missions to be staffed by Belgian rather than by French or Portuguese. His convention with the Vatican of May 1906 granted each Catholic mission station from 100 to 200 hectares (about 250 to 500 acres) of land for an indefinite length of time. In return the mission was to establish a school that would submit its syllabus to the governor-general for approval.[27] The arrangement recommended itself to Belgium on grounds of economy when Belgium annexed the Congo in 1908. But the prime reason advanced for extensive reliance on the Catholic church was that only by such means could education be guaranteed to have a positive moral purpose as stressed in Belgium's educational reform after the war. It was decided in 1925 that the government should aid and develop what were called "national" mission schools. (In practice, all such schools were Catholic.) The schools should be of three types: first-grade schools, which would give instruction for at least two years; second-grade schools, established chiefly in industrialized areas, which would provide instruction for three years, and special schools, which would train clerks, teachers, and artisans over a period of three years. But in each type of school moral education was placed at the head of the curriculum, for it was believed that in Africa the schools must inculcate character traits that in Europe were taught at home: "In Belgium the primary function of the school is to instruct. In the Congo, its purpose must be essentially to educate."[28]

By the time of the Congo's independence Belgium had achieved the highest literacy rate in sub-Saharan Africa, yet little in the way of secondary education. This was strictly in line with Belgium's threefold paternalism: the Catholic notion of society as hierarchical with rulers charged to provide the conditions for a "good life" for their subjects, the big industrial corporations' concept of welfare as a means to good labor relations and high productivity, and the colonial rulers' viewpoint that it was right to concentrate on increasing the material prosperity of the African masses and to educate them to play useful, though subordinate, roles in modern society before creating a secondary school and university elite and granting political rights. As in virtually all colonial education, there was no role for the educated woman. Girls' education was strictly limited to the primary level and was meant to inculcate obedience.

Nearly all missionary teachers shared the cultural arrogance of the West and so made no attempt to teach Christianity in a positive relationship to African traditional religion or to render the culture of Europe meaningful in terms of African culture. Africans accepted that education should be utilitarian, for they saw it as a means to acquire technical expertise. Education became a matter of skills to be learned rather than culture to be imbibed.[29]

The British

In the British colonies education traditionally was left to Christian missionaries, except for very special cases such as Northern Nigeria, where the policy of indirect rule involved working with the emirs. Thus colonial educational institutions duplicated the pattern of Anglican, Dissenting, and Roman Catholic schools that prevailed in mid-nineteenth-century Britain. The missionaries naturally saw the schools principally as powerful engines of evangelization, and therefore they concentrated on rapid, and often highly competitive, expansion with little regard to the vocational opportunities available to their graduates in later life.[30] The proliferation of schools through uncontrolled expansion was not, however, haphazard; it followed the pattern of African demand. The mission schools also had to adjust the nonreligious part of their training to the wishes of their pupils and their parents. Originally they usually emphasized training in farming and elementary technical skills, but eventually they were to gain a reputation for "bookish" curricula in response to pressure from the Africans for a more literary education. Literacy paid more than artisanship, so Africans preferred to become clerks rather than carpenters. The Basel Mission schools in the Gold Coast frequently were favorably contrasted by British officials there with the Church Missionary Society and Wesleyan schools on the grounds that the former offered vocational training directly relevant to the colony's manpower needs. But the carpenters and masons from the Basel Mission learned that they could receive higher wages as clerks.[31]

In the period between the two world wars the governments of the various British colonies sought to supervise educational development through grants-in-aid given on a per capita basis. Nevertheless, any group could and still did open schools, although the government would not offer grants unless the schools met minimal standards. The consequence was a more rapid proliferation of schools than in the French territories, where output was carefully related to vocational opportunity.

When the British adopted indirect rule as the preferred mode of local administration, there seemed some danger to their authority in privately run schools.[32] The government tried to overcome this not by clamping controls on missionary expansion — again excepting the special but of course very important case of Northern Nigeria — but by concentrating their effort on traditional elites, "the sons of chiefs," and by stressing "adapted" education that would blend elements from indigenous culture with relevant western educational procedures. Sierra Leone was the laboratory where assimilationist theory had been tested earlier. The Creoles who were the products of the experiment, however, came to irritate British officials by their very success in imitating the British way of life. They were made the scapegoats for the 1898 rising in the protectorate. Adapted education was designed to prevent the protectorate peoples from modeling themselves on the Creoles. They were to be kept apart and "unspoiled."

The British, therefore, relied heavily on ruling the Sierra Leone protectorate through traditional authorities. In educational policy this led in 1906 to the creation of the Bo School for chief's sons and nominees, who had hitherto risked being "creolized" if sent to Freetown schools. At Bo, as Christopher Fyfe has commented, "the doctrines of Blyden, Burton and Rousseau united uneasily to inculcate the dignity of labour"[33] in the shape of agricultural training, which was stressed as much for character building as to increase farm productivity. In order to counter detribalization "Mendi pupils will be taught in such a way as to make them prefer Mendi land to any other country, so with Temenes and all the various tribes represented in the school." Indeed, the obvious escape route for an ambitious youth, entry into government service, was closed to Bo schoolboys in order to force them to return to their home villages. The chiefs had no liking for this ban, or so the district commissioners thought, and when the number of boys sponsored by them began to drop, the government in 1916 agreed to rescind it.[34]

World War I shook European self-assurance. Greater sympathy toward African beliefs and practices was strengthened by the development of the social sciences, especially anthropology. Tanganyika, as a League of Nations mandate, inevitably had to be treated as a showpiece of enlightened British imperial administration. The arrival of Sir Donald Cameron in 1925 signaled an attempt to embody such cultural relativism within the framework of indirect rule.

Malangali School, founded in 1927 in the Southern Highlands Province, epitomized this approach in the educational field. W. Bryant Mumford, the headmaster from 1928 to 1931, set the stamp of his cultural relativist ideas upon the development of the school.[35] Mumford earlier had experimented with secular moral education through the Boy Scout movement when he was in charge of the Bukoba government school, but he had decided that scouting was too remote from African traditions. Although Malangali had sections devoted to both the academic English-language training practiced in the existing mission schools and to industrial or craft training, Mumford focused attention on the third section, which was characterized as a tribal school to educate boys from the aristocracy for their positions as chiefs, utilizing traditional forms of instruction. Mumford advertised his school as equivalent to the traditional *wigendo* institutions by which youths were sent for craft training to the dwelling of some "big man," whose elders would then indoctrinate them in the customs, virtues, and folklore of their people. To reconstruct the *wigendo* system, Mumford recruited old men to be the moral mentors of his students. The curriculum included spear throwing, tribal dancing, and tribal lore. The students wore the traditional togalike dress, and their dormitories were constructed in quadrangles resembling local housing.

Once this experimental school was set up, Mumford took leave to write a thesis for the University of Toronto and to publicize his anthropological approach to education in articles and lectures. He returned to find morale at the school sapped by a barrage of criticism, directed especially at the school's cultural conservatism. Nevertheless, he managed to rally the support of the director of education, Stanley Rivers-Smith, and began a second round of cultural experimentation late in 1930 by requesting that anthropologists be attached to the school to investigate the feasibility of linking moral education with initiation ceremonies.

Malangali had already aroused strong missionary opposition on the grounds that the elders, in their capacity as moral tutors, were instructing the pupils in non-Christian beliefs. Now Mumford's rather abstract theism, stressing that "we are all aware of the Supreme Being and of the Spirits of those who have passed on," raised objections from even the comparatively tolerant Moravian leader, Oskar Gemuseus.[36] There were other causes for missionary hostility. The political motive for founding Malangali, as distinct from the cultural theory of indirect rule, was anxiety because so many missionaries responsible for education in the area were not British. Moreover, the mission schools were assisted by government grants, so that they were competing against Malangali for scarce funds during the depression.

Mumford, with a reputation based on Malangali and his writing, eventually left Tanganyika for the influential post of head of the colonial department at the London University Institute of Education. Soon after his departure from Malangali his traditionalist innovations were watered down, and Malangali began to offer a much more orthodox English curriculum. Ironically, Gemuseus had to watch his own Rungwe School, a hundred miles to the west, being converted into a vernacular teacher training center as a result of pressure from new German missionaries who were intent on retarding westernization because they considered a tribal and racially separatist approach proper for emissaries of the Third Reich. The Moravians' African teaching staff faced a reduction of pay once the English branch of the school was closed. In 1936, therefore, the African teachers and pupils, protesting this restriction in the scope of their opportunities, departed for the reformed Malangali.[37]

The checkered histories of the Malangali and Rungwe schools, together with the effects of local calculations of vocational advantage in the Gold Coast and Sierra Leone, indicated that African aspirations, as well as imperial policies, shaped the pattern of education in the colonial period. Raum has pointed out that "the difficulties experienced by early missionaries in attracting buyers for their educational wares is shown in the desperate attempts made by them to induce children to attend. Bribes in the form of food, clothes, even money payments, were common; chiefs had to be persuaded to accept education for children."[38] Later, when the colonial regime was better established and more mission schools were available, Africans could at least shape curricula by their choice of school. Traditional kinship patterns may also have influenced the development of education. Remi Clignet, when comparing the patrilineal Bété with the matrilineal Abouré in the Ivory Coast, discovered that Bété parents placed much more significance on the academic success of their children than did the Abouré, despite the much greater contact of the Abouré with Europeans. He suggests that the Abouré could not respond so positively as the Bété because of tensions between paternal and avuncular authority within a matrilineal system.[39]

CHAPTER 14

The Shaping of South African Civilization

The frontier of white settlement had already penetrated far into the interior of southern Africa when European colonization elsewhere amounted to little more than a series of trading and governmental outposts strung along the coast. Even during the scramble, when European states developed a novel appetite for land all over the continent, the force and scope of the imperial impact was immeasurably greater in the south. For now, to the shock waves of white settlers intent on carving out their own six-thousand-acre farms in the African hinterland were added the consequences of South Africa's own mineral revolution, drawing workers from hundreds of miles away to labor at Kimberley and on the Rand. The profits generated by the continent's first industrial revolution created new and powerful African-based imperialisms, epitomized in their very different ways by Cecil Rhodes and President Paul Kruger of the Transvaal. Although the full program of South African political expansion was to be frustrated—in that after unification in 1910 only South-West Africa, in the guise of a League of Nations mandate, was formally brought under political control—South Africa's high level of previous industrialization meant that all the surrounding territories were cast in the role of economic satellites, even if they were as far distant as Nyasaland or, like Mozambique, were under a different European flag.[1]

The Rand

The mineral revolution transformed southern Africa in the last quarter of the nineteenth century. Kimberley diamonds were supplemented by the discovery in 1886 of the major gold-bearing reef, the Witwatersrand, within the frontiers of the Afrikaner republic of the Transvaal. Although the technology of the Afrikaner farmers was quite unable to develop the goldfields, the Transvaal government could drain off some of the profits of the mining industry that quickly developed on the Rand. The Transvaal, which hitherto had been virtually bankrupt, now threatened to become the major political force in southern Africa, potentially able to dominate both the African majority and the British settler minority alike.

The mining compounds in which the African workers were imprisoned for the period of their contract were first introduced at Kimberley with a view to preventing diamond thefts. But it was soon obvious that such labor barracks had further advantages for the mineowners.[2] African workers confined to such compounds were not free to spend their pay on cheap, potent liquor, through which they had often lost two working days per week in the times when they lived in the slums and shanties around Kimberley. This was doubtless one reason why Colored and western-educated African politicians supported the compound system. It was "as near perfection as it was possible to make it," declared John Tengo Jabavu, the editor of *Imvo* and the most influential African in Cape politics, when he visited Kimberley in 1906 to collect money to establish the South African Native College at Fort Hare.[3] But miners who lived in shantytowns acquired the urban sharpness and sophistication that Trollope had seen developing in Kimberley before it had any compounds.[4] Furthermore, long hours of dangerous toil in an unpleasant work place naturally led workers to break their contracts by seeking alternative employment or returning home, unless confined within labor barracks.

The mining compounds therefore preserved a system of migrant labor. African miners, especially those drawn from outside the boundaries of the Transvaal and, later, the Union of South Africa, shifted repeatedly throughout their careers between family life in their rural homelands and such all-male mining compounds. This repeated migration prevented the development of class and national consciousness because the workers tended to regard their period of service in the labor barracks as only a raid on the white man's economy to secure cash for taxes, the bride-price, a gun, a bicycle, or simply the wherewithal for survival before returning home. From the employer's standpoint the system was considerably more profitable than slavery because it gave control over the worker in these compound-jails without buying and being responsible for him for life. The rural homeland was expected to support the worker's family; hence he need not be paid a wage sufficient to reproduce the working force. Moreover, the homelands were expected to serve as a kind of welfare state when a worker became sick, disabled, or aged.[5]

But the more the mines drew off the most productive rural labor, men in the prime of life, the more the homeland fields became neglected. Under the traditional division of labor by sex and age, much of the heavy work needed to keep the land productive had been done by precisely those men now recruited to the mines.[6] Year by year the homelands could support only a decreasing population, or the same population but at a lower level. Much of the history of South African labor relations is explained by the conquering group, the whites, launching ventures in capitalist agriculture, mining, and manufacturing with a labor force only recently conquered and expropriated. In 1913 Africans, who formed almost three-quarters of the population, possessed only 7 percent of the land in South Africa and that, scarcely ever the best, was rapidly deteriorating through erosion.

To the "desperate self-interest of the severely deprived"[7] living within the bounds of South Africa was added the reserve army of labor from less developed territories beyond them. The badly neglected British High Commission Territories—Basutoland, Bechuanaland, and Swaziland, especially Basutoland, whose men had earlier acquired notable skill and experience as miners—served South African employers well in this respect. So also did Mozambique, whose Portuguese rulers had drawn up their first formal agreement with the Transvaal government in 1897 to provide workers for the gold mines, although the Thonga peoples in the southern part of the colony had been migrating to work in South Africa since the 1860s.[8]

Partition and Unification

The British government left the occupation of central Africa largely to Cecil Rhodes and his British South Africa Company, incorporated by royal charter in 1889. In 1888 Rhodes had obtained a monopoly of all minerals in the Ndebele kingdom of Lobengula in exchange for a thousand rifles, a hundred thousand rounds of ammunition, an annual pension of £1,200, and a steamboat to be used on the Zambezi River. Unfortunately for Rhodes, the second Rand he had hoped for in this area, which was later to bear his name, was not to materialize. Rhodes's Pioneer Column, consisting of 380 white men plus their African and Colored servants, had originally skirted Lobengula's kingdom to occupy Mashonaland, but once their hopes of a mineral bonanza in Mashonaland were thwarted, they invaded the Ndebele kingdom. Perhaps, they hoped, they would strike mineral riches there; anyway that area seemed a better prospect for white ranch-style farming. Lobengula died shortly after his army was defeated in 1893. The seizure of their land and cattle and the general maltreatment by European settlers led the Ndebele and the Mashona to make common cause, guided by Shona spirit mediums, in a desperate attempt to drive the whites out in 1896, but machine guns finally shattered the African resistance.[9]

The failure to find a second Rand in Rhodesia and the military hubris induced by machine gunning down Ndebele warriors tempted Rhodes and his confederates into the adventure of the Jameson Raid in 1895 against the Transvaal republic. The Transvaal—also known as the South African Republic, indicating its own ambitions to political hegemony in the area—exasperated some of the whites who flocked to the goldfields by refusing them political rights because the conservative Afrikaners feared they would be swamped by an influx of cosmopolitan, loose-living Uitlanders (British, American, and other immigrants). Owners of deep-level mines, who were faced with heavy expenses, also seemed to have found that the Transvaal government could not supply the framework of industrial law and order that they deemed necessary for efficient labor coercion and thus the protection of their profits.[10] With the mineowners' powerful backing and with hopes for support from the Uitlanders, Leander Starr Jameson, Rhodes's principal lieutenant, invaded the Transvaal at the end of 1895. But he had planned badly and was forced to surrender on the fifth day of his invasion, January 2, 1896, when his troops were surrounded by Afrikaner commandos.[11]

The raid ended Rhodes's political career, but those within British government circles who had been implicated in the plot were now more than ever determined to force the Transvaal into a trial of strength. The Cape was regarded as the linchpin of the empire, controlling a much more secure route to India and Australasia than the Suez Canal, which would be comparatively easy for a hostile power to close. However, such a strategy depended on the Cape Colony's remaining British and dominating the rest of southern Africa. The danger, from the British point of view, was that the Rand would render the Transvaal sufficiently wealthy and powerful to attract or coerce the white settlers of southern Africa into a United States of South Africa under Afrikaner domination. The British high commissioner in South Africa, Sir Alfred Milner, manipulated the Uitlander grievances to provoke the Transvaal to war. In October 1899 a battle broke out, with the Orange Free State rallying to the side of its fellow republic. The Afrikaner forces were defeated in the field, but they reconstituted themselves as guerrilla commandos and fought the military might of the British Empire with skill and courage for two and a half years. There was much loss of life and destruction of property, especially in the phase of guerrilla fighting and scorched-earth tactics, before the British annexed both the Transvaal and the Orange Free State as crown colonies to be administered by imperial officials under Milner as governor.[12]

Both the British and the Afrikaners were generally careful to conduct their campaigns in such a way that African fighting forces did not become involved.[13] The British had a chance but refused to recruit Indian, Chinese, and Hausa troops from West Africa, doubtless because they feared that help from these groups would alienate white settler opinion. Similarly, although the rich farmlands of the Caledon River valley constituted the granary of the Orange Free State and much of the Transvaal, the British never supported a Basuto movement to retake their "conquered territories," although the Basuto paramount chief, Lerotholi, favored the British side.[14] They also refused to provide arms for the Zulu and some other groups who offered to fight the republics. The republics, for their part, refused to arm the Swazi, their old allies against the Zulu, and some Basuto and other factions that offered to help. In general, the major African leaders were pro-British, and minority opposition factions gravitated to the Afrikaner side. As a result, it was very much in the republics' interest to ensure that Africans remained noncombatant, although they were employed as personal servants, wagon drivers, and, especially by the British, as scouts.

The Anglo-Boer War had an uneven effect economically on the African majority in southern Africa. The British army paid relatively high wages in comparison with those obtained before the war. The average price paid by the British for a Basuto pony was £16, although some fetched as high as £50. Meat and grain also sold well so that the war "was, for the Basuto, a period of unexampled prosperity."[15] In other areas, too, the emergent African peasantry was able to make quick profits by selling at inflated prices to the British army.[16] Other Africans seized the chance to steal European cattle. The Bakgatla, for example, had by the end of the war "gone a long way towards making good the cattle they had lost during the rinderpest epidemic of 1896."[17] On the other hand, the scorched-earth tactics practiced by both sides in the guerrilla campaigns destroyed the herds and farms of Africans as well as Afrikaners. And the Africans themselves suffered from looting and requisitioning by the white combatants. In general, those who still possessed some facets of political independence in Basutoland and Bechuanaland fared best; those in the Cape Colony and Natal could at least exploit favorable market opportunities; and those in the republics fared worst, especially in losing considerable quantities of livestock.[18]

The war opened the way for new leaders among the Afrikaners. The original republican armies had been led by older men, who failed to exploit their initial successes and the time lag in British mobilization and settled down to leisurely and totally unnecessary siege operations. (One cultural by-product of such sieges was that the Boer forces, surrounding Mafeking, learned to play cricket.[19]) These old leaders were discredited when Bloemfontein and Pretoria fell to the British. They were succeeded by younger and generally better educated men drawn from business, the professions, and the ranks of prosperous and progressive farmers.[20] Unlike the conservative military leaders they replaced, the new men had a war plan: to destroy the gold mines and to invade the Cape, thus arousing Britain's Afrikaner subjects to rebellion.

The strategy might have been successful if employed at the outset of war in 1899, but by 1900 the British had mobilized sufficient forces to withstand the invasion of the Cape. Furthermore, they responded to the Afrikaner war of movement and guerrilla tactics by utilizing more and more Africans and Coloreds as scouts and employing republican turncoats as "National Scouts." Here they were able to turn the incipient Afrikaner class divisions to their advantage.[21] Because a six-thousand-acre farm could be claimed as every white man's birthright, the Afrikaners had rapidly taken up all available land and had created as a by-product a class of landless whites, known as *bywoners*, who were dependent upon the goodwill of their landed relatives. Such *bywoners* were considered indispensable reinforcements to the local commando as long as semiautonomous African groups remained in the vicinity. But the increasing efficiency of the state's own apparatus of coercion, and the concomitant disarmament of the republics' African subjects, deprived the *bywoners* of their traditional role and led to increasingly uneasy relationships with their patrons. These landless men, including for example, Piet, the brother of the great Afrikaner guerrilla leader, Christian de Wet, constituted natural recruits to the National Scouts. With this kind of local help the British could at last travel and fight at night, thus cancelling out what had hitherto been one of the main Afrikaner advantages.[22]

Although it was the Afrikaner commanders who eventually surrendered in 1902, their long fight effectively demonstrated the weaknesses of British imperial power. In contrast to the experience of the Royal Navy in the American Revolution, British seapower went unchallenged by rival European navies while the empire geared itself to suppress the Afrikaner republics. Nevertheless, the British were uncomfortably aware of how long it had taken them to organize the defeat of two relatively small states and of how vulnerable such a commitment of their forces rendered them, given the quickening great power rivalry at the turn of the century. Nor could the British, who planned their careers within the total imperial framework, display the same commitment to winning a local colonial war as the Afrikaners, to whom it was a matter of national survival. In December 1900 Lord Roberts had hurried away from the battlefields without taking the trouble to mop up Afrikaner resistance in order to avail himself of the chance to be commander in chief. His successor, Lord Kitchener, was similarly impatient, somewhat to the disgust of Milner, for a quick armistice in 1902, lest he miss his opportunity to be commander in chief in India. King Edward VII, seeking a coronation that could truly celebrate the Pax Britannica, also hurried the process of making peace, thus strengthening the Afrikaners' bargaining position. Finally, the Afrikaners had decisively won the propaganda battle, at least in Europe and North America, where it mattered to the British. The spectacle of bullying imperialists suppressing small white nations became immeasurably more shameful when the British resorted to what they termed "concentration camps," in which Afrikaner women and children were imprisoned to prevent them from harboring the commandos. A storm of domestic and international protest broke out when the camp inmates were decimated by disease. Plainly an empire that had to be enforced by such means contradicted the moral professions by which the British justified their imperialism. Although formally defeated, the Afrikaners had called Britain's bluff, exposing the relatively feeble powers of coercion possessed by any empire with pretensions to moral authority and thus foreshadowing the midcentury politics of decolonization.[23]

The Afrikaners' indispensable equipment in shattering the myth of empire was their white skin. At the end of the war some 56,000 Africans in the Transvaal were imprisoned in concentration camps, suffering at one stage a death rate as high as 32 percent per annum.[24] But they wore a different uniform of color, so this provoked no great scandal or commission of inquiry from London. At the outset of the war in 1899 both Prime Minister Salisbury and Colonial Secretary Chamberlain had attacked the institutionalized color discrimination of the republics, but even by 1900 this view had become an embarrassment to imperial officials, who wished to appease white settler opinion. Clause 8 of the Vereeniging treaty of 1902 registered the surrender by barring the imperial authorities from extending the franchise beyond the white community before the introduction of responsible self-government. In the process of formal surrender, therefore, the Afrikaners forced Britain to renege on its paternalist pretensions.[25]

In 1906 and 1907 Britain granted self-government to the two conquered Afrikaner territories. The new sophisticated leaders, who had emerged as war heroes in the guerrilla struggle, now applied their talents to politics. The "age of the generals" in South Africa's history had begun, with political power passing once more into Afrikaner hands in the Transvaal and the Orange River Colony — the old Orange Free State — so that all but whites were permanently excluded from voting.[26]

The discussion on what should be the relationship of the four colonies and the associated debate on African political rights preoccupied South African political leaders. The results of the 1906 rising among the Zulu gave evidence of the interdependence of all the white colonial governments, for the other three colonies had feared the extension of the rising from Zululand to their own African subjects and had sent reinforcements to strengthen the hundred thousand whites in Natal. The Natal government's handling of the rising — which it had done much to provoke, by its insensitive piling on of taxes, rents, and oppressive labor legislation in the face of warnings by its own native administration, and to spread by its brutal and panicky suppression of a small initial insurrection — gave scant confidence in its capacity to handle race relations.[27] The Cape, the Orange River Colony, and Natal itself also sought unification to be able to tap the wealth of the Transvaal for the general economic expansion of South Africa, and the Transvaal rulers themselves could appreciate the benefits of the coordinated transport and customs policy.[28]

In order to achieve the Union of South Africa the differing white policies toward Africans had to be reconciled. The racial exclusiveness of the two ex-republics' *baasskap*, reinforced by Natal, was set against the Cape's token political integration for Africans. Under Cape Liberalism western-educated Africans who owned or leased property of a certain value could register to vote. In 1909 Africans amounted to 4.7 percent of the Cape electorate. Eventually the colonies agreed that each should take into the Union its existing franchise regulations, which would remain in force until such time as a two-thirds majority of both houses of the South African parliament decided to change them. The ex-republics hoped that they would eventually command enough support to disenfranchise African and Colored voters in the Cape, while the Cape Liberals were, like their metropolitan British counterparts, equally convinced that "progress" was on their side and that it was merely a matter of time before they converted the northerners to their own approach to politics. The

British government itself exercised its residual paternalism in southern Africa by refusing to allow the Union government to incorporate the High Commission Territories of Basutoland, Bechuanaland, and Swaziland until their inhabitants signified their agreement, which in 1910 they certainly did not. African opinion, at least in the High Commission Territories, might therefore exercise some influence on the racial policies of the Union government.[29]

The creation of the Union led Africans in 1912 to build from earlier organizations the Union-wide South African Native Congress, which later changed its name to the better known African National Congress.[30] The architect of the new movement was Pixley Ka Izaka Sema, related by marriage to the Zulu royal house, a graduate of Columbia University, and a member of the Middle Temple who practiced law in Johannesburg. There was, he claimed, a general desire for a national organization: "We are one people. Let us forget the differences between Xhosa-Fingo, Zulus, and Tongas, Basutos and other Natives."[31] The main opponent of the new movement was Jabavu, who feared the congress threatened his own position as the recognized spokesman for Africans. The congress sought to attract the traditional chiefs by creating an "upper house" for them. That it was far from subversive in its aims is shown by its inviting the government to send a representative to open it. Nevertheless, the trend of legislation within South Africa forced the congress into an adversary position. The first law it denounced was the Native Land Act of 1913, which prevented Africans, except in the Cape, from acquiring land outside their own areas.[32] Solomon Plaatje, a Tswana journalist and author and the secretary general of the congress, summarized the impact of this act: "Awakening on Friday morning, June 20th, 1913, the South African Native found himself, not actually a slave, but a pariah in the land of his birth."[33]

Electoral Politics in the Union

With an overwhelmingly white electorate parliamentary politics in South Africa reflected divisions within the white community, especially the cleavage between the Afrikaners and those South Africans of British descent. No British party could hope to win a majority, because the British South Africans were always a minority within the white population and suffered from constituency demarcations that favored the Afrikaner-dominated rural areas. The predominant party from 1910 to 1924 was the South African party, which was a blend of British South Africans and more liberal-minded Afrikaners. It was led by General Louis Botha until his death in 1919 and thereafter by General Jan Smuts, both successful Afrikaner war leaders, who sought to create a united white South Africa within the British Empire through a policy of reconciliation and economic development. They expected to move that empire toward a commonwealth of autonomous self-governing white dominions, which would provide Smuts with a sufficiently substantial base from which to operate as an international statesman. Originally the official opposition to the South African party was the Unionist party, led by Rhodes's old lieutenant, Jameson. But in 1913 the first Afrikaner party was founded by General James Hertzog, who feared the assimilation of the Afrikaner people by the South African party's policies of reconciliation and the general subordination of South Africa to British interests.[34] Hertzog's Nationalist party managed to attract more and more Afrikaners, helped along by their dislike of South African participation on the British side in World War I—which had provoked a small Afrikaner rebellion. At the same time the South African party expanded its British South African support when it joined a coalition with the Unionist party in 1915 and went on to absorb it in 1921.

In 1922 the white miners struck and seized control of the Rand gold mines because the owners had proposed to cut labor costs by replacing some of the skilled workers with Africans at lower wages. Early in 1922 a general strike of whites began, enveloping the whole Witwatersrand area, with the strikers rallying behind the powerful cry, "Workers of the World Unite—for a White South Africa." Smuts, who firmly believed that South Africa faced economic disaster without a prosperous capitalist mining sector, used troops to suppress this "Rand rebellion."[35]

In the election of 1924 the workers took their revenge. The Labor party, led by Colonel Frederic Creswell, drew its support largely from urban workers of British descent and now allied itself with Hertzog's Nationalists against Smuts. It doubled in strength from nine to eighteen seats, and the Nationalists cut further into the strength of the South African party in the rural districts, so that the Nationalist-Labor pact gained a decisive majority and formed a government that was pledged to color bar and segregationist policies.[36]

In 1929 Hertzog's Nationalists won a clear majority and seemed set for an indefinite period of control. But the depression led to a demand from the white electorate for a government composed of both Nationalist and South African party leaders. In 1934 most of the Nationalist party joined with most of the South African party to form the United party, which held power until 1948. A small British group led by Colonel Charles Stallard broke away from Smuts to form the Dominion party, and a larger group of Afrikaners, led by Dr. D. F. Malan, rejected the coalition and formed the Purified Nationalist party. The

United party, however, enjoyed huge electoral support between the Afrikaner and British South African extremes, winning 111 seats in the 1938 election while the Dominion party won only eight, the Purified Nationalists only twenty-seven, and Labor a mere three.

Immediately after the 1938 election there was a remarkable manifestation of Afrikaner nationalism when thousands of Afrikaners grew beards and wore voortrekker costume to greet the ox-drawn wagons that trundled through the countryside during the centenary celebration of the Great Trek. Orators like Dr. Malan eloquently claimed that the Afrikaner people were still beset by their traditional enemies, the British and the Bantu, who had confronted their ancestors. On the arrival of the wagons in Pretoria, writes an Afrikaner historian, D. W. Kruger, "an extraordinary spirit of fervid patriotism, bordering on adoration, swept over the country. Enthusiam became nearly religious and sometimes hysterical, women bringing their babies to be baptised in the shadow of the waggons."[37] Such was the situation at the outbreak of war in 1939.

Politics and Poverty

After 1870 there was no longer sufficient land available to supply young Afrikaners with farms of their own. Many therefore drifted into *bywoner* status or made do with their portion of a family estate, generally shared out equally among the many progeny. By the early twentieth century repeated subdivision produced some remarkable examples of fragmentation. In 1908 the Transvaal Indigency Commission revealed the case of an heir entitled to 296,387,007/ 4,705,511,234,760 of a 5,347-acre farm—in fact, under half an acre![38] Wagon driving did provide an acceptable alternative occupation to farming, but once the railroads reached the Rand, first from the Cape in 1892, and then from Natal and Delagoa Bay in 1895, these opportunities were curtailed. The turn of the century brought a succession of disasters: rinderpest in 1896; war in 1899, breaking many landowner-*bywoner* relationships as well as causing vast physical damage to farmlands; finally drought and depression in 1903.[39] The concentration camps were hated as a symbol of coercive British imperialism; yet ten thousand Afrikaners stayed on in them for months—they simply had no place else to go.[40]

Nor did the Afrikaners who were forced off the land find it easy to make their way in the urban-industrial sector. It was assumed, at least by the Afrikaners themselves, that they lacked any capacity for business.[41] Skilled managerial work in the mines was monopolized by white expatriates, who supervised the ill-paid African laborers. English-speaking South Africans, who dominated the urban sector, watched with distaste as both white and black shanty-towns developed. An English-speaking commission to investigate poverty in Pretoria in 1905 noted that "the poor white class is chiefly drawn from the original European settlers of South Africa whose function *should essentially be that of cultivators of the soil*."[42] The Bloemfontein English-language news-paper, *The Friend*, on the occasion of the 1923 Poor White Congress, called, according to Dr. Malan, for increased British immigration to protect existing city dwellers against the Afrikaner influx.[43] Until World War II the Afrikaners themselves accepted the idea that they were unfitted for urban life. Many individuals saved for the day when they might go back to the land.[44]

The Afrikaners took advantage of the 1907 strike by English-speaking miners (against the owners' decision that each white miner should operate three instead of two drills) to break into the mines.[45] By 1913 they made up a majority of white miners, although not until November 1948 did Afrikaner Nationalists succeed in seizing control of the Mineworkers' Union.[46]

In other areas the Afrikaners relied heavily on their political strength to make economic progress. The old Transvaalers had shown the way, regarding all those connected with the mines as species of Uitlanders. Whether they were cosmopolitan capitalists with offices in Park Lane, or black and white employees of the capitalists, or target workers from Basutoland, Wales, and Cornwall, they appeared to be plundering the Afrikaners' patrimony and bearing it off to the outside world. Hence the miners were fair game to be taxed to provide civil service salaries for displaced *bywoners* and even greater perquisites for political notables.[47]

In the Union of South Africa the gold mines subsidized the white, over-whelmingly Afrikaner farmers both through the heavy burden of taxation they bore and the discriminatory charges of the state-owned railways. (In turn, heavy taxation on the mining industry was possible largely through the depression of black miners' wages.) South Africa's black peasantry was also disadvantaged in competition with white farmers through government trans-portation policy, for, as W. M. Macmillan observed, "to locate the native re-serves, it is no bad rule . . . to look for the areas circumvented or entirely missed even by branch lines."[48]

The 1924 Nationalist-Labor government won power because Smuts was identified with the mineowners' attempt to substitute lower-paid black labor for white labor, whereas Hertzog offered the white electors a directly opposite "civilized labor" policy under which white workers might be substituted for Africans wherever possible. The state-owned railways once more were the chief means by which the whites were favored, raising their percentage of unskilled white workers from 9.5 to 39.3, while the proportion of Africans was cut from 76 to 48.9 percent between 1924 and 1933. Other branches of central government, such as the post office, also implemented the "civilized labor" policy, and municipalities that followed suit were reimbursed for the extra expense out of state funds. Similarly private employers were subsidized if they increased the proportion of white workers they employed.[49]

In all such cases the Afrikaners making the "Second Trek" to the city used their political strength to win out at the expense of Africans and Coloreds, who in many cases possessed greater urban and industrial skills — the Coloreds were South Africa's traditional artisan class, groups like the Basuto had acquired mining expertise, and the Tswana had a tradition of living in relatively large townships — and in any case could nearly always be forced to accept lower wages. Long before the Nationalist-Labor pact government's "civilized labor" policy came into being, Africans and Coloreds had faced various forms of harassment that limited their bargaining power. The pass laws in South Africa stretched back to Governor Caledon's 1809 proclamation designed to fix the domicile of Khoi migrants: those without a pass were treated as vagrants, liable to be hired out by the local officials to anyone they pleased and on the farmer's own terms. From that date on, a battery of such laws subjected various categories of Africans and Coloreds to controls.[50] The 1923 Natives (Urban Areas) Act, passed under the Smuts regime, made use of the pass system to control entry into the towns. The act was denounced by the African National Congress as reducing Africans to perpetual serfdom.[51] Hertzog's "civilized labor" policy ostentatiously built on these foundations after 1924.

The African National Congress continued to hold its annual conventions and to attack such measures, but in 1938 it still had under four thousand members. The Industrial and Commercial Workers' Union, which was founded in 1919 by Clements Kadalie, the clerk from Nyasaland, won considerably more support for much of the interwar period. Starting in the Cape and moving into the Transvaal, it gained more than a hundred thousand members as well as many thousands of supporters at its peak. Kadalie never decided whether it should be a strictly trade union organization or should constitute a political protest movement, which is hardly surprising given the labor-repressive framework the organization had to operate within. The central organization of the union was too weak to control the proliferating membership, and faction fights developed, especially between Communist and moderate leaders. The mineowners were able to use state power to block effective organizing operations in the massive labor force. After the union had split into three factions, Kadalie moved to East London, where he led a dock strike that was eventually broken after he and eight other leaders were jailed.[52]

The Afrikaners' political power was reflected in the privileged and protected status of the "poor whites" in the towns. "Civilized laborers" were paid about double the wages of those they replaced, but this still left them far behind British South Africans. As late as 1948, after the industrial boom of World War II had benefited them, the annual per capita income of Afrikaners in the Rand was computed at £182 compared to £349 for English-speaking whites.[53] Afrikaners in the cities, where English was the language of wealth and authority, were made sharply aware of their inferiority, illustrated, as Adrian Leftwich points out, "by the English-speakers' cruel caricature of the Afrikaner child's limp admission of social inadequacy: *My papa werk op die spoorwëe*' (My father works on the railways.)"[54] Afrikaners countered with lampoons of "Hoggenheimer," a figure portrayed as the archetypal Anglo-Jewish capitalist. Despite the "civilized labor" policy there was ample economic distress for Dr. Malan's Purified Nationalist party to work upon.

CHAPTER 15

Urbanization and Interwar Politics

There was no industrial revolution in tropical Africa in the interwar years to match that in the white-dominated south. Nevertheless, there was spectacular growth of a few great commercial and administrative centers. In French West Africa the population of the modern port and governmental nerve center of Dakar mushroomed from 24,914 in 1910 to 53,882 in 1931 and to 92,000 in 1936.[1] In British West Africa the population of Lagos, originally an African city, although geared to the transatlantic slave trade, shot up from 74,000 inhabitants in 1910 to 99,690 in 1921 and to 126,608 in 1931. The massive Yoruba city of Ibadan, which was estimated to have 70,000 inhabitants in 1850, reached 175,000 by the 1911 census, 238,094 by 1921, and 387,133 by 1931.[2] Freetown's population was 20,000 in 1870, 33,000 by 1914 and 55,509 by 1931.[3] In East and Central Africa the interwar populations of the cities were never so large, although in Kenya the African population of Nairobi grew from 12,000 in 1921 to 27,000 in 1931 and to 40,000 in 1938.[4]

When African townspeople banded together to protest against imperial policies, colonial officials habitually retorted that they were unrepresentative because the true grass roots of African politics were in rural areas. Speaking before the Nigerian Council in 1920, Sir Hugh Clifford dismissed the National Congress of British West Africa as "a self-selected and . . . self-appointed congregation of educated African gentlemen. . . . it can only be described as farcical to suppose that . . . continental Nigeria can be represented by a handful of gentlemen drawn from a half-dozen Coast tribes—men born and bred in British administered towns situated on the sea-shore, who in the safety of British protection have peacefully pursued their studies under British teachers."[5] Similarly in Sierra Leone officials drew a sharp distinction between Creoles and countrymen, and in the Gold Coast they cited ideas of the Omanhene (head chief) of Akim Abuakwa, Nana Ofori Atta, to cancel out the political aspirations of the British-trained lawyer, writer, and early African nationalist, Casely Hayford.[6] In terms of sheer numbers the officials were right, of course: the town populations were heavily outnumbered by those of the rural areas, which were safely, it was assumed, in the control of their traditional rulers. Yet by the end of the interwar period the towns in several parts of Africa were serving as coordinating centers for politics that reached deep into the rural areas.[7]

Orthodox British colonial administration in the interwar years subscribed to notions of indirect rule that were originally formulated in Northern Nigeria. There urban settlements, some of which had existed for over a millennium, dominated the trade and politics of the surrounding areas. Several Hausa city-states, loosely incorporated within the framework of the Sokoto empire, continued to function as the religious, administrative, and economic centers of existing polities, symbolizing "not the negation, but the synthesis of the values held by the peoples of the surrounding countryside."[8] Newcomers, or "native aliens," traditionally had belonged to a district of the town known as the Sabon Gari, and Lugard was careful to exclude these districts from the jurisdiction of the local Hausa courts. Europeans also tended to segregate themselves, ostensibly for health reasons. With such alien influences suitably quarantined to the satisfaction of both the Hausa-Fulani and the British colonial elites, the towns of Northern Nigeria continued to exercise their traditional coordinating functions, suggesting that there was no necessary incompatibility between urban development and rural stability. Colonial administrators were therefore lulled into a false sense of security that made it easy for them to dismiss protest movements as the work of marginal, unrepresentative men. But in many other areas of West Africa the majority of towns were colonial creations, which also, eventually, came to play a coordinating role in African politics. As centers of intellectual innovation they inevitably threatened both traditional and imperial authorities.

British West Africa

On the night of July 18, 1919, celebrations to mark the conclusion of the peace treaty suddenly exploded into race riots in Freetown.[9] The shops and houses of Syrian traders were simultaneously attacked in each ward of the city. The background to the violence was the deadly influenza epidemic of 1919 and the peacetime discharge of many workers attracted to Freetown when it was an important naval base, all compounded by food shortages and soaring prices. In particular, the Syrian and Lebanese merchants (generally referred to as Syrians) were accused of manipulating the price of rice, which was in short supply because of the failure of the 1919 crop as the result of heavy rains and the depletion of the labor force by the epidemic. A laborer who earned one shilling a day found that the price of a cup of rice had risen from a penny (or a twelfth of a day's pay) to five pence. The Syrians also were unpopular among local merchants for what were held to be unfair business practices. They were charged, furthermore, with calling Sierra Leoneans "niggers" and "slaves" and with allegedly corrupting "young girls attending the higher seminaries" and "girls of reputed respectability."[10] Nor were the British themselves devoid of responsibility in Sierra Leonean eyes: "There was considerable indignation in some parts of the City at the report of the racial disturbances in Liverpool, Cardiff, and a few other places in England and Wales which gave rise to considerable apprehension that the 'Sea-boys' [African sailors] repatriated from those places with a deep sense of injury would instigate reprisals in Sierra Leone against the white residents."[11]

The riots, in which three people were killed and considerable damage was done to property, spread into the protectorate towns and lasted, somewhat sporadically, for about a month. The available military and police forces were stretched to a point where little could be done to prevent further violence; indeed, a few soldiers joined in the looting. The British colonial secretary, Viscount Alfred Milner, took a very stern view. In sending troops from the Gold Coast, he declared, "It seems to me that it is a case for strong measures to restore the authority of the law and to mark the distinction between the civilization of the British and the Ottoman Empire."[12] On July 14, four days before the outbreak of the riots, the technical staff and laborers employed by the government railway and public works department had struck, demanding a war bonus similar to that given the clerical staff. R. A. Maude, the attorney general, thought the rioters, all of who were suffering from the rising cost of living, "had the idea that the loot was their bonus."[13] The strike and the rice riots seemed to have been confused by both the authorities and many Sierra Leoneans — "trek," the Krio word for "strike," tends to denote anything from a walkout to a rebellion under arms. J. Ayodele Langley comments:

Consequently, "bonus" became the battle-cry of the hungry lumpenproletariat, assisted by a depressed urban petty bourgeoisie (and an unemployed clerkly

class which at last was applying its useless Latin to colonial politics) and the
refrain of a rather cleverly constructed song:

> Strike don cam for Bonus
> We unite for bonus;
> Creole Boy ner danger Boy,
> Bonus, Bo-Bonus!
>
> Kaiser make Bonus,
> When we take Bonum:
> Peace Terms wan Bonam up,
> Bonus, Bo-Bonus!
>
> Milner say pay Bonus,
> Barker say bite first,
> Maud say make Red-belleh shoot,
> Bonus, Bo-Bonus!
>
> Bonus Bona Bonum
> Boni Bone Bona
> We want small Bonus
> Bonus, Bo-Bonus! . . .
>
> Last year we say ner Flu,
> This year we call am Strike;
> When all dem Coral go,
> Then Bonus, Sweet Bonus!

The Kaiser referred to was Wilhelm of Germany, Barker was the acting general
manager of the railway, and "coral" was a term for early Syrian and Lebanese
peddlers who sold such beads.[14]

The threat of mass insurrection, exemplified by the 1919 race riots, prompted "progressive" administrators to seek accommodation with the western-
educated elite in British West Africa on the matter of representative political
institutions.[15] The first colony to be given a new constitution was Nigeria in
1922, and it provided for the election of four legislative council members from
Lagos and one from Calabar. There also were to be fifteen unoffical members,
who would be nominated by the governor to represent business interests and
the various provinces of Southern Nigeria. But there were to be twenty-three
colonial civil servants who were automatically members and three other officials nominated by the governor, who also was president of the council with a
casting vote and power of veto. Sierra Leone followed with a new constitution in 1924, which provided for a legislative council of twenty-one members,
of whom eleven were colonial officials. Three others were to be elected directly
by the colony, and five were to be nominated by the governor—two from the

colony and three protectorate paramount chiefs. The remaining two unofficial members represented European business and generally voted with the colonial administration. In 1925 the Gold Coast was given a somewhat more complicated constitution with fifteen official members and fourteen unofficial ones on the legislative council. Three unofficial members were directly elected from Accra, Cape Coast, and Sekondi. Three provincial councils, composed of the Omanhene of each province, elected two of their number to serve as unofficial legislative councillors. This provision led to bitter opposition from western-educated Africans and prevented the Gold Coast legislative council from coming into operation until 1927.[16]

Legislative council elections were based on a limited male franchise. In Sierra Leone, for example, an elector resident in an urban area had to own real estate with an annual rental value of £10 per year or had to earn £100 a year, and an elector resident in a rural area had to own real estate valued at £6 per year or had to earn £60.[17] These constitutions remained virtually unchanged throughout the interwar period, although in 1938 a standing financial committee was established in Sierra Leone with an unofficial African majority—the first case of an institution of colonial government being so organized in Africa.[18]

Many of the youngsters who came to Freetown from the protectorate in search of western education ended up assuming a Creole identity. While at school they often lived as wards in Creole households, and once at work they found their colleagues would not tolerate protectorate men as fellow clerks unless they "turned Creole," which involved a change of name and the curtailment of associations with their original ethnic groups. With the skimming off of this potential modernizing elite, the Mende, Temne, and other "ethnic" sections of Freetown, presided over by officially recognized tribal headmen, tended to be unmoved by the formal protest politics of the National Congress. Precisely because the Creoles were in an important sense an open society, prepared to admit individual countrymen who conformed to their criteria, the cultural boundaries between Creoledom and the protectorate as a whole were kept sharp, and the stereotype of them as polar opposites, so dear to British colonial officials, was reinforced.[19]

Temne imigrants, from an area already infiltrated by Islam, naturally settled alongside one of the mosques of East Freetown. Here the more ambitious immigrants had an alternative to full creolization, which would mean accepting Christianity. Instead of becoming Christian Creoles, they passed themselves off as Mandinka or Aku, the descendants of Yoruba recaptives who were Muslim and who retained their ancestral folkways more obviously than their Christian counterparts. The urban sophistication and greater Islamic knowledge of these long-established groups was such that, as one of the younger Temne leaders deplored, "every bright young Temne is lost to the other tribes and the word Temne is associated with the uncivilized people."[20] In particular, the Mandinka dance societies, introduced by the Mandinka headmen after a visit to French Guinea in 1930, captured many young Temne with their mutual welfare features, their inventive music, and proliferation of opportunities for both sexes to hold office in them.[21] "The serious educated Temne began to think about their tribe and to seek emancipation from low prestige. The problem is very great as there is no means of approach. The Tribal Administration is effective only with the low educated classes; the better class of Temnes looked with disdain on their less favoured brothers. . . . The problem was made more difficult as the leaders of the Temne commonly were not educated and most of them of limited means. Their appeals to the youths were ineffective."[22]

The solution devised by the author of this diagnosis was to create a new organization, the Ambas Geda society, bypassing the illiterate elders. "Ambas" in Temne means "we have," and "geda" is Krio for "together." The society's title was, in effect, a rallying cry to Temne patriots: "We, the Temne, have the people and must bring them in."[23] Songs were composed in Temne, a new dance rhythm was devised, and many of the innovations of the successful Mandinka societies were adapted for Temne use. Just as the continuation of the Temne and Krio languages in the name of this society typified the blend of traditional and city culture, so the chief executive was the "Sultan" and his female counterpart was the "Mammy Queen," a title originally bestowed by Creoles on Queen Victoria.[24]

Some songs were designed to uphold Temne by using ridicule to ensure social conformity:

> "The shame of it, Ai Kamara, the shame of it!
> Ai Kamara bore a child:
> He had no sooner grown up than she made him her husband.
> Ah friends, let us come together
> And consider if this is done in Temne-land!"[25]

Temne songs also could be a vehicle for straightforward patriotic sentiment:

> "Eh! In this Temne land
> Do you all see this land?
> Oh, the Temne used to have it
> But now the Government has snatched it from us."[26]

This was a reminder to the Temne that they could claim precedence based on their original occupation of the land over all other ethnic groups in Freetown and over the British colonial government itself.

Other Ambas Geda songs expressed the conflict between the older and younger generations:

> "Ah, look what is being said,
> Look what is being done,
> How they envy our play
> Ah, I do believe [in the play],
> As the old folk envy the geda,
> Let them just go on envying."[27]

About two years after the founding of the Ambas Geda one of the most popular members was expelled for having seduced a woman member on the society's premises. Elaborate measures had been taken to prevent such an occurrence lest husbands refuse to bring their wives and fathers forbid their daughters to attend. In addition to his expulsion, the guilty member was ordered to pay the parents £5 compensation and to marry the woman. The officials gave him every assistance, however, to found a new society along similar lines. He called it "Boys London" to emphasize the members' sophistication, and it quickly became popular. Other groups of this sort were formed, and the most successful ones established branches in different sections of the city. In 1953, Banton counted about thirty such bodies in Freetown.[28]

Using this organizational network, the young men wrested control of the formal political apparatus from their illiterate elders. During World War II the post of the Temne tribal headman fell vacant, and the young men determined, after prolonged deliberation, to put forward the schoolmaster-founder of Ambas Geda, Kande Bureh. His open campaigning suggested to his much older opponents that he could not be a serious contender but was merely making himself known in preparation for the next election. Although he had formally resigned from Ambas Geda when his candidacy was announced, he kept in close touch with his supporters there and in the other societies, transforming them, Banton claimed in 1957, into the most effective party machine Freetown had yet seen.[29] As the campaign funds did not stretch to hiring enough transport, Kande Bureh's Freetown supporters rode to the polling field in the other candidate's trucks. Once there, they unfurled large banners and attached four thousand small flags to their clothing, advertising their support of Kande Bureh. They did, however, hire trucks to bring in supporters from out-of-town groups. Although not allowed to vote, these additional backers contributed to an impression of overwhelming support for the young men's candidate, and he was elected.[30]

The mobilization of the Temne was to provide the protectorate-based Sierra Leone People's party with an organization with which to capture Freetown, hitherto dominated by Creole political organizations, in the elections that marked the period of decolonization.[31] Meantime, on the eve of the outbreak of World War II, the Creole journalist and "agitator" I. T. A. Wallace-Johnson succeeded in uniting younger, more radical Creoles and the same age-group of protectorate-born men and women into the Sierra Leone branch of the West African Youth League. Briefly, Freetown was thrilled and shocked by Wallace-Johnson's Marxist ideas, rhetoric, and organizational skill before the colonial authorities were able to use wartime security legislation to jail him and repress his movement.[32]

Wallace-Johnson's more famous ally during his Gold Coast days had been Nnamdi Azikiwe. Azikiwe had returned to Nigeria from the United States in 1934 as the first Ibo with an advanced college degree.[33] During the interwar years educational facilities in Iboland expanded rapidly as the Ibo, forced to migrate by the overpopulation of their homeland, realized that schooling was the key to prosperity in the growing towns and cities of colonial Nigeria. Observing the advantages the Yoruba had derived from their long years of contact with missionary educators, the Ibo became even more opportunistic, commonly remarking, "An Ibo would accept education from anyone, even from the Devil."[34]

Margery Perham pointed to Azikiwe's American academic background to draw attention to the problem of the western-educated African who sought employment within the framework of indirect rule: "The governement does not, of course, want to encourage the hope that all those educated overseas have a prescriptive right to government employment, yet the assistance of government is necessary, if highly educated men are to find openings in the Protectorate. When they fail to obtain encouragement in this direction they settle in the towns in a mood of embitterment which finds its main object in the government's native policy. This loss or perversion of talent is so unfortunate that the British authorities would be wise to make considerable efforts to create openings for such men . . ."[35]

Although the British colonial administration denied Azikiwe a career in its ranks, it had other blandishments to offer when he moved to Accra as the editor of the radical *African Morning Post*. He reported that Sir Arnold Hodgson, who had earned the nickname of "the Sunshine Governor" while in Sierra

Leone, liked to "open the gates and garden of Christiansborg Castle to the leading members of the Accra community, and all delighted in strutting in the precincts of the Castle." The revue, "The Downfall of Zachariah Fee," written by the governor and featuring the song, "Teddy Bears' Picnic," was another fondly remembered event. Finally, the governor presented Azikiwe with the collected speeches of Stanley Baldwin as a wedding present.[36] In 1937 Azikiwe and Wallace-Johnson were convicted of sedition for an article in the *Post* ("Has the African a God?") written by Wallace-Johnson, in which he roundly condemned Christianity and imperialism. Azikiwe's sentence was ultimately suspended. In that same year he published his book, *Renascent Africa*, and returned to Nigeria to found a daily newspaper, the *West African Pilot*.[37]

In Nigeria Azikiwe at once became an important political force. His book, his articles in learned journals, and his supremely successful popular journalism, which publicized the Nigerian Youth League, made him a folk hero, particularly to the Ibo but also to many other young activists. Margery Perham's question about what scope the Ibo groups could offer to one of the tribe who was so highly qualified—a question raised when colonial authorities failed to give him a job—was now answered. Young Ibo, forced by immigration to make their way in towns far from their ancestral homelands had set up political and social organizations of "Sons Abroad" from villages and townships all over Nigeria.[38] The Sons Abroad did not only apply themselves to mutual self-help and the new urban politics. They sought to improve their hometowns and villages by offering scholarships and funding schools, hospitals, and community centers. Whereas the officially sponsored traditional rulers were charged with such duties as enforcing tax collection and compelling obedience to the white man's laws, the emissaries of the Sons Abroad appeared to the villagers in altogether more benevolent capacities. Thus the Sons Abroad were able to form a bond between town and country that shattered the colonial officials' cherished belief in a dichotomy between the new urban protest politics and the grass roots politics of the rural areas. It was to be Azikiwe's achievement to preside over this development.[38]

The Copper Belt

Many West African towns and cities were centuries old, rooted in African traditions rather than European needs. Where they did grow up in response to western contact, the long years of the Atlantic slave trade and the subsequent legitimate trade allowed West Africans a much greater period in which to adjust to urbanization than was possible elsewhere. Nor, at least for the urban elite, should such social amenity as Governor Hodgson displayed be discounted. White manners in West Africa certainly contrasted sharply with the *baasskap* attitudes imported from the south into East and Central Africa. In racially stratified Northern Rhodesia, for example, Governor Sir Ronald Storrs had indicated that the paramount chief of Barotseland was the only African with whom a white man was supposed to shake hands.[40] The raw race relations in the camp towns of the copper belt led a British official in 1933 to observe, "I have the impression that the attitude of the Europeans to natives at Nkana is neither politic nor in the best interests of the mine."[41]

In 1935 a number of African miners in the copper belt withdrew their labor in protest against conditions of work, low pay, and high taxes. African unions were forbidden, so any such group action was illegal. Members of the police force called in to handle the situation panicked, opened fire, and killed seven strikers and wounded twenty-two others. Many survivors were jailed. In testimony before the resultant commission of inquiry African workers vented their grievances. Eliti Tuli Phili, a Thonga clerk from Nyasaland, was one spokesman: "The natives have seen that they started work at the same time as the European and the European at once is able to buy a motor car and he gets a lot of food at the hotel. The natives complain about this. They compare the wages of the Europeans with the wages of the natives. They do the same kind of work, for instance, the natives working underground are supervised by a European who only points out to them the places where they should drill the holes. After doing this the European sits down and the natives drill the holes. The natives know where the holes should be drilled, they have been doing that work for some time and they know and understand the work."[42]

Alarmed by the strike and such ideas, the European miners sought advice from unions in South Africa, which operated under the color bar. By 1937 these white miners had formed their own trade union to enforce rigid racial discrimination in jobs where hitherto there had been only an informal color bar. In the short run, therefore, the strike was in some ways counterproductive with regard to immediate conditions of employment. It did, however, call attention to the limited social welfare suggestions of John Merle Davis's *Modern Industry and the African*. It also suggested that the copper belt was an obvious area in which social scientists, such as the anthropologists of the Rhodes-Livingstone Institute (founded in 1937), could study the impact of urbanization and industrialization "including the nature of African ambition and aspirations in a white-dominated society."[43] In the perspective of African political history the strike marked the beginning of mass involvement, which quickly progressed to the development of a specifically anticolonial program.[44]

French Territories

In French West and Equatorial Africa the basic political division was between Senegal, where there were "riots, demonstrations, strikes, imprisonment of candidates and impassioned speeches," and the rest, save for Dahomey with its large western-educated elite, where Africans had neither the right of assembly nor freedom of speech. With regulations such as were in force at Bouaké in Ivory Coast in 1926, Africans were kept under close control: "Order regulating the circulation of natives in the town of Bouaké after 8 p.m. Article I: Every native circulating after 8 p.m. in the streets of Bouaké must have a lamp of sufficient force to signal his presence (15 days plus 100 francs summarily imposed for contravention)."[45]

Blaise Diagne's political rise in the four communes of Senegal has already been described. By 1919 he had Africanized all representative institutions in Senegal and had been returned to the deputyship with the backing of the Republican Socialist party, which had been formed around a nucleus of returned war veterans. But in about 1922 Diagne came to terms with the existing French interests. In 1921 he opposed the creation of a state bank and so helped the Banque de l'Afrique Occidentale to retain its exclusive privilege of issuing currency for French West Africa. In 1923 he signed a pact with the Bordeaux merchant houses, in which he agreed to cease attacking them in return for their political support. In 1930 he defended French forced-labor policies before the International Labor Conference of the League of Nations, arguing that France was totally opposed to such practices and that "the presence of the delegate of France in my person is already symbolic; it signifies that my country has intended to show through my presence here [at Geneva] what her feelings are." He defended French policies at a time when it was known that women were forced in the French Congo to work on road building with their bare hands, while carrying their babies on their backs, because the administration had issued no tools. In 1931 Diagne became the undersecretary of state for the colonies at the price of absolute cooperation with the French regime and the suppression of his old program for extending the political system of the four communes to the rest of Senegal. By the time of his death in 1934 he was so far absorbed into the life of metropolitan France that he rarely visited Senegal.[46]

In 1937 the Popular Front government permitted limited freedom to *sujets* — that is, those outside the privileged circle of the four communes — for the formation of associations, including trade unions and professional organizations, by those who were literate in French and who held primary school certificates, although the associations were always subject to the approval of the local French authorities. By November 1937, a total of 119 trade unions had been formed, of which 42 were professional associations. But this burst of activity was short lived, for the Vichy regime sharply repressed any such popular organization in French West Africa.[47]

CHAPTER 16

The Second World War

The years of World War II were a watershed in the history of modern Africa. European empires buckled and collapsed under the strain. After a few months' fighting, Italy's East African empire was captured by British forces that included many Africans and a contingent of the Force Publique from the Belgian Congo aided by guerrilla forces operating within Ethiopia. On May 5, 1941, five years to the day after the Italian forces entered Addis Ababa, Emperor Haile Selassie returned to his capital. With France defeated and occupied, French West Africa came under the control of the Vichy regime, but the authorities in French Equatorial Africa opted for the Free French regime under General Charles de Gaulle. The German army invaded Belgium on May 10, 1940, and on May 27 the Belgian army surrendered, but the governor-general of the Congo sided with the Allies. African troops fighting for Britain in Southeast Asia at the height of the nationalist "Quit India" movement were led to wonder whether the Japanese were their real enemy. Although Britain emerged victorious, it had to sell most of its foreign investments to finance the war, and its postwar power was obviously dwarfed by that of the United States and the Soviet Union, both of which then believed in rapid decolonization. With many Africans mobilized, with key military bases developed through massive importation of modern equipment, and with expensive health services designed to eradicate hitherto endemic diseases, the pace of change in Africa quickened. For masses of men and women in all walks of life in tropical Africa, the advent of the personnel and paraphernalia of European and American conscript armies dramatized the crude power of the industrialized West on a scale hitherto encountered only in the white-dominated south. But although western power was dramatized, it was at the same time demystified, as for the first time Europeans were seen, stripped and sweating, working with their hands rather than sitting at their desks in crisp colonial "whites." Off-duty, they were liable to be similarly unbuttoned, drinking and womanizing in public bars as well as in discreet "Europeans-only" clubs.

Such was the impact of the war that the colonial powers were to find the trend toward change uncontrollable, although it took time for European imperialists and even many African nationalists to realize how fundamentally their relationships were altered. First, however, Africa was presented with a foretaste of fascism and western appeasement in the Italo-Ethopian war of 1935-36, which not only tragically affected Ethiopians but heightened political consciousness throughout Africa.

The Italo-Ethiopian Crisis

In 1935 the Italian fascist dictator Mussolini instigated a series of disputes with Ethiopians as a preliminary to an Italian invasion. Emperor Haile Selassie referred these matters to the League of Nations, but the European powers temporized, and sanctions against the aggressor were halfhearted and ineffective. Italian forces attacked Ethiopia in October 1935. Helped by air power, which was used to drop bombs and poison gas and to fly reconnaissance missions, Mussolini's armies entered Addis Ababa in May 1936. Haile Selassie fled, first to Palestine, then to Britain.

In terms of international law the invasion involved the sovereignty of an independent state and the effectiveness of collective security measures aimed at the peaceful settlement of a dispute through the use of sanctions against an aggressor. However, to Africans—as well as to Afro-Americans and Afro-West Indians—Ethiopia was not just any independent state but one of great symbolic significance. The Italo-Ethiopian crisis produced a sharp rise in radical Pan-Africanism, especially after Britain and France, the chief colonial powers in Africa, failed to make sanctions work through a determined embargo on oil for Italy.

Mussolini himself forced such a development by basing his international case on alleged Ethiopian racial inferiority: "Has the League of Nations become the tribunal before which the Negroes and uncivilised peoples, all the world's savages, can bring the great nations which have revolutionised and transformed history?"[1] In an important early study of the development of African nationalism Lord Hailey noted the radicalizing effect of the Ethiopian controversy

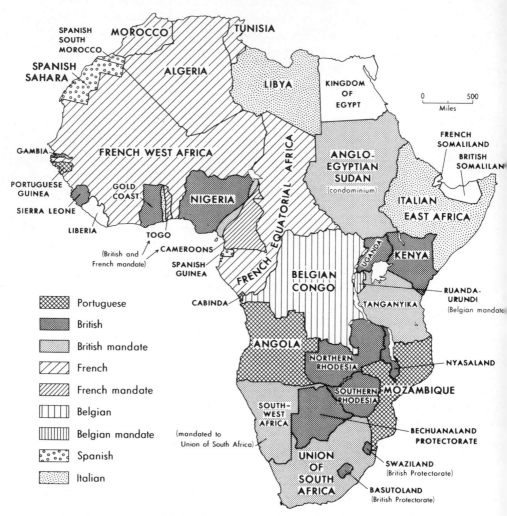

Map 7. Africa in 1939, indicating areas controlled by European powers at that date

SPANISH
SOUTH
MOROCCO

SPANISH
SAHARA

MOROCCO

TUNISIA

ALGERIA

LIBYA

KINGDOM
OF
EGYPT

0   500
Miles

GAMBIA

FRENCH WEST AFRICA

PORTUGUESE
GUINEA

SIERRA LEONE

LIBERIA

GOLD
COAST

NIGERIA

FRENCH SOMALILAND

BRITISH
SOMALILAND

ANGLO-
EGYPTIAN
SUDAN
(condominium)

ITALIAN
EAST AFRICA

TOGO

(British and
French mandate)

CAMEROONS

SPANISH
GUINEA

FRENCH EQUATORIAL AFRICA

BELGIAN
CONGO

UGANDA

KENYA

RUANDA-
URUNDI
(Belgian mandate)

CABINDA

TANGANYIKA

Portuguese

British

British mandate

French

French mandate

Belgian

Belgian mandate

Spanish

Italian

ANGOLA

NORTHERN
RHODESIA

SOUTHERN
RHODESIA

MOZAMBIQUE

NYASALAND

SOUTH-
WEST
AFRICA

(mandated to
Union of South Africa)

UNION
OF
SOUTH
AFRICA

BECHUANALAND
PROTECTORATE

SWAZILAND
(British Protectorate)

BASUTOLAND
(British Protectorate)

on African political thought throughout the African continent.[2] In Nigeria the larger ethnic groups banded together in protest for the first time ever. West Indians and Afro-Americans offered to fight in the Ethiopian army, and in Harlem in New York City there were bitter racial clashes with policemen of Italian descent.[3]

In the Gold Coast the *African Morning Post* on April 27, 1936, castigated the failure of the League to apply sanctions, for "had Ethiopia been a European country, or a country inhabited exclusively by the Caucasoid races, the League of Nations would have been much more energetic in this policy. . . . We make bold to say that had Ethiopia been a white country like Belgium, Holland or Greece, not only would the League have imposed economic and financial sanctions, but military and diplomatic sanctions would have been in order. . . . Now is the time for Africans to think of race not grace."[4] The *Gold Coast Spectator*'s editorial on May 9, 1936, was even more bitter: "Force, the white man's god, is again supreme. . . . Poison gas, British oil and the white man's duplicity all combined to make the Italian advance victorious. . . . After the Great War the League lent money to some of the small Central powers to rehabilitate them. But these are whites. The League refused funds to Ethiopia, even though Article XVI stipulates it. Ethiopia being black, could not be supported, even in affliction, and her financial solicitations were treated with derision. This is the Christian nations at work!"[5] I. T. A. Wallace-Johnson, who was himself a Christian but a member of an independent African church, rather than a European mission church, and who was also an anticolonial Marxist, believed that the episode should promote political consciousness:

The white man—yea the European in this instance—has proved that Christianity and barbarism are identical. He has proved that European Christian ethics are nothing but a farce and that after all, the sum total of the Christian faith and doctrine is Blessed are the strong for they shall weaken the weak. . . . The whole Ethiopian Empire may be annexed by Italy. But it is just the beginning of a new struggle. It is just the opening of a new page in the history of African nationalism for which every African should be justly proud. The name of Haile Selassie should be the slogan of Africans throughout the length and breadth of this great continent. . . . Africa's children should take a lesson from this Italo-Ethiopian war and be awake to national consciousness.[6]

To the future leader of the Pan-African and national liberation movement, Kwame Nkrumah, the news of Italy's invasion was all he needed. "At that moment it was almost as if the whole of London had suddenly declared war on me personally. For the next few minutes I could do nothing but glare at each impassive face wondering if those people could possibly realise the wickedness of colonialism, and praying that the day might come when I could play my part in bringing about the downfall of such a system. My nationalism surged to the fore."[7]

The invasion galvanized African thinking because "Ethiopia had come to symbolise all the things which Blacks were constantly being reminded they did not possess: an ancient history stretching back into the Biblical era, a venerable monarchy, a Christian Church from apostolic times, a decisive military victory over a European army during the partition and, most of all, the dignity of independence and international recognition. In fact, in African thinking, the adjective 'Ethiopian' meant not so much a country as a condition of independence."[8]

Inside Ethiopia a "law in defence of the race" embodying fascist ideas of racial purity prohibited contact between Italians and Ethiopian women but was often flouted. In February 1937 an attempt to assassinate Rodolpho Graziani, the Italian viceroy who had been commander on the southern front, led to a violent reaction in which several young western-educated Ethiopians were executed. But in November 1937 Graziani was replaced by the Duke of Aosta, a cousin of the Italian king, who inaugurated a conciliatory policy. An effort to attract Ethiopian notables to the colonial regime met with some spectacular successes, especially in regions where the Italians were able to exploit Muslim resentment of Haile Selassie's ostentatiously Christian rule. Schools offering education in local languages, Italian, and even Arabic were set up. Considerable sums were spent by the Italians on roads, hospitals, clinics, and agricultural stations to make their new conquest a colonial showpiece, and many Italian farmers also were brought to Ethiopia as colonists in an effort to increase Ethiopia's agricultural exports. But resistance continued, especially in the mountains to the east of Addis Ababa and in Gojjam along the border with the Sudan.[9]

War and Diplomacy in Tropical Africa

At the outbreak of war in September 1939 the French sought to mobilize a force similar to the 180,000 African soldiers who had served on the European front in World War I. A total of 80,000 troops already had been dispatched when France fell in June 1940, and a further 118,000 were still in Africa—many of them reservists conscripted in 1939 and 1940—although only 20,000 of these were considered fit for battle.[10] In 1914-18 the British, with the large, well-trained Indian army at their disposal, used African soldiers much less than the French. World War II proved much more truly global, necessitating many more African reinforcements for Britain's hard-pressed imperial garrisons, including a sizable deployment to defend India itself. In British West Africa the Royal West African Frontier Force was expanded from 8,000 to 146,000 without any formal mechanism for conscription. The bulk of the troops were recruited in Northern Nigeria through the agency of the chiefs. "No pressure was employed," according to Sir Ahmadu Bello, although some district officers suspected that press-gang methods and subtler forms of persuasion were applied.[11] Britain's East African forces were increased from seven battalions — approximately 5,000 men — at the outbreak of war to 280,000 by the end.[12]

Taking advantage of the imminent fall of France, Mussolini in June 1940 declared war on France and Britain. Italian troops scored an immediate success by capturing British Somaliland, then denuded of defense forces. The British countered by encouraging Haile Selassie to set up his base at Khartoum, from where he sent emissaries into Ethiopia to rally resistance. A unit made up of Ethiopian exiles named from the Bible, "Gideon's Force," by General Orde Wingate, the British commander, invaded Ethiopia through Gojjam. Meanwhile, British, Nigerian, Free French, Belgian, and South African forces also invaded, and Haile Selassie was able to reenter his capital in May of 1941.

Britain withdrew the West African troops from the East African campaign before the fighting was over because of fears for the security of Freetown, which was regarded as an essential link in Allied communications. The colonial administration of French West Africa had opted for alignment with the Vichy regime, which was avowedly neutral, rather than with de Gaulle's Free French forces. The British feared, however, that German pressure would lead to an attack on Freetown from Dakar. On the other hand, the regime in French Equatorial Africa, headed by Governor Félix Eboué, a black Guyanese, sided with de Gaulle in defiance of High Commissioner Pierre-François Boisson at Dakar, giving the Allies an important staging-post at Fort Lamy that could be used to link Nigeria with East and North Africa.[13] Soon afterwards the French Cameroons was seized for the Free French in a spectacular thrust from Nigeria by Colonel Jacques Leclerc. The administration of the Congo at Brazzaville then followed by siding with de Gaulle, and the pro-Vichy officials of Gabon were ousted.

Meanwhile, Boisson at Dakar clung to the Vichy policy of neutrality. An inopportune British and Free French raid in September 1940 was repelled, serving only to harden opinion there against de Gaulle. But in 1942, when the Allies landed in West Africa, Boisson decided the time was ripe to rally to the Allied side with a well-trained force of a hundred thousand African soldiers, a half brigade of Foreign Legionnaires, and a European battalion, all accompanied by planes and ships.

Gaullist propaganda made much of African loyalty. Jacques Stern, Free French minister of the colonies, published a eulogy of the French colonial regime in which he declared that there was no racial discrimination and speculated that the unknown French soldier buried beneath the Arc de Triomphe might be black.[14] But Mbella Sonne Diponko, the Cameroons novelist, has caught the dominant mood better, remembering

as a child seeing Camerounian men being conscripted by non-Camerounian Bambara soldiers [from the French Sudan]. Some hid in the bush. Many others who were taken clearly went against their will, not because they didn't want to fight against Nazi Germany and on the side of France, but simply because they couldn't be bothered one way or the other. . . .

It wasn't Africans who vacillated between the Free French Movement and the Vichy regime. The *right* even to vacillate was denied them because, although French forces had been defeated in France, French-speaking Africans were still a colonised people, there were French-speaking officials on the spot to carry on with the job of autocratic rule. It was these officials who were, with the hand-picked *notables* associated with them, for or against de Gaulle. And once they had decided one way or the other, all they did was to issue orders for the rank and file to follow suit.[15]

The transfers of allegiance to de Gaulle registered diplomatic maneuvers and military coups rather than any manifestation of the popular will. In the context of African political history the Gaullist putsches of the 1940s anticipated the military takeovers of the independent regimes two decades later, demonstrating to the mass of Africans then under arms the ability of disciplined fighting forces to seize power swiftly, especially in conditions of relative political apathy.

The oscillations of the bureaucratic elite fed the cynicism depicted by Diponko. While Dakar was aligned with Vichy, Governor Léon Geisemar, along with other Jewish officials, was rendered destitute but emerged as secretary-general of the government under the Free French, while Boisson in his turn was disgraced and jailed. Colonial loyalties were also eroded as Vichy engaged in propaganda warfare with the Allies. The chief newspaper in French West Africa, *Paris-Dakar*, was careful to report any items that showed that all was not well in British West Africa, and at the same time the French authorities banned the public's listening to the British Broadcasting Corporation.[16]

Wartime Economics

World War II had a severe economic impact on most areas of Africa because of the shortage of consumer imports and the abrupt closure of European export markets. The loss of cheap Japanese imports led to a fivefold increase in the price of textiles in Uganda, for example.[17] In West Africa it has been estimated that the barter terms of trade declined further, and, even worse, real income also showed a downward trend, so that the war had in fact a more serious impact than the depression of the 1930s.[18] "By the end of the war West Africa's total importing capacity was lower than at any time since 1900 (with the possible exception of 1921), though population and public debts had both increased greatly since the beginning of the century."[19]

On the other hand, shortages of imported cloth and other manufactures led to a revival of indigenous weaving and blacksmithing in areas like Senegal. Similarly, wartime conditions led to the beginnings of industrialization in Senegal, where metropolitan interests hitherto had effectively checked the development of peanut processing. In order to economize on shipping space, a 1938 agreement enforcing restrictions on the amount of peanut oil processed in Senegal was rescinded in 1939. By 1941 the quota allowed had risen from 5,800 tons in 1938 to 45,000 tons.[20]

When French West Africa came over to the Allied side, the Free French regime proclaimed the slogan, "Work = Victory = Liberation of the Motherland," and in Senegal began a "battle of the groundnuts" to raise peanut production to prewar levels.[21] But the administration failed to reach its target of 400,000 tons. Only 275,000 were produced—partly because a higher price was paid across the border in British-ruled Gambia.[22]

In Ivory Coast, where the African farmers were all *sujets* and therefore did not have the limited but real constitutional means of protest of some Senegalese, the Free French regime was particularly harsh. Farmers were forced to switch crops at the behest of the administration, and plantations were destroyed, ostensibly because their crops were diseased, though such measures were often initiated because the Africans were competing with European plantation owners, who were also favored by the bonus that was paid to the owners of larger farms.[23]

In British territories the state intervened directly in the economy to support the war effort with increased African cash crops and minerals, which became especially valuable to the Allies after the loss of Southeast Asia to the Japanese. Quotas and fixed prices were employed by bodies like the West African Produce Marketing Board, which collaborated closely with the larger European firms organized into the Association of West African Merchants. The smaller firms, owned by Africans and Levantines, tended to suffer from this state interference in the free market.[24] Prices were kept low and thus the African farmer contributed, willy-nilly, to the British war effort by being paid a lower price than his tropical produce could have commanded on the world market.[25]

The Belgian Congo and the Portuguese Territories

The war made no drastic political impact on territories held by Belgium and Portugal. After the conquest of Belgium by the Germans in 1940 the Belgian government in exile resolved to continue the fight, and Governor-General Pierre-Marie-Joseph Ryckmans aligned the Congo on the side of the Allies. The Force Publique was expanded and a contingent was sent, as we have seen, to the Ethiopian campaign. Garrison and support troops were furnished for the Middle East and West Africa. Because of the German occupation of Belgium, the Force could only be enlarged from the Congo, which meant in practice depleting the colonial administration by taking away experienced officials. This contributed to a general decline in the numerical strength and quality of the administration from 1940 onward.[26]

The shortage of seasoned officials was especially serious because the Congo was called upon to make a major contribution to the Allied war effort after the loss of Malayan rubber and tin to the Japanese. Tin production was expanded from 2,750 tons in 1939 to 17,300 tons in 1945 and rubber production from 1,142 tons in 1939 to 11,337 tons in 1944. Katanga supplied the uranium for America's first atomic bomb.[27] Moreover, the workers in these rapidly growing export sectors had to be fed, which entailed the expansion of food production for the internal market. In order to meet these demands, the period of compulsory farm labor was doubled from 60 to 120 days per annum. Officials of the overworked administrative service tended to be judged by the productivity of their areas, and any qualms that this policy of forced production might bear too harshly on African farmers were dismissed in the face of the government's determination to defeat Nazi Germany.[28] To escape the system, many of the most vigorous farmers left the villages for the towns; those who remained bore an even heavier work burden and had less time to devote to producing foodstuffs for themselves or engaging in the round of customary political and ceremonial activities. Ryckmans himself caught the gloom of the villages in a memorable phrase, "At each full moon, the circle of dancers grows smaller."[29]

The war served as a catalyst, generally increasing the pace of social and economic change. But scant attempt was made to facilitate adjustment to such changes through political action. In 1939 Simon Mpadi had founded the Mission des Noirs, or "khaki movement," a breakaway group that had its origins in the Salvation Army, and many of his adherents hoped for a German victory. Apart from this, the Congolese had not yet demonstrated any obvious political aspirations.[30] After 1945 the Belgians, preoccupied with reconstruction in the homeland, repaired the old colonial framework by filling vacancies in the ranks and counted themselves lucky that, unlike other European powers, they were not harassed by a surge of nationalism among their colonial subjects.[31]

If Belgium's paternalism and the lack of any ideological schism equivalent to the Free French-Vichy divide muffled African politics in the Congo, this was even more true of the Portuguese territories. Prime Minister Antonio Salazar's brand of Portuguese fascism — *Estada Nova*, "the new state" — skillfully avoided involvement in the fighting. *Estada Nova* was even strengthened by the war, profiting from trade with the belligerents, especially in such strategic metals as wolfram, allowing the Portuguese administration to tighten its control in Africa. It is unique in the historiography of Africa that accounts of Mozambique, Angola and Guinea Bissau scarcely mention World War II, and still less do they treat it as a watershed.[32] The significance of the war was therefore to keep Portuguese Africa, like Portugal itself, aloof from the main forces of change elsewhere.

The White-Dominated South

When war broke out, the ministry of the United party government, which had held power since 1934, split irrevocably. Six ministers backed the premier, General James Hertzog, who sought neutrality; seven sided with his deputy, General Jan Smuts, who urged involvement with Britain and the Commonwealth. In the subsequent debate, Hertzog, equating Germany's defeat in 1918 and treatment at Versailles with the Afrikaner sufferings in the Anglo-Boer War, compromised his neutralism and alienated support by defending Hitler's diplomatic record. Smuts argued that South Africa could not afford to remain in neutral isolation while Germany still coveted its old South-West Africa territory. In the final tally Hertzog was defeated by 80 votes to 67. Patrick Duncan, the high commissioner, refused him a dissolution of parliament, and Smuts, still vigorous at 69, was once more prime minister.[33]

Deprived of office for the first time in fifteen years, Nationalist Afrikanerdom appeared in disarray. There was considerable disagreement among the Nationalists as to how far they should oppose the war. Some, like Dr. D. F. Malan, leader of the Purified Nationalist party, wanted strict neutrality; whereas others, like Hendrik Verwoerd, would not have objected to a Nazi victory, and some, like John Vorster, who was interned during the war, would positively have welcomed it. The future of Afrikanerdom was disputed in parliament by Malan's Purified Nationalists and the rump of the Hertzogites and outside by the Black Shirts, the Gray Shirts, the *Broederbond* secret society, *Ossewabrandwag*, or "ox-wagon sentinel," and Pirow's New Order, all of which were influenced by the Nazi example. The old leader, Hertzog, was bitterly disillusioned by such personal, organizational, and ideological factionalism. He renounced party politics in favor of the new "world-revolution," National Socialism. In the 1943 election, facing this Nationalist confusion, Smuts's United party won 89 seats and its Dominion party allies a further 7 while 9 went to Labor and 2 to Independents, leaving the Nationalists with 33. Yet the weakness of Nationalist Afrikanerdom was deceptive. There was some evidence that Hertzog would have won an election on the neutrality issue in 1939. Furthermore, with the politics of "fusion" discredited through the fall of Hertzog, when once Afrikanerdom regrouped, it was likely to be of the militant type exemplified by Malan.[34]

The war produced a burst of economic development. The sharp curtailment of imports combined with South Africa's war effort to stimulate local industry, especially in the iron, steel, and engineering sectors. The huge Allied convoys to the Middle and Far Eastern fronts were provisioned as they rounded the Cape, turning South Africa's agricultural problems from those of surpluses to shortages and leading to a rapid increase in the price of farm products. Ironically, this "English war" to which so many Afrikaners were bitterly opposed produced an economic boom that allowed Afrikaner farmers to begin the process of agricultural mechanization and virtually eliminated the Poor White — essentially a "Poor Afrikaner" — problem. As a result of this newfound prosperity community institutions for savings and investment, such as the Volksas Bank, which dates from 1945, were founded, facilitating the emergence of an Afrikaner commercial and industrial bourgeoisie, closely tied to Nationalist politics.[35]

In Southern Rhodesia the war also spurred economic development, similarly eliminating the poor whites as the country built up its own iron and steel industry and many lesser enterprises. An air training scheme was developed, in association with the British government, whereby Southern Rhodesia was called upon to supply airports and ancillary buildings. "Farmers and industrial firms suddenly found an almost insatiable market," wrote the biographers of Sir Godfrey Huggins, Southern Rhodesia's wartime prime minister.[36] Southern Rhodesia's industrial revolution, like that in South Africa, was presided over by local politicians who were linked to, and often drawn from, local capitalists.

Hence the wealth generated was utilized for general economic development in the interests of an emergent national bourgeoisie rather than for the kind of enclave development so characteristic of much of the rest of colonial Africa, where crucial investment decisions were made by expatriate businessmen.[37] The white settler regime also acquired efficient fighting services, including air power, as a legacy of this wartime program.[38]

Wartime Radicalization

World War II marked the decline in power of the major European colonial states, Britain and France, and the rise of the superpowers, the United States and Soviet Russia, both avowedly anticolonial. Article III of the 1941 Atlantic Charter, which declared "the right of all peoples to choose the form of government under which they live," proved an especial embarrassment to Britain and France when Afro-Asian nationalist leaders, including Nnamdi Azikiwe and other West African radicals, claimed that it should apply to the colonies in the form of responsible self-government. Both Winston Churchill, the British prime minister, and General de Gaulle, the leader of the Free French, insisted that Article III should apply only to the European countries liberated from the Axis powers. President Franklin D. Roosevelt, on the other hand, declared that the right of self-determination should apply to all peoples and that the United States would actively support it.[39] In 1944 Sumner Welles, one of the president's chief lieutenants, indicated America's approach to the postwar settlement: "Unless the forces of nationalism, which are fast growing and more and more powerful in all these vast areas of the earth, are canalized into constructive channels, a devastating state of chaos will ensue. The determination of some of these peoples to secure their freedom cannot longer be thwarted."[40]

The unabashed imperialism of Churchill and de Gaulle, backed by a multitude of experiences demonstrating that the British and French had no intention of promptly applying Article III to their African territories, contributed to a quickening radical spirit among African nationalists. In November 1944 at Camp Faidherbe, close to Dakar, Senegalese *tirailleurs*, protesting the failure of the authorities to honor the terms on which they had enlisted, mutinied. They were brutally suppressed with at least a hundred casualties.[41]

For many Africans military service amounted to a crash course in comparative imperialism and colonial nationalism. In the jungles of Southeast Asia the Japanese war in which so many African troops fought taught them anticolonialist lessons. A Gold Coast soldier in Burma hoped to send some of the books and pamphlets he had been reading there to nationalist leaders back home. The Japanese had been defeated, but the war was not over:

We have finished the war physically, but morally it is not over. We have to struggle for liberty; at home the suppression is great. We have been spared back to life from the fighting front: but unless God gives us grace we shall fight to death about the suppressive mode of Rule we are encountering out here. In comparisin [sic] we are regarded less human: as to our lowliness in this sphere of the world, it is worse.

We are discovering the truths of Wallace-Johnson's writings: and I would to God that He gives us more Wallace-Johnsons when we come back home.

We have made up our minds to help build the country, free from all oppression, and in our oath to the Lord, we shall never miss you in all our plans to build our motherland. . . .[42]

West Africans serving on the other side of the continent, especially in Kenya, were shocked to find that, despite the presence of so many Europeans, their fellow Africans rarely were able to converse with them in English and were condemned to fill the most menial roles in a society dominated by white settlers, backed by Indian merchants and clerks. In a burst of Pan-Africanist sentiment some of them reported back to the *West African Pilot* in December 1940 that it was unacceptable that one part of the continent should become free while others were kept in bondage. These West African servicemen therefore had resolved to convince whites "that the African can do as much as any other member of the human race, if only given equal opportunities.[43]

In 1942 shattering defeats by the Japanese in the Far East led the British to send the King's African Rifles overseas for the first time. The Kenya government prudently began planning for their demobilization almost at once. The "economical and political flux" in the recruits' homelands and their development of a sense that wage employment opportunities ought to be available, even before their enlistment, led the government to create a subcommittee on postwar employment of Africans in 1943. The subcommittee warned that, unlike its World War I predecessors who had fought only in Africa, the present generation of soldiers would be unsettled by acquaintance with radically different cultures overseas. Moreover, whereas the World War I Kenya soldier was in almost every case a rank-and-file infantryman or carrier, his successor enjoyed more varied opportunities: "His capacity for taking responsibility and his skilled work have surprised those who knew him only as a manual labourer. He has shown his worth and it will not be surprising if he expects to see it acknowledged. . . He has been well clothed and shod; he has been fed on a balanced and ample diet; and his medical and material needs have been carefully tended. His pay has been comparatively high and on discharge the habits of the standard of life he has acquired will not easily fall from him. His desires will be such that he will not generally be content with the low standard with which most Africans were content before the war."[44]

Some postwar nationalist leaders have testified to the radicalizing effect of service overseas. Waruhiu Itote—"General China" of the Mau Mau—recalled a chance encounter with an Indian girl, reared in East Africa, in an Indian railway station. She explained how Indian nationalists had extracted a promise of self-government from the British and, after quizzing him as to what he believed he was fighting for, upbraided him as a mercenary. He also recollected long political discussions with a black American soldier, attacking their mutual problem of the color bar, at a leave camp in India.[45]

Dedan Mugo Kimani became an instructor in an army hygiene section and later a sergeant major teaching Swahili to Europeans of all ranks including majors and colonels. After a year's service in Ethiopia he was promoted to senior sergeant major as a hygiene instructor back in Kenya. He recalled, "I began to be a politician because the treatment of African non-commissioned officers was discriminating. Clothes, rations, quarters, were different from Asians and Europeans. I tried to agitate inside the Army but I was court-martialed for this in Gilgil in 1944 and sentenced to three months detention." Discharged on medical grounds in December 1945, he found employment at Kiambu in the African Demobilization Unit. He was elected president of the Kenya Ex-Servicemen in September 1946 and to the Kiambu Local Native Council in October. In February 1947 he was further elected president of All-Kikuyu Age Groups.[46]

Bildad Mwaganu Kaggia served in the Middle East and Britain—where he met Jomo Kenyatta—and reached the rank of staff sergeant before demobilization: "I first became really interested in politics when I was in the Middle East. Previously I had been a keen student of religion, but after seeing the Holy Land I looked at Christianity in a different way. I saw the establishment of foreign religion through missions as a stepping-stone to colonialism, and I therefore thought that the first move in the struggle for independence must be [to] liberate our people from foreign religious beliefs. These missions used slogans that supported the colonial authorities, such as 'The Government or Powers that be are ordained by God.' Many of our people, fed by this, believed it and could not be expected to fight with their lives for their real rights while still believing it. The missions on their side also found certain advantages in the preservation of colonial rule." After his demobilization he clashed with the Church Missionary Society at Kahuhia, from whose primary school he had graduated, and then launched a movement attacking all missionary churches. It spread rapidly in central Kenya.[47]

In certain crucial ways the Kenya to which these radicalized ex-servicemen returned appeared even more a "white man's country" than what they had left. European farmers did well out of the war. The British government offered them guaranteed prices and subsidies in order to feed its large East African forces and cope with the loss of vital Asian sources of tropical supply. Spurred on by a combination of material and patriotic motives, the European farmers' production of cereals, coffee, tea, and sisal soared. A series of interterritorial boards was established to coordinate production, with white settlers strongly represented; thus they assumed unprecedented influence over the development of East Africa as a whole. Defense regulations were exploited to curb Indian immigration and competition, while compulsory African labor on European farms was allowed as an "essential undertaking" for the war effort. By 1945 European farmers "were financially and psychologically more secure than they had ever been before."[48]

In March 1944 the Europeans established the Electors' Union, superseding earlier organizations that were considered either too local or were semimoribund. The Electors' Union insisted that leadership must remain in European control and sought to safeguard the White Highlands as a permanent area of European settlement. The wartime trend must continue, the Electors' Union exhorted, with white settlers gradually replacing the influence of the British Colonial Office in the councils of government. It hoped that the heads of departments would try to participate in the Electors' Union's conferences, which they did. It was not that Africans' interests would be ignored; rather, so the argument ran, the Nairobi secretariat and the European settlers were the proper agents of imperial trusteeship. It is worth emphasizing that the settler conception of trusteeship was sharply selective. The settler-secretariat alignment was explicitly designed to reduce Colonial Office influence and to diminish, also, by implication, the trusteeship roles of district officials and missionaries, who had frequently defended African interests in Kenya. (Significantly, when Archdeacon—later Archbishop—L. J. Beecher was appointed to the legislative council as a representative of African interests in 1943, he quickly clashed with settler spokesmen.)

In August 1945 Major Sir Ferdinand Cavendish-Bentinck, one of the settlers' more aristocratic spokesmen, became a quasi minister under the title of member for agriculture with responsibility for settling postwar British ex-servicemen in Kenya. Africans and Indians united in protesting his appointment as a move towards consolidation of white settler hegemony.[49]

Settler rhetoric ran to an extremism that exaggerated the realities of European power. Although the settlers talked about "home rule," they assumed this would involve a permanent tie with Britain—somewhat on the model of Ulster—entailing continuing military, administrative, and economic support. A few, notably the editor of the *Kenya Weekly News*, Commander F. J. Couldrey, urged the Europeans to come to terms with African political aspirations.[50] Couldrey's suggestion that an African be appointed to the legislative council was indeed adopted by Governor Sir Henry Moore in 1944, but his liberalism alienated most settlers. Africans were more likely to be aware of the image of settler power projected by the Electors' Union: thus Kenya politics tended to polarize along racial lines.

In 1944 after all the French colonies had rallied to the Free French cause de Gaulle summoned his senior administrators to a conference at Brazzaville, the capital of French Equatorial Africa, in order to formulate plans for the postwar development of the French empire. Governors, parliamentarians, and colonial experts all participated, but there were no negotiations or even consultations with the Africans.[51] Many Frenchmen were deeply moved by the involvement of the African dependencies, especially French Equatorial Africa, in the Free French war effort. There was consequently much talk of reform and some discussion of federal assemblies, but these were to be merely consultative. Indeed, the preamble to the conference's final resolution flatly rejected any radical move towards decolonization: "The aims of the civilizing work accomplished by France in the colonies exclude any thought of autonomy. . . . the idea of establishing, even in the distant future, 'self government' in the colonies must be discarded."[52] Britain, on the other hand, had the experience of the earlier progress of white settler colonies towards self-government as a storehouse of constitutional and administrative precedent when it came to coping with African political ferment. Britain, therefore, planned for the postwar future of Africa by means of a series of commissions on which Africans were represented and in which the aim of ultimate decolonization was implicit.[53]

As the end of the war drew near, just as in 1918, the prospect of a large-scale international settlement and the formation of a new international organization prompted African spokesmen to formulate their ideas on postwar political development. Pan-Africanism, which had languished since the Fourth Pan-African Congress in New York in 1927, was revived when a number of black welfare organizations and student groups resident in Britain joined in 1944 to form the Pan-African Federation. In April 1944 the new federation, in cooperation with such groups as the League of Coloured Peoples and the West African Students' Union, addressed a manifesto to the United Nations Conference at San Francisco. The manifesto reminded the world powers that they had subscribed to the Atlantic Charter and had advocated the development of Africa through United Nations agencies in which Africans would participate to bring about "full self-government within a definite time limit" and to eradicate mass illiteracy. Fastening on the characterization of the war as an antifascist struggle, the manifesto insisted:

United Nations must free themselves of the evils against which they are fighting.
    Africa is a land of varied political forms, economic interests and social and cultural standards. This is complicated by the fact that among the powers with imperial possessions in Africa are fascist Spain and fascist Portugal. It is further complicated by the colour-bar laws and practices obtaining within the territories of some of the United Nations themselves, notably the Union of South Africa. The United Nations are pledged to secure in addition to the military defeat of fascism, the eradication of its moral and political manifestations, chief of which is the theory of the master-race against inferior races. If the principles for which we fight do not apply to Europe, then it is the duty of the United Nations to eliminate the influence of the Spanish and Portuguese fascist regimes and to remove from their own territories those theories and practices for the destruction of which Africans have died on many battlefields.[54]

    The Fifth Pan-African Congress was held in Manchester in October 1945. Kwame Nkrumah, who had just returned from his university studies in the United States, wrote its "Declaration to the Colonial Peoples of the World":

We believe in the rights of all peoples to govern themselves. We affirm the right of all colonial peoples to control their own destiny. All colonies must be free from foreign imperialist control, whether political or economic. The peoples of the colonies must have the right to elect their own government, a government without restrictions from a foreign power. . . .

The object of the imperialist powers is to exploit. By granting the right to the colonial peoples to govern themselves, they are defeating that objective. Therefore, the struggle for political power by colonial and subject peoples is the first step towards, and the necessary pre-requisite to, complete social, economic and political emancipation.

The Fifth Pan-African Congress, therefore, calls on the workers and farmers of the colonies to organize effectively. Colonial workers must be in the front lines of the battle against imperialism.

This Fifth Pan-African Congress calls on the intellectuals and professional classes of the colonies to awaken to their responsibilities. The long, long night is over. . . . Today there is only one road to effective action—the organization of the masses.

COLONIAL AND SUBJECT PEOPLES OF THE WORLD—UNITE![55]

George Padmore, the Afro-West Indian socialist who was responsible for much of the preliminary organizational work, made certain that trade union and peasant representatives would attend, largely by timing the congress to take advantage of the presence of colonial trade unionists in Europe for the World Trade Union Conference in Paris.[56] Looking back, Nkrumah saw this social transformation as decisively radicalizing the movement for independence; the Manchester congress "shot into the limbo the gradualist aspirations of our African middle classes and intellectuals and expressed the solid-down-to-earth will of our workers, trade unionists, farmers and peasants . . ."[57] Manchester marked the zenith of the Pan-African movement. The inclusion of working class delegates was a master stroke by a nationalist movement advertising its popular support to the newly elected British Labour government. In contrast with earlier Pan-African congresses, white well-wishers of the missionary type were absent. Moreover, the proportion of Africans, as against Afro-West Indians and Afro-Americans, was much greater. The impression was that this time the black Africans had taken charge.

Yet even at Manchester weaknesses could be discerned. Only at the most generalized level, for example, could Pan-Africanism transcend the Anglophone-Francophone divide. Raphael Armattoe, the Togolese poet, reported on the situation in Francophone Africa south of the Sahara, including the Belgian Congo. He spoke about the higher level of education in French colonies in comparison with their British equivalents and refrained from criticism of the French colonial authorities. He reflected, "It is sometimes questioned whether French West Africans have any feeling of national consciousness, but I can say that French West Africans would be happier if they were governing themselves. They sometimes envy the British Africans their intense national feeling—oppression has bound them together. A French West African should feel that he is an African first, before he is anything else."[58] If French colonial officials had not developed constitutional guidelines to cope with the notion of African independence, it was partly because they faced nothing equivalent to the new popular nationalism in British West Africa. Further, reflecting the advanced state of West African politics, the focus was largely regional—West African—rather than truly continental.

Ironically, West Africa's pride of place, and Britain's comparatively liberal response to developments there, quickly deflected the radicalism exhibited at

Manchester into local rather than Pan-African channels. The British had already initiated plans for greater popular participation in the government of their West African colonies in the hope of securing African cooperation in the war effort. The Manchester congress, under Nkrumah's inspiration, denounced "the artificial divisions and territorial boundaries created by the imperialist powers which are deliberate steps to obstruct the political unity of the West African peoples,"[59] just at the time when representative institutions were being fashioned for each colony that would very shortly incorporate him, along with other popular leaders, into separate political arenas, circumscribed by those same artificial boundaries.[60]

In South Africa the strong Christian commitment of many black leaders and the state's suppression of mass organizations and agitation had combined to create a politics of moral assertion that sought to capitalize on the Allies' avowed commitment to antifascism and democracy. Dr. Alfred B. Xuma, president of the African National Congress, established the sizable Atlantic Charter Committee, composed of "leaders of African thought"—physicians, attorneys, teachers, ministers, and an editor—to prepare plans for the "postwar reconstruction of Africa with special reference to Southern Africa." The committee produced "The Atlantic Charter from the Standpoint of Africans within the Union of South Africa" and also a bill of rights. These were combined as *Africans' Claims in South Africa*, which was adopted as a guideline by the annual conference of the African National Congress in December 1943.[61]

The declarations in *Africans' Claims* committed the congress—which had sometimes seemed to prefer a qualified, nonracial franchise in the tradition of the Cape—to political democracy. It also suggested sweeping reforms designed to promote greater equality in employment and education, to allow more freedom of movement and residence, and to create a health service along the lines of that advocated by the British Labour party. But, in significant contrast to their contemporary, the Nigerian nationalist Dr. Nnamdi Azikiwe, whose *Atlantic Charter and British West Africa* was framed as a memorandum to the British colonial secretary, demanding full independence within fifteen years, the congressmen stipulated no timetable or program of action. Instead, Dr. Xuma forwarded *Africans' Claims* to Prime Minister Smuts along with a request for an interview.

In some ways this seemed a propitious time for such an approach. The United party was shorn of its extreme Afrikaner Nationalist wing, and Jan Hofmeyr, the most respected spokesman for South African liberalism, was back in the cabinet with responsibility for domestic affairs. Denys Reitz, the minister for native affairs, had himself referred to the Atlantic Charter as the basis for future reform.[62] Altogether the war had tended to polarize white opinion on race relations. When Afrikaner Nationalists were influenced by Nazi ideology, this caused some white groups to redouble their efforts toward interracial cooperation in order to give practical meaning to antifacism in the South African context.

But Smuts rejected both the African National Congress's interpretation of the Atlantic Charter and Xuma's request for an interview. In the aftermath of the 1943 election he was concerned to promote white unity, and he was piqued at the congress's initiative. Meanwhile, the congress had *Africans' Claims* printed, with a preface by Xuma, challenging Africans "to organize themselves and unite into a mass liberation movement . . ." It sold "like hot cakes."[63] In 1944 the African National Congress authorized the formation of its Youth League, which became committed, under the charismatic influence of Anton Lembede, to shifting the emphasis from interracial collaboration to militant and self-reliant African nationalism. Disturbances in Pretoria in 1942 and Johannesburg in 1944, as well as sixty illegal African strikes between 1942 and the end of 1944, indicated potential grass-roots support for such militancy. There was also the prospect of arraigning South Africa before world opinion. In 1945 Xuma forwarded *Africans' Claims* to the United Nations at San Francisco. The following year he had the satisfaction of being present in person at the United Nations when the General Assembly rejected, by 36 votes to nil, the Union of South Africa's request to incorporate South-West Africa and censured the Union for racially discriminatory legislation. It was at the same session of the United Nations that Smuts and Xuma met for the first time face to face. It was apparently an accidental encounter at a reception. Smuts was reported to have drawn Xuma aside, saying, "Look here, Xuma, these people do not understand us. Let us go back home and sit down together and solve our problems." But before the conversation could go any further, a protective aide, doubtless worried about the effect of the meeting on white South African opinion, took Smuts away.[64]

CHAPTER 17

Decolonization

On December 7, 1938, the British colonial secretary, Malcolm MacDonald, proclaimed the commitment of Britain to self-government for its colonies: "The great purpose of the British Empire is the gradual spread of freedom among all His Majesty's subjects in whatever part of the world they live. That spread of freedom is a slow evolutionary process. In some countries it is more rapid than in others. In some parts of the Empire, in the Dominions, that evolutionary process has been completed, it is finished. Inside the Colonial Empire the evolutionary process is going on all the time. . . . It may take generations, or even centuries for the peoples in some parts of the Colonial Empire to achieve self-government. But it is a major part of our policy, even among the most backward peoples of Africa, to teach them and to encourage them always to be able to stand a little more on their own feet."[1] MacDonald's commitment to ultimate African self-government—however remote in time—was the first official statement of its kind, in the view of Margery Perham, who also records the relief felt by a senior colonial official at a conference in 1939 that "at any rate in Africa [in contrast to Asia] we can be sure that we have unlimited time to work."[2]

A quarter of a century earlier the Reverend Attoh Ahuma, a spokesman for Gold Coast nationalism, also could envisage such slow-paced progress from imperial tutelage because he believed that contemporary Africa had only reached the level of economic and social development of medieval Europe.[3] By 1943 the accepted leader of Gold Coast nationalism, J. B. Danquah, put his estimate on the time needed to catch up at a mere decade. Such accelerated

290

modernization would need massive legislation, but, he argued, "must we be afraid of a lot of legislation? They did it in Russia in 25 years. There is no reason we should not do it in the Gold Coast in 10 years."[4] The Gold Coast became independent as Ghana in 1957. In a sense, therefore, the ideas of Danquah with regard to the pace of mid-twentieth-century change triumphed over those of MacDonald, though in the process Danquah himself was super-seded by the much more radical nationalist leader, Kwame Nkrumah.

If MacDonald's notion of deliberate, carefully prepared constitutional pro-gress went out of fashion in the 1950s—although he himself had a remarkable postwar career as a peripatetic troubleshooter for successive British govern-ments concerned with decolonization—Nkrumah himself was to be overthrown by an army and police coup d'état that enjoyed much popular support. In December 1966 the University of East Africa held a social science conference where historians prepared a series of papers on African protest movements and the development of nationalism, "only to find that hardly a single political scientist was now concerned with them. 'Nationalism is a dead subject'—so one distinguished author of a book on African politics announced: he himself had moved on to the politics of economic planning."[5] Frantz Fanon, very much the hero figure of young African radicals in the late 1960s, dismissed the leaders who took power at independence as "spoilt children of yesterday's colonialism and of today's national governments, [who] organized the loot of whatever national resources exist."[6]

In white-dominated southern Africa changes of perspective were equally rapid. On February 3, 1960, British Prime Minister Harold Macmillan delivered the famous "wind of change" speech to the South African parliament at Cape Town, in which he condemned *apartheid* and urged the settler societies to come to terms with African nationalism. For the whites in Kenya and in the Central African Federation territories of Northern Rhodesia and Nyasaland his speech warned that the Conservative government, which had returned to power in October 1959, was in the process of discarding many hitherto accepted im-perialist dogmas.[7] Some, at least, took the cue and participated in smoothing the transition from white domination to black independence—notably Sir Michael Blundell, whose autobiography, *So Rough a Wind*, develops Macmil-lan's metaphor with reference to the political transformation of Kenya.[8]

Farther south, Macmillan's prophecies seemed to be falsified by events. On March 21, 1960, a demonstration against the pass laws by the Pan-African Congress at Sharpeville was forcibly dispersed by the police. Sixty-seven Afri-cans were killed and 180 were wounded. There were no police casualties.

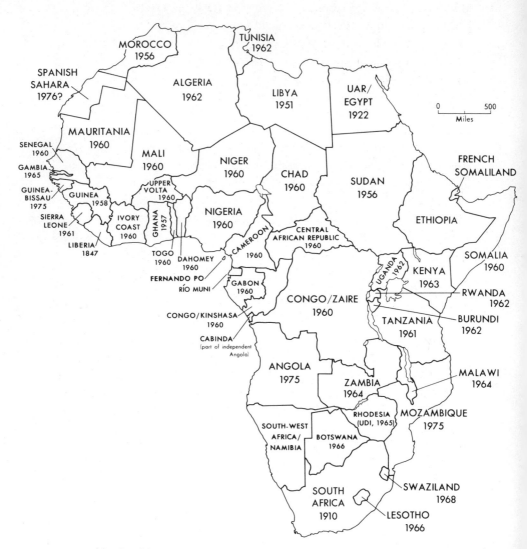

Map 8. African independence, indicating the chronology of independence

Liberals in South Africa and elsewhere expected that the South African government would be shocked into reversing its trend toward authoritarianism. But in March Chief Albert Luthuli, the leader of the African National Congress, was arrested for condemning the Sharpeville massacre as genocide. The government then instituted a series of strong-arm measures designed to repress protest. The era of nonviolent resistance closed with a three-day "stay-at-home" organized by African nationalists to coincide with the proclamation of the republic by the government in May 1961. But, anticipated by massive counteraction by the government, the strike failed. A subsequent brief period of sabotage was ended by arresting such key leaders as Nelson Mandela in 1963 and sentencing them to life imprisonment in the Rivonia trial in 1964. On November 11, 1965, Ian Smith's government in Southern Rhodesia made a unilateral declaration of independence from British rule. Harold Wilson's Labour government failed to intervene militarily, relying instead on economic sanctions. These have failed to topple Smith, who remains in power at the time of writing. By the end of the 1960s several well-informed studies were published examining the development of southern Africa in terms of the stability of white control, and there was some evidence that western foreign policy had tilted toward an acceptance of prolonged white domination.[9] However, the overthrow of the Portuguese dictatorship in 1974, prompted by losses in the long war against African guerrilla fighters, and the subsequent changes in Mozambique radically revised such prognostications of continued white control. It is a truism that is perhaps worth restating that historians depend, when interpreting any event, on being sufficiently distant from it in time to be able to locate it in its historical sequence. To see the present as history is, in a sense, literally impossible, and certainly it is very difficult as the changing fashions in interpretation just chronicled indicate. Nevertheless, looking at the process of decolonization as a stage in Europe's ongoing impact on Africa, certain aspects stand out.

International Opinion and Institutions

The fluidity of accepted interpretations of decolonization, with one orthodoxy scarcely crystallizing before collapsing into its successor, reflects an underlying evolution in international values as well as the haste with which African area studies are improvised and the sheer velocity of the processes they are required to explain. The scope of international law has been highly permissive, tending to recognize as legitimate whatever has been enforceable. Since the American Declaration of Independence in 1776, at least, it has been feasible to assume that those subject to alien rule might revolt; yet, like the right of revolution in general, this has been a right that would come to full recognition only if the revolution were successful. In a sense, the question of whether the rebels have been regarded as punishable traitors or founding fathers has rested upon the fate of their movement. Later imperialists, with the benefit of hindsight, have usually proved more flexible than George III, as the procession of "prison graduates" to positions of ministerial responsibility during British decolonization testifies. More recently, Portugal, hitherto the most obstinate of European colonial powers, has welcomed last year's "terrorists" as patriotic freedom fighters, worthy to grasp the levers of government.[10]

Neither the North American and Latin-American revolutions nor the introduction of responsible government in 1847 into Canada undermined the idea that any state that conquered or otherwise acquired a dependent territory was entitled to maintain control by standard coercive procedures of blockade, punitive expedition, court-martial, and full-scale colonial war. It was still accepted by western opinion that one of the most obvious expressions of national prowess was to achieve control over the land and lives of other peoples as exemplified by the thrust across the continent and the subjugation of native Americans by the newly independent United States. During the scramble for Africa European invaders equipped with prophylactic quinine and tremendous superiority in firepower regarded black rule as somehow inherently illegitimate, degrading the status of black rulers whom they had once considered as kings to mere chiefs. Yet only a few decades later it was white rule in Africa that was held to be illegitimate by much of articulate, institutionalized world opinion.

The nature of organized international opinion had of course greatly changed between 1885 and 1945. The role of the United Nations in accelerating decolonization requires special attention. The preamble to the United Nations Declaration of Human Rights indicated that its signatories lived in a very different political world from that of the old interwar League of Nations. The preamble virtually recognized a contingent right of revolution when it stated that "it is essential, if man is not to be compelled to have recourse, as a last resort, to rebellion against tyranny and oppression, that human rights should be protected by the rule of law."[11] At the outset in San Francisco in 1945 certain key members of the United Nations displayed an anticolonial stance that caused deep apprehension among the imperial powers. Two of the permanent members (the "big five") of the Security Council, the Soviet Union and Nationalist China, were fervently opposed to colonialism. So also had been President Franklin Roosevelt, and even after his death the cold war solidarity with the United

States' European allies did not immediately displace the sense of an anticolonial tradition stemming from 1776 or the natural feeling that metropolitan traders enjoyed unfair advantage over their American rivals in their countries' dependencies. The charter of the United Nations, therefore, committed members in Article 73 to "recognize that the interests of the inhabitants of these territories are paramount, to develop self-government, to take due account of the political aspirations of the peoples, and to assist them in the progressive development of their free political institutions."

The fundamentally different approaches of the League and the United Nations are exhibited in their contrasting policies toward "enemy" colonies after the two world wars. Whereas Germany's colonies in 1919 had been divided between the victorious powers, Italy's possessions after World War II were treated very differently: Libya was granted independence in 1951, Eritrea was attached to the independent African state of Ethiopia, and Italian Somaliland was returned to Italy in order to be prepared for independence within a strict ten-year deadline.

The Trusteeship Council set up by the United Nations was very different from the Permanent Mandates Commission of the League of Nations, which had been dominated by experts in imperial rule, such as Lugard, who sought to promote "professional" standards of colonial administration. It had possessed only advisory powers, which were exercised with due tact and reserve. An anticolonial Australian delegation brought foreboding to all the imperial powers by proposing that all dependencies be brought under United Nations trusteeship. Although this was averted, the composition of the Trusteeship Council was much less attuned to imperial interests than that of its predecessor had been because, alongside representatives of the administering powers, it included permanent members of the Security Council as well as elected members, who were generally chosen from the Afro-Asian and Latin-American states. Members of the Trusteeship Council, moreover, sat as representatives of their governments rather than as spokesmen for "enlightened" standards of colonial bureaucracy. The Trusteeship Council, therefore, included an important anticolonial membership, which increasingly saw its role as speeding the process of decolonization.

Petitioners from nationalist movements were allowed to testify before the Trusteeship Council, thus gaining a forum from which to broadcast their claims. Pressure for the establishment of firm timetables for independence grew as the council dispatched visiting missions, which, especially from 1954 onward, were sharply critical of the pace of political advance formulated by the trust powers.

In Togo and the Cameroons, for example, the French found themselves tied to schedules of decolonization worked out for the neighboring British-controlled territories. Because the British portion of Togo was timed to become independent in 1957 after absorption into the Gold Coast, following a referendum conducted by the United Nations, the French were forced to grant a special status of autonomy for French-administered Togo. This put the territory in the vanguard of nationalist progress and forced the pace of advance elsewhere. Similarly the plans for Nigerian independence approved by the British were partly responsible for the French proposing full and speedy independence for the Cameroons. The imminence of a referendum in the British-administered Cameroons to choose between permanent integration into Nigeria and reunification with the French mandate led the French to offer full independence in order to attract votes for the reunification alternative that they supported.[12]

The General Assembly of the United Nations provided a further arena in which the anticolonial struggle could be waged. In 1960 Kwame Nkrumah, president of the Republic of Ghana, demanded that the assembly call upon all the colonial powers to free their African dependencies and even asserted that the "possession of colonies is now quite incompatible with the membership of the United Nations."[13] In the same year the assembly called for immediate steps to transfer all power to the people of non-self-governing territories in a unanimous declaration: "The subjection of peoples to alien subjugation, domination and exploitation constitutes a denial of fundamental human rights, is contrary to the Charter of the United Nations, and is an impediment to the promotion of world peace and co-operation."[14] The voting then was eighty-nine for with none against, but the remaining colonial powers and their close allies — Australia, Belgium, the Dominican Republic, France, Portugal, South Africa, Spain, Great Britain, and the United States — were among those abstaining.

Even the Security Council, long dominated by the powerful western industrialized states, is no longer quite so secure a forum for expounding opposition to militant anticolonialism. In 1961, when India annexed Goa from Portugal by armed force, the United States spokesman, Adlai Stevenson, claimed that this was as much an act of aggression as the invasion of Egypt to seize the Suez Canal by a combined British, French, and Israeli force or as the suppression of the Hungarian uprising in the same year, 1956, by Soviet Russia. He rejected the Indian representative's view that "there can be no question of aggression against your own frontier, or against your own people whom you want to liberate."[15] Eventually a resolution deploring the use of force against Goa and calling for an end to hostilities, introduced by the United States,

Great Britain, France, and Turkey, won by a vote of seven to four, but it was vetoed by the Soviet Union. A counterresolution supporting India, offered by Ceylon, Libya, and the United Arab Republic, received the support of only the Soviet Union. Yet none of the opponents of India took the question to the General Assembly, where it was presumed that India would have the support of the anticolonial majority. Thirteen years later what Rupert Emerson has termed the "new higher law" of anticolonialism had won such support in the Security Council that the United States, Great Britain, and France were forced to exercise the veto there to prevent the expulsion of South Africa for being in persistent breach of the United Nations charter.

In such debates the spokesmen for subjugated peoples have usually held the moral and logical initiative because the right of self-determination under discussion was implicit in the West's own avowed political principles: nationalism, liberty, democracy, and equality. In fact, upholders of the status quo rarely mounted a direct challenge to the principle of self-determination. Even the spokesmen for white-dominated southern Africa—whose Afrikaner and Portuguese rulers were most insulated from western "progressive" political ideas—usually sought formulae that avoided an outright defense of colonialism. South Africa claimed that *apartheid* offered the Bantu homelands phased decolonization. Portugal, on the other hand, blandly altered the constitutional designation of its dependencies from "colonies" to "overseas provinces" when it sought entry into the United Nations in the early 1950s without wishing to open its territories to international inspection.

The other imperial powers—Britain, France, and Belgium—were too much in the mainstream of the western political tradition and took its tenets too seriously to manipulate its concepts so uninhibitedly in the face of African insistence on self-determination. True, France with its parliamentarism and tradition of citizenship went much further than Portugal in linking colonies and metropolis in common political institutions. But the presence in Paris of a few black deputies simply underlined the undemocratic character of such concessions. Equality in representation would mean the French being vastly outnumbered by their erstwhile colonial subjects, and this they were plainly not prepared to contemplate. Hence, the de Gaulle government shifted to endorsement of territorial nationalism at the end of the 1950s.

Meanwhile, in the context of Anglo-American relations, the British already had pioneered what was to become one of the standard imperial defenses against the anticolonial lobby. The traditional sympathy of the United States for Indian and other colonial nationalism, irritating enough to the British political elite before 1939, became much more ominous when prominent American spokesmen attacked British imperialism just when the Anglo-American "special relationship" was taking shape during the war. In October 1942 *Life* magazine published an "Open Letter from the Editors . . . to the People of England" stating bluntly that "Great Britain had better decide to part with her Empire, for the United States is not prepared to fight in order to keep it."[16] Vice-President Henry Wallace and Republican leader Wendell Willkie also forthrightly condemned British imperial policy. Winston Churchill, more than anyone else the architect of the "special relationship" and also, especially in 1942, the year of the fall of Singapore, the spokesman for an embattled British nationalism and imperialism, indignantly objected to the idea of American cheek "coming to school-marm us into proper behaviour."[17] Nevertheless, the British political and official elite had a strongly felt need to explain, and justify, imperial policy to their powerful ally.

The standard British defense tended to construe American criticism as a demand for "immediate liberation." It was then a relatively easy matter for someone knowledgeable to detail the practical difficulties in the way of any such instant decolonization. The best of the British colonial experts, such as Lord Hailey and Margery Perham, used the controversy to clarify British thinking about imperial ends as well as administrative means and to push the government toward reform and development.[18] Nevertheless, the nature of the encounter meant that the British generally based their case on knowledge of the rich variety of local colonial situations and general expertise over detail and timing.

Soon after the war the United States, as leader of the western alliance, abandoned its anticolonial position for a more conservative stance. In retrospect the wartime Anglo-American debate over the future of the British Empire provided British spokesmen with a dress rehearsal for their defense against postwar accusations of procrastination over decolonization in the United Nations General Assembly and Trusteeship Council. Lord Hailey's own account of the rise of international interest in the colonies makes the continuity between the American and the United Nations confrontation clear. He pointed out that chapters 11 to 13 of the United Nations charter focused on the "imperialist egotism" of the colonial powers as the chief obstacle to decolonization. "But," he argued, "the real problem does not lie here. It lies in the improvement of the material and social conditions of the people of the territories themselves. Were these adequately improved, the civilized world could rest assured that they might safely be left to secure for themselves what changes they felt to be needed in their political status."[19] In fact, British policy makers felt aggrieved because the notion of preparation for independence through development was not just a ploy in international debate but a guiding concept of their administration from about 1940 onward.[20]

In addition to the argument in favor of realistic, phased decolonization—essentially a plea for time—some opponents of the anticolonial groups at the United Nations counterattacked vigorously, maintaining that focusing on the freedom and welfare of peoples under white colonial rule while ignoring other oppressed minorities amounted to operating a double standard. Belgian representatives at the United Nations elaborated this idea so that it became known as *la thése Belge*. Stressing their special responsibility for groups like the Pygmies of the equatorial rain forest, who were much less involved in the modern sector than their neighbors, the Belgians developed an updated version of the arguments by Sir Hugh Clifford and other officials of the previous generation in favor of metropolitan trusteeship on behalf of such groups. Belgium's retreat from the Congo in 1960 and the rapid growth in the number of independent states that might be offended by the expression of such views have meant that this thesis has been heard less frequently in the United Nations in recent years. Nevertheless, it is still used by conservative editorial writers in chiding liberation movements. Similarly, in the standard rhetoric of upholders of the South African regime the argument against "immediate liberation" has become "this can't be done overnight"—usually with the implication that if something cannot be changed overnight, it cannot or should not be changed at all.

West African Breakthrough

By 1945 the British finally had made up their minds to concede to their brown Commonwealth in Asia the independence that the white Commonwealth already possessed. The sequel of African colonization therefore involved no great debate over principle but rather questions of preparation and timing.[21] Dennis Austin, the historian of the evolution of Commonwealth status and the development of Gold Coast independence, has outlined the strategic steps involved: "The guiding principle behind the different stages of this advance—from an elementary form of Crown Colony administration to a complete system of cabinet responsible government—lies in the changing balance of power between British officials and representatives of the local community. By these means a colony is led to independence by a gradual process of emancipation through the careful training of the 'unofficials' in the techniques of self-government."[22] He added the caution, "This, at least, is the theory."

The strategy was highly ambitious, an extreme example of the assumption that it was both feasible and desirable to transfer western political institutions and patterns of behavior to nonwestern environments. Such an approach was in sharp contrast to much that had hitherto characterized British colonial policy. Central to the corporate self-esteem of the colonial bureaucracy had been the notion that "good government" — which they believed was exemplified in their upholding the rule of law and fostering limited economic development — was preferable to African self-government. By temperament and training many such men were quite unfitted for the task they were now expected to perform. Arthur Creech-Jones, the new Labour secretary of state for the colonies, set great store by local government reform. Yet domination of the district by the district commissioner was unlike the British domestic system, and many district officials knew little about that system anyway.[23] Insofar as they recognized any African capacity for self-rule, they believed it had already been incorporated within the colonial system in the form of indirect rule. But African nationalists, even those who were considered moderate, such as Azikiwe's Yoruba rival, Chief Awolowo, opposed indirect rule because they suspected, on the whole rightly, that it had been consigned to them as an alternative to the development of parliamentary institutions on the Westminster model.[24] Writing of Uganda, the anthropologist Aidan Southall explained the ambiguity of indirect rule: "It is still, after nearly forty years of European rule, not possible to be true to Alur and European values at one and the same time. Administrators are compelled on the logic of the situation to view the chief's loyalty to them as right, and to consider the disloyalty to his people and their values, in which support of the British government involves him, as a stand for enlightenment. But they cannot force his subjects to view it so. There will always be moments of critical decision in which what is officially required of the chief will be seen as treachery by many of his subjects."[25] Those devotees of indirect rule who did manage to transcend bureaucratic authoritarianism were prone to a conservative attachment to traditional African institutions, nourished by their understanding of contemporary functionalist anthropological studies, which was totally at odds with the optimistic assumptions behind the concept of preparation.[26]

Nationalist leaders mounted their first successful thrust toward self-government in the Gold Coast.[27] The circumstances confronting them there were relatively favorable. The leaders of Clement Attlee's postwar Labour government already had been won over by Indian nationalists in the debate over decolonization. A series of new constitutions was introduced into most African colonies in the immediate postwar period, which initiated or increased African representation on legislative councils and gave greater scope for African political parties. Secretary of State Creech-Jones in 1947 issued a circular instructing colonial administrations to replace the "native administration" system based on the chiefs with elected local councils, which both opened the way for the new nationalists to penetrate the rural areas and forced the chiefs to politicize themselves. In 1948 he followed this up with an explicit declaration: "The central purpose of British colonial policy is simple. It is to guide the colonial territories to responsible government within the Commonwealth in conditions that ensure to the people concerned both a fair standard of living and freedom from oppression from any quarter."[28] When the Tories returned to power in 1951, they did not call their predecessors' aims into question.

The people of the Gold Coast approached these developments in British policy with a comparatively prosperous economy based on the boom in cocoa prices, so that, for example, their national income was nearly double that of Uganda, which had approximately the same population size. Nor did the movement for independence suffer from the division between northerners and southerners, as in Nigeria, or between colony and protectorate, as in Sierra Leone. In demographic terms the Gold Coast dwarfed the relatively homogenous Gambia.

Nkrumah manipulated this situation brilliantly. British plans for stately progress toward decolonization were disrupted, first by the 1948 riots in Accra and then by the overwhelming success of Nkrumah's Convention People's party in the 1951 election. "How is it possible . . . ," Nkrumah asked himself, "for a revolution to succeed without arms and ammunition? After months of studying Gandhi's policy and watching the effect it had, I began to see that, when backed by a strong political organization, it would be the solution to the colonial problem."[29]

Governor Sir Charles Arden-Clarke, who had the benefit of Southeast Asian experience from which to view such developments, felt that he had no alternative but to release Nkrumah from jail to take office as the leader of government business in the wake of his electoral triumph. Nkrumah accepted, thereby boldly short-circuiting the process of decolonization by taking office at a very much earlier stage in the nationalist encounter than did the Indian leaders on whom he partly modeled himself. Moreover, he adopted Gandhi's strategy of confrontation, adroitly varying the alternatives of the threat of "positive action" and the limited collaboration of "tactical action," in order to shift the British in the direction he wished. Hence, it was a bare ten years between

Nkrumah's return to the Gold Coast from his studies abroad and the independence of Ghana in 1957. Once that was achieved, it was only a matter of timing and some resolution of their internal divisions before Nigeria, Sierra Leone, and the Gambia were similarly decolonized.

France had formulated a postwar policy of reform, not independence, at Brazzaville in January and February 1944.[30] Heavily influenced by Félix Eboué, the conference recommended the abolition of forced labor and the status of *sujet*, along with the abitrary code of laws, the *indigénat*, which governed that demeaning status. It advocated greater participation by the African elite in administration and in representative political institutions, while economic and social reform would cater to the general welfare. At a time when their Anglophone contemporaries were demanding outright independence, the Francophone African leaders worked within the framework of the Brazzaville proposals, concentrating on a generous implementation of them by French postwar governments.

In 1946 the Fourth Republic reversed the traditional ruling that the colonies should finance their development from their own sources by establishing Funds for Investment in Economic and Social Development (FIDES). It has been reckoned that between 1946 and 1958 nearly three-quarters of the total public investment and nearly one-third of civil and military recurrent expenditure were financed by France.[31] Many Africans benefited by the new trend, but it also tied the colonies almost inextricably to France. Moreover, unlike their equivalents in British West Africa, bureaucrats in the French colonies could and did play an active role in politics. Sixty-one out of seventy elected members of the territorial assembly of Upper Volta and forty out of sixty of those in Niger were civil servants, for example, in March 1957.[32] By then a law passed on the initiative of the veteran Senegalese politician Lamine Gueye equalizing the terms of service for Africans and Europeans was swallowing as much as 60 percent of the recurrent budget in civil servants' salaries.[33]

But events outside the confines of French West and Equatorial Africa combined to force the pace of decolonization. After seven years' hard fighting in Indochina, the humiliation of Dien Bien Phu brought into office Pierre Mendès-France, who successfully fulfilled his pledge to negotiate peace within thirty days. The long Algerian war from 1955 to 1962, in which at its height half a million French soldiers were committed, further broke the will of French governments to oppose national liberation movements in prolonged bloody confrontation. In 1955 the delegates at the Afro-Asian conference at Bandung pledged to help all subject peoples struggling for independence, while from West Africa itself, Kwame Nkrumah had become one of the most powerful voices exhorting a global struggle against imperialism. His emergence as the leader of government business in the Gold Coast in 1951 and finally as the prime minister of Ghana in 1957 brought decolonization close to hand, especially through Togo's status as a United Nations trust territory. These developments within the British sphere "certainly contributed to the growth of impatience among the peoples of French West and Equatorial Africa," as Gaston Deferre, the minister of overseas France, acknowledged in March 1956.[34] Deferre was responsible for introducing *loi cadre*, that part of Mendès-France's solution to his country's imperial problems that was aimed at sub-Saharan Africa. Deferre insisted that the reforms of the *loi cadre* would "maintain and reinforce the necessary Union between Metropolitan France and the peoples of the overseas territories."[35] Nor did the African political leaders protest the continuation of the union, only the form it would take. Yet the reform of the *loi cadre* by the introduction of universal suffrage and the establishment of councils of government in retrospect marks an important stage in the shift to political independence.

In order to keep pace with the rapid progress of the Gold Coast, France offered its territories membership in a Francophone community. Only Guinea, rallying behind Sékou Touré, stayed out. A series of groupings was patched together by African leaders aware of the perils of "balkanization." The Federation of Mali was established, comprising Senegal, Sudan, Upper Volta, and Dahomey, although Upper Volta and Dahomey quickly dropped out. The notion of a Senegambian union also was floated as well as one comprising Ghana, Guinea and Mali. Personal rivalries shattered all such projects, and the colonies finally became independent in 1960 through a series of bilateral agreements with France.

Whereas constitutional change in Nigeria and the Gold Coast had accelerated French concessions in the Cameroons and Togo, de Gaulle's 1958 declaration precipitated British decolonization in Sierra Leone and the Gambia. Quite quickly the concept of "viability"—involving size and economic capacity to bear the burden of defense—was scrapped. Sierra Leone, with under three million people, became independent in 1961 and the Gambia, with less than half a million, followed in 1965. The concept of preparation itself had been undermined ever since Nkrumah seized the initiative in 1951. Just as indirect rule, in practice, usually meant "find the chief," so, for successive British governments, the concept of preparation was reduced to one simple rule: find a leader and hand over to him.[36] Preparation for independence became "a paper exercise of Lancaster House conferences, a challenge to chairmanship rather than a duty to find a constitutional framework genuinely acceptable to the people of the country concerned and relevant to their needs and conditions."[37]

The British and the Settlers' Realm

The Mau Mau rebellion of the 1950s was decisive in the decolonization of British East Africa. Some two thousand Kikuyu took up arms in 1952, and by the following year there were twenty thousand fighting in the forests. The main rebel force had been crushed with great severity by 1956 — the British officially admitting that there were some ten thousand Kikuyu deaths and that eighty thousand Kikuyu were held prisoner — but the guerrilla activities lasted until 1960. Despite this military defeat the movement was politically victorious, breaking settler solidarity so that the moderates began to entertain the idea of an eventual African majority rule and exploding the presumptuous notion that Kenya was a "white man's country." The Mau Mau uprising was essentially concerned with land. As Donald L. Barnett put it, "It is not only the brute fact of landlessness, land hunger and insecurity of tenure which conditioned Kikuyu involvement in the nationalist movement and peasant revolt; it is also the fact that for a people who attach such sacred meaning to the land the areas alienated remained within their field of experience, unattainable yet in considerable measure unused by its new [white] owner."[38] The Mau Mau rebellion not only opened the territory to the dispossessed but ended the sacrilegious myth of the White Highlands.

The Colonial Office responded with the Lyttleton constitution of 1954, and despite divisions between the radical and centralist Kenya African National Union and the moderate and federalist Kenya African Democratic Union, which feared Kikuyu domination, there was relatively steady progress toward independence. Jomo Kenyatta, the president of the Kenya African National Union, was released from detention in 1961, where he had been kept since the Mau Mau emergency, and became the prime minister in 1963, when Kenya became independent. Shortly afterward Kenya adopted a single-party constitution.

But the British response to force, evident in the decolonization of Kenya after Mau Mau, ill fitted them to cope with more powerful and better armed white settler groups elsewhere. In Rhodesia a steady shift to the right culminated in the electoral victory — on a restricted, largely white franchise — of the Rhodesia Front in 1962. Efforts to maneuver concessions for the African majority were thwarted, and the Front's leader, Ian Smith, declared independence unilaterally in 1965.[39]

Modes of decolonization supply no sure guide to the structure of the African successor regime or its relationship to the former metropolitan power. On October 20, 1952, the British declared a state of emergency because of the Mau Mau rebellion in Kenya. The different political stance taken two decades later by the three presidents of the independent states that developed out of the British East African High Commission Territories could hardly have been predicted by their roles in the process of political decolonization. Kenya's president was Kenyatta, whom the British colonial authorities had convicted on charges of helping to found and direct the Mau Mau cause. Uganda was presided over by Idi Amin, who had been a loyal soldier of the colonial forces and had participated in the war against the Mau Mau guerrilla fighters. The president of Tanzania was Julius K. Nyerere, who had abhorred the violence of both sides in the 1950s and had encouraged a nonviolent nationalist movement in his own country. Twenty years later Amin, who had fought with the colonial troops in Kenya, was actively engaged in drastically reducing British influence and power in independent Uganda. Kenyatta, on the other hand, was much closer to the British in sympathy than Amin, the man who had once helped chase desperate Kikuyu fighters. Meanwhile, through the Arusha Declaration of 1967, which nationalized a number of industries in Tanzania and provided guidelines for a new national ethic, Nyerere had charted perhaps the most radical and socialist, if least violent, route to economic independence.

Imperial rulers and nationalist leaders devised appropriate ceremonies for the final transfer of power from the European colonial governments to indigenous African rulers. Each country had its own traditions and procedures for rendering such acts of state solemn and significant. Perhaps the British, with the help of their long experience of decolonization stretching back to the Canadians in the nineteenth century and the loss of the thirteen American colonies in the eighteenth century, and with the ceremonial continuity supplied by their monarchy, stage managed it best: "A special meeting of an elected body is held at which representatives of the two governments make speeches, both in impeccable English; one flag replaces another, one anthem asking God to bless a beloved person is followed by another asking Him to bless a piece of land or a mythical figure, the populace is entertained with fireworks, and the day ends with a formal ball, at which a middle-aged politician dances warily with an English princess, as if to show that, in one magical instant, the barriers erected by power have disappeared and all men are equal once again."[40]

The process of decolonization in Africa was not always so cordial. When 97 percent of the voters in French Guinea rallied behind Sékou Touré and voted against de Gaulle's proposed French Community, the French countered by cancelling all financial aid and ordering all French colonial servants to return home at once. French medical personnel stripped hospitals and clinics of supplies in one of a number of drastic actions taken in a futile attempt to demonstrate to other French colonies that a small and relatively poor state could not survive without continued metropolitan help.[41]

King Baudouin in person, rather than any proxy prince or princess, graced the independence ceremony of the Belgian Congo on June 30, 1960. But his eulogistic account of Leopold II's achievements struck the wrong note. Prime Minister Patrice Lumumba riposted by denouncing Belgian imperial exploitation. In this case, at least, there was no attempt to camouflage the starkly different interpretations of the European colonial heritage.[42]

Occassionally human error and inclement weather disrupted even the stately proceedings in those colonies Britain was leaving. The night before the ceremony of Sierra Leonean independence on April 27, 1961, the splendidly bedecked stage was drenched in a sudden tropical downpour. A Sierra Leonean laborer, working late on the site, hastily mopped up in order that everything might be seemly for the morrow. Unfortunately, he was not aware that the large piece of blue, white, and green cloth he used was the new national flag. Clearly it would be some time before the symbols of Sierra Leone's new political condition could create a coherent nation-state within the administrative shell left by the retreating colonial rulers. This was the nub of the problem of decolonization: the more seemly the proceedings, the more they tended to disguise the problems facing the new states. The formality and dignity of the ceremony might make it appear to the Europeans that nothing very much was going to change. The British might believe that their political civilization would be preserved and the French that their culture and language would remain. But to the newly independent Africans the solemn event might give a quite different impression. In the 1960 election in the Belgian Congo the Parti Solidaire Africain, a regional mass party for the Kwilu district in the southwestern Congo, had sought immediate implementation of a platform involving complete elimination of unemployment, free primary and secondary education, all-round wage increases, improvement of housing in rural areas, and free medical care for all non-wage-earners.[43] Such extravagant platform promises were likely to become even more exaggerated in the heat of campaigning. Both Africans and Europeans were prone to unrealistic optimism at the moment of independence. The Europeans thought very little would change; the Africans thought that everything would be different.

CHAPTER 18

Aftermaths of Empire

Sierra Leone became independent on April 27, 1961. The date singled out by the first prime minister, Dr. (later Sir) Milton Margai, was no accident. He had been born in 1895, a year before the British declared their protectorate, and the event he chose to commemorate now as Sierra Leone's national day was the rebellion of the Mende people, or the Hut Tax War, against British overlord-ship that had occurred when he was a boy of three years. The Mende's loss of independence and their enforced aggregation under the imperial yoke with other hitherto separate ethnic groups thus lasted less than a lifetime. Dr. Mar-gai's remembrance of the heroes of 1898 offered the state a hallowed past. But, given the diverse histories of the various sections of Sierra Leone, no heroes could command universal approval. Even among the Mende some sections had found it prudent to collaborate with the British, while the Sierra Leone Creoles were the chief victims, especially in Mende country, of the insurrection. A Creole intellectual who chose to name one of his children Bai Bureh, after the Temne war leader, was berated by his aged mother for flouting his community's traditions.[1] And similarly in Guinea, where Sékou Touré usually could benefit by pointing to his relationship with Samori, this led certain audiences, in cer-tain cases, to fear that he might seek to enslave them as Samori had done.[2]

In Kenya the bitter and bloody antecedents of independence were played down in the immediate aftermath. The Mau Mau rebellion was considered more as evidence of Kikuyu dissatisfaction than as an all-embracing symbol of nation-al liberation. It had been a civil war as well—a revolt of poor Kikuyu against their more fortunate fellows—so overemphasis could be doubly divisive. Jomo

Kenyatta, too, it has been surmised, may have harbored deep, half-conscious resentments against the movement whose eruption precipitated his own long detention. Moreover, precisely because Mau Mau had given Kenya a bad western press, an image of barbaric blancophobia, Kenyatta and his lieutenants felt obliged to reassure white settlers and potential investors that the new Kenya government would conform to "respectable," rather than radical, standards of international behavior: "The Government of an independent Kenya will not be a gangster Government. Those who have been panicky about their property —whether land or buildings or houses—can now rest assured that the future African Government, the Kenya Government, will not deprive them of their property or rights of ownership."[3] Institutionalized international opinion's "new higher law" set its impress on Africa by prescribing decorous norms of decolonization not only for imperialists but for their nationalist successors as well.

The power and authority of the independence regimes was quite fragile. The governments were new and therefore, despite such transitional positions as leader of government business, had neither much experience nor much scope to acquire a time-tested loyal following. Given such scant opportunity, it is remarkable that so much was achieved. Dr. Margai, as the first medical doctor in the protectorate, was frequently called upon by chiefs for technical and political advice during the 1930s and 1940s. This role of confidential adviser gave him the chiefs' devoted support during his postwar career as a party political leader. Jomo Kenyatta's long-standing reputation as a nationalist was especially important in legitimizing the postindependence government of Kenya. Indeed, wherever the nationalist struggle was especially arduous, as for example in Ghana and Guinea, as well as in Kenya, the postindependence regimes tended to acquire a special legitimacy from the drive for self-rule. Nkrumah, Sékou Touré, and Kenyatta all brought special charisma to their administrations. But this could also work negatively. Patrice Lumumba dead—murdered —was more powerful than Lumumba alive. The membership cards of his party, the Mouvement National Congolais, carried a red spot symbolic of the blood of the martyr. Judged by the uncompromising standards of militant "Lumumbism," the mundane postindependence regime was condemned by rebels seeking a "second independence."[4]

Congo-Kinshasa: Zaire

The Belgian Congo hardly merited mention in the discussion of decolonization. Although the image of Congolese independence, compounded of disintegration and bloodshed, was to dominate much of western thinking for the rest of the independence decade, preparation for it had been minimal. The first call to action had come from Professor A. A. J. Van Bilsen, who published a moderate plan for a thirty-year phased decolonization in 1955. He was rewarded by being ostracized in many government and academic circles for his hardihood.[5] In general, the authorities took great care to keep "their" Africans cut off from political currents in the rest of the world. In marked contrast to the vigorous African press that developed in British West Africa in the nineteenth century, the first independent African newspaper was not founded in the Belgian Congo until 1957. Nor was freedom of association allowed until 1959. Open political parties could only operate, therefore, in the last months of colonial rule.

Van Bilsen's proposals were adopted for discussion by a group of Catholic *evolués*. They were, however, denounced for their moderation by ABAKO (Alliance des Ba-Kongo), which had begun in 1950 as a cultural association in this ethnic group because of the administration's ban on political parties but which now rapidly grew into a militant nationalist party. Barred from ABAKO by its ethnic identification, members of other groups formed their own regional or ethnic parties, such as Balubakat and CONAKAT (Confédération des Associations Tribales du Katanga). There was also the Mouvement National Congolais, the national party headed by Lumumba, which gained significant support in four of the Congo's six provinces owing to Lumumba's charisma and, ironically, his success in making tactical alliances with small ethnic parties.[6]

Quite quickly the elaborate colonial apparatus began to disintegrate, as the triple alliance between church, state, and the big concessionary companies started to fall apart. The tradition that issues of the Congo should be removed from Belgian party politics had already been breached when in 1956 anticlericalism was one of the few joint tenets on which the Liberal-Socialist coalition government was based. When the government attacked the mission-dominated educational system of the Congo, the Catholic bishops retorted with a strong statement in favor of "emancipation" of the Congo. Meanwhile, the Socialists were determined not to be drawn into a Belgian equivalent of the Algerian war on behalf of the concessionary companies; "not a single soldier for Union Minière" became a potent slogan. The once powerful administration centered on Léopoldville was stunned by the double politicization of the Congo both in the Belgian parliament and through the mushrooming of African political parties. Decolonization, therefore, became something to be arranged between Belgian and Congolese politicians, with the colonial administration cast in a very minor role.[7]

Belgium's rapid surrender in the face of Congolese nationalism encouraged the tendency of the nationalists to splinter along regional and ethnic lines by apparently eliminating the need for African solidarity against a powerful enemy. But the multiplicity of parties also escalated nationalist demands as each group felt it necessary to maintain its appeal by outbidding its rivals. Three days of leaderless rioting in Léopoldville (January 4-6, 1959) completed the demoralization of the Belgian administration. In the aftermath thousands of the unemployed were expelled from Léopoldville, effectively politicizing the countryside without squelching nationalism in the capital. The Belgian government now abandoned responsibility for the decisive negotiations preceding independence to a round table conference in early 1960 between the African parties and the three major Belgian parties. With the opposition Socialist party acting as arbiter between the nationalists and the two government parties, the Belgians agreed to grant complete independence by June 30 of that year. Patrice Lumumba was to be the prime minister, and Joseph Kasavubu of ABAKO was to be president.

In effect, this meant that a completely Africanized set of political institutions was to be grafted onto a European-controlled administration supported by a European-officered army. Given such bureaucratic and military continuity and the expectation that these would permit progress at a stately pace toward Africanization in each sector, some Belgians felt that they could remain reasonably optimistic despite the radical rhetoric of the local politicians. On July 5, 1960, the colonial correspondent of *La Libre Belgique* wrote: "The *Force Publique* remains the miracle of the Congo which was Belgian. The F. P. today is the only solid institution of this country. Its soldiers have an *esprit de corps*. They are no longer Bangala, Bayaka, or Bakongo, they are from the *Force Publique*. They all have the same martial air, the same ear-to-ear smile, the same efficiency too. The *Force Publique* has made a prodigious demonstration: well led, well trained, the Congolese are capable of achieving great things."[8] The day that this article was published the Force Publique mutinied, leading to assaults on Europeans and the consequent flight of nearly all the Belgian administrators. Moise Tshombe's CONAKAT party took the opportunity to lead the wealthy province of Katanga into secession. United Nations' assistance was invoked as a kind of surrogate colonialism to check the disintegration of governmental authority. On September 5, 1960, President Kasavubu dismissed Lumumba. A week later the army under Colonel Joseph Mobutu seized power from the politicians and set up a caretaker administration of university graduates, which held power until February 1961. In January of that year Lumumba, having once escaped arrest, was sent to Katanga where he was murdered.

Even without the remarkable chain of events begun by the mutiny of July 5, 1960, it is difficult to imagine that the Belgian gamble could have succeeded. Belgian bureaucrats were scarcely the best personnel to implement the radical nationalist policies that triumphed in the 1960 elections. The failure to match political Africanization with bureaucratic and military equivalents produced dangerous built-in contradictions in the new state.

The immediate causes of the mutiny were the provocative policies and attitudes of the Force Publique's last European commander, General E. Janssens, well known for his right-wing opinions. By early 1960 there was a growing discontent within the Force Publique that his plans for gradual Africanization, which would not have produced the first Congolese officers until 1963, would prevent them from enjoying their rightful share of the benefits of independence. (At independence the Force Publique had three Congolese sergeants major but no commissioned officers.) Janssens claimed that he was merely concerned to safeguard standards, but his autobiography indicates a deeper motive: "The strict and absolute discipline . . . was based essentially on the prestige of the leaders and . . . the prestige of the officer was reinforced by the prestige of being white. . . . One could not sap, later, the prestige of the European without sapping that of the officer. An Africanization which could only be achieved by a devaluation of the ranks would necessarily compromise this indispensable discipline."[9]

The Congolese politicians themselves deeply distrusted the army, whose soldiers had hitherto been encouraged to take great pride in their loyalty to the Belgian crown. They feared that Janssens might use the pretext of their own divisions to turn the army loose upon them. As an insurance measure the nationalists sought out soldiers from their own ethnic groups who would apprise them of any future danger; thus they themselves were involved in politicizing the army.[10]

Although as independence approached the parties backed the soldiers' demands for Africanization, Lumumba had declared in Brussels, just after the ending of the round table conference, "It is not because the Congo is independent that we can turn a private into a general."[11] A campaign of anonymous letters from the troops began just before independence. Several of them were printed in Congolese political journals: "Dear Lumumba, friend of the Europeans . . . we guarantee you the infernal ruin of your powers as long as you insult us as ignorant and incapable of taking the places of your white brothers . . ."[12]

On July 5, 1960, Janssens summoned the Congolese noncommissioned officers of the Léopoldville garrison to a meeting, following the first act of indiscipline the day before. He wrote on a blackboard, "After Independence = Before Independence," and stated flatly, "The *Force Publique* continues as before." That evening the soldiers from Thysville who were ordered to march on Léopoldville to curb the insubordination refused to go and arrested their officers instead. The mutiny was on. Overnight the expatriate officer corps disappeared and discipline crumbled.

Prime Minister Lumumba sought to maintain some control by promoting all soldiers one grade and dismissing Janssens. But still the mutiny spread. On July 8 the government decided to Africanize the entire officer corps, retaining only a small group of politically acceptable Belgian officers as advisers. But as panic spread through the European community, the Belgian government decided to use metropolitan troops to protect Belgian lives and property. In Elizabethville five European civilians, including the Italian vice-consul, were ambushed and shot by mutineers. On July 11 Belgian naval forces bombarded Matadi after the Europeans had been evacuated. Although only nineteen African deaths were finally attributed to this shelling, the Force Publique transmitted the news as a general massacre of civilians to its garrisons all over the country. Almost immediately mutineers in widely separated areas began hunting down Europeans to avenge Matadi. On the same day Belgian forces intervened in Katanga to expel all Congolese troops who did not support Moise Tshombe's bid for "independence," thus conniving at the breakup of the new Congo state. The intervention of the United Nations froze the situation and set limits to disorder and foreign intervention.[13]

The political class failed to fill the vacuum of power and authority. The party machines, so active in selling membership cards and setting up branches in the run-up to independence, found no incentive to operate in the countryside with no prospect of new elections before 1963. Key issues now seemed to be decided by combinations and maneuvers within the elite, as well as by foreign influence, and the African leadership, absorbed in ministerial and assembly politics, found little profit in cultivating a mass base. It would have been difficult to gratify popular expectations aroused by the 1960 election in any case, but the central parliament and the provincial assemblies gravely damaged their popularity by quintupling their own salaries in July of 1960. "Politician" swiftly became a perjorative term signifying one who had usurped all the material benefits of independence. When parliament was forced to adjourn indefinitely by Mobutu in September 1963, there was hardly any protest.[14]

The mass exodus of Belgian administrators and army officers also opened the way for ten thousand clerks and noncommissioned officers to be promoted. Several thousand other well-paid "political" positions were created in 1960 at the central and provincial levels. Indpendence also brought fine opportunities for Congolese businessmen with political contacts, especially through favoritism in the granting of import licenses and foreign exchange quotas, both highly profitable during the currency instability that followed independence. In all, Crawford Young estimates that there were roughly only 150,000 financial beneficiaries of independence out of a total population of about twelve million.[15] The enrichment of the new elite took place against a background of general economic distress. The 1957 recession in the Congo had led to cyclical unemployment, which became massive structural unemployment in the 1960 crisis. Between December 1959 and December 1961, it is estimated, the proportion of wage earners who lost their jobs rose from 29 to 58 percent, a situation exacerbated by the vast influx to the cities in 1960 of young Congolese seeking the rewards of independence.[16] The sense of relative economic deprivation was reflected in the actions of a trade union, which appealed for a general strike against the privileged class, i.e., the new African elite, in 1962.[17]

The Belgian colonial order that had been so unpopular in 1959-60 was invested with nostalgia as *Kongo ya lelo* — "present day Congo" — became a saying that was symbolic of disorder between 1961 and 1964.[18] Some disillusion with the realities of independence was largely inevitable, of course, given the utopian expectations engendered in the heady electioneering of 1959-60.[19] Not all such apocalyptic visions of the new order simply faded to be replaced by gilded memories of Belgian rule in the face of the actualities of the new regime. There was a strong demand for a "second" or "true" independence that found expression in the mass support for Pierre Mulele's rebellion, especially in the poorer regions, in 1964. But the same divisions that weakened the state worked against the rebellion, rendering it self-sealing along the lines of ethnic and regional fission. By 1965 the rebellion was crushed, but Tshombe, who had been invited by Kasavubu to form a government, provoked a crisis by seeking to dismiss the president. The army under Mobutu intervened once more in a bloodless coup to end the deadlock.

Nigeria

Concluding a pioneer study of elections in colonial Africa on the eve of independence, the British political scientist W. J. M. Mackenzie commented: "[There is] a sentiment among Europeans that if they are to go it must be with honour, honour defined by European standards of good government and democracy.

The withdrawing powers and their administrators wish to leave behind democratic government and decent administration. Perhaps the administrators on the spot care most for the latter, and are not much impressed by the value of party politics, either at home or in Africa. But political opinion at home demands democracy."[20] Nigeria tended to be regarded by some British colonial officials and sympathetic western observers as a successful example of the transplantation of British political institutions. The spectacular contrast, in the early sixties, with the disorders of the Congo—heightened by the fine impression made by British-trained Nigerian soldiers in the United Nations force there—seemed to vindicate the deliberate pace of British decolonization.[21] The British were prepared to admit, however, that there was something fortuitous about the successful transference of the concept of "Her Majesty's opposition" to the Nigerian environment. Mackenzie himself, commenting on the Western Region election in May 1956 and the Eastern Region election in March 1957, observed, "Nigeria has for the moment found a tolerably free system by which the N.C.N.C. [National Council of Nigeria and the Cameroons] organizes dissidents in Yorubaland, Action Group does the same in Iboland, and both are interested in sustaining some opposition to the regime in the Northern region." But he added that it was not certain that "this curious arrangement of checks and balances" would remain stable in a self-governing Nigeria.[22]

In a study of the 1959 preindependence election Ken Post discovered enough corruption and ballot rigging to conclude pessimistically that fair elections would be unlikely in the future. "Faced with the task of organizing an election expatriate officials fell back upon the rules of the game as they knew them in Britain and were able to enforce some observation of these rules on the politicians. Yet this was the result of a particular situation at a particular time, and these conditions will not occur again. In a sense the Federal election of 1959 was the last great act of the British Raj."[23]

During the period of decolonization from the late 1940s until 1960 the British had insisted on retaining the three regions into which they had divided Nigeria in 1939. They successfully resisted all demands for the division of the Northern Region, dominated by the Northern People's Congress. They believed partition of this powerful region would undermine the stability of an independent Nigeria. Ultimately both the "nationalist" parties of Azikiwe, the National Council of Nigeria and the Cameroons, and Chief Awolowo's Action Group accepted the British colonial regional structure and gave up the idea of redivision. In 1954 a federal system was introduced, theoretically to prevent any single region from dominating the others. Yet the massive size and large population of the north gave it the voting strength increasingly to dominate the federation. The nationalist movement as an inclusive political force in Nigeria proved short lived once it became apparent, around 1950, that the British intended to get out. The dominant forces henceforth were those of Hausa-Fulani, Yoruba, and Ibo solidarity as the party leaders mobilized their followings on the basis of ethnic ties. The conscious traditionalism of the British in preserving established political units within the framework of Lugardian Indirect Rule was, of course, partly responsible. Indeed, only on the eve of World War II did the British seriously consider how to integrate such units into a larger political system.[24]

Indirect rule was, however, only one aspect, though a very important one, of the emphasis on ethnic identification by the British. Different peoples had been considered the best recruits for certain occupations within the colonial order. For example, the Tiv were thought to make good soldiers, the Yoruba good clerks, and the Kru such good manual workers that it was worthwhile to import them from Liberia. The accidents of geography, along with African values and British stereotypes, were also important. In particular, those Nigerians living in the south had a greater chance of finding a colonial career than those living in the hinterland. Chief Awolowo, who was to become one of the country's most important politicians, noted this differential in the mid-1940s from his own standpoint: "In embracing Western culture, the Yorubas take the lead, and have benefited immensely as a result. The Efiks, the Ijaws, the Ibibios and the Ibos come next. The four last named are particularly keen and ambitious, and are doing all they can to overtake the Yorubas. The Hausas and Fulanis on the other hand are extremely conservative, and take very reluctantly to Western civilization. Their eyes are turned to the East from whence light and inspiration have come to them in ages past; and they seem to spurn to look westward. And if the race is to the swift, in spite of their lower cultural background, the Ibos or the Ibibios would certainly qualify for self-government, long before the Hausas."[25] Each group's sense of separateness was intensified, as Awolowo noted, by its understanding that it was now in competition with others with whom it had been agglomerated within a common imperial framework.

The British sought to export to Nigeria and their other colonies the rudiments of the British welfare state and parliamentary democracy. It was regarded as axiomatic that laissez-faire liberalism had been discredited by the interwar depression and mass unemployment, whereas central planning had been vindicated by wartime experience. The various statutory marketing boards, had, moreover, piled up surpluses (in effect, export taxes levied on African farmers) that could be used to finance such amenities as schools, hospitals, transportation development, electricity, and piped water. The Nigerian politicians enthusiastically adapted such welfare colonialism in their electioneering. But not every community could be supplied with these desirable services at once, and minority factions increasingly found themselves being "punished" by the withholding of social welfare investments for voting the wrong way.[26]

The marketing boards and other public corporations by which the government participated in commerce proved a boon to the politicians. The split in the ruling Action Group in the Western Region in 1962 led to the revelation that it had invested around £6.5 million of public funds in the National Investment and Properties Company, which had four party leaders as its directors. Between April 1959 and November 1961 one of the directors gave £3,696,036 to the party in the form of "special donations."[27] Similar intrigues involving government, party, public corporations, and private business were revealed in other parts of the federation after the army coup. While bureaucratic norms of integrity and objectivity had been fairly well established in the civil service proper, the corporations lacked any such tradition and were openly used as instruments of patronage. The minister of finance at the time of the overthrow of the civilian administration, Chief Festus Okotie-Eboh, caught this mood of the times when, discussing a trade union issue in the house of representatives, he declared, "It is stated even in the Bible that to those that have, more shall be given, and from those that do not have shall be taken even the little they have."[28]

Minority ethnic groups, unable or unwilling to come to terms with the dominant regional party in their areas, suffered badly under this system. In the Northern Region the Northern People's Congress created a vast coalition that excluded the Tiv. In response, Tiv rioters in 1960 fired the houses of chiefs, court members, and tax collectors who had supported the Northern People's Congress. Sporadic violence continued, swelling into an armed uprising in February 1964, which the army and police suppressed with the loss of several hundred Tiv lives. Robin Cohen considers that the use of the soldiers against the Tiv by the First Republic was decisive in giving the army a new sense of its power at the same time as it was politicized and drawn into the arena of ethnic competition.[29]

The army was also used in the 1964 strike and the 1965 Yoruba rebellion. Thrice, therefore, the army had been called upon to act in support of the political elite. For soldiers to suppress the politicians was to breach their own rules of conduct. But the open dissent of other alienated groups suggested that a cumulative collapse of public agreement on proper procedures had occurred and that military intervention against the unpopular politicians might be justified in terms of the national interest. The coup of January 15, 1966, was the victory of the military and administrative elites over the political class. The new military regime was pledged to eliminate corruption, and it did succeed for a time in reducing it. In much of the country the military takeover was highly popular, but the politicized army reflected within itself all the divisions and crises of Nigerian society. When, after another coup and the massacre of the Ibo in the north, Nigeria threatened to fall apart, General J. A. Ankrah of Ghana, prompted by Britain, sought to hold the two sides together on the basis of military esprit de corps: "There will be no war because the two old boys will meet at the frontier and tell each other—Old boy, we are not going to commit our boys to fight, come on, let us keep the politicians out—and that is the end."[30] He was wrong. The army's corporate sense, instilled by discipline and training, fared no better than that of other elite groups under pressure of the crisis.

Poverty and Development

Poverty was at the center of the new states' problems. The metropolitan countries exported ideas and institutions of parliamentary democracy and social welfare in order to render the process of decolonization decent by their own standards. Whereas countries like Britain had achieved their own industrialization with a very limited franchise and laissez-faire ideas of the government's functions, the successor states of colonialism in Africa were equipped at the outset with the mechanisms of universal suffrage and an ethic of state welfare, while their economies were still agricultural and extractive and their prospects for development problematic. The relatively favorable terms of trade for agricultural products and African minerals in the fifties and the buildup of reserves by the produce marketing boards in the ex-British territories at first masked the economic constraints on political performance. Subsequently, some states, notably Nigeria and Zaire (as Congo-Kinshasa was renamed by President Mobutu in 1971), have benefited from the exploitation of oil reserves and the effectiveness of the Organization of Petroleum Exporting Countries (OPEC) in forcing up petroleum prices. But even in such fortunate cases the problem of industrialization before their precious mineral reserves are depleted remains.

It was not only that the new states were poor in absolute terms. The disproportionate inequalities within their boundaries, inflaming ethnic or regional jealousies, created severe strains—in the Ivory Coast, for example, per capita income in the south was over ten times that in the north.[31] Saddled with fragile state apparatus and uncertain revenue, the new political elites resorted to the kind of "welfare tribalism" so evident in the worsening crises of the first Nigerian republic in a desperate attempt to hang on to office. With the state crucially important as a source of both consumption income and investment capital "politics turned out to be very largely a zero-sum game. Either you were in power or you were out (very likely in exile or jail)."[32] Eventually, with the politicians escalating their stakes and risks, the system toppled over the edge of brinkmanship, and the soldiers took control of the two largest sub-Saharan African states, Nigeria and Zaire.[33]

Caught in such dilemmas most African states have professed some brand of African socialism. Usually this has meant simply the acceptance of the social welfare and state enterprise ideas of terminal colonialism, providing ideological justification for the practices of the new elite. But some governments, notably that of Tanzania, have sought more radical solutions to the problems of African poverty.

The Tanzanian Experiment

In mid-1960 Julius Nyerere was about to become the chief minister of an internally self-governing Tanganyika. Independence was close and some observers sought reassurance that the troubles that accompanied independence in the Congo would not be repeated in Tanganyika. Nyerere was emphatic: "These things cannot happen here. First, we have a strong organization, TANU [Tanganyika African National Union]. The Congo did not have that kind of organization . . . [and further] there is not the slightest chance that the forces of law and order in Tanganyika will mutiny."[34] On January 19, 1964, just over two years after Tanganyika became independent, Nyerere faced the worst crisis of his career when a mutiny occurred of the First Battalion of the Tanganyika Rifles at Colito barracks outside Dar es Salaam. Led by an education sergeant, Hingo Ilogi, the mutineers locked their British and African officers in the guardroom, seized the radio station, set up some roadblocks, and went on a rampage through the town. About twenty people were killed. President Nyerere was prevailed upon to go into hiding, and the government came to a halt. Oscar Kambona, the minister of defense, managed, however, to make contact with the mutineers, and two days later Nyerere emerged from hiding. But it was only when, at Nyerere's request, a British Royal Marine commando unit landed on January 25 and rounded up the mutineers that the government's authority was restored.[35]   .

The fragility of the government's position had been brutally exposed. Less than a thousand soldiers, for not all members of the First Battalion mutinied, had caused the collapse. In a nationwide broadcast following the disarming of the Tanganyika Rifles by British troops, Nyerere said, "I am told that there is already foolish talk that the British have come back to rule Tanganyika again. This is rubbish. . . . Any independent country is able to ask for the help of another independent country. Asking for help in this way is not something to be proud of. I do not want any person to think that I was happy in making this request. This whole week has been a week of the most grievous shame for our nation."[36] Events in Tanganyika had provoked sympathetic mutinies in some Uganda and Kenya army units. But it was Tanganyika, already seen as a radical Pan-Africanist state nonaligned in the cold war, which experienced the most humiliation from needing the help of ex-imperial forces.

Despite the suspicion of the British foreign secretary, Sir Alec Douglas-Home, that Communist influence was at work—which partly explains his zeal in supporting the new African civilian regime—it seems that the mutineers acted on behalf of no one but themselves. The East African armies were behaving in the manner of trade unions, holding their paymaster, the state, to ransom. There is no evidence that in Tanganyika they secured any popular support. But in a real sense the mutineers represented everyone in Tanganyika who was outside the new ruling elite. When Tanganyika became independent in December 1961, there were only three African commissioned officers in the army, although a further fifteen were on training courses. A request for a crash training program, presented a few weeks before the mutiny, produced a scheme by the British commander for an Africanized army within ten years. But a government circular issued shortly before the mutiny announced a slowing down of Africanization in order to accommodate non-Africans who had opted for Tanganyika nationality under the citizenship provisions of the independence consitution. "The nation," the circular stated, "must use the entire reservoir of skill and experience. It would be wrong for us to distinguish between Tanganyikan citizens on any ground other than their character and ability. We cannot allow the growth of first and second class citizenship. Africanization is dead."[37] Confronted by this flat statement from the government, Tanganyika's dissident soldiers demanded for themselves the three things—better conditions, better pay, and Africanization—that the new ruling elite had secured for its members at independence. Later the minister of finance said that the legitimate grievances of the soldiers were "part of the grievances of all our people which is poverty."[38]

After the sympathetic uprising by his own troops Jomo Kenyatta rebuked

Kenya's mutineers on January 26, 1964: "During the colonial days the men of the King's African Rifles served the British government loyally. Now that we have our own African government the world and our own people are justified in expecting even greater loyalty from the Kenya Army." But, as the East African political scientist Ali Mazrui commented, "If these soldiers had indeed been so loyal to the colonial regime there must have been times when the Kenya soldiers and the Kenya nationalists were in opposing camps."[39] The East African armies inherited by the new states were essentially mercenary forces, recruited and trained by the British. Certain groups tended to be preferred as soldiers and they themselves came to favor military careers. In Uganda the northern peoples — Acholi, Teso, and Lango — predominated. In Tanganyika the disparities were not so great, but a few peoples, such as the Kuwe and Hehe, provided many recruits. Certainly much needed to be done before the armies were integrated into the mainstream of national life.

The top ranks of the army in Tanganyika were quickly Africanized, and pay raises were voted. Many mutineers and some civilians were put in detention. President Nyerere summed up the crisis: "It will take months and even years to erase from the mind of the world what they have heard about the events of this week."[40] He felt it necessary, in order to preserve his and Tanganyika's place in the vanguard of the liberation movement, to go before a specially called meeting of the Organization of African Unity and explain why he had requested British troops. He was given a vote of confidence by the organization and by the national executive of the Tanganyika African National Union on January 31, 1964. Demonstrations were held to show that the country was behind the president and that as a people they were ashamed of letting him down. When Nyerere addressed the women's league and told them he was sorry he had to call in British troops, several women shouted, "We forgive you!"

Both Nyerere and the last British governor, Sir Richard Turnbull, had been conscious of the tenuousness of authority in Tanganyika. British rule had not presented the new independent regime with stable local government units. Two radical revisions of the structure of the government — first, from a system of direct rule by appointed chiefs, based on an Arab model that the Germans had adapted, to the indirect rule introduced by Sir Donald Cameron in the 1920s, and second, a change in the 1950s to a variety of local councils, some of which were multiracial — meant that the new state inherited no deep-rooted local government authorities. Nor, because Tanganyika gained its independence relatively quickly, was TANU a strongly disciplined party. Indeed, within weeks after independence in December 1961 Nyerere took the remarkable step of resigning his prime ministership in order to consolidate his control over TANU. The first legislation of the new state provided for party officials to be appointed to the posts of regional and area commissioners. Shortly afterward, when chieftainships were abolished, the most reliable chiefs were assimilated into a new centrally controlled administrative structure. Such reforms produced solid benefits in the 1964 crisis. With very few exceptions the regions and districts away from Dar es Salaam stayed remarkably calm. And in Dar es Salaam the political and bureaucratic leadership remained quite solid both at the top and in the middle echelons.[41]

The problem of the army remained. Nyerere now questioned the principle inherited from the British that the army must be politically "neutral" in domestic politics. Because Nyerere perceived the mutiny as a failure in political and personal loyalty to nation and ruler, he called for a new army to be built around the TANU Youth League. By June 1964 the second vice-president of what was now the United Republic of Tanganyika and Zanzibar—later Tanzania—Rashidi Kawawa, explained to new army recruits, "You are just as much citizens of the country as are farmers or fishermen. There is no reason therefore for refusing any citizen of the country permission to have a say in the politics of the country."[42] Political discussions between officers and soldiers were to be encouraged, and the army was to be represented on the national executive of TANU. Police and soldiers responded to TANU's invitation to join the party. In fact they enrolled as whole units with officers entrusted with the responsibility for liaison between the army and the party. On November 6, 1964, a political commissar of the Tanzania defense forces was appointed. The army, too, would be integrated into the mainstream of national life by becoming a developmental militia, trained not merely in the use of force but also for the tasks of economic and social development.[43] Shortly after the mutiny Nyerere decided to diversify his military advisers by accepting the help of Communist China. The arrival of a Chinese training team caused great consternation in the West. In an angry press conference the president emphasized that Tanzania's links with the West were still very strong and that his diversification simply gave fresh meaning to Tanzania's nonalignment. The worst that could happen as a result of Chinese influence, he pointed out, was that the soldiers might be inclined to rebel against authority, but Tanzania had already experienced such a rebellion, although the training had been provided by the British.[44]

Nonalignment, symbolized in the diversification of military advice, was to be the guiding principle of Tanzanian foreign policy. Canada, Israel, West Germany, and (indirectly) East Germany were all involved, along with the Chinese.

In some cases these foreign connections were revised or severed in the light of subsequent international developments. But the clue to such apparent volatility lay in Nyerere's determination after the mutiny to advertise his international neutrality. Such consciously wrought internationalism also offset the inevitable parochialism of the imperial nexus. In place of a single national culture, refracted through the behavior of British colonials abroad, the general acceptance of the Cambridge School Certificate as proof of educational achievement, and the cultural activities of the British Council, Tanzanians now had a multiplicity of linkages, each to a country with its own national traditions and its striking images of other cultures.

The international neutrality of Tanzania forced Nyerere to create a separate domestic armed unit to act as a countervailing force against his own professional army, a role the British forces had played in 1964. The institution that Nyerere developed was national service, which, by spreading military training, breached the professional soldiers' monopoly of military skills. In May 1965 the president appealed to the youth of Tanzania to volunteer for the National Youth Service. But by October 1966 fewer than twenty-five educated people had volunteered, and so national service was made compulsory for sixth form (high school) graduates, those who had attended university, and those who graduated from professional institutions. The young people spent part of their time in manual work, often farming, and part in basic military training. Informally referred to by President Nyerere as "the Green Guards," they were to fill the country's military and developmental needs.[45]

Compulsory national service was, therefore, one of the chief steps taken by the president to curb the pretensions of the educated elite. At the 1965 elections he instituted an ingenious arrangement by which, although Tanzania was by now a single-party state, the electors could choose in each constituency between two rival candidates from TANU. In the Arusha Declaration of 1967 and in various other statements which followed, he committed the government to a consciously egalitarian policy. This was not simply an expression of his own considerable political idealism. He was also very much aware of the fragility of the political authority of his government and of the need to develop a new social and economic basis for his regime.[46]

Nyerere's ideas were hammered out in the midst of a sharp debate, centering on Anglophone East Africa in particular but Pan-African in scope, on the direction taken by the postindependence regimes.[47] The contrast between the conspicuous rewards of the new rulers and the general poverty was generally sharply resented:

"And when they have fallen into things
They eat the meat from the chest of bulls
And their wives grow larger buttocks
And their skins shine with health,
They throw themselves into soft beds
But the hip bones of the voters
Grow painful sleeping on the same earth
They slept before Uhuru."[48]

Tanzanians coined the term "Nizers" and "Nizations" to identify the new elite and the material benefits of Africanization, and in East Africa generally the beneficiaries were known as "Wabenzi," the tribe in the Mercedes Benz cars.[49] Powerful, mechanized, and luxurious, the car perfectly symbolized the fruits of modernization as popularly understood. Grass-roots cynicism found support in radical critiques of the new regimes from within the ranks of the intelligentsia itself. In 1967 Okot p'Bitek, writing in the Kampala magazine *Transition*, defined African socialism as "the government of the people by the educated, for the educated" and dismissed the revolutionary rhetoric of East African university students thus: "They are committed and conservative. They have vested interests. They look forward to graduation, the circumcision ceremony before joining the 'big car' tribesmen. Our universities and schools are nests in which black exploiters are hatched and bred, at the expense of the tax payers, or perhaps heart payers."[50]

While the attractions of the Mercedes for the elite have often been denounced by East African politicians and writers, popular reactions have been ambivalent, blending envy and emulation with outrage. But in 1969 in Kenya Tom Mboya defended the Mercedes and its place in the popular culture of a country that allowed social mobility. New levels of luxury, colorful proofs "that things were going to happen," were necessary incentives: "If I can afford it there is no reason why I shouldn't buy one. We don't all have to go on bicycles to show that we are committed to our people. In fact our people need to have some ambition as a driving force in their efforts to self improvement. . . . You can't really think you are going to try and create a colourless society in this country. . . . It has been tried before in Russia and it was decided that no one should earn more than three hundred roubles regardless of his job, his station in life and so on. This is the kind of attitude or approach which is really negative because it can lead people to assuming that things are not going to happen."[51]

Nyerere in Tanzania, by contrast, saw uncontrolled technological opulence as divisive. On August 5, 1967, at a teach-in on the Arusha Declaration at University College in Dar es Salaam, he stated it thus: "Our future lies in the development of our agriculture and our rural areas. But because we are seeking to grow our own roots and to preserve what is valuable in our traditional past, we have also to stop thinking in terms of massive agricultural mechanization and the proletarianization of our rural population. We have, instead, to think in terms of development through the improvement of the tools we now use, and through the growth of cooperative systems of production. Instead of aiming at large farms using tractors and other modern equipment and employing agricultural labourers, we should aim at having ox ploughs all over the country. The jembe [hoe] will have to be eliminated by the ox plough before the latter can be eliminated by the tractor."[52] Technological gradualism and a general emphasis on farming, then, were part of his recipe for avoiding the kind of enclave development that was producing fissures along ethnic, regional, and incipient class lines elsewhere.[53]

The Liberation of Portuguese Africa

Not all of Africa is yet decolonized. But even the present rulers of South Africa have seen the need for a more flexible diplomacy following the overthrow of the Portuguese dictatorship in April 1974 and the imminent independence of Mozambique. It was ironical that the hero of the fascist regime, General António Spinola, should recommend a political rather than a military solution to Portugal's imperial problems by recognizing the rights of self-determination and by establishing democratic institutions in the colonies, and this fact was not lost on the Portuguese. His *Portugal and the Future* appeared in Lisbon bookshops in February 1974, and by the end of April the regime had collapsed in a bloodless revolution as the Portuguese people claimed for themselves the popular participation and democracy he was proposing for Africans. But revolutions, however popular, still require armed force to carry them through. Portugal's African wars had created this force — an increasingly radical army with a divided hierarchy, which more and more came to understand that the campaigns against African freedom fighters could not be won.[54]

Here Africans had shaped the course of European history. Now with the immense prestige of their military victory, the freedom movements, which in March 1974 were chiefly concerned with guerrilla warfare and the administration and welfare of large, though scattered, rural populations, have to take responsibility for large states such as Mozambique. They therefore now face the usual crop of postcolonial problems including those of immigrant minorities, dependence upon migrant workers, and runaway urbanization. During the guerrilla phase of the struggle Amilcar Cabral of Guinea went so far as to describe political independence as a western stratagem designed to produce reliable allies. But he also argued consistently that Portugal's domestic economy and her brand of colonialism were too weak to follow such policies. Portuguese business could not compete with more efficient rivals without the protection of tight political control over the colonies. This thesis needs reexamination in view of economic changes in Portugal during the Premier Marcelo Caetano regime and the increasing foreign investment from the United States and South Africa as well as Europe in Angola and to a lesser extent in Mozambique.[55]

In the course of their guerrilla wars Cabral and his comrades began to restructure society in the territories they controlled. Within the liberated areas, according to Marcelino dos Santos, the guerrillas thrashed out the future of their countries: "Which ways should we follow? It was in that phase that the contradictions appeared and those who were mainly fighting for their own individual interests or for the interest of a narrow group, came more openly to the surface. If we do not follow collectivist attitudes we will not be able to face the enemy successfully. In this sense it is true to say that the internal dynamic of the struggle is such that conditions generate collective thinking. Even if the origins of such collective attitudes are partly pragmatic, there is certainly a strong possibility that in the course of collective effort a situation is created from which it is difficult to withdraw."[56] Such ideas, invested with the immense prestige of victory through force of arms, are likely to be increasingly canvassed in other areas of Africa, while in Guinea Bissau, Mozambique, and Angola those who hold them already are implementing them as they grapple with the problems that confront newly free states. Ironically, the very success of the national liberation movements against alien domination has prompted a new phase of great power intervention, this time by the Soviet Union, China, and the United States, rather than the Europeans.

Our radically foreshortened time perspective on the postcolonial period forces discussion of it to be tentative. Yet already at this point in history the apparent shape and direction taken by African societies in the aftermath of empire prompts certain questions. For example, agriculture remains the most important, in some cases almost the only, basis of economy in most independent African nations. This, and the increasing awareness by agricultural scientists of the relevance of African farming practices, gives urgency to the study of the history of African food production systems and their modification, for good or ill, through the western impact. Africa's continued economic dependence after the abrogation of formal European political control has given a new thrust to the study of the development of Africa's economic links with Europe and the Americas over a longer time span.[57] The creation of lively schools of historiography both within Africa and without, equipped with better knowledge of both what went before and what came after, is bringing the imperial episode into clearer perspective.

Notes

Notes

Chapter 1. The Continent and Its Regions

1. I have found two general works, George F. Carter, *Man and the Land: A Cultural Geography*, 2d ed. (New York: Holt, Rinehart and Winston, 1968), and Richard A. Watson and Patty Jo Watson, *Man and Nature: An Anthropological Essay in Human Ecology* (New York: Harcourt, Brace and World, 1969), especially stimulating on this theme.

2. William A. Hance, *The Geography of Modern Africa* (New York: Columbia University Press, 1964), and L. D. Stamp, *Africa: A Study in Tropical Development*, 2d ed. (New York: John Wiley, 1964), extend the discussion of African geography that follows.

3. Pierre Gourou, *The Tropical World*, 4th ed. (London: Longmans, 1966), is crucial for a general understanding of tropical geography.

4. Paul Bohannan, *African Outline* (Harmondsworth: Penguin Books, 1966), p. 47.

5. W. B. Morgan and J. C. Pugh, *West Africa* (London: Methuen, 1969).

6. Philip D. Curtin, *The Image of Africa: British Ideas and Action, 1780-1850* (Madison: University of Wisconsin Press, 1964), is a brilliant exposition of the interplay between image and reality. George Basalla, "The Spread of Western Science," *Science*, 156: 611-622 (1967), proposes a model for the spread of western science.

7. Smeathman's importance is stressed by Curtin. See also Elizabeth Smeathman (his sister-in-law) to Dr. John Coakley Lettsom, London, January 3, 1787, in Thomas Joseph Pettigrew, *Memoirs of the Life and Writings of the Late John Coakley Lettsom*, 3 vols. (London, 1817), II, 252-262; Ellen Gibson Wilson, *The Loyal Blacks* (New York: G. P. Putnam's Sons, 1976), p. 140.

8. Cited in Curtin, *Image*, p. 61.

9. For Buxton, see Curtin, *Image*, pp. 298-303, 414-438.

10. Roy Lewis, *Sierra Leone* (London: Her Majesty's Stationery Office, 1954), pp. 74-84.

11. William J. Talbot, "Land Utilization in the Arid Regions of Southern Africa: Part 1, South Africa," in L. D. Stamp, ed., *A History of Land Use in Arid Regions* (Paris: UNESCO, 1961), p. 304.

12. Henry S. Wilson, ed., *Origins of West African Nationalism* (London: Macmillan, 1969), pp. 37-39.

13. John C. Ene, *Insects and Man in West Africa* (Ibadan: Ibadan University Press, 1963).

14. Robert F. Gray, "Medical Research: Some Anthropological Aspects," in Robert A. Lystad, ed., *The African World* (London: Pall Mall Press, 1965), p. 364.

15. In addition to the works by Curtin and Basalla cited above, I have found two works on the general history of science especially useful: Thomas S. Kuhn's stimulating and controversial *The Structure of Scientific Revolutions* (Chicago: University of Chicago Press, 1962), and George W. Stocking, Jr., *Race, Culture and Evolution* (New York: Free Press, 1968), which is a model for historians on how to handle the scientific ideas of the past without "anachronistic patronization" (Stocking's own phrase, p. 42).

16. Jacques Maquet, *Africanity* (London: Oxford University Press, 1972), p. 141, and George P. Murdock, *Africa: Its Peoples and Their Culture History* (New York: McGraw-Hill, 1959).

17. Jacques Maquet, "The Cultural Units of Africa: A Classificatory Problem," in Mary Douglas and Phyllis M. Kaberry, eds., *Man in Africa* (London: Tavistock Publications, 1969), pp. 3-13, discusses the generally pragmatic approach of the *Ethnographic Survey*.

18. Melville J. Herskovits, "Peoples ar.d Cultures in Sub-Saharan Africa," originally published in 1955, reprinted in Peter J. M. McEwan and Robert B. Sutcliffe, eds., *The Study of Africa* (London: Methuen, 1965), p. 20. See also Melville J. Herskovits, *The Human Factor in Changing Africa* (New York, Knopf, 1962), pp. 30-112, which represents his most considered application of the culture area concept to Africa.

19. Barrington Moore, Jr., *Social Origins of Dictatorship and Democracy* (Harmondsworth: Penguin, 1966), p. 486. Anthony Atmore and Nancy Westlake, "A Liberal Dilemma: A Critique of the Oxford History of South Africa," *Race*, 14:111-112 (1972), also cite this passage from Barrington Moore in a forceful criticism of the assumption of precolonial stasis.

20. J. F. A. Ajayi, "A Survey of the Cultural and Political Regions of Africa at the Beginning of the Nineteenth Century," in Joseph C. Anene and Godfrey N. Brown, eds., *Africa in the Nineteenth and Twentieth Centuries: A Handbook for Teachers and Students* (Ibadan: Ibadan University Press, 1966), p. 74. Also J. F. A. Ajayi, "Colonialism: An Episode in African History," in Lewis H. Gann and Peter Duignan, eds., *Colonialism in Africa, 1870-1960* (Cambridge: Cambridge University Press, 1969), I, 497-508; and J. F. A. Ajayi, "The Continuity of African Institutions under Colonialism," in Terence O. Ranger, ed., *Emerging Themes of African History* (Nairobi: East African Publishing House, 1968), pp. 189-200.

21. Ajayi, "Colonialism: An Episode," p. 505.

22. Samir Amin, "Underdevelopment and Dependence in Black Africa," *Journal of Modern African Studies*, 10:503-524 (1972).

23. Herskovits, *The Human Factor*, pp. 59-62.

24. Hastings Beck, *Meet the Cape Food* (Cape Town: Purnell, 1956), p. 32, also pp. 3, 4.

25. Donald Denoon, *Southern Africa since 1800* (London: Longman, 1972), pp. 12-14.

26. Melville J. Herskovits, "The Cattle Complex in East Africa," *American Anthropologist*, n.s. 28:230-273, 361-388, 494-528, 633-664 (1926). He had already formulated "A Preliminary Consideration of the Culture Areas of Africa," *American Anthropologist*, n.s. 26:50-64 (1924).

27. J. D. Omer-Cooper, *The Zulu Aftermath: A Nineteenth Century Revolution in Bantu Africa* (London: Longmans, 1966).

28. Richard Gray and David Birmingham, eds., *Pre-Colonial African Trade: Essays on Trade in Central and Eastern Africa before 1900* (London: Oxford University Press, 1970), indicates the kind of developments that should be borne in mind.

29. Harold K. Schneider, "The Subsistence Role of Cattle among the Pakot and in East Africa," *American Anthropologist*, n.s. 59:278-301 (1957).

30. Herskovits, *The Human Factor*, p. 79. East Sudanese recalcitrance reduces Herskovits's perception of African history for once to something very like Trevor-Roper's famous "purposeless gyrations."

31. Colin Turnbull, *The Forest People* (New York: Simon and Schuster, 1961).

32. Herskovits, *The Human Factor*, p. 84.

33. Claude Meillassoux, ed., *The Development of Indigenous Trade and Markets in West Africa* (London: Oxford University Press, 1971).

34. Ellen G. Wilson, *A West African Cook Book* (New York: M. Evans, 1971), provides a general introduction to West African food for Americans.

35. Jack Goody and Joan Buckley, "Inheritance and Women's Labour in Africa," *Africa*, 43:108-121 (1973), discusses aspects of the relatively neglected topic of the role of women.

36. Herskovits, *The Human Factor*, p. 105.

37. *Ibid*., pp. 56-58.

38. John I. Clarke, *Population Geography and the Developing Countries* (Oxford: Pergamon, 1971), pp. 130-131.

39. Charles M. Good, Jr., *Dimensions of East African Culture* (East Lansing: African Studies Center, Michigan State University, 1966).

40. Paul Bohannan and Laura Bohannan, *Tiv Economy* (London: Longmans, 1968); E. E. Evans-Pritchard, *The Nuer* (Oxford, Clarendon Press, 1940); Max Gluckman, *The Judicial Process among the Barotse* (Manchester: Manchester University Press, 1954); Mary Douglas, *The Lele of the Kasai* (London: Oxford University Press, 1963).

41. Amin, "Underdevelopment and Dependence," pp. 503-504.

42. Warren L. d'Azevedo, "Some Historical Problems in the Delineation of a Central West Atlantic Region," *Annals of the New York Academy of Sciences*, 96:514 (1962).

43. *Ibid*., pp. 512-538, and H. D. Gunn's comment on d'Azevedo's paper on p. 577 of the same volume.

44. Boyd C. Shafer, *Faces of Nationalism* (New York: Harcourt Brace Jovanovich 1972), especially pp. 333-336, throws light on the relationship between nationalism and historiography.

Chapter 2. Before Partition

1. Catherine Coquéry-Vidrovitch and Henri Moniot, *L'Afrique noire de 1800 à nos jours* (Paris: Presses Universitaires de France, 1974), especially pp. 257-261, discusses this point perceptively. Also see chapter 1.

2. See Paul Bohannan and Philip D. Curtin, *Africa and Africans* (New York: Natural History Press, 1964), pp. 277-294, for a brief, yet comprehensive, discussion of such political developments, which they term "the Secondary Empires of the pre-colonial century." Also J. B. Webster, "Tribalism, Nationalism and Patriotism in Nineteenth and Twentieth Century Africa," in H. L. Dyck and H. P. Krosby, eds., *Empire and Nations* (Toronto: University of Toronto Press, 1969).

3. J. D. Omer-Cooper, *The Zulu Aftermath: A Nineteenth Century Revolution in Bantu Africa* (London: Longmans, 1966), is indispensable. Also very useful are Monica Wilson, "The Nguni People," in Monica Wilson and Leonard Thompson, eds., *The Oxford History of South Africa*, vol. 1, *South Africa to 1870* (Oxford: Clarendon Press, 1969), pp. 75-130, and Donald Denoon, *Southern Africa since 1800* (London: Longmans, 1972), pp. 15-42.

4. Alan Smith, "The Trade of Delagoa Bay as a Factor in Nguni Politics, 1750-1835," in Leonard Thompson, ed., *African Societies in Southern Africa* (London: Heinemann, 1969), pp. 171-189.

5. W. G. Randles, "L'Afrique du Sud et du Zambèze, 1800-1880," in Hubert Deschamps, *Histoire générale de l'Afrique noire, de Madagascar et des Archipels*, vol. 2, *De 1800 à nos jours* (Paris: Presses Universitaires de France, 1971), pp. 247-259, is extremely interesting on Shaka's youth cult.

6. See Eric A. Walker, *The Great Trek* (London: A. and C. Black, 1934; reprint 3d ed., London: Longmans, 1957); also Denoon, *Southern Africa*, pp. 43-54, and Leonard Thompson, "Co-operation and Conflict: The High Veld," in Wilson and Thompson, *Oxford History*, pp. 405-424.

7. Eric A. Walker, *A History of Southern Africa* (London: Longmans, 1959), p. 208.

8. See further discussion elsewhere in this chapter and in chapter 14.

9. See chapter 4.

10. What follows is largely based on Murray Last, *The Sokoto Caliphate* (London: Longmans, 1967). See also John Ralph Willis, "Jihad fi Sabil Allah, Its Doctrinal basis in Islam and Some Aspects of Its Evolution in Nineteenth Century West Africa," *Journal of African History*, 8:395-415 (1967).

11. See chapters 4, 7, and 12 for the subsequent history of Islamic politics.

12. See chapter 4.

13. See John S. Galbraith, *The Reluctant Empire: British Policy on the South African Frontier, 1834-1854* (Berkeley: University of California Press, 1963), for a lucid analysis of the mechanics of the turbulent frontier.

14. For what follows, see Wilson and Thompson, *Oxford History*, and Denoon, *Southern Africa*.

15. For Philip, see W. M. Macmillan, *Bantu, Boer and Briton* (London: Faber and Faber, 1929).

16. For the British and the preoccupation with the route to India, the classic work is Ronald E. Robinson and John Gallagher with Alice Denny, *Africa and the Victorians: The Official Mind of Imperialism* (London: Macmillan, 1961).

17. Stanley Trapido, "The Origins of the Cape Franchise Qualifications of 1853," *Journal of African History*, 5:37-54 (1964) is most illuminating. See W. L. Burn, *Age of Equipoise* (London: Routledge & Kegan Paul, 1964), for a profound analysis of the mid-Victorian politics of improvement. For the parallels and connections between contemporary British franchise politics and colonial ideas of representative government, see Henry S. Wilson, ed., *Origins of West African Nationalism* (London: Macmillan, 1969), Introduction, especially pp. 33-34.

18. Trapido, "Origins of the Cape Franchise," p. 54.

19. See chapter 14 for South Africa's political developments.

20. Anthony Trollope, *South Africa* (1878; reprint ed., London: Dawson, 1968), pp. 187-188.

21. See chapter 4.

22. See Elliot J. Berg, "Backward-Sloping Labor Supply Functions in Dual Economies—The African Case," *Quarterly Journal of Economics*, 75:468-492 (1961), for an elegant refutation of this theory.

23. H. J. Simons and R. E. Simons, *Class and Colour in South Africa, 1850-1950* (Harmondsworth: Penguin, 1969), pp. 36-37.

24. On the Portuguese colonies I have chiefly employed Richard J. Hammond, *Portugal and Africa, 1815-1910: A Study in Uneconomic Imperialism* (Stanford: Stanford

University Press, 1966), and Ronald H. Chilcote, *Portuguese Africa* (Englewood Cliffs, N.J.: Prentice-Hall, 1967).

25. James Duffy, *A Question of Slavery* (Oxford: Clarendon Press, 1967), pp. 4-6.

26. Herbert Feis, *Europe: The World's Banker, 1870-1914* (New Haven: Yale University Press, 1935), p. 257.

27. V. R. Dorjahn and Christopher Fyfe, "Landlord and Stranger: Change in Tenancy Relations in Sierra Leone," *Journal of African History*, 3:391-417 (1962).

28. The reasons that prompted the Europeans to such attacks are discussed elsewhere in this chapter. For the alteration in status between African and imperial polities during the nineteenth century, see chapter 4.

29. On general Gold Coast history, David Kimble, *A Political History of Ghana, 1850-1928* (Oxford: Clarendon Press, 1963), contains a fund of information.

30. Grey's proposals for the Gold Coast are cited in Wilson, *Origins*, pp. 123-128.

31. For the development of the stereotype of the "educated African" among British officials, see Kimble, *Ghana*, pp. 87-93. For the Fanti Confederation, *ibid.*, pp. 222-263; Christopher Fyfe, *Africanus Horton, 1835-1883: West African Scientist and Patriot* (New York: Oxford University Press, 1972), and Wilson, *Origins*, pp. 30 33, 208-225.

32. On Senegal, the best brief study is Michael Crowder, *Senegal: A Study in French Assimilation Policy* (London: Oxford University Press, 1962). G. Wesley Johnson, Jr., *The Emergence of Black Politics in Senegal* (Stanford: Stanford University Press, 1971), also has a most useful introductory section, pp. 3-89. Roger Pasquier provides a succinct summary, partly based on his own extensive research, in "Mauritanie et Senegambie," in Deschamps, *Histoire générale*, II, 51-84.

33. Cited in John D. Hargreaves, *Prelude to the Partition of West Africa* (London: Macmillan, 1963), p. 94.

34. Rita Cruise O'Brien, *White Society in Black Africa: The French of Senegal* (London: Faber and Faber, 1972), pp. 29-47, is helpful on social structure, as is Johnson, *Emergence*, pp. 3-89, and H. O. Idowu, "Café-au-lait: Senegal's Mulatto Community in the Nineteenth Century," *Journal of the Historical Society of Nigeria*, 6:271-288 (1972).

35. Johnson, *Emergence*, pp. 38-62.

36. A. S. Kanya-Forstner, *The Conquest of the Western Sudan: A Study in French Military Imperialism* (Cambridge: Cambridge University Press, 1969), pp. 1-44, sets Faidherbe's career in the general context of French expansion.

37. For the subsequent development of French military imperialism, see C. W. Newbury and A. S. Kanya-Forstner, "French Policy and the Origins of the Scramble for West Africa," *Journal of African History*, 10:253-276 (1969).

38. For the Fingo, see Omer-Cooper, *Zulu Aftermath*, chapter 11, and R. A. Moyer, "Some Current Manifestations of Early Mfengu History," *Collected Seminar Papers on the Societies of Southern Africa in the Nineteenth and Twentieth Centuries* (London: Institute of Commonwealth Studies, University of London, 1973), III, 144-154.

39. Rev. John Ayliff and Rev. Joseph Whiteside, *History of the Abambo, Generally Known as Fingos* (1912; reprint ed., Cape Town: Struik, 1962).

40. *Ibid.*, pp. 29-30.

41. H. M. Robertson, "150 Years of Economic Contact between White and Black," *South African Journal of Economics*, 2:411 (1934).

42. Ayliff and Whiteside, *History of the Abambo*, p. 46.

43. Charles Brownlee, *Reminiscences of Kaffir Life and History*, pp. 380-381, cited in Robertson, "150 Years," p. 419.

44. *Ibid.*

45. Moyer, "Early Mfengu History," p. 152, note 14.

46. For the Creoles, see Christopher Fyfe's monumental *A History of Sierra Leone* (London: Oxford University Press, 1962), and John Peterson's work stressing their "Africanism," *Province of Freedom: A History of Sierra Leone, 1787-1870* (London: Faber and Faber, 1969). P. E. H. Hair, "Africanism: The Freetown Contribution," *Journal of Modern African Studies*, 5:521-539 (1967).

47. For Abeokuta, see S. O. Biobaku, *The Egba and Their Neighbours, 1842-1872* (Oxford: Clarendon Press, 1957); Earl Phillips, "The Egba at Abeokuta: Acculturation and Political Change, 1830-1870," *Journal of African History*, 10:117-131 (1969); Agneta Pallinder-Law, "Aborted Modernization in West Africa? The Case of Abeokuta," *Journal of African History*, 15:65-82 (1974).

48. For a sensitive explanation of this dilemma, see Philip Ehrensaft, "The Political Economy of Informal Empire in Pre-Colonial Nigeria, 1807-1884," *Canadian Journal of African Studies*, 6:451-490 (1972).

49. United Kingdom, *Parliamentary Papers*, 1865, 5(412), Report from Select Committee on West African Settlements, p. xvi. The best discussion of the 1865 committee is in Hargreaves, *Partition of West Africa*, pp. 64-90.

Chapter 3. Background to the Scramble

1. Ronald E. Robinson and John Gallagher, "The Partition of Africa," in F. H. Hinsley, ed., *New Cambridge Modern History* (Cambridge: Cambridge University Press, 1962), XI, 620.

2. S. B. Saul, *The Myth of the Great Depression, 1873-1896* (London: Macmillan, 1969).

3. Henri Brunschwig, "Politique et économie dans l'empire français d'Afrique noire," *Journal of African History*, 11:404-405 (1970). Brunschwig's article supplies several other examples of such sanguine speculation.

4. Anthony G. Hopkins, *An Economic History of West Africa* (London: Longman, 1973). Chapter 4, "The Economic Basis of Imperialism," is excellent here.

5. C. W. Newbury and A. S. Kanya-Forstner, "French Policy and the Origins of the Scramble for Africa," *Journal of African History*, 10:253-274 (1969), is particularly enlightening. See also A. S. Kanya-Forstner, *The Conquest of the Western Sudan: A Study in French Military Imperialism* (Cambridge: Cambridge University Press, 1969), and Henri Brunschwig, *French Colonialism, 1871-1914: Myths and Realities* (London: Pall Mall Press, 1964).

6. John E. Flint, "Britain and the Partition of West Africa," in John E. Flint and Glyndwr Williams, eds., *Perspectives of Empire* (London: Longmans, 1973), pp. 93-111, is very useful.

7. Tom Kemp, *Economic Forces in French History* (London: Dobson, 1971).

8. Kanya-Forstner, *Conquest of the Western Sudan*, chapters 2 and 3, gives an acute analysis of French policy in Senegal.

9. *Ibid.*, p. 57.

10. C. W. Newbury, "The Protectionist Revival in French Colonial Trade," *Economic History Review*, 2d ser., 21:337-341 (1968).

11. Flint, "Britain and the Partition," p. 103.

12. For what follows, see Donald V. McKay, "Colonization in the French Geographical Movement," *Geographical Review*, 33:214-232 (1943).

13. Brunschwig, "Politique et économie," pp. 403-409.

14. *Ibid.*, pp. 406-407. For Leroy-Beaulieu's ideas, see Agnes Murphy, *The Ideology of French Imperialism* (Washington: Catholic University Press, 1948).

15. W. B. Thorson, "Charles de Freycinet, French Empire-Builder," *Research Studies of the State College of Washington*, 12:257-282 (1943).

16. *Ibid.*; Brunschwig, "Politique et économie," p. 406.

17. Newbury and Kanya-Forstner, "French Policy and the Origins," p. 262.

18. *Ibid.*

19. *Ibid.*

20. Kanya-Forstner's *Conquest of the Western Sudan* is indispensable for what follows. But see B. Olatunji Oloruntimehin, "Theories of 'Official Mind' and 'Military Imperialism' as Related to the French Conquest of the Western Sudan," *Journal of the Historical Society of Nigeria*, 5:419-434 (1970), for qualifications and criticisms arising from intensive study of the "local crisis."

21. Newbury and Kanya-Forstner, "French Policy and the Origins," pp. 268-273.

22. D. C. M. Platt, "The National Economy and British Imperial Expansion before 1914," *Journal of Imperial and Commonwealth History*, 2:3-14 (1931).

23. Gerald S. Graham, *Peculiar Interlude* (Sydney: University of Sydney Press, 1959).

24. D. C. M. Platt, *Finance, Trade, and Politics in British Foreign Policy, 1815-1914* (Oxford: Clarendon Press, 1968), p. 261.

25. D. C. M. Platt, "British Policy during the 'New Imperialism,'" *Past and Present*, 39:127 (1968).

26. Flint, "Britain and the Partition," pp. 93-111.

27. Platt, "British Policy," p. 128.

28. *Ibid.*

29. Cited in Sir John Clapham, *An Economic History of Modern Britain* (Cambridge: Cambridge University Press, 1963), III, 9.

30. *Ibid.*, p. 16.

31. Platt, *Finance, Trade, and Politics*, p. 82

32. Quoted by Jean Stengers, "The Partition of Africa. I. L'Impérialisme colonial de la fin du XIXe siècle: Mythe ou réalité," *Journal of African History*, 3:487 (1962).

33. F. Crouzet, "Commerce et empire: L'Expérience britannique du libre-échange à la première guerre mondiale," *Annales*, 19:281-310 (1964).

34. S. B. Saul, *Studies in British Overseas Trade, 1870-1914* (Liverpool: Liverpool University Press, 1960).

35. This account of German policy is based primarily on: Henry A. Turner, Jr., "Bismarck's Imperialist Venture," in Prosser Gifford and William Roger Louis, eds., *Britain and Germany in Africa: Imperial Rivalry and Colonial Rule* (New Haven: Yale University Press, 1967); William O. Aydelotte, *Bismarck and British Colonial Policy* (Philadelphia: University of Pennsylvania Press, 1937); Alan J. P. Taylor, *Germany's First Bid for Colonies, 1884-1885* (Hamden, Conn.: Archon Books, 1967); Sybil E. Crowe, *The Berlin West African Conference, 1884-1885* (London: Longmans, 1942); Harmut Pogge von Strandmann, "Germany's Colonial Expansion under Bismarck," *Past and Present*, 42:140-159 (1969); and Hans-Ulrich Wehler, "Bismarck's Imperialism, 1862-1890," *Past and Present*, 45:119-155 (1970).

36. Hans-Ulrich Wehler, "Industrial Growth and Early German Imperialism," in Roger Owen and Bob Sutcliffe, eds., *Studies in the Theory of Imperialism* (London: Longmans, 1972), p. 91.

37. Hopkins, *Economic History*, pp. 159-160.

38. *Ibid.*

39. Von Strandmann, "Germany's Colonial Expansion," pp. 150-152.

40. Turner, "Bismarck's Imperialist Venture," pp. 53-57.

41. *Ibid.*, pp. 54-82.

42. *Ibid.*, and Crowe, *Berlin West African Conference*, chapter 3.

43. Wehler, "Bismarck's Imperialism."

44. Turner, "Bismarck's Imperialist Venture," pp. 68-82.

45. This account of Portuguese policy is based on Eric Axelson, *Portugal and the Scramble for Africa, 1875-1891* (Johannesburg: Witwatersrand University Press, 1967); Richard J. Hammond, *Portugal and Africa, 1815-1910: A Study in Uneconomic Imperialism* (Stanford: Stanford University Press, 1966); James Duffy, *Portuguese Africa* (Cambridge: Harvard University Press, 1959); Victor G. Kiernan, "The Old Alliance: England and Portugal," in Ralph Miliband and John Saville, eds., *The Socialist Register 1973* (London: Merlin Press, 1974); Jean Stengers, "King Leopold and Anglo-French Rivalry, 1882-1884," in Prosser Gifford and William Roger Louis, eds., *France and Britain in Africa: Imperial Rivalry and Colonial Rule* (New Haven: Yale University Press, 1971), p. 147.

46. See chapter 2, p. 34.

47. Cited in George Shepperson, "Africa, the Victorians and Imperialism," *Revue belge de philologie et d'histoire*, 40:1228-1238 (1962).

48. Stengers, "Leopold and Anglo-French Rivalry," p. 147.

49. *Ibid.*, p. 149.

50. C. W. Newbury, "The Tariff Factor in Anglo-French West African Partition," in Gifford and Louis, *France and Britain in Africa*, p. 237.

51. This section on Leopold II and the Congo Free State is based primarily on Roger Anstey, *Britain and the Congo in the Nineteenth Century* (Oxford: Clarendon Press, 1962); Neal Ascherson, *The King Incorporated* (London: Allen and Unwin, 1963); Stengers, "Leopold and Anglo-French Rivalry."

52. Ascherson, *King Incorporated*, chapters 11-14.

53. Stengers, "L'Impérialisme colonial," pp. 469-491.

54. This discussion of the Berlin Conference is based primarily upon Crowe, *Berlin West African Conference*; William R. Louis, "The Berlin Congo Conference," in Gifford and Louis, *France and Britain in Africa*, pp. 167-220; R. J. Gavin and J. A. Betley, eds., *The Scramble for Africa: Documents on the Berlin West African Conference and Related Subjects, 1884-1885* (Ibadan: Ibadan University Press, 1973).

55. Ascherson, *King Incorporated*, pp. 112-114.

56. This point will be developed in my forthcoming book, *Dr. Blyden and the Negro Race*.

57. Ascherson, *King Incorporated*, pp. 129-131.

58. *Ibid.*, pp. 131-132.

59. *Ibid.*, p. 132.

60. Granville to Malet, November 15, 1884, cited in Gavin and Betley, *Scramble*, pp. 71-72.

61. *Ibid.*, pp. 77-78.

62. Cited in Louis, "Berlin Congo Conference," p. 202.

63. Geoffroy de Courcel, *L'Influence de la Conférence de Berlin de 1885 sur le droit colonial international* (Paris: Editions Internationales, 1935).

64. F. H. Hinsley, *Sovereignty* (London: C. A. Watts, 1966), p. 205.

65. *Ibid.*, especially chapters 1, 5, 6.

66. Minute by Sir Edward Malet, leader of the British delegation, to Granville, January 17, 1885, F.O. 343/6, cited in Louis, "Berlin Congo Conference," p. 210.

67. *Ibid.*, p. 211.

68. *Ibid.*, p. 213-214.

69. The classic study is by John E. Flint, *Sir George Goldie and the Making of Nigeria* (London: Oxford University Press, 1960).

70. John S. Galbraith, *Mackinnon and East Africa* (Cambridge: Cambridge University Press, 1972), is the first installment of what promises to be a major reappraisal of the chartered companies.

Chapter 4. The European Occupation of the Interior

1. A comprehensive account of the development of protectorate administration by the European powers during the process of partition is badly needed. Two important accounts of the legal side came to hand only in the final stages of writing: C. H. Alexandrowicz, "The Partition of Africa by Treaty," in K. Ingham, ed., *Foreign Relations of African States* (London: Butterworths, 1974), pp. 129-157, and W. Ross Johnston, *Sovereignty and Protection: A Study of British Jurisdictional Imperialism in the Late Nineteenth Century* (Durham, N.C.: Duke University Press, 1973). H. F. Morris, "Protection or Annexation? Some Constitutional Anomalies of Colonial Rule," in H. F. Morris and James S. Read, *Indirect Rule and the Search for Justice: Essays in East African Legal History* (Oxford: Clarendon Press, 1972), pp. 41-70, is most enlightening for East Africa, as is Claire Palley, *The Constitutional History and Law of Southern Rhodesia* (Oxford: Clarendon Press, 1966).

2. Johnston, *Sovereignty*, p. 313.

3. Alexandrowicz, "Partition of Africa," pp. 138-143. Cf. "In all treaties from the foundation of the Colony [of Sierra Leone] . . . to the present day, the character of the chiefs as owners and sovereigns and as independent contracting powers is unequivocally and universally recognized. Only in a few of the later treaties is there provision for the English crown assuming sovereignty and full control in the event of chiefs not fulfilling treaty engagements." United Kingdom, *Parliamentary Papers*, 1899, 60 (c. 9388; c. 9391), Report on the Insurrection in the Sierra Leone Protectorate (usually referred to as the Chalmers Report), p. 15.

4. Henry Maine, *International Law* (London, 1888), p. 58. For the controversy over Jenkyns's views, see Johnston, *Sovereignty*, pp. 214-225, and Palley, *Southern Rhodesia*, pp. 57-60.

5. Johnston, *Sovereignty*, p. 222.

6. Palley, *Southern Rhodesia*, p. 60. In fact, the United States did not ultimately ratify the 1885 Berlin Act.

7. *Ibid.*, p. 61.

8. Joseph C. Anene, *Southern Nigeria in Transition, 1885-1906: Theory and Practice in a Colonial Protectorate* (Cambridge: Cambridge University Press, 1966), p. 66; Johnston, *Sovereignty*, pp. 315-316.

9. Johnston, *Sovereignty*, pp. 325-326.

10. T. J. Alldridge, *The Sherbro and Its Hinterland* (London: Macmillan, 1901), pp. 165-251, is a very informative account of the author's treaty making in Sierra Leone, which reveals the sense of independence and equality displayed by the African signatories.

11. Christopher Fyfe, *A History of Sierra Leone* (London: Oxford University Press, 1962), pp. 552-553.

12. It would be interesting to establish the meaning of the terms "protectorate" and "protection" in African languages.

13. Pierre Alexandre, "Chiefs, *Commandants* and Clerks," in Michael Crowder and Obaro Ikime, eds., *West African Chiefs* (New York: Africana Publishing Corp., 1970), pp. 3 and 12, note 3.

14. *Ibid.*, p. 5.

15. Elizabeth M. Chilver, "Paramountcy and Protection in the Cameroons: The Bali and the Germans," in Prosser Gifford and William Roger Louis, eds., *Britain and Germany*

in Africa: Imperial Rivalry and Colonial Rule (New Haven: Yale University Press, 1967), pp. 479-511, is virtually unique, among studies of Afro-German relationships in West Africa, in making it apparent as John D. Fage has aptly put it "that the Germans as well as making Cameroons history, were themselves to some extent prisoners of that history." *Ibid.*, p. 694. The following section therefore relies primarily on this account.

16. *Ibid.*, p. 493.

17. For the subsequent development of the Bali-German relationship, see chapter 7.

18. Morris, "Protection or Annexation?" p. 50.

19. Alexandrowicz, "Partition of Africa," pp. 144-145.

20. Helmut Bley, *South-West Africa under German Rule, 1894-1914* (London: Heinemann, 1971), especially pp. 86-91, 174-201. "Old Germans" were among those few German men spared by the Herero in the 1905 revolt. See chapter 8.

21. For Alldridge, see note 10 in this chapter.

22. The classic work is Captain Charles E. Callwell, *Small Wars: Their Principles and Practice* (London: Her Majesty's Stationery Office, 1896), and the 3d edition (1906), much enlarged, in which Callwell, by now Colonel, includes information on post-1896 campaigns as well as material culled from the notes that Lt. Col. Septans of the French marine infantry incorporated in his translation of the first edition.

23. Brian Bond, *Victorian Military Campaigns* (London: Hutchinson, 1967), p. 20.

24. Obaro Ikime, "Colonial Conquest and Resistance in Southern Nigeria," *Journal of the Historical Society of Nigeria*, 4:268 (1972). Ikime's article and three symposia, Michael Crowder, ed., *West African Resistance: The Military Response to Colonial Occupation* (London: Hutchinson, 1971); Bethwell A. Ogot, ed., *War and Society in Africa: Ten Studies* (London: Frank Cass, 1972); and Robert I. Rotberg and Ali Mazrui, eds., *Protest and Power in Black Africa* (New York: Oxford University Press, 1970), examine the "small wars" from the African side.

25. Bond, *Victorian Military Campaigns*, p. 20.

26. Yves Person, "Guinea-Samori," in Crowder, *West African Resistance*, p. 134. Sven E. Rubenson, "Adwa in 1896: The Resounding Protest," in Rotberg and Mazrui, *Protest and Power*, p. 121.

27. Callwell, *Small Wars*, 1906 ed., p. 33.

28. *Ibid.*, pp. 505, 373.

29. Anthony Atmore, J. M. Chirenje, and S. I. Mudenge, "Firearms in South Central Africa," *Journal of African History*, 12:545-556 (1971); H. A. C. Cairns, *Prelude to Imperialism: British Reactions to Central African Society, 1840-1890* (London: Routledge & Kegan Paul, 1965), pp. 109-110.

30. Crowder, *West African Resistance*, p. 16.

31. Callwell, *Small Wars*, 1896 ed., pp. 238-239.

32. Eric A. Walker, *A History of Southern Africa* (London: Longmans, 1959), p. 429.

33. Monica Hunter, *Reactions to Conquest*, 2d ed. (London: Oxford University Press, 1961), p. 412, note 2.

34. Crowder, *West African Resistance*, p. 16.

35. Callwell, *Small Wars*, 1906 ed., p. 440.

36. Person, "Guinea-Samori," pp. 111-143, especially p. 133. See also J. B. Webster, A. A. Boahen, and H. O. Idowo, *The Growth of African Civilization: The Revolutionary Years—West Africa since 1800* (London: Longmans, 1967), pp. 241-253.

37. Anthony Atmore and Peter Sanders, "Sotho Arms and Ammunition in the Nineteenth Century," *Journal of African History*, 12:535-544 (1971).

38. Henri Brunschwig, "De la résistance africaine à l'impérialisme européen," *Journal*

of African History, 15:58 (1974). For the development of French military imperialism, see chapter 2.

39. B. Olatunji Oloruntimehin, "Anti-French Coalition of African States and Groups in the Western Sudan, 1889-1893," *Odu*, 3:18 (1970).

40. For Maji-Maji, see chapter 8.

41. Margery Perham, *Lugard*, vol.2, *The Years of Authority* (London: Collins, 1960), p. 90.

42. Lugard's speech is cited in A. H. M. Kirk-Greene, *The Principles of British Administration in Nigeria* (London: Oxford University Press, 1965), pp. 43-44.

43. See chapter 7.

Chapter 5. Frontiers and Boundaries

1. Cited in the cogent study by Joseph C. Anene, *The International Boundaries of Nigeria* (London: Longmans, 1970), p. 3. Sir Edward Hertslet, *The Map of Africa by Treaty*, 3 vols. (London: His Majesty's Stationery Office, 1909; reprint 3d ed., London: Frank Cass, 1967), is the classic work. My understanding of this topic has also been helped by Saadia Touval, *The Boundary Politics of Independent Africa* (Cambridge: Harvard University Press, 1972); Carl G. Widstrand, ed., *African Boundary Problems* (Uppsala: Scandinavian Institute of African Studies, 1969); Yves Person, "L'Afrique noire et ses frontières." *Revue française d'études politiques africaines*, 80:18-43 (1972). Good general studies are J. R. V. Prescott, *The Geography of Frontiers and Boundaries* (London: Hutchinson, 1965), which contains much African material; S. Whittemore Boggs, *International Boundaries* (New York: Columbia University Press, 1940); Stephen B. Jones, *Boundary-Making* (Washington, D.C.: Carnegie Endowment for International Peace, 1945); J. Ancel, *Géographie des frontières* (Paris: Gallimard, 1938).

2. Alastair Lamb, *Asian Frontiers* (London: Pall Mall Press, 1968), p. 4.

3. *Ibid.*, p. 6.

4. Ancel, *Géographie*, pp. 8-13, 20-27.

5. Prescott, *Geography*, pp. 19-20.

6. Anene, *International Boundaries*, p. 5.

7. Allen M. Howard, "Big Men, Traders and Chiefs: Power, Commerce and Spatial Change in the Sierra Leone-Guinea Plain, 1865-95" (Ph.D. thesis, University of Wisconsin, 1972).

8. Anthony G. Hopkins, "Economic Imperialism in West Africa," *Economic History Review*, 21:580-600 (1968). Martin A. Klein, "Social and Economic Factors in the Muslim Revolution in Senegambia," *Journal of African History*, 13:419-442 (1972).

9. William Tordoff, *Ashanti under the Prempehs* (London: Oxford University Press, 1965).

10. Cited in W. David McIntyre, *The Imperial Frontier in the Tropics, 1865-1875* (New York: St. Martins Press, 1967), p. 3.

11. *Ibid.*, p. 8.

12. Prescott, *Geography*, p. 88; Harry R. Rudin, *Germans in the Cameroons* (New Haven: Yale University Press, 1938), pp. 60-68.

13. Notably by Saadia Touval, "Treaties, Borders and the Partition of Africa," *Journal of African History*, 7:279-292 (1966).

14. Boggs, *Boundaries*, pp. 161-163.

15. Person, "L'Afrique noire," puts the point especially forcefully.

16. Hubert Deschamps, "Les Frontières de la Senegambie," *Revue française d'études politiques africaines*, 80:44-57 (1972), is the best discussion of this unique case.

17. Elizabeth Hopkins, "The International Boundary as a Factor in the Extension of Colonial Control," in Daniel F. McCall, Norman R. Bennett, Jeffrey Butler, eds., *Boston University Papers on Africa*, vol. 2, *Eastern African History* (Boston: Boston University Press, 1962), pp. 208-245, is a revealing study. The quotation is from p. 225.

18. *Ibid*.

19. *Ibid*.

20. I owe this point to Malcolm McCall, research student, University of York.

21. Hertslet, *Map of Africa*, p. 861.

22. Malcolm McCall, "Luawa under British Rule" (Ph.D. thesis, University of York, 1974).

23. Touval, *Boundary Politics*, p. 8.

24. Prescott, *Geography*, p. 63. For the vicissitudes of the Alaketu, see chapter 7.

25. David M. Abshire and Michael A. Samuels, eds., *Portuguese Africa: A Handbook* (London: Pall Mall Press, 1969).

26. Derwent Whittesley, *The Earth and the State*, 2d ed. (New York: Henry Holt, 1944), especially pp. 335-341.

27. Touval, *Boundary Politics*, pp. 9-10.

28. *Ibid*., pp. 19-20.

29. For Ajayi's arguments, see chapter 1.

30. Boggs, *Boundaries*, pp. 79-80.

Chapter 6. The Theory and Practice of Empire, 1885-1914

1. C. H. Stigand, *Native Administration* (London: Constable, 1914), pp. 5-6.

2. C. H. Stigand, *The Land of Zinj* (London: Thomas Nelson, 1913), p. 312.

3. Hubert Deschamps, "Et Maintenant Lord Lugard?" *Africa*, 23:296-306 (1963).

4. M. Semakula Kiwanuka, "Colonial Policies and Administrations in Africa: The Myths of the Contrasts," *African Historical Studies*, 3:295-313 (1970).

5. Georges Balandier, "La Situation coloniale: Approche théorique," *Cahiers internationaux de sociologie*, 11:44-79 (1951). See also E. A. Brett, *Colonialism and Under-development in East Africa* (London: Heinemann, 1973), pp. 1-34, which ranges over much modern discussion in the social sciences.

6. John Rex, *Race Relations in Sociological Theory* (London: Weidenfeld and Nicholson, 1970), especially chapters 2 and 3, is illuminating on the institutions of colonialism generally. See also Brett, *Colonialism*, pp. 1-34; Balandier, "La Situation coloniale."

7. See chapter 7.

8. Philip D. Curtin, " 'Scientific Racism' and the British Theory of Empire," *Journal of the Historical Society of Nigeria*, 2:40-51 (1960).

9. D. A. Low, *Lion Rampant* (London: Frank Cass, 1973), chapter 2, "Empire and Social Engineering,"

10. Henry S. Wilson, ed., *Origins of West African Nationalism* (London: Macmillan, 1969), p. 38.

11. Philip D. Curtin, ed., *Imperialism* (New York: Harper and Row, 1971), pp. xix-xxi.

12. Edward W. Blyden, *Christianity, Islam and the Negro Race* (London, 1887), discusses such views.

13. Cited in Low, *Lion Rampant*, p. 63.

14. See chapter 3.

15. Sir Charles Eliot, "The East Africa Protectorate," in Charles S. Golden, ed., *The Empire and the Century* (London: John Murray, 1905), pp. 861-876.

16. Sir Harry H. Johnston, *The Negro in the New World*, (London: Methuen, 1910).

Maurice S. Evans, *Black and White in South East Africa* (London: Longmans, 1911), and *Black and White in the Southern States of America* (London: Longmans, 1915).

17. Suzanne Miers, "The Brussels Conference of 1889-1890: The Place of the Slave Trade in the Policies of Great Britain and Germany," in Prosser Gifford and William Roger Louis, eds., *Britain and Germany in Africa: Imperial Rivalry and Colonial Rule* (New Haven: Yale University Press, 1967), p. 92.

18. *Ibid.*, p. 111.

19. Francis Wilson and Dominique Perrot, eds., *Outlook on a Century, 1870-1970* (Braamfontein: Lovedale Press, 1973), pp. 133-134.

20. Alfred P. Hillier, "The Native Races of South Africa," *Proceedings of the Royal Colonial Institute*, 31:45-48 (1898-99). For the present day consequences of the Colored's "truly heroic rate of alcoholism," see Jim Hoagland, *South Africa: Civilizations in Conflict* (London: Allen and Unwin, 1973), pp. 111-112.

21. Miers, "Brussels Conference," p. 83.

Chapter 7. The Consolidation of Colonial Rule in West Africa and the Congo Basin

1. Sir Frederick Graham, assistant undersecretary at the Colonial Office, in July 1906, cited in Ronald Hyam, *Elgin and Churchill at the Colonial Office* (London: Macmillan, 1968), p. 381.

2. The point is made by John Fage in concluding observations, "British and German Colonial Rule: A Synthesis and Summary," in Prosser Gifford and William Roger Louis, eds., *Britain and Germany in Africa: Imperial Rivalry and Colonial Rule* (New Haven: Yale University Press, 1967), pp. 691-706, and Leonard Thompson, "France and Britain in Africa: A Perspective," in Prosser Gifford and William Roger Louis, eds., *Britain and France in Africa: Imperial Rivalry and Colonial Rule* (New Haven, Yale University Press, 1971), pp. 777-784.

3. On developments in France during this period, see especially Jean Ganiage, *L'Expansion coloniale de la France sous la Troisième République* (Paris: Payot, 1968), and for a brief survey, Catherine Coquéry-Vidrovitch, "French Colonization in Africa to 1920: Administration and Economic Development," in L. H. Gann and Peter Duignan, eds., *Colonialism in Africa, 1870-1960* (Cambridge: Cambridge University Press, 1969), I, 165-198, which summarizes several specialist studies.

4. William B. Cohen, *Rulers of Empire: The French Colonial Service in Africa* (Stanford: Hoover Institution Press, 1971), p. 81. The theme of the contrast between French West and French Equatorial Africa emerges strongly from Coquéry-Vidrovitch's "French Colonization."

5. Cohen, *Rulers of Empire*, pp. 37-56.

6. Raymond F. Betts, *Assimilation and Association in French Colonial Theory, 1890-1914* (New York: Columbia University Press, 1961); Hubert Deschamps, *Les Méthodes et doctrines coloniales de la France* (Paris: Armand Colin, 1953).

7. See chapter 4.

8. Cohen, *Rulers of Empire*, p. 75.

9. Pierre Alexandre, "Chiefs, *Commandants* and Clerks," and "Chieftaincy in French West Africa," in Michael Crowder and Obaro Ikime, eds., *West African Chiefs* (New York: Africana Publishing Corporation, 1970), pp. 2-13, 24-78, are, especially the former, incisive and witty on these relationships.

10. I. A. Aswiaju, "The Alaketu of Ketu and the Onimeko of Meko: The Changing Status of Two Yoruba Rulers under French and British Rule," in Crowder and Ikime,

West African Chiefs, pp 134-160, an exemplary comparative history of the colonial impact.

11. *Ibid.*, p. 142.

12. *Ibid.*, p. 144.

13. *Ibid.*, p. 146.

14. Elliott P. Skinner, *The Mossi of the Upper Volta* (Stanford: Stanford University Press, 1964); also his very useful chapter, "The Mossi under Colonial Rule," in Crowder and Ikime, *West African Chiefs*, pp. 98-123.

15. Martin A. Klein, *Islam and Imperialism in Senegal: Sine-Saloum, 1847-1914* (Edinburgh: Edinburgh University Press, 1968), p. 205.

16. S. B. Saul, "The Economic Significance of 'Constructive Imperialism,'" *Journal of Economic History*, 17:173-192 (1957); Hyam, *Elgin and Churchill*, pp. 367-427; Lady Flora Lugard, *A Tropical Dependency* (facsimile of 1905 ed.; London: Frank Cass, 1964), p. 419.

17. Aswiaju, "The Alaketu of Ketu," pp. 136-137.

18. *Ibid.*, pp. 149-150.

19. See chapter 10.

20. Margery Perham, *Lugard*, vol. 2, *The Years of Authority* (London: Collins, 1960), p. 27, is meticulous and indispensable. Also valuable is Perham's *Native Administration in Nigeria* (London: Oxford University Press, 1937). I. F. Nicolson, *The Administration of Nigeria, 1900-1960: Men, Methods, and Myths* (Oxford: Clarendon Press, 1969), much more critical of Lugard, and Mary Bull, "Indirect Rule in Northern Nigeria, 1900-1911," in Kenneth Robinson and Frederick Madden, eds., *Essays in Imperial Government* (Oxford: Basil Blackwell, 1963), are also very useful.

21. E. D. Morel, *Nigeria: Its Peoples and Its Problems* (London: Smith Elder and Co., 1911), p. 190.

22. Lugard, *Tropical Dependency*, p. 334.

23. See chapter 4.

24. Perham, *Lugard*, p. 149.

25. *Ibid.*, pp. 149-150.

26. Lugard's *Political Memoranda* of 1906, cited in John Smith, "The Relationship of the British Political Officer to His Chief in Northern Nigeria," in Crowder and Ikime, *West African Chiefs*, p. 15. One officer informed Lugard in 1918, "Reading them [the *Memoranda*] is like reading the Bible, the more you read it, the more you find there was in it!" Perham, *Lugard*, p. 524.

27. Smith, "British Political Officer," p. 16.

28. Cohen, *Rulers of Empire*, p. 77.

29. Perham, *Lugard*, p. 260.

30. Bull, "Indirect Rule;" Perham, *Lugard*, pp. 469-488.

31. Perham, *Lugard*, p. 472, and Perham, *Native Administration*, pp. 70-71.

32. For his views, see Charles L. Temple, *Native Races and Their Rulers* (Cape Town: Argus Publishing Co., 1918).

33. A. H. M. Kirk-Greene, ed., *Lugard and the Amalgamation of Nigeria: A Documentary Record* (London: Frank Cass, 1968), pp. 8-9. The introduction, pp. 1-44, is very helpful on the process of amalgamation.

34. *Ibid.*, p. 21. For crown colony constitutionalism, see discussion elsewhere in this chapter and in chapter 2.

35. Kirk-Greene, *Amalgamation*, pp. 22-24.

36. Helen Lackner, "Social Anthropology and Indirect Rule: Eastern Nigeria 1920-1940," in Talal Asad, ed., *Anthropology and the Colonial Encounter* (London: Ithaca Press. 1973), pp. 133-134.

37. In noting the divergency between Northern and Southern Nigeria, the cluster of quite outstanding Nigerian historians who have studied the origins and nature of Indirect Rule have created an exemplary historiography. They are well represented in Crowder and Ikime, *West African Chiefs*, but anyone wishing to take this subject further must consult the files of the *Journal of the Historical Society of Nigeria*.

38. The most accessible, up-to-date analysis of the constitutional and political context of German imperialism is John Iliffe, *Tanganyika under German Rule, 1905-1912* (Cambridge: Cambridge University Press, 1969), pp. 30-39.

39. For the initial involvement between the Bali and the Germans, see chapter 4. For the working out of that relationship, Elizabeth M. Chilver, "Paramountcy and Protection in the Cameroons: The Bali and the Germans," in Gifford and Louis, *Britain and Germany*, pp. 479-511, is again indispensable. Her article on "Native Administration in the West Central Cameroons, 1902-1954," in Robinson and Madden, *Essays*, pp. 89-139, is also helpful.

40. Chilver, "Paramountcy and Protection," p. 501.

41. *Ibid.*, p. 504.

42. *Ibid.*, p. 507.

43. *Ibid.*, pp. 509-510.

44. Research on German East Africa, especially by John Iliffe, also modifies the earlier accounts of Dernburg's reforms. See chapter 8.

45. The two handiest accounts of Togo are Michael Crowder's chapter, "The Model Colony," in his *West Africa under Colonial Rule* (London: Hutchinson, 1968), pp. 241-251, and D. E. K. Amunemey, "German Administration in Southern Togo," *Journal of African History*, 10:623-639 (1969).

46. Chilver, "Native Administration," pp. 94-95.

47. Perham, *Lugard*, pp. 611-612, and C. W. Newbury, "Partition, Development and Trusteeship," in Gifford and Louis, *Britain and Germany*, pp. 455-477.

48. Ruth Slade, *King Leopold's Congo* (London: Oxford University Press, 1962), and Roger Anstey, *King Leopold's Legacy: The Congo under Belgian Rule, 1908-1960* (London: Oxford University Press, 1966), are both very illuminating, and I have relied heavily upon them.

49. A. B. Keith's phrase, cited in Slade, *Leopold's Congo*, p. 172.

50. *Ibid.*, cited on p. 175.

51. *Ibid.*, cited on p. 176.

52. Anstey, *Leopold's Legacy*, chapter 1, especially p. 30.

53. Slade, *Leopold's Congo*, p. 174.

54. Anstey, *Leopold's Legacy*, p. 6.

55. *Ibid.*

56. *Ibid.*, p. 7.

57. *Ibid.*

58. *Ibid.*, p. 9.

59. Slade, *Leopold's Congo*, p. 188.

60. For a discussion of the Colonial Charter, see Lord Hailey, *An African Survey Revised 1956* (London: Oxford University Press, 1957), pp. 345-349, and Anstey, *Leopold's Legacy*, pp. 38-40.

61. Anstey, *Leopold's Legacy*, p. 48.

62. *Ibid.*, pp. 53-54.

63. Marvin Miracle, *Agriculture in the Congo Basin* (Madison: University of Wisconsin Press, 1967), p. 240.

64. *Ibid.*, p. 238.

65. Anstey, *Leopold's Legacy*, pp. 47-55.

66. See further discussion elsewhere in this chapter and in chapter 2.

67. Richard Symonds, *The British and Their Successors: A Study in the Development of Government Services in the New States* (London: Faber and Faber, 1966), pp. 119-127; David Kimble, *A Political History of Ghana, 1850-1928* (Oxford: Clarendon Press, 1963), pp. 93-195; Christopher Fyfe, *A History of Sierra Leone* (London: Oxford University Press, 1962), pp. 523-524, 532-534, 537-538, 615.

68. Kimble, *Ghana*, pp. 330-357.

69. See chapter 2. See also Agneta Pallinder-Law, "Aborted Modernization in West Africa? The Case of Abeokuta," *Journal of African History*, 15:65-82 (1974).

70. Fyfe, *Sierra Leone*, p. 555.

71. G. Wesley Johnson, Jr., *The Emergence of Black Politics in Senegal* (Stanford: Stanford University Press, 1971), pp. 123-218, a penetrating analysis on which the following account is based.

72. *Ibid.*, p. 133.

73. See chapter 12 on the Mourides.

Chapter 8. Establishing the White Man's Realm

1. Ronald Hyam, *The Failure of South African Expansion, 1908-1948* (London: Macmillan, 1972), p. 123. Chapters 1 and 2 are especially useful on this.

2. *Ibid.*, p. 14.

3. *Ibid.*, p. 23.

4. The classic discussion of the issues involved is W. K. Hancock, *Survey of British Commonwealth Affairs*, vol. 2, *Problems of Economic Policy* (London: Oxford University Press, 1942), part 2.

5. On German East Africa, I have relied heavily on John Iliffe, *Tanganyika under German Rule, 1905-1912* (Cambridge: Cambridge University Press, 1969); Ralph A. Austen, *Northwest Tanzania under German and British Rule: Colonial Policy and Tribal Politics, 1889-1939* (New Haven: Yale University Press, 1968); Aylward Shorter, *Chiefship in Western Tanzania: A Political History of the Kimbu* (Oxford: Clarendon Press, 1972). For a general survey, I. N. Kimambo and A. J. Temu, eds., *A History of Tanzania* (Nairobi: East African Publishing House, 1969).

6. Iliffe, *Tanganyika*, p. 56.

7. *Ibid.*, p. 57.

8. *Ibid.*, p. 131.

9. *Ibid.*, p. 123.

10. *Ibid.*, p. 144.

11. *Ibid.*, p. 143-144.

12. Austen, *Northwest Tanzania*, p. 34.

13. *Ibid.*, p. 38.

14. *Ibid.*

15. Iliffe, *Tanganyika*, pp. 157-159.

16. Shorter, *Chiefship, passim.*

17. Aylward Shorter, "The Kimbu," in Andrew Roberts, ed., *Tanzania before 1900* (Nairobi: East African Publishing House, 1968), p. 112.

18. Shorter, *Chiefship*, pp. 327-332.

19. Iliffe, *Tanganyika*. Chapter 2 is the most accessible account of the rising.

20. *Ibid.*, p. 25.

21. *Ibid.*

22. *Ibid*., p. 24.

23. *Ibid*.

24. *Ibid*., p. 28.

25. *Ibid*., p. 55.

26. *Ibid*.

27. *Ibid*., p. 70

28. *Ibid*., citations on pp. 71, 54.

29. *Ibid*., p. 84.

30. Helmut Bley, *South-West Africa under German Rule, 1894-1914* (London: Heinemann, 1971), p. 3. Bley offers a profound analysis of the structures and psychology of imperialism and "settlerdom," which I have found indispensable. See also his "Social Discord in South West Africa," in Prosser Gifford and William Roger Louis, eds., *Britain and Germany in Africa: Imperial Rivalry and Colonial Rule* (New Haven: Yale University Press, 1967), pp. 607-630.

31. Bley, "Social Discord," p. 623.

32. Bley, *South-West Africa*, p. 143.

33. *Ibid*., p. 162.

34. *Ibid*.

35. *Ibid*., p. 164.

36. *Ibid*., pp. 163-164.

37. *Ibid*., p. 166.

38. *Ibid*., p. 167.

39. On the British in East Africa, the chapters by D. A. Low, "Uganda: The Establishment of the Protectorate, 1894-1919"; C. C. Wrigley, "Kenya: The Patterns of Economic Life, 1902-1945"; George Bennett, "Settlers and Politics in Kenya, up to 1945"; and Cyril Ehrlich, "The Uganda Economy, 1903-1945," in Vincent Harlow, E. M. Chilver, and Alison Smith, eds., *History of East Africa*, vol. 2 (Oxford: Clarendon Press, 1965), are essential. See also G. H. Mungeam, *British Rule in Kenya, 1895-1912: The Establishment of Administration in the East African Protectorate* (Oxford: Clarendon Press, 1966); M. P. K. Sorrenson, *Origins of European Settlement in Kenya* (Nairobi: Oxford University Press, 1968); D. A. Low, *Buganda in Modern History* (London: Weidenfeld and Nicholson, 1971); D. A. Low and R. C. Pratt, *Buganda and British Overrule, 1900-1955* (London: Oxford University Press, 1960), and Richard D. Wolff, *The Economics of Colonialism: Britain and Kenya, 1870-1930* (New Haven: Yale University Press, 1974).

40. On the settlement issue, see Sorrenson, *Origins of European Settlement*.

41. Cited in Bennett, "Settlers and Politics in Kenya," pp. 270-271.

42. Wrigley, "Kenya: The Patterns of Economic Life," p. 217.

43. Cited in Bennett, "Settlers and Politics in Kenya," p. 283.

44. *Ibid*., pp. 282-283.

45. *Ibid*., p. 276, for Bennett's phrase.

46. See chapters by Ehrlich and Wrigley, in Harlow, Chilver, and Smith, *History*. See also Hugh Fearn, *An African Economy: A Study of the Economic Development of Nyanza Province of Kenya* (Oxford: Oxford University Press, 1961); C. C. Wrigley, *Crops and Wealth in Uganda*, East African Studies, no. 12 (Kampala: East African Institute of Social Research, 1959). The literature is usefully summarized in C. M. Elliott, "Agriculture and Economic Development in Africa: Theory and Experience, 1880-1914," in E. L. Jones and S. J. Woolf, eds., *Agrarian Change and Economic Development* (London: Methuen University Paperbacks, 1974), pp. 123-150.

47. Wrigley, "Kenya: The Patterns of Economic Life," p. 224.

48. *Ibid.*

49. *Ibid.*, p. 226.

50. Ehrlich, "The Uganda Economy," p. 414.

51. The phrase was coined by anthropologist Hilda Kuper for her study of the Swazi, *The Uniform of Colour* (Johannesburg: Witwatersrand University Press, 1947).

52. See chapter 13 for general discussion of missions.

53. Bley, *South-West Africa*, p. 43.

54. *Ibid.*, p. 68.

55. *Ibid.*

Chapter 9. The First World War

1. J. Ayodele Langley, *Pan-Africanism and Nationalism in West Africa, 1900-1945* (Oxford: Clarendon Press, 1973), judiciously analyzes Du Bois's impact upon African politics. For Chilembwe's response to the war, see his moving letter to the *Nyasaland Times* in November 1914, "The Voice of African Natives in the Present Time," included in the penetrating study of Chilembwe's life and times by George Shepperson and Thomas Price, *Independent African* (Edinburgh: Edinburgh University Press, 1958), pp. 234-235. See also chapter 12.

2. For the high morale of Germans captured in the Cameroons—"all convinced that the Allies were already defeated in Europe and that London was in flames"—see Margery Perham, *Lugard*, vol. 2, *The Years of Authority* (London: Collins, 1960), p. 537.

3. See chapter 2.

4. Cited in Jean Suret-Canale, *French Colonialism in Tropical Africa, 1900-1945* (London: Hurst, 1971), p. 135.

5. *Ibid.*

6. *Ibid.*, pp. 134-138; Michael Crowder, "The 1914-1918 European War and West Africa," in J. F. A. Ajayi and Michael Crowder, eds., *History of West Africa* (London: Longman, 1974), II, 484-513, analyzes French recruitment policy and its effects.

7. Crowder, "The 1914-1918 European War," p. 493.

8. *Ibid.*, pp. 494, note 21, citing unpublished research by I. A. Aswiaju.

9. *Ibid.*, pp. 498-499.

10. *Ibid.*, p. 500; also Suret-Canale, *French Colonialism*, pp. 139-143, and Jacques Lombard, *Autorités traditionelles et pouvoirs européens en Afrique noire* (Paris: Armand Colin, 1967), pp. 120-123.

11. Crowder, "The 1914-1918 European War," p. 500.

12. For Diagne and the 1914 election, see G. Wesley Johnson, Jr., *The Emergence of Black Politics in Senegal* (Stanford: Stanford University Press, 1971), pp. 104-129, and Crowder, "The 1914-1918 European War," pp. 496-497.

13. Crowder, "The 1914-1918 European War," pp. 500-503.

14. *Ibid.*, pp. 501-503, and Suret-Canale, *French Colonialism*, pp. 136-139.

15. Crowder, "The 1914-1918 European War," p. 502.

16. The handiest brief account of the campaign is by W. O. Henderson, "German East Africa," in Vincent Harlow, E. M. Chilver, and Alison Smith, eds., *History of East Africa* (Oxford: Clarendon Press, 1965) II, 155-162.

17. Cited in Marcia Wright, *German Missions in Tanganyika, 1891-1941: Lutherans and Moravians in the Southern Highlands* (Oxford: Clarendon Press, 1971), p. 142.

18. Bethwell A. Ogot, "Kenya under British Rule," in B. A. Ogot and J. A. Kieran, eds., *Zamani: A Survey of East African History* (Nairobi: East African Publishing House, 1968), p. 268.

19. Cited in Henderson, "German East Africa," p. 162.

20. Wright, *German Missions*, pp. 143-145.

21. Terence O. Ranger's illuminating "The Movement of Ideas," in I. N. Kimambo and A. J. Temu, eds., *A History of Tanzania* (Nairobi: East African Publishing House, 1969), pp. 179-180, examines the effects of the war on Islam.

22. *Ibid.*, p. 176.

23. *Ibid.*, p. 177.

24. *Ibid.*, and John Iliffe, "The Age of Improvement and Differentiation," in Kimambo and Temu, *History of Tanzania*, pp. 123-160.

25. Cited in J. M. Lonsdale's important article, "Some Origins of Nationalism in East Africa," *Journal of African History*, 9:132-133 (1968). The forthcoming publication of Lonsdale's thesis, "A Political History of Nyanza, 1883-1945" (Ph.D. thesis, Cambridge University, 1966), will elucidate this issue.

26. Ogot, "Kenya under British Rule," p. 266.

27. See chapter 8.

28. William Roger Louis, *Great Britain and Germany's Lost Colonies, 1914-1915* (Oxford: Clarendon Press, 1967), especially pp. 68-76, 157-159.

29. *Ibid.*, pp. 78-160.

30. Maynard W. Swanson, "South West Africa in Trust," in Prosser Gifford and William Roger Louis, eds., *Britain and Germany in Africa: Imperial Rivalry and Colonial Rule* (New Haven: Yale University Press, 1967), pp. 630-664.

31. Harry R. Rudin, *Armistice, 1918* (New Haven: Yale University Press, 1944), pp. 183-184.

32. Langley, *Pan-Africanism*, pp. 63-68, 108-133.

Chapter 10. Changes in Government between World Wars

1. *The African World and Cape-Cairo Express*, March 17, 1923, p. 251, cited in Michael Crowder, "The 1914-1918 European War and West Africa," in J. F. A. Ajayi and Michael Crowder, eds., *History of West Africa* (London: Longman, 1974), II, 495.

2. Margery Perham, *Colonial Sequence, 1930-1949: A Chronological Commentary upon British Colonial Policy Especially in Africa* (London: Methuen, 1967), pp. xii-xiii; Hubert Deschamps, "French Colonial Policy in Tropical Africa between Two World Wars," in Prosser Gifford and William Roger Louis, eds., *France and Britain in Africa: Imperial Rivalry and Colonial Rule* (New Haven: Yale University Press, 1971), pp. 543-569.

3. Sir Frederick D. Lugard, *The Dual Mandate in British Tropical Africa* (Edinburgh: William Blackwood and Sons, 1922). For Lugard's work on the Permanent Mandates Commission, see Margery Perham, *Lugard*, vol. 2, *The Years of Authority* (London, Collins, 1960), pp. 645-655.

4. Margery Perham, "Some Problems of Indirect Rule in Africa," an address to the Royal Society of Arts, March 24, 1934, reported in Perham, *Colonial Sequence*, pp. 92-93.

5. K. A. Korsah, "Indirect Rule — a Means to an End," *African Affairs*, 43:182 (1944).

6. Perham, "Problems of Indirect Rule," pp. 101-102.

7. P. C. Lloyd, "Kings, Chiefs and Local Government," *West Africa*, January 31, 1953, cited in Michael Crowder, "Indirect Rule — French and British Style," *Africa*, 34:198 (1964).

8. Lugard, *Dual Mandate*, pp. 200-201, 219, 250.

9. Perham, "Problems of Indirect Rule," p. 101.

10. "Our Task in Africa," *The Times*, February 12, 1936, reported in Perham, *Colonial Sequence*, p. 150.

11. Lugard, *Dual Mandate*, pp. 69-70.

12. Perham, *Colonial Sequence*, p. 108.

13. Recently there has been considerable debate on the links between Indirect Rule and "functional" social anthropology. Talal Asad, ed., *Anthropology and the Colonial Encounter* (London: Ithaca Press, 1973), is the best introduction to this discussion. Philip E. Mitchell, "The Anthropologist and the Practical Man: A Reply and a Question," *Africa*, 3:217-223 (1930), puts the viewpoint of the "practical man." Wendy James, "The Anthropologist as Reluctant Imperialist," in Asad, *Anthropology*, pp. 41-69, is a brief, judicious analysis of the discussion.

14. Bronislaw Malinowski, *The Dynamics of Culture Change* (New Haven: Yale University Press, 1945), p. 138. See introduction by Phyllis M. Kaberry, p. vi, for Malinowski's seminar. On his ideas generally, Raymond Firth, *Man and Culture: An Evaluation of the Work of Malinowski* (London: Routledge & Kegan Paul, 1957), is valuable.

15. Perham, "Problems of Indirect Rule," p. 104.

16. *Gold Coast Leader*, Supplement, July 17, 1926, cited in Raymond Leslie Buell, *The Native Problem in Africa* (1928; reprint ed., London: Frank Cass, 1965), p. 771.

17. Cited in Perham, *Colonial Sequence*, p. 46.

18. See chapter 8.

19. United Kingdom, *Parliamentary Papers*, 1923, 18 (c. 1922), Memorandum on Indians in Kenya.

20. George Bennett, "British Settlers North of the Zambezi," in L. H. Gann and Peter Duignan, eds., *Colonialism in Africa 1870-1960*, vol. 2, *The History and Politics of Colonialism* (Cambridge: Cambridge University Press, 1970), pp. 53-91, is the best brief introduction. The sentence cited is on p. 62.

21. *Ibid*., p. 63.

22. Jan C. Smuts, *Africa and Some World Problems* (Oxford: Clarendon Press, 1930), p. 56. The first of his 1929 Rhodes Memorial Lectures, "African Settlement," *ibid*., pp. 37-67, forcefully expounds the settler case.

23. The phrase is in Perham, *Colonial Sequence*, p. xi.

24. Jacques Lombard, *Autorités traditionelles et pouvoirs européens en Afrique noire* (Paris: Armand Colin, 1967), pp. 127-128.

25. Cited in William B. Cohen, *Rulers of Empire: The French Colonial Service in Africa* (Stanford: Hoover Institution Press, 1971), p. 129, a mine of information on policies and personnel.

26. Albert Sarraut, *La Mise en valeur des colonies françaises* (Paris: Payot, 1923). Sarraut's ideas are discussed in Cohen, *Rulers of Empire*, pp. 109-110; Also by Ralph A. Austen, "Varieties of Trusteeship: African Territories under British and French Mandate, 1919-1939," pp. 519-521, and Deschamps, "French Colonial Policy," pp. 552-554, both in Gifford and Louis, *France and Britain in Africa*.

27. Cohen, *Rulers of Empire*, p. 129.

28. *Ibid*., p. 113.

29. *Ibid*., pp. 100-101.

30. *Ibid*., p. 113.

31. *The Times*., May 18, 1933, reported in Perham, *Colonial Sequence*, p. 74.

32. Cohen, *Rulers of Empire*, p. 133. For Deschamps's own retrospective comments, see "French Colonial Policy," p. 562, and his Lugard Memorial Lecture, "Et Maintenant Lord Lugard?" *Africa*, 23:295-306 (1963).

33. On Belgian policy, especially Franck's reforms, the handiest account in English is again Roger Anstey, *King Leopold's Legacy: The Congo under Belgian Rule, 1908-1960* (London: Oxford University Press, 1966), pp. 62-84.

34. Cited in Lord Hailey, *An African Survey: A Study of Problems Arising in Africa South of the Sahara* (London: Oxford Press, 1938), p. 1271.

35. Anstey, *Leopold's Legacy*, p. 65.

36. Perham, *Colonial Sequence*, p. 74.

37. For general discussions of the myth or reality of the differences, see chapter 6.

38. Perham, *Colonial Sequence*, p. 72.

39. I. A. Aswiaju, "The Alaketu of Ketu and the Onimeko of Meko: The Changing Status of Two Yoruba Rulers under French and British Rule," in Michael Crowder and Obaro Ikime, eds., *West African Chiefs* (New York: Africana Publishing Corp., 1970), p. 135.

40. A. E. Afigbo, "West African Chiefs during Colonial Rule and After," *Odu*, 5:105-106 (1971).

41. Ralph A. Austen, *Northwest Tanzania under German and British Rule: Colonial Policy and Tribal Politics, 1889-1939* (New Haven: Yale University Press, 1968), p. 255.

42. Colin M. Turnbull, *The Lonely African* (London: Chatto and Windus, 1963), pp. 57-70. Masoudi tells his story on pp. 29-43.

43. James W. Fernandez, "Fang Representations under Acculturation," in Philip D. Curtin, ed., *Africa and the West: Intellectual Responses to European Culture* (Madison: University of Wisconsin Press, 1972), pp. 11-14. The quotation is from p. 12 of Fernandez' sympathetic study.

44. Martin A. Klein, "Traditional Political Institutions and Colonial Domination," *African Historical Studies*, 4:665 (1971).

45. Jacques Kuoh Moukouri, *Doigts noirs: Je fus écrivain-interprète au Cameroun* (Montreal: Editions à la page, 1963), pp. 28-30, cited in Cohen, *Rulers of Empire*, p. 123.

46. Lord Hailey, *Native Administration and Political Development in British Tropical Africa* (London: His Majesty's Stationery Office, 1942), pp. 22. See also Perham, *Colonial Sequence*, pp. xviii-xix.

47. Hubert Deschamps, "Les Empires coloniaux et les nationalités d'outre-mer" (mimeographed copy of course given at the Sorbonne in 1947-48), p. 45, and his "La France d'outre-mer et la Communauté" (mimeographed copy of lectures at the Institut d'Etudes Politiques in 1948-49), p. 60, cited in Cohen, *Rulers of Empire*, p. 108.

48. See chapter 15.

Chapter 11. The Colonial Economy

1. Symposia and readers are legion. Two of the best are D. K. Fieldhouse, *The Theory of Capitalist Imperialism* (London: Longmans, 1967); Roger Owen and Bob Sutcliffe, eds., *Studies in the Theory of Imperialism* (London: Longmans, 1972). And see further discussion elsewhere in this chapter and in chapter 18.

2. S. Herbert Frankel, *Capital Investment in Africa* (London: Oxford University Press, 1938), p. 210.

3. *Ibid.*, pp. 289-299. See also S. E. Katzenellenbogen, *Railways and the Copper Mines of Katanga* (London: Oxford University Press, 1973).

4. Robert E. Baldwin, *Economic Development and Export Growth: A Study of Northern Rhodesia* (Berkeley: University of California Press, 1966), written by one of the most astute and lucid students of development economics, provides a model analysis of the "costs" and "benefits" of copper belt development.

5. Lord Hailey, *An African Survey: A Study of Problems Arising in Africa South of the Sahara* (London: Oxford University Press, 1938), p. 274.

6. Roger Anstey, *King Leopold's Legacy: The Congo under Belgian Rule, 1908-1960* (London: Oxford University Press, 1966), pp. 118-120, is a handy account in English of

labor stabilization. See also L. Mottoulle, *Politique sociale de l'Union Minière du Haut-Katanga pour sa main d'oeuvre indigène* (Brussels: I. R. C. B., 1946).

7. Lucy Mair, *Native Policies in Africa* (London: George Routledge, 1936), p. 232.

8. Anstey, *Leopold's Legacy*, p. 119.

9. Mair, *Native Policies*, pp. 232-233.

10. *Ibid.*, p. 233.

11. Anstey, *Leopold's Legacy*, p. 120.

12. A. L. Epstein, *Politics in an Urban African Community* (Manchester: Manchester University Press, 1958), p. 21. Written by an anthropologist, this is one of the seminal works on the history of African industrialization.

13. Ian Henderson, "The Limits of Colonial Power: Race and Labour Problems in Colonial Zambia, 1900-1953," *Journal of Imperial and Commonwealth History*, 2:300 (1974). Henderson's article, pp. 294-307, brings out the conflicting aims of the various European groups as well. See chapter 12 for missionary policies.

14. Henderson, "Limits of Colonial Power."

15. E. D. Morel, *Affairs of West Africa* (London: Heinemann, 1902), pp. 367-370, provides an interesting contemporary account of the boom and its bursting.

16. Cited in Roger G. Thomas, "Forced Labour in British West Africa: The Case of the Northern Territories of the Gold Coast, 1906-1927," *Journal of African History*, 14:86, n. 48 (1973). Thomas's whole article, pp. 79-103, is essential for appreciating the problems of chiefs, miners, administrators, and mineowners.

17. *Ibid.*, p. 103.

18. *Ibid.*, p. 102.

19. Geoffrey B. Kay, ed., *The Political Economy of Colonialism in Ghana: A Collection of Documents and Statistics, 1900-1960* (Cambridge: Cambridge University Press, 1972), in his introduction forcefully argues this, especially pp. 20-25, 35-36.

20. For general mining statistics, *ibid.*, pp. 334-340.

21. Anthony G. Hopkins, *An Economic History of West Africa* (London: Longman, 1973), pp. 170-171, 210-214, referring back to W. K. Hancock, *Survey of British Commonwealth Affairs*, vol. 2, *Problems of Economic Policy* (London: Oxford University Press, 1942), part 2, pp. 175-200. See also chapter 8.

22. See chapter 10.

23. Hopkins, *Economic History*, pp. 210-211.

24. The political objections to plantations are dealt with in chapter 10.

25. Hopkins, *Economic History*, p. 213.

26. *Ibid.*, p. 216.

27. Polly Hill, *The Migrant Cocoa-Farmers of Southern Ghana* (Cambridge: Cambridge University Press, 1963), is based on extensive field work and is quite indispensable.

28. Hopkins, *Economic History*, p. 216.

29. R. H. Green and Stephen Hymer, "Cocoa in the Gold Coast: A Study in the Relations between African Farmers and Agricultural Experts," *Journal of Economic History*, 36:312 (1966). The confusion was between the West Indian *criollo* and the Amelorado type grown in the Gold Coast.

30. Allan W. Cardinall, *The Gold Coast, 1931* (Accra: Government Printer, 1931), p. 84.

31. Hopkins, *Economic History*, p. 212. See also Abeudu Bowen Jones, "The Republic of Liberia," in J. F. A. Ajayi and Michael Crowder, eds., *History of West Africa* (London: Longman, 1974), II, 320-322.

32. J. Gus Liebenow, *Liberia: The Evolution of Privilege* (Ithaca: Cornell University Press, 1970).

33. The contrast between the Congo Basin and West Africa has been sharply drawn by Samir Amin, and the following material owes much to his formulation. For a general discussion of his ideas on regionalization, see chapter 1 and his article "Underdevelopment and Dependence in Black Africa: Historical Origins," *Journal of Peace Research*, 2:106-119 (1970).

34. For French policy, Cathérine Coquéry-Vidrovitch, *Le Congo au temps des grandes compagnies concessionaires, 1899-1930* (Paris: Mouton, 1972), is essential. For a succinct account of the "economy of pillage," see Cathérine Coquéry-Vidrovitch and Henri Moniot, *L'Afrique noire de 1800 à nos jours* (Paris: Presses Universitaires de France, 1974), pp. 182-185.

35. Jean Suret-Canale, *French Colonialism in Tropical Africa, 1900-1945* (London: Hurst, 1971), p. 280.

36. Hopkins, *Economic History*, p. 266, and Norman A. Cox-George, *Finance and Development in West Africa: The Sierra Leone Experience* (London: Dobson, 1961), pp. 265-272.

37. Hopkins, *Economic History*, pp. 260-261, persuasively argues the limited influence of the colonial governments in the depressed economies.

38. J. O. Oye Makinde, "West Africa between the World Wars: The Economics of the Colonial Impact," *Ghana Social Science Journal*, 2:85 (1972).

39. Cox-George, *Finance and Development*, p. 272.

40. Leo Spitzer and La Ray Denzer, "I. T. A. Wallace-Johnson and the West African Youth League. Part II: The Sierra Leone Period, 1938-1945," *International Journal of African Historical Studies*, 6:566 (1973).

41. Suret-Canale, *French Colonialism*, p. 279.

42. *Ibid.*

43. William B. Cohen, *Rulers of Empire: The French Colonial Service in Africa* (Stanford: Hoover Institution Press, 1971), p. 139.

44. George C. Abbott, "A Re-examination of the 1929 Colonial Development Act," *Economic History Review*, 24: 68-81 (1971), corrects earlier writers who tended to read post-World War II ideas on development into the act.

45. Frankel, *Capital Investment*, pp. 170-171.

46. Ralph G. Saylor, *The Economic System of Sierra Leone* (Durham, N.C.: Duke University Press, 1967), pp. 75-76, deals with the schemes for rice improvement

47. *Ibid.*, p. 139.

48. Cox-George, *Finance and Development*, pp. 241 and 272.

49. *Ibid.*, p. 240.

50. W. M. Macmillan, "African Development," in C. K. Meek, W. M. Macmillan, and E. R. J. Hussey, *Europe and West Africa*, University of London Heath Clark Lectures, 1939 (London: Oxford University Press, 1940), pp. 48 and 54.

51. Spitzer and Denzer, "Wallace-Johnson," p. 570.

52. Macmillan, "African Development," pp. 41-71. The quotation is on p. 49. But see Saylor, *Economic System*, pp. 141-142, where it is argued that the effect of the 1945 Wages Board Ordinance was to force "high wages" on the Sierra Leone Development Company, leading to the adoption of labor-saving techniques, and consequently, unemployment.

53. Spitzer and Denzer, "Wallace-Johnson," pp. 570-571.

54. *Ibid.*, p. 571.

55. Cited in Donald Winch's *Economics and Policy: A Historical Survey* (London: Fontana, 1972), p. 76, an indispensable account of the triumph of "Keynesianism" in both Britain and the United States.

56. Austin Robinson, *Fifty Years of Commonwealth Development* (Cambridge: Cambridge University Press, 1972), p. 9.

57. *West Indies Royal Commission Report, 1938-1939* (London: His Majesty's Stationery Office, Cmd. 6607, 1945).

58. Robinson, *Fifty Years*, p. 9.

59. Cohen, *Rulers of Empire*, p. 139.

60. Robinson, *Fifty Years*, p. 29, pinpoints the paradox very well.

61. *Ibid.*, pp. 29-31.

62. W. K. Hancock, *Wealth of Colonies* (Cambridge: Cambridge University Press, 1950), pp. 8-17. But see also Eric Stokes, "Late Nineteenth Century Colonial Expansion and the Attack on the Theory of Economic Imperialim: A Case of Mistaken Identity?" *Historical Journal*, 12:285-301 (1969), which stresses that, for Lenin, imperialism could mean economic domination without formal political control, a point that is significant for the following discussion.

63. Samir Amin and Walter Rodney are probably the two most influential scholars working along such lines. See espeically Samir Amin, *Neo-Colonialism in West Africa* (Harmondsworth: Penguin, 1973), and Walter Rodney, *How Europe Underdeveloped Africa* (London: Bougle-L'Ouverture, 1972). See also Immanuel Wallerstein, "Africa in a Capitalist World," *Issue: A Quarterly Journal of Africanist Opinion*, 3:1-11 (1973), and E. A. Alpers, "Re-thinking African Economic History: A Contribution to the Discussion of the Roles of Underdevelopment," *Ufahumu*, 3:97-129 (1973), for well-informed, perceptive discussions of such ideas.

64. Kenneth O. Diké, *Trade and Politics in the Niger Delta* (London: Oxford University Press, 1950), p. 18.

65. Hopkins, *Economic History*, pp. 182-185, 237-238. See also the review by Patrick Manning in *Canadian Journal of African Studies*, 8:177-179 (1974).

Chapter 12. Religion and Imperialism

1. See especially the review of Geoffrey Parrinder, *Religion in Africa* (Harmondsworth: Penguin African Library, 1969), by B. A. Ogot, in *African Historical Studies*, 3:182-183 (1970).

2. Notably Edward A. Alpers, "Towards a History of the Expansion of Islam in East Africa," in T. O. Ranger and Isaria Kimambo, eds., *The Historical Study of African Religion* (London: Heinemann, 1972), pp. 172-201; T. O. Ranger, "Missionary Adaptation of African Religious Institutions, the Masasi Case," in Ranger and Kimambo, *Historical Study*, pp. 221-251; M. Schoffeleers, "The Resistance of the Nyau Societies to the Roman Catholic Missions in Colonial Malawi," in Ranger and Kimambo, *Historical Study*, pp. 252-273; Anthony J. Dachs, "Missionary Imperialism—the Case of Bechuanaland," *Journal of African History*, 13:647-658 (1972).

3. Robin Horton, "African Conversion," *Africa*, 61:85-108 (1971).

4. See especially Ranger and Kimambo, *Historical Study*, Introduction, pp. 15-17, 195-196, and Humphrey J. Fisher, "Conversion Reconsidered," *Africa*, 63:27-40 (1973).

5. Horton, "Conversion," p. 101.

6. *Ibid.*, p. 100.

7. *Ibid.*, p. 104.

8. Hilda Kuper, *The Uniform of Colour* (Johannesburg: Witwatersrand University Press, 1947), p. 80.

9. James W. Fernandez, "Fang Representations under Acculturation," in Philip D. Curtin, ed., *Africa and the West: Intellectual Responses to European Culture* (Madison:

University of Wisconsin Press, 1972), p. 18. See also chapter 10 for Fang problems with colonial jurisprudence.

10. Fernandez, "Fang Representations," pp. 18-19.

11. *Ibid.*, p. 19.

12. J. D. Y. Peel, *Aladura: A Religious Movement among the Yoruba* (London: Oxford University Press, 1968).

13. Horton, "Conversion," pp. 86-87. Note the point made earlier in chapter 11 that the barter terms of trade were generally moving against West Africans in these years.

14. Bengt G. M. Sundkler, *Bantu Prophets in South Africa*, 2d ed. (London: Oxford University Press, 1961).

15. See Jane Linden and Ian Linden, "John Chilembwe and the New Jerusalem," *Journal of African History*, 12:629-651 (1971). The quotation is on p. 630. See also the perceptive review of this article by T. O. Ranger, *African Religious Research*, 2:56-61 (1972).

16. On missionaries and the Tswana, Dachs, "Missionary Imperialism," is illuminating. See also Anthony Sillery, *Botswana* (London: Methuen, 1974), for a succinct historical survey.

17. Dachs, "Missionary Imperialism," p. 648

18. *Ibid.*, p. 650.

19. *Ibid.*

20. *Ibid.*, p. 651.

21. *Ibid.*, pp. 651-652.

22. *Ibid.*, p. 652.

23. *Ibid.*, pp. 653-654.

24. For Khama, see Isaac Schapera, *Tribal Innovators: Tswana Chiefs and Social Change, 1795-1940* (London: University of London Press, 1970).

25. *Ibid.*, p. 122.

26. *Ibid.*, p. 245.

27. James Bryce, *Impressions of South Africa*, 2d ed. (London, 1898), pp. 262-264.

28. Robert I. Rotberg, *Christian Missionaries and the Creation of Northern Rhodesia, 1880-1929* (Princeton: Princeton University Press, 1965), pp. 24-26.

29. J. Merle Davis, ed., *Modern Industry and the Africans: An Enquiry into the Effect of the Copper Mines of Central Africa upon Native Society and the Work of the Christian Missions*, 2d ed. (London: Frank Cass, 1967), has a very useful introduction by Robert I. Rotberg.

30. *Ibid.*, p. xv.

31. *Ibid.*, p. xvi.

32. *Ibid.*, p. 371.

33. *Ibid.*, p. 370.

34. *Ibid.*, p. xx.

35. *Ibid.*, p. 97.

36. *Ibid.*, p. xxii.

37. See chapters 15 and 17 for the development of African politics on the copper belt.

38. For a general discussion of the reasons, see the introductory section to this chapter.

39. The historiography on Chilembwe is extensive. See especially George Shepperson and Thomas Price, *Independent African* (Edinburgh: Edinburgh University Press, 1958); Gideon Simeon Mwase, ed., with introduction by Robert I. Rotberg, *Strike a Blow and Die: A Narrative of Race Relations in Colonial Africa* (Cambridge: Harvard University Press, 1967); Robert I. Rotberg, "Resistance and Rebellion in British Nyasaland and German East Africa, 1888-1915: A Tentative Comparison," in Prosser Gifford and William

Roger Louis, eds., *Britain and Germany in Africa: Imperial Rivalry and Colonial Rule* (New Haven: Yale University Press, 1967), pp. 667-690; Robert I. Rotberg, "Psychological Stress and the Question of Identity: Chilembwe's Revolt Reconsidered," in Robert I. Rotberg and Ali A. Mazrui, eds., *Protest and Power in Black Africa* (New York: Oxford University Press, 1970), pp. 337-373; Jane Linden and Ian Linden, "John Chilembwe," pp. 629-651.

40. Jane Linden and Ian Linden, "John Chilembwe," p. 651.

41. *Ibid.*, p. 633.

42. *Ibid.*, p. 635.

43. Rotberg, "Resistance and Rebellion," p. 685; Shepperson and Price, *Independent African*, pp. 234-235.

44. Cited in Rotberg, "Psychological Stress," pp. 343 and 344.

45. Cited in Rotberg's introduction to Mwase, *Strike a Blow*, p. 5.

46. *Ibid.*, p. 29.

47. Rotberg, "Resistance and Rebellion," especially pp. 689-690, and Jane Linden and Ian Linden, "John Chilembwe," p. 647.

48. *Ibid.* On millenarianism in Africa generally, see Ranger and Kimambo, *Historical Study*, Introduction, pp. 18-19.

49. The Mourides have been the subject of three important recent studies: Cheikh Tidiane Sy, *La Confrérie sénégalaise des Mourides* (Paris: Présence Africaine, 1969); Lucy C. Behrman, *Muslim Brotherhoods and Politics in Senegal* (Cambridge: Harvard University Press, 1970); Donal B. Cruise O'Brien, *The Mourides of Senegal: The Political and Economic Organization of an Islamic Brotherhood* (Oxford: Clarendon Press, 1971). What follows is based upon them.

50. Martin Klein's review of Cruise O'Brien, *The Mourides of Senegal, Journal of African History*, 13:158 (1972), clarifies the chronology.

51. Cruise O'Brien, *The Mourides of Senegal*, pp. 141-158, presents the handiest account of the Bay Fall. Sy, *La Confrérie*, is full of perceptions on the parallels between the Bay Fall and the role of the *tyeddo* in the old Wolof kingdoms.

52. Cruise O'Brien, *The Mourides of Senegal*, p. 3.

53. *Ibid.*, pp. 224-225, 296-300.

Chapter 13. Theory and Practice of Colonial Education

1. Sir Frederick D. Lugard, *The Dual Mandate in British Tropical Africa* (Edinburgh: William Blackwood and Sons, 1922), p. 437.

2. A. Victor Murray, *The School in the Bush* (London: Frank Cass, 1967), p. 19.

3. *Ibid.*, pp. 323-325.

4. Bo School Prospectus, reproduced in Christopher Fyfe, ed., *Sierra Leone Inheritance* (London: Oxford University Press, 1964), pp. 304-307.

5. Cited in L. Gray Cowan, James O'Connell, and David G. Scanlon, eds., *Education and Nation-Building in Africa* (London: Pall Mall Press, 1965), pp. 45-52.

6. *Methodist Herald*, February 27, 1887.

7. *Ibid.*, June 29, 1887.

8. *Ibid.*, August 10, 1887.

9. Philip J. Foster, *Education and Social Change in Ghana* (London: Routledge & Kegan Paul, 1965); David B. Abernethy, *The Political Dilemma of Popular Education: An African Case* (Stanford: Stanford University Press, 1969); Robert Koehl, "The Uses of the University: Past and Present in Nigerian Educational Culture," *Comparative Education Review*, 15:116-131 (1971); Barbara Yates, "African Reaction to Education: The Congolese Case," *Comparative Education Review*, 15:158-171 (1971); Remi Clignet and Philip J. Foster,

The Fortunate Few: A Study of Secondary Schools and Students in the Ivory Coast (Evanston Ill.: Northwestern University Press, 1966).

10. Melville J. Herskovits, *The Human Factor in Changing Africa* (New York: Knopf, 1962), p. 222. Chapter 8, "The School," is especially good, although by discussing A. Victor Murray's views outside the context of the political situation when *The School in the Bush* was written, Herskovits does scant justice to that delightful book.

11. *Ibid.*

12. Koehl, "Uses of the University," p. 116.

13. The scale of his state and its flexible balance between Islam and "traditional" religion impressed Edward Blyden and were decisive in the development of his political thought.

14. Denise Bouche, "Autrefois, notre pays s'appelait la Gaule . . . ," *Cahiers d'études africaines*, 8:110-122 (1968), shrewdly probes the myth, as do Prosser Gifford and Timothy C. Weiskel in their very informative "African Education in a Colonial Context," in Prosser Gifford and William Roger Louis, eds., *France and Britain in Africa: Imperial Rivalry and Colonial Rule* (New Haven: Yale University Press, 1971), pp. 633-711.

15. For the general development of French imperial policy, see chapters 6 and 7. Michael Crowder, *West Africa under Colonial Rule* (London: Hutchinson, 1968), pp. 17-19, offers a similar division of the colonial era by periods.

16. Gifford and Weiskel, "African Education," pp. 672-673.

17. Georges Hardy, *Une Conquête morale: L'Enseignement en Afrique Occidentale Française* (Paris: Armand Colin, 1917), p. 187.

18. Gifford and Weiskel, "African Education," pp. 674-675.

19. For assimilation, see chapters 6 and 7 and Priscilla Blakemore, "Assimilation and Association in French Educational Policy and Practice," in Vincent M. Battle and Charles H. Lyons, eds., *Essays in the History of African Education* (New York: Teachers College Press, Columbia University, 1970), pp. 89-90.

20. For Hardy, see Gifford and Weiskel, "African Education," pp. 690-694. Also William B. Cohen, *Rulers of Empire: The French Colonial Service in Africa* (Stanford: Hoover Institution Press, 1971), pp. 87-90.

21. Hardy, *Une Conquête morale*, p. 62.

22. Remi Clignet, "Inadequacies of the Notion of Assimilation in African Education," *Journal of Modern African Studies*, 8:425-444 (1970), deals perceptively with the relationship between metropolitan and colonial educational institutions.

23. The songs are cited in Gifford and Weiskel, "African Education," p. 695.

24. Bouche, "Autrefois, notre pays," p. 118.

25. Gifford and Weiskel, "African Education," p. 696.

26. Richard Dodson, "Congo-Léopoldville," in David G. Scanlon, ed., *Church, State and Education in Africa* (New York: Teachers College Press, Columbia University, 1966), pp. 61-108. The role of the concessionary companies in Belgian paternalism is also dealt with in chapter 11 of the present volume.

27. Dodson, "Congo-Léopoldville," p. 68.

28. *Projet d'organisation de l'enseignement au Congo Belge avec le concours des sociétés des missions nationales* (Brussels: Société Anonyme, 1925), p. 4.

29. Roger Anstey, *King Leopold's Legacy: The Congo under Belgian Rule, 1908-1960* (London: Oxford University Press, 1966), pp. 135-136.

30. Foster's *Education and Social Change* is a fine pioneer study that reaches beyond formal policy statements to educational realities. Among the better works that have followed Foster's example are Kenneth J. King, *Pan-Africanism and Education: A Study of*

Race, Philanthropy and Education in the Southern States of America and East Africa (Oxford: Clarendon Press, 1971), and Abernethy, *Political Dilemma.*

31. Foster, *Education and Social Change*, pp. 90-91.

32. See Otto F. Raum, "Indirect Rule as a Political Education," *Internationale Zeitschrift für Erziehung*, 5:97-107 (1936), for an interesting contemporary discussion. There is also much material in O. W. Furley and T. Watson, "Education in Tanganyika between the Wars," *South Atlantic Quarterly*, 65:471-490 (1966). Christopher Fyfe, *A History of Sierra Leone* (London: Oxford University Press, 1962), p. 616.

33. Bo School Prospectus, in Fyfe, *Inheritance*, pp. 304-307.

34. I owe this point to Mark Walton of the University of York, who is preparing a dissertation on Bo School.

35. W. Bryant Mumford, "Education and the Social Adjustment of Primitive Peoples of Africa to European Culture," *Africa*, 2:138-159 (1929); W. Bryant Mumford, "Malangali School," *Africa*, 3:265-290 (1930). See also Furley and Watson, "Education in Tanganyika," pp. 481-483.

36. Marcia Wright, *German Missions in Tanganyika, 1891-1941: Lutherans and Moravians in the Southern Highlands* (Oxford: Clarendon Press, 1971), pp. 169-171.

37. *Ibid.*, p. 195.

38. Otto F. Raum, "The Demand for and Support of Education in African Tribal Society," *Year Book of Education* (London: Evans Brothers, 1956), p. 537, cited in Foster, *Education and Social Change*, p. 57, who confirms that bribes were frequently used by the Basel Mission in its first ten years.

39. Remi Clignet and Philip J. Foster, "French and British Colonial Education in Africa," *Comparative Education Review*, 8:191-198 (1964), where Clignet indicates the findings of his "Tradition et évolution de la vie familiale en Côte d'Ivoire," (Ph.D. thesis, University of Paris, 1963).

Chapter 14. The Shaping of South African Civilization

1. See chapters 8 and 11.

2. John Rex, *Race, Colonialism and the City* (London: Routledge & Kegan Paul, 1973), pp. 257-283, is penetrating on the South African migrant labor system. See also the indispensable study by H. J. Simons and R. E. Simons, *Class and Colour in South Africa, 1850-1950* (Harmondsworth, Penguin, 1969).

3. H. J. Simons and R. E. Simons, *Class and Colour*, p. 46.

4. See chapter 2.

5. The points are argued cogently in Rex, *Race, Colonialism*, pp. 273-277.

6. G. Tylden, *The Rise of the Basuto* (Cape Town: Juta, 1950), p. 207.

7. The phrase is from p. 310 of Stanley Trapido's seminal article, "South Africa in a Comparative Study of Industrialization," *Journal of Development Studies*, 7:309-320 (1971). Some of Trapido's ideas are challenged in a lively study by Norman Bromberger, "Economic Growth and Political Change in South Africa," in Adrian Leftwich, ed., *South Africa: Economic Growth and Political Change* (London: Allison and Busby, 1974), pp. 61-123.

8. On Mozambique, see especially Marvin Harris, "Labour Migration among the Mozambique Thonga: Cultural and Political Factors," *Africa*, 29:50-66 (1959). A. Rita Ferreira, "Labour Migration among the Mozambique Thonga, *Africa* 30:243-245 (1960), is a reply to Harris.

9. L. H. Gann, *A History of Southern Rhodesia: Early Days to 1934* (London: Chatto and Windus, 1965), and Philip Mason, *The Birth of a Dilemma* (London: Oxford Univer-

sity Press, 1958), are standard works on the area. Terence O. Ranger, *Revolt in Southern Rhodesia, 1896-1897* (London: Heinemann, 1967), is a fine, pioneering study.

10. G. Blainey, "Lost Causes of the Jameson Raid," *Economic History Review*, 18:350-366 (1965), is a brilliant examination of the importance of the deep-level mines.

11. J. G. Lockhart and C. M. Woodhouse, *Cecil Rhodes: The Colossus of Southern Africa* (New York: Macmillan, 1963), is the latest biography.

12. J. S. Marais, *The Fall of Kruger's Republic* (Oxford: Clarendon Press, 1961), is the best general survey. Donald Denoon, *A Grand Illusion* (London: Longman, 1973), is a comprehensive study of Milner's reconstruction policy.

13. Donald Denoon, "Participation in the 'Boer War,'" in Bethwell A. Ogot, ed., *War and Society in Africa: Ten Studies* (London: Frank Cass, 1972), makes this point.

14. C. R. de Wet, *Three Years' War* (Westminster: Constable, 1902), is an illuminating, lively account of the guerrilla war. He points out the importance of this Afrikaner granary on p. 113.

15. Tylden, *Rise of the Basuto*, p. 205.

16. Colin Bundy, "The Emergence and Decline of a South African Peasantry," *African Affairs*, 71:369-388 (1972).

17. Isaac Schapera, *A Short History of the Bakgatla-bagaKgafela* (Cape Town: School of African Studies, University of Cape Town, 1942), p. 20.

18. Denoon, "Participation," p. 115. Peter Warwick of the University of York is preparing a doctoral thesis on the war's effects on Africans, and my understanding of it has been helped by discussion with him.

19. Denoon, "Participation," p. 119.

20. *Ibid.*, pp. 119-120.

21. Stanley Trapido, "The South African Republic: Class Formation and the State, 1850-1900," in *Collected Seminar Papers on the Societies of South Africa in the Nineteenth and Twentieth Centuries* (London: Institute of Commonwealth Studies, University of London, 1973), III, 53-65, is an important study of Afrikaner stratification.

22. de Wet, *Three Years' War*, p. 324.

23. There is much of interest on thise points in Rayne Kruger, *Good-Bye Dolly Gray* (London: Cassell, 1961), but the Anglo-Boer War still lacks a modern, comprehensive treatment from the imperial standpoint.

24. Denoon, "Participation," p. 115.

25. Denoon, *Grand Illusion*, pp. 1-26.

26. Leonard M. Thompson, *The Unification of South Africa, 1902-1910* (Oxford: Clarendon Press, 1960), carefully studies this process.

27. Shula Marks, *Reluctant Rebellion: The 1906-8 Disturbances in Natal* (Oxford: Clarendon Press, 1970), is an excellent and comprehensive account.

28. Thompson, *Unification*, clarifies the economic aspects of unification.

29. *Ibid.* See also Ronald Hyam, "African Interests and the South Africa Act, 1908-1910," *Historical Journal*, 13:85-105 (1970).

30. Peter Walshe, *The Rise of African Nationalism in South Africa: The A. N. C., 1912-1952* (London: Hurst, 1970), pp. 1-43, skillfully analyzes the origins of the African National Congress.

31. Cited in H. J. Simons and R. E. Simons, *Class and Colour*, p. 133.

32. The Cape was excluded because land owning was a qualification for the franchise and therefore to change the rules amounted to a constitutional issue inviting a special two-thirds vote by both houses.

33. H. J. Simons and R. E. Simons, *Class and Colour*, p. 132. See also Walshe, *Rise of African Nationalism*, pp. 44-50.

34. D. W. Kruger, *The Age of the Generals: A Short Political History of the Union of South Africa, 1910-1948* (Johannesburg: Dagbreek Book Store, 1958), and René de Villiers, "Afrikaner Nationalism," in Monica Wilson and Leonard Thompson, eds., *The Oxford History of South Africa*, vol. 2, *South Africa 1870-1966* (Oxford: Clarendon Press, 1971), are very useful on political developments.

35. A comprehensive study of the Rand revolt is lacking, but·H. J. Simons and R. E. Simons, *Class and Colour*, pp. 271-299, is useful.

36. See further discussion elsewhere in this chapter.

37. Kruger, *Age of the Generals*, p. 5. This passage is also cited on p. 221 of Laurence Salomon, "The Economic Background of the Revival of Afrikaner Nationalism," in Jeffrey Butler, ed., *Boston University Papers in African History* (Boston: Boston University Press, 1966), I, 219-242, a succinct analysis. Boyd C. Shafer, *Faces of Nationalism* (New York: Harcourt Brace Jovanovich, 1972), carefully sets Afrikaner and other African nationalisms in a world perspective.

38. Cited in Salomon, "Economic Background," p. 227.

39. Richard B. Ford, "The Urban Trek: Some Comparisons of American and South African Mobility," in Heribert Adam, ed., *South Africa: Sociological Perspectives* (London: Oxford University Press, 1971), p. 258.

40. Salomon, "Economic Background," p. 230.

41. David Welsh, "The Political Economy of Afrikaner Nationalism," in Leftwich, *South Africa*, p. 525. Welsh·'s perceptive article is packed with useful information.

42. Cited in Salomon, "Economic Background," who supplies the italics, p. 232.

43. *Ibid.*, p. 233.

44. Welsh, "Political Economy," p. 250.

45. *Ibid.*, p. 251.

46. *Ibid.*, pp. 234, 256-257.

47. Trapido, "South African Republic," is illuminating on this.

48. W. M. Macmillan, *Complex South Africa* (London: Faber and Faber, 1930), p. 387, cited in Bundy, "South African Peasantry," p. 387.

49. Salomon, "Economic Background," p. 234.

50. Lord Hailey, *An African Survey: A Study of Problems Arising in Africa South of the Sahara* (London: Oxford University Press, 1938), pp. 664-669, contains a lucid summary of pass law legislation.

51. R. H. Davenport, *The Beginnings of Urban Segregation in South Africa: The Natives (Urban Areas) Act of 1923 and Its Background* (Grahamstown: Institute of Social and Economic Research, Rhodes University, 1971), is indispensable.

52. On Clements Kadalie and the Industrial and Commercial Workers' Union, see his autobiography, *My Life and the ICU: The Autobiography of a Black Trade Unionist in South Africa*, ed. Stanley Trapido (London: Frank Cass, 1970), with a useful introduction by Stanley Trapido, and Sheridan W. Johns III, "Trade Union, Political Pressure Group or Mass Movement? The Industrial and Commercial Workers' Union of Africa," in Robert I. Rotberg and Ali Mazrui, eds., *Protest and Power in Black Africa* (New York: Oxford University Press, 1970), pp. 695-754.

53. Salomon, "Economic Background," p. 235.

54. Adrian Leftwich, "The Constitution and Continuity of South African Inequality: Some Conceptual Questions," in Leftwich, *South Africa*, p. 168.

Chapter 15. Urbanization and Interwar Politics

1. See the useful comparative table in Thomas Hodgkin's pioneer study, *Nationalism in Tropical Africa* (London: Muller, 1956), p. 67, for Dakar and Lagos.

2. A. L. Mabogunje, *Yoruba Towns* (Ibadan: Ibadan University Press, 1962), p. 1, table 1.

3. Christopher Fyfe and Eldred Jones, eds., *Freetown: A Symposium* (Freetown: Sierra Leone University Press, 1968), p. 30.

4. Figures cited in John Middleton, "Kenya: Administration and Changes in African Life," in Vincent Harlow, E. M. Chilver, and Alison Smith, eds., *History of East Africa* (Oxford: Clarendon Press, 1965), II, 345.

5. Cited in Joan Wheare, *The Nigerian Legislative Council* (London: Faber and Faber, 1950), pp. 31-32.

6. See David Kimble, *A Political History of Ghana, 1850-1928* (Oxford: Clarendon Press, 1963), pp. 379-396, for the clash between Ofori Atta and Casely Hayford.

7. See further discussion elsewhere in this chapter.

8. Prosser Gifford, "Indirect Rule: Touchstone or Tombstone for Colonial Policy?" in Prosser Gifford and William Roger Louis, eds., *Britain and Germany in Africa: Imperial Rivalry and Colonial Rule* (New Haven: Yale University Press, 1967), p. 361, makes this point. For Hausa urbanization, see Horace Miner, "Urban Influences on the Hausa," in Hilda Kuper, ed., *Urbanization and Migration in West Africa* (Berkeley: University of California Press, 1965), p. 110-130.

9. See J. Ayodele Langley, *Pan-Africanism and Nationalism in West Africa, 1900-1945* (Oxford: Clarendon Press, 1973), pp. 199-215, which provides a perceptive analysis in the general context of West African politics.

10. *Ibid.*, p. 208.

11. *Ibid.*

12. *Ibid.*, p. 209. Doubtless Britain's being entrusted by the League of Nations with the Palestine mandate made Milner especially sensitive to the comparison when Syrians and Lebanese also came from ex-Ottoman territories, though, in their case, under French mandate.

13. *Ibid.*, p. 211.

14. *Ibid.*, pp. 211-212.

15. Martin Kilson, *Political Change in a West African State: A Study of the Modernization Process in Sierra Leone* (Cambridge: Harvard University Press 1966), has made this point effectively; see especially pp. 284-286. Langley, *Pan-Africanism and Nationalism*, notably pp. 278-280, deals astutely with Sir Hugh Clifford's response to pressure.

16. Michael Crowder, *West Africa under Colonial Rule* (London: Hutchinson, 1968), pp. 454-460, presents a succinct account of these constitutional changes.

17. Kilson, *Political Change*, p. 123.

18. Crowder, *West Africa*, p. 450.

19. Michael Banton, "Social Alignment and Identity in a West African City," in Kuper, *Urbanization and Migration*, pp. 136-137. Banton's whole article is helpful, and his book, *West African City* (London: Oxford University Press, 1957), is a mine of information.

20. Banton, *West African City*, p. 163.

21. *Ibid.*, pp. 164-165.

22. *Ibid.*

23. *Ibid.*, p. 166.

24. *Ibid.*, p. 171.

25. *Ibid.*, p. 175.

26. *Ibid.*

27. *Ibid.*, p. 166.

28. *Ibid.*, p. 168.

29. *Ibid.*, p. 176.

30. *Ibid.*, pp. 176-177.

31. Kilson, *Political Change*, pp. 227-280.

32. Leo Spitzer and La Ray Denzer, "I. T. A. Wallace-Johnson and the West African Youth League. Part II: The Sierra Leone Period, 1938-1945," *International Journal of African Historical Studies*, 6:565-601 (1973).

33. Margery Perham, *Native Administration in Nigeria* (London: Oxford University Press, 1937), p. 361.

34. James Coleman, *Nigeria: Background to Nationalism* (Berkeley: University of California Press, 1958), p. 224.

35. Perham, *Native Administration*, p. 361.

36. Nnamdi Azikiwe,*My Odyssey: An Autobiography* (London: Hurst, 1970), pp. 281-282.

37. *Ibid.*, pp. 260-308.

38. Coleman, *Nigeria*, pp. 75-77, 332-343.

39. See chapter 17.

40. L. H. Gann, *A History of Northern Rhodesia: Early Days to 1953* (London: Chatto and Windus, 1964), p. 282.

41. Robert I. Rotberg, *The Rise of Nationalism in Central Africa* (Cambridge: Harvard University Press, 1966), p. 161. Rotberg presents the handiest account of the 1935 copper belt protest on pp. 161-168.

42. *Ibid.*, p. 167.

43. Richard Brown, "Anthropology and Colonial Rule: Godfrey Wilson and the Rhodes-Livingstone Institute, Northern Rhodesia," in Talal Asad, ed.,*Anthropology and the Colonial Encounter* (London: Ithaca Press, 1973), pp. 173-197.

44. A. L. Epstein, *Politics in an Urban African Community* (Manchester: Manchester University Press, 1958), is a thoughtful study of the development of political consciousness and organization on the copper belt.

45. Cited in Crowder, *West Africa*, p. 433. Crowder's account of French interwar politics, pp. 433-453, is the most readily available in English.

46. *Ibid.*, pp. 434-437. For radical opposition to Diagne, often operating outside of Africa, see Langley, *Pan-Africanism and Nationalism*, pp. 286-325.

47. Crowder, *West Africa*, pp. 438, 441-443.

Chapter 16. The Second World War

1. He was cited in the *Nigerian Daily Telegraph*, September 24, 1935, p. 3, quoted by J. B. Webster, "Political Activity in British West Africa, 1900-1940," in J. F. A. Ajayi and Michael Crowder, eds., *History of West Africa* (London: Longman, 1974), II, 591.

2. Lord Hailey, "Nationalism in Africa," *African Affairs*, 36:134-147 (1937); see especially p. 143.

3. Webster, "Political Activity," p. 591, and for the Harlem riot, Clive Barnes, "The Harlem Riot" (Seminar paper, University of York, 1971).

4. Cited in J. Ayodele Langley, *Pan-Africanism and Nationalism in West Africa, 1900-1945* (Oxford: Clarendon Press, 1973), p. 333. Langley's account, pp. 327-337, and Webster's "Political Activity," pp. 591-592, are the most useful analyses of the impact of the crisis on African political consciousness.

5. Langley, *Pan-Africanism and Nationalism*, p. 334.

6. *Ibid.*, p. 335.

7. Kwame Nkrumah, *Ghana: The Autobiography of Kwame Nkrumah* (Edinburgh: Thomas Nelson, 1959), p. 27.

8. Webster, "Political Activity," p. 591.

9. Hubert Deschamps, "L'Afrique Occidentale, Centrale et du Nord-Est," in Jean Ganiage, Hubert Deschamps, and Odette Guitard, *L'Afrique au XXe Siècle* (Paris: Sirey, 1966), pp. 482-485.

10. Michael Crowder, "The 1939-1945 War and West Africa," in Ajayi and Crowder, *History of West Africa*, p. 598. Crowder's chapter, pp. 596-621, is very useful.

11. *Ibid.*

12. Carl G. Rosberg and John Nottingham, *The Myth of Mau Mau: Nationalism in Kenya* (New York: Praeger, 1966), p. 191.

13. Crowder, "The 1939-1945 War," p. 600.

14. *Ibid.*, p. 604. But see Jean Suret-Canale, *French Colonialism in Tropical Africa, 1900-1945* (London: Hurst, 1971), pp. 471-473, for the development of institutionalized racism during the Vichy regime.

15. Cited in Crowder, "The 1939-1945 War," p. 604.

16. *Ibid.*, p. 603.

17. Cyril Ehrlich, "The Uganda Economy, 1903-1945," in Vincent Harlow, E. M. Chilver, and Alison Smith, eds., *History of East Africa* (Oxford: Clarendon Press, 1965), II, 473.

18. Anthony G. Hopkins, *An Economic History of West Africa* (London: Longman, 1973), p. 184.

19. *Ibid.*, p. 185.

20. Suret-Canale, *French Colonialism*, p. 482.

21. Crowder, "The 1939-1945 War," pp. 606-607.

22. *Ibid.*, p. 607.

23. *Ibid.*

24. *Ibid.*, pp. 608-609.

25. *Ibid.*

26. Roger Anstey, *King Leopold's Legacy: The Congo under Belgian Rule, 1908-1960* (London: Oxford University Press, 1966), pp. 143-145.

27. *Ibid.*, p. 144.

28. *Ibid.*, pp. 146-147.

29. *Ibid.*, p. 156.

30. *Ibid.*, pp. 133-134.

31. *Ibid.*, pp. 157-158. In 1947 the Belgians did, however, react to United Nations ideas on decolonization. See chapter 17.

32. See Ronald H. Chilcote's fine, brief *Portuguese Africa* (Englewood Cliffs, N.J.: Prentice-Hall, 1967).

33. W. P. Hancock, *Smuts: The Fields of Force* (Cambridge: Cambridge University Press, 1968), II, 284-285.

34. For a full discussion of the 1943 election, see Kenneth A. Heard, *General Elections of South Africa, 1943-1970* (London: Oxford University Press, 1974), pp. 15-29. For its wider implications, see Newell M. Stultz, *Afrikaner Politics in South Africa* (Berkeley: University of California Press, 1974), pp. 60-96.

35. David Welsh, "The Political Economy of Afrikaner Nationalism," in Adrian Leftwich, ed., *South Africa: Economic Growth and Political Change* (London: Allison and Busby, 1974), pp. 249-285, especially p. 260, sets the wartime changes in context. For African political developments in the war years, see discussion elsewhere in this chapter.

36. Lewis H. Gann and Michael Gelfand, *Huggins of Rhodesia: The Man and His Country* (London: Allen and Unwin, 1964), p. 153.

37. For a clear neo-Marxist analysis of these processes, see Giovanni Arrighi, "The Political Economy of Rhodesia," in Giovanni Arrighi and John S. Saul, *Essays on the Political*

Economy of Africa (New York: Monthly Review Press, 1973), pp. 336-377, especially pp. 348-352, for wartime developments.

38. See chapters 17 and 18 for the development of Rhodesian postwar politics.

39. Rudolf von Albertini, *Decolonization: The Administration and Future of the Colonies, 1919-1960* (New York: Doubleday, 1971), pp. 22-23.

40. Sumner Welles, *The Time of Decision* (1944), p. 383, cited in *ibid.*, p. 23.

41. Jean Suret-Canale, *Afrique noire occidentale et centrale: De la colonialism aux indépendance, 1945-1960* (Paris: Editions Sociales, 1972), p. 211.

42. Langley, *Pan-Africanism and Nationalism*, pp. 345-346, citing a letter from NCO Emil K. Sackey, 835 Company, W.A.A.S.C. Indian Command, to Kobina Sekyi, the nationalist leader, September 4, 1945.

43. Cited in G. O. Olusanyu, *The Second World War and Politics in Nigeria, 1939-1953* (London: Evans Bros., for the University of Lagos, 1973), p. 95.

44. Cited in Rosberg and Nottingham, *Myth of Mau Mau*, p. 194.

45. *Ibid.*, p. 192.

46. *Ibid.*, pp. 193-194.

47. *Ibid.*, pp. 192-193.

48. *Ibid.*, p. 196.

49. *Ibid.*, pp. 195-198.

50. George Bennett, *Kenya: A Political History* (London: Oxford University Press, 1963), pp. 97-98.

51. This point and the general contrast with British procedures is made forcefully by von Albertini, *Decolonization*, pp. 368-369.

52. Cited in W. A. Nielson, *The Great Powers and Africa* (London: Pall Mall Press, 1969), p. 84.

53. von Albertini, *Decolonization*, especially pp. 158-175, and chapter 17 in this book.

54. Cited in Langley, *Pan-Africanism and Nationalism*, p. 349.

55. Cited *ibid.*, p. 55.

56. James R. Hooker, *Black Revolutionary* (London: Pall Mall Press, 1967), p. 94.

57. *Ibid.*, p. 95.

58. Langley, *Pan-Africanism and Nationalism*, pp. 353-354, and Imanuel Geiss, *The Pan-African Movement* (London: Methuen, 1974), pp. 405-406.

59. Langley, *Pan-Africanism and Nationalism*, p. 354.

60. See chapter 17.

61. Thomas Karis and Gwendolen M. Carter, *From Protest to Challenge*, vol. 2, *Hope and Challenge* (Stanford: Hoover Institution Press, 1973), pp. 87-90, 209-223, prints the documents and supplies indispensable commentary.

62. Peter Walshe, *The Rise of African Nationalism in South Africa: The A. N. C., 1912-1952* (London: Hurst, 1970), p. 272.

63. *Ibid.*, p. 274.

64. *Ibid.*, p. 330.

Chapter 17. Decolonization

1. *Hansard*, 342:1246 (December 7, 1938), cited in Rudolf von Albertini, *Decolonization: The Administration and Future of the Colonies, 1919-1960* (New York: Doubleday, 1971), p. 85.

2. Margery Perham, *Colonial Sequence, 1930-1949: A Chronological Commentary upon British Colonial Policy Especially in Africa* (London: Methuen, 1967), p. 310, and Margery Perham, *The Colonial Reckoning* (London: Fontana, 1961), pp. 85-86.

3. "The Future of West Africa with Special Reference to Cape Coast Castle," *Gold Coast Nation*, August 15, 1912.

4. J. B. Danquah, *Self-help and Expansion* (Accra: Gold Coast Continuation Committee, Gold Coast Youth Conference, [1943]), p. 16.

5. Terence O. Ranger, ed., *Emerging Themes of African History* (Nairobi: East African Publishing House, 1968), p. xix.

6. Cited, significantly, in the opening paragraph of the editorial inaugurating the *Review of African Political Economy*, 1:1 (1974), which is avowedly "Marxist . . . using a method which analyses a situation in order to change it," *ibid.*, p. 2.

7. Sir Roy Welensky, *Welensky's 4,000 Days* (London: Collins, 1964), especially pp. 170-189.

8. Sir Michael Blundell, *So Rough a Wind* (London: Weidenfield and Nicholson, 1964).

9. Heribert Adam, *Modernizing Racial Domination: South Africa's Political Dynamics* (Berkeley: University of California Press, 1971), is perhaps the most perceptive study stressing the stability of the regime. On the "tilt" toward the white-dominated regimes, see, for example, Murrey Marder, "Nixon Altered U.S. Policy in Southern Africa," *International Herald Tribune* (Paris), October 14, 1974, and Andrew Wilson, "Why the U.S. Tilted towards Vorster," *Observer* (London), January 5, 1975.

10. On the development of a political theory of anticolonialism, see Rupert Emerson, *Self-Determination Revisited in the Era of Decolonization*, Occasional Papers, no. 9 (Cambridge: Center for International Affairs, Harvard University Press, 1964). Also on the politics of decolonization within the United Nations, see M. Crawford Young, "Decolonization in Africa," in L. H. Gann and Peter Duignan, eds., *Colonialism in Africa, 1870-1960* (Cambridge: Cambridge University Press, 1970), II, especially pp. 455-488.

11. Cited in Emerson, *Self-Determination*, p. 11.

12. Young, "Decolonization," pp. 457-458.

13. Cited in Emerson, *Self-Determination*, p. 12.

14. *Ibid.*, p. 2.

15. *Ibid.*, p. 20.

16. Cited in Lord Hailey, *An African Survey Revised 1956* (London: Oxford University Press, 1957), p. 245.

17. Cited in J. M. Lee, *Colonial Development and Good Government* (Oxford: Clarendon Press, 1967), p. 22.

18. Rita Hinden, *Empire and After* (London: Essential Books, 1949), pp. 140-150, illuminates these wartime arguments from this standpoint.

19. Lord Hailey, *African Survey Revised*, p. 251.

20. Lee, *Colonial Development*, makes this clear.

21. Bernard B. Schaffer, "The Concept of Preparation," in his *The Administrative Factor* (London: Frank Cass, 1973), pp. 194-219, is an astute analysis in the light of modern administrative theory. W. P. Kirkman, *Unscrambling an Empire* (London: Chatto and Windus, 1966), by the former African correspondent of the London *Times* conveys the tempo of decolonization well. See also Lee, *Colonial Development*, pp. 195-240.

22. Dennis Austin, "Institutional Problems of the Gold Coast," in *What Are the Problems of Parliamentary Government in West Africa?* (London: Hansard Society, 1958), p. 7.

23. See Schaffer, "Concept of Preparation," pp. 204-205, for significant examples.

24. Obafemi Awolowo, *Path to Nigerian Freedom* (London: Faber and Faber, 1947).

25. Aidan W. Southall, *Alur Society* (London: East African Institute of Social Research, 1956), p. 307.

26. Talal Asad, ed., *Anthropology and the Colonial Encounter* (London: Ithaca Press, 1973).

27. Dennis Austin, *Politics in Ghana, 1946-1960* (London: Oxford University Press, 1964), is a mine of information. D. A. Low, *Lion Rampant* (London: Frank Cass, 1973), pp. 172-176, is a concise evaluation of the significance of Ghanian independence. Kwame Nkrumah, *Ghana: The Autobiography of Kwame Nkrumah* (Edinburgh: Thomas Nelson, 1959), is, of course, indispensable.

28. Cited in Sir Charles J. Jeffries, *The Transfer of Power* (London: Pall Mall Press, 1960), p. 15.

29. Nkrumah, *Ghana*, pp. v-vi.

30. For the decolonization of French West and Equatorial Africa the most useful, succinct account is Michael Crowder and Donal Cruise O'Brien, "French West Africa, 1945-1960," in J. F. A. Ajayi and Michael Crowder, eds., *History of West Africa* (London: Longman, 1974), II, 664-699. Also of interest is H. Grimal, *La Décolonisation, 1919-1963* (Paris: Armand Colin, 1969), and for a large-scale account, Edward Mortimer, *France and the Africans, 1944-1960* (London: Faber and Faber, 1969).

31. Crowder and Cruise O'Brien, "French West Africa," p. 676.

32. *Ibid.*, p. 687.

33. *Ibid.*, p. 686. See also Elliot J. Berg's prescient article, "The Economic Basis of Political Choice in West Africa," *American Political Science Review*, 44:391-405 (1960).

34. Crowder and Cruise O'Brien, "French West Africa," p. 685.

35. *Ibid.*

36. The introduction to Sir Hugh Foot, *A Start in Freedom* (London: Hodder and Stoughton, 1964), pp. 15-16, makes this clear.

37. Kirkman, *Unscrambling an Empire*, p. 13.

38. Donald L. Barnett and Karari Njama, *Mau Mau from Within* (New York: Monthly Review Press, 1967), p. 34. See also Carl G. Rosberg and John Nottingham, *The Myth of Mau Mau: Nationalism in Kenya* (New York: Praeger, 1966), which sets the movement in context.

39. For the Rhodesian unilateral declaration of independence and the Portuguese territories, see chapters 17 and 18.

40. Albert Hourani, "Independence and the Imperial Legacy," *Middle East Forum*, 42:5-27 (1966), is penetrating and suggestive. The quotation is from p. 5.

41. von Albertini, *Decolonization*, p. 450.

42. Roger Anstey, *King Leopold's Legacy: The Congo under Belgian Rule, 1908-1960* (London: Oxford University Press, 1966), pp. 259-260, comments on the significance of the Baudouin-Lumumba confrontation.

43. For the Parti Solidaire Africain platform, see Young, "Decolonization," p. 461. M. Crawford Young, *Politics in the Congo* (Princeton: Princeton University Press, 1965), is a very thorough examination.

Chapter 18. Aftermaths of Empire

1. Information privately supplied in Freetown.

2. For the problems of history and patriotism generally, see J. F. A. Ajayi's important article, "The Place of African History and Culture in the Process of Nation-Building in Africa South of the Sahara," *Journal of Negro Education*, 30:206-213 (1960). Also Ali A. Mazrui's wide-ranging discussion in his *Cultural Engineering and Nation-Building in East Africa* (Evanston, Ill.: Northwestern University Press, 1972), pp. 3-22, and the brief general analysis in Boyd C. Shafer, *Faces of Nationalism* (New York: Harcourt Brace Jovanovich, 1972), pp. 333-336.

3. Kenyatta's speech on August 25, 1961, cited in Robert Buijtenhuis, *Mau Mau Twenty Years After* (The Hague: Mouton, 1973), p. 55. Robert Ruark's sensational *Uhuru* (Lon-

don: Transworld Publishers, 1970), which was first published in 1962, is both a symptom of the white problem in understanding Mau Mau and a large contributor to the stereotype that emerged.

4. M. Crawford Young's "Rebellion and the Congo," in Robert I. Rotberg, ed., *Rebellion in Black Africa* (London: Oxford University Press, 1971), pp. 209-245, especially pp. 229-230 and 236-237, gives an able and brief description of "Lumumbism."

5. M. Crawford Young, *Politics in the Congo* (Princeton: Princeton University Press, 1965), p. 22. Young's study is an invaluable resource on Belgian policy.

6. *Ibid*., pp. 232-306.

7. *Ibid*., pp. 140-161.

8. Cited *ibid*., p. 438.

9. *Ibid*., p. 444, citing E. Janssens, *J'étais le général Janssens*, 1961, p. 153.

10. Young, *Politics in the Congo*, p. 314.

11. Cited *ibid*., p. 315.

12. Cited, with other examples, *ibid*.

13. *Ibid*., p. 316.

14. *Ibid*., p. 576.

15. Young, "Rebellion and the Congo," p. 218.

16. *Ibid*., p. 219.

17. Young, *Politics in the Congo*, p. 577.

18. See also Guy Bernard's brief, mordant "Perspectives pour un sociologie dialectique de la décolonisation du Congo," *Canadian Journal of African Studies*, 6:33-43 (1971), especially p. 34, which should be supplemented by Young's "Rebellion and the Congo," p. 215.

19. Young, "Rebellion and the Congo," pp. 244-245.

20. W. J. M. Mackenzie and Kenneth Robinson, eds., *Five Elections in Africa* (Oxford: Clarendon Press, 1960), p. 465.

21. For example, the *New York Times*, January 2, 1965, was confident that Nigerians would compose their differences by a "typical recourse to the democratic process." Cited in Ken W. J. Post and Michael Vickers's incisive *Structure and Conflict in Nigeria, 1960-1966* (London: Heinemann, 1973), p. 1, along with other notions of Nigeria as the "last stronghold of democracy" in Africa.

22. Mackenzie and Robinson, *Five Elections*, pp. 484-485.

23. Ken W. J. Post, *The Nigerian Federal Election of 1959: Politics and Administration in a Developing Political System* (London: Oxford University Press, 1963), p. 439.

24. Post and Vickers, *Structure and Conflict*, pp. 21-22.

25. Obafemi Awolowo, *Path to Nigerian Freedom*, 1947, p. 49, cited in Post and Vickers, *Structure and Conflict*, p. 20, which has an excellent discussion of ethnicity, pp. 11-35. See also Robin Cohen, *Labour and Politics in Nigeria* (London: Heinemann, 1974), pp. 24-34, for a lucid analysis.

26. S. K. Panter-Brick, ed., *Nigerian Politics and Military Rule: Prelude to the Civil War* (London: Athlone Press, 1970).

27. Post and Vickers, *Structure and Conflict*, p. 54.

28. Cohen, *Labour and Politics*, p. 199.

29. *Ibid*., p. 28.

30. Cited in Ruth First's *The Barrel of a Gun* (London: Allen Lane, 1970), p. 334, a comprehensive study of African military coups.

31. Richard Stryker, "Developmental Strategy in the Ivory Coast," in Michael F. Lofchie, ed., *The State of the Nations* (Berkeley: University of California Press, 1971), pp. 119-139, a careful, sober appraisal of the problems of the new states by American political scientists.

32. Immanuel Wallerstein, "The Range of Choice," in Lofchie, *State of the Nations*, p. 22.

33. An important pioneer work, predicting the likelihood of the civilian system breaking down *before* it happened, was Martin Kilson, *Political Change in a West African State: A Study of the Modernization Process in Sierra Leone* (Cambridge: Harvard University Press, 1966).

34. Cited in Ali A. Mazrui, *Violence and Thought* (London: Longmans, 1969), p. 3.

35. Henry Bienen, "National Security in Tanganyika after the Mutiny," *Transition*, 5:39-48 (1965), an indispensable account reprinted in the very useful collection edited by Lionel Cliffe and John S. Saul, *Socialism in Tanzania* (Nairobi: East African Publishing House, 1972), I, 216-225.

36. Cited in Mazrui, *Cultural Engineering*, p. 169.

37. Cited in First, *Barrel of a Gun*, pp. 205-206.

38. Cited in Bienen, "National Security," p. 220.

39. Cited, with commentary, in Mazrui, *Violence and Thought*, p. 5.

40. Cited in Bienen, "National Security," p. 219.

41. *Ibid.*, pp. 216-225.

42. Cited in Mazrui, *Cultural Engineering*, p. 171.

43. *Ibid.*, pp. 169-173 and 230-233.

44. *Ibid.*, p. 172.

45. *Ibid.*, p. 231.

46. For Nyerere's ideas, see *The Arusha Declaration and TANU's Policy on Socialism and Self-Reliance* (Dar es Salaam: TANU, 1967), and Julius K. Nyerere, *Nyerere on Socialism* (Dar es Salaam: Oxford University Press, 1969). I. A. Shivji, "Tanzania: The Silent Class Struggle," along with much else that is relevant, is printed in Cliffe and Saul, *Socialism in Tanzania*, II, 304-330.

47. For parallels in other areas of Africa, see J. P. N'Diaye, *La jeunesse africaine face à l'impérialisme* (Paris: Maspero, 1971), for Francophone Africa, and Ukpabi Asika, "The Uses of Literacy: Notes towards a Definition of the Nigerian Intellectual," *Nigerian Opinion*, 3:154 (1967), cited in Lofchie, *State of the Nations*, pp. 20-21.

48. Okot p'Bitek, "Indigenous Ills," in Cliffe and Saul, *Socialism in Tanzania*, II, 293.

49. *Ibid*. For a sympathetic discussion of "Nizers," John S. Saul, "The State in Post-Colonial Societies: Tanzania," in Ralph Miliband and John Saville, eds., *The Socialist Register, 1974* (London: Merlin Press, 1974), pp. 349-372.

50. Okot p'Bitek, "Indigenous Ills," II, 293.

51. Tom Mboya, "This So-Called Elite," interview by Viviene Barton, *Sunday Nation* (Nairobi), April 27, 1969, cited in Mazrui, *Cultural Engineering*, p. 254.

52. Julius K. Nyerere, *Freedom and Socialism* (London: Oxford University Press, 1965), p. 320.

53. Mazrui, *Cultural Engineering*, pp. 252-255, discusses Nyerere's ideas on socialism through technological gradualism.

54. The collapse of the Portuguese dicatatorship has excited much comment. I have found Kenneth Maxwell, "Portugal: A Neat Revolution," *New York Review of Books*, June 13, 1974, pp. 16-21, especially enlightening.

55. Lionel Cliffe, Peter Lawrence, and Richard Moorsome, "Western Economic and Political Involvement in Portugal and the Colonies in the 1970s," *Ufahumu*, 4:145-165 (1973).

56. Cited in Ruth First's shrewd assessment, "Southern Africa after Spinola," *Ufahumu*, 5:88-108 (1974).

57. See Bibliography: Selected Supplementary Reading.

Bibliography

Bibliography

Works Cited

OFFICIAL PAPERS

United Kingdom, *Parliamentary Papers*:
1865, 5 (412). Report from Select Committee on West African Settlements.
1899, 60 (c. 9388; c. 9391). Report on the Insurrection in the Sierra Leone Protectorate.
1923, 18 (c. 1922). Memorandum on Indians in Kenya.

BOOKS

Abernethy, David B. *The Political Dilemma of Popular Education: An African Case*. Stanford: Stanford University Press, 1969.
Abshire, David M., and Michael A. Samuels, eds. *Portuguese Africa: A Handbook*. London: Pall Mall Press, 1969.
Adam, Heribert. *Modernizing Racial Domination: South Africa's Political Dynamics*. Berkeley: University of California Press, 1971.
———, ed. *South Africa: Sociological Perspectives*. London: Oxford University Press, 1971.
Ajayi, J. F. A. "Colonialism: An Episode in African History," in Lewis H. Gann and Peter Duignan, eds. *Colonialism in Africa, 1870-1960*. Vol. 1. Cambridge: Cambridge University Press, 1969.
———. "The Continuity of African Institutions under Colonialism," in Terence O. Ranger, ed. *Emerging Themes of African History*. Nairobi: East African Publishing House, 1968.
———. "A Survey of the Cultural and Political Regions of Africa at the Beginning of the Nineteenth Century," in Joseph C. Anene and Godfrey N. Brown, eds. *Africa in the Nineteenth and Twentieth Centuries: A Handbook for Teachers and Students*. Ibadan: Ibadan University Press, 1966.
———, and Michael Crowder, eds. *History of West Africa*. Vol. 2. London: Longman, 1974.
Alexandre, Pierre. "Chiefs, *Commandants* and Clerks" and "Chieftaincy in French West Africa," in Michael Crowder and Obaro Ikime, eds. *West African Chiefs*. New York: Africana Publishing Corp., 1970.

369

Alexandrowicz, C. H. "The Partition of Africa by Treaty," in K. Ingham, ed. *Foreign Relations of African States*. London: Butterworths, 1974.

Alldridge, T. J. *The Sherbro and Its Hinterland*. London: Macmillan, 1901.

Alpers, Edward A. "Towards a History of the Expansion of Islam in East Africa," in T. O. Ranger and Isaria Kimambo, eds. *The Historical Study of African Religion*. London: Heinemann, 1972.

Amin, Samir. *Neo-Colonialism in West Africa*. Harmondsworth: Penguin, 1973.

Ancel, J. *Géographie des frontières*. Paris: Gallimard, 1938.

Anene, Joseph C. *The International Boundaries of Nigeria*. London: Longmans, 1970.

———. *Southern Nigeria in Transition, 1885-1906: Theory and Practice in a Colonial Protectorate*. Cambridge: Cambridge University Press, 1966.

———, and Godfrey Brown, eds. *Africa in the Nineteenth and Twentieth Centuries: A Handbook for Teachers and Students*. Ibadan: Ibadan University Press, 1966.

Anstey, Roger. *Britain and the Congo in the Nineteenth Century*. Oxford: Clarendon Press, 1962.

———. *King Leopold's Legacy: The Congo under Belgian Rule, 1908-1960*. London: Oxford University Press, 1966.

Arrighi, Giovanni. "The Political Economy of Rhodesia," in Giovanni Arrighi and John S. Saul. *Essays on the Political Economy of Africa*. New York: Monthly Review Press, 1973.

———, and John S. Saul. *Essays on the Political Economy of Africa*. New York: Monthly Review Press, 1973.

Arusha Declaration and TANU's Policy on Socialism and Self-Reliance, The. Dar es Salaam: Publicity Section of TANU, 1967.

Asad, Talal, ed. *Anthropology and the Colonial Encounter*. London: Ithaca Press, 1973.

Ascherson, Neal. *The King Incorporated*. London: Allen and Unwin, 1963.

Aswiaju, I. A. "The Alaketu of Ketu and the Onimeko of Meko: The Changing Status of Two Yoruba Rulers under French and British Rule," in Michael Crowder and Obaro Ikime, eds. *West African Chiefs*. New York: Africana Publishing Corp., 1970.

Austen, Ralph A. *Northwest Tanzania under German and British Rule: Colonial Policy and Tribal Politics, 1889-1939*. New Haven: Yale University Press, 1968.

———. "Varieties of Trusteeship: African Territories under British and French Mandate, 1919-1939," in Prosser Gifford and William Roger Louis, eds. *France and Britain in Africa: Imperial Rivalry and Colonial Rule*. New Haven: Yale University Press, 1971.

Austin, Dennis. "Institutional Problems of the Gold Coast," in *What Are the Problems of Parliamentary Government in West Africa?* London: Hansard Society, 1958.

———. *Politics in Ghana, 1946-1960*. London: Oxford University Press, 1964.

Awolowo, Obafemi. *Path to Nigerian Freedom*. London: Faber and Faber, 1947.

Axelson, Eric. *Portugal and the Scramble for Africa, 1875-1891*. Johannesburg: Witwatersrand University Press, 1967.

Aydelotte, William O. *Bismarck and British Colonial Policy*. Philadelphia: University of Pennsylvania Press, 1937.

Ayliff, Rev. John, and Rev. Joseph Whiteside. *History of the Abambo, Generally Known as Fingos*. 1912. Reprint ed., Cape Town: Struik, 1962.

Azikiwe, Nnamdi. *My Odyssey: An Autobiography*. London: Hurst, 1970.

Baldwin, Robert E. *Economic Development and Export Growth: A Study of Northern Rhodesia*. Berkeley: University of California Press, 1966.

Banton, Michael. "Social Alignment and Identity in a West African City," in Hilda Kuper, ed. *Urbanization and Migration in West Africa*. Berkeley: University of California Press, 1965.

———. *West African City*. London: Oxford University Press, 1957.

Barnett, Donald L., and Karari Njama. *Mau Mau from Within*. New York: Monthly Review Press, 1967.

Battle, Vincent M., and Charles H. Lyons, eds. *Essays in the History of African Education*. New York: Teachers College Press, Columbia University, 1970.

Beck, Hastings. *Meet the Cape Food*. Cape Town: Purnell, 1956.

Behrman, Lucy C. *Muslim Brotherhoods and Politics in Senegal*. Cambridge: Harvard University Press, 1970.

Bennett, George. "British Settlers North of the Zambezi," in L. H. Gann and Peter Duignan, eds. *Colonialism in Africa, 1870-1960*. Vol. 2. Cambridge: Cambridge University Press, 1970.

———. *Kenya: A Political History*. London: Oxford University Press, 1963.

———. "Settlers and Politics in Kenya, up to 1945," in Vincent Harlow, E. M. Chilver, and Alison Smith, eds. *History of East Africa*. Vol. 2. Oxford: Clarendon Press, 1965.

Betts, Raymond F. *Assimilation and Association in French Colonial Theory, 1890-1914*. New York: Columbia University Press, 1961.

Biobaku, S. O. *The Egba and Their Neighbours, 1842-1872*. Oxford: Clarendon Press, 1957.

Blakemore, Priscilla. "Assimilation and Association in French Educational Policy and Practice," in Vincent M. Battle and Charles H. Lyons, eds. *Essays in the History of African Education*. New York: Teachers College Press, Columbia University, 1970.

Bley, Helmut. "Social Discord in South West Africa," in Prosser Gifford and William Roger Louis, eds. *Britain and Germany in Africa: Imperial Rivalry and Colonial Rule*. New Haven: Yale University Press, 1967.

———. *South-West Africa under German Rule, 1894-1914*. London: Heinemann, 1971.

Blundell, Sir Michael. *So Rough A Wind*. London: Weidenfeld and Nicholson, 1964.

Blyden, Edward W. *Christianity, Islam and the Negro Race*. London, 1887.

Boggs, S. Whittemore. *International Boundaries*. New York: Columbia University Press, 1940.

Bohannan, Paul. *African Outline*. Harmondsworth: Penguin Books, 1966.

———, and Laura Bohannan. *Tiv Economy*. London: Longmans, 1968.

———, and Philip D. Curtin. *Africa and Africans*. New York: Natural History Press, 1964.

Bond, Brian. *Victorian Military Campaigns*. London: Hutchinson, 1967.

Brett, E. A. *Colonialism and Underdevelopment in East Africa*. London: Heinemann, 1973.

Bromberger, Norman. "Economic Growth and Political Change in South Africa," in Adrian Leftwich, ed. *South Africa: Economic Growth and Political Change*. London: Allison and Busby, 1974.

Brown, Richard. "Anthropology and Colonial Rule: Godfrey Wilson and the Rhodes-Livingstone Institute, Northern Rhodesia," in Talal Asad, ed. *Anthropology and the Colonial Encounter*. London: Ithaca Press, 1973.

Brownlee, Charles. *Reminiscences of Kaffir Life and History*. Lovedale, 1896.

Brunschwig, Henri. *French Colonialism, 1871-1914: Myths and Realities*. London: Pall Mall Press, 1964.

Bryce, James. *Impressions of South Africa*. 2d ed. London, 1898.

Buell, Raymond Leslie. *The Native Problem in Africa*. 1928. Reprint ed., London: Frank Cass, 1965.

Buijtenhuis, Robert. *Mau Mau Twenty Years After*. The Hague: Mouton: 1973.

Bull, Mary. "Indirect Rule in Northern Nigeria, 1900-1911," in Kenneth Robinson and Frederick Madden, eds. *Essays in Imperial Government*. Oxford: Basil Blackwell, 1963.

Burn, W. L. *Age of Equipoise*. London: Routledge & Kegan Paul, 1964.

Butler, Jeffrey, ed. *Boston University Papers in African History.* Vol. 1. Boston: Boston University Press, 1966.

Cairns, H. A. C. *Prelude to Imperialism: British Reactions to Central African Society, 1840-1890.* London: Routledge & Kegan Paul, 1965.

Callwell, Charles E. *Small Wars: Their Principles and Practice.* London: Her Majesty's Stationery Office, 1896, and 3d ed., enlarged, 1906.

Cardinall, Allan W. *The Gold Coast, 1931.* Accra: Government Printer, 1931.

Carter, George F. *Man and the Land: A Cultural Geography.* 2d ed. New York: Holt, Rinehart and Winston, 1968.

Chilcote, Ronald H. *Portuguese Africa.* Englewood Cliffs, N.J.: Prentice-Hall, 1967.

Chilver, Elizabeth M. "Native Administration in the West Central Cameroons, 1902-1954," in Kenneth Robinson and Frederick Madden, eds. *Essays in Imperial Government.* Oxford: Basil Blackwell, 1963.

———. "Paramountcy and Protection in the Cameroons: The Bali and the Germans," in Prosser Gifford and William Roger Louis, eds. *Britain and Germany in Africa: Imperial Rivalry and Colonial Rule.* New Haven: Yale University Press, 1967.

Clapham, Sir John. *An Economic History of Modern Britain.* Vol. 3. Cambridge: Cambridge University Press, 1963.

Clarke, John I. *Population Geography and the Developing Countries.* Oxford: Pergamon, 1971.

Cliffe, Lionel, and John S. Saul, eds. *Socialism in Tanzania.* Nairobi: East African Publishing House, 1972.

Clignet, Remi, and Philip J. Foster. *The Fortunate Few: A Study of Secondary Schools and Students in the Ivory Coast.* Evanston, Ill.: Northwestern University Press, 1966.

Cohen, Robin. *Labour and Politics in Nigeria.* London: Heinemann, 1974.

Cohen, William B. *Rulers of Empire: The French Colonial Service in Africa.* Stanford: Hoover Institution Press, 1971.

Coleman, James. *Nigeria: Background to Nationalism.* Berkeley: University of California Press, 1958.

Collected Seminar Papers on the Societies of South Africa in the Nineteenth and Twentieth Centuries. Vol. 3. London: Institute of Commonwealth Studies, University of London, 1973.

Coquéry-Vidrovitch, Catherine. *Le Congo au temps des grandes compagnies concessionaires, 1899-1930.* Paris: Mouton, 1972.

———. "French Colonization in Africa to 1920: Administration and Economic Development," in L. H. Gann and Peter Duignan, eds. *Colonialism in Africa, 1870-1960.* Vol. 1. Cambridge: Cambridge University Press, 1969.

———, and Henri Moniot. *L'Afrique noire de 1800 à nos jours.* Paris: Presses Universitaires de France, 1974.

Cowan, L. Gray, James O'Connell, and David G. Scanlon, eds. *Education and Nation-Building in Africa.* London: Pall Mall Press, 1965.

Cox-George, Norman A. *Finance and Development in West Africa: The Sierra Leone Experience.* London: Dobson, 1961.

Crowder, Michael. "The 1914-1918 European War and West Africa," in J. F. A. Ajayi and Michael Crowder, eds. *History of West Africa.* Vol. 2. London: Longman, 1974.

———. "The 1939-1945 War and West Africa," in J. F. A. Ajayi and Michael Crowder, eds. *History of West Africa.* Vol. 2. London: Longman, 1974.

———. *Senegal: A Study in French Assimilation Policy.* London: Oxford University Press, 1962.

————. *West Africa under Colonial Rule*. London: Hutchinson, 1968.

————, ed. *West African Resistance: The Military Response to Colonial Occupation*. London: Hutchinson, 1971.

————, and Donal Cruise O'Brien. "French West Africa, 1945-1960," in J. F. A. Ajayi and Michael Crowder, eds. *History of West Africa*. Vol. 2. London: Longman, 1974.

————, and Obaro Ikime, eds. *West African Chiefs*. New York: Africana Publishing Corp., 1970.

Crowe, Sybil E. *The Berlin West African Conference, 1884-1885*. London: Longmans, 1942.

Curtin, Philip D. *The Image of Africa: British Ideas and Action, 1780-1850*. Madison: University of Wisconsin Press, 1964.

————, ed. *Africa and the West: Intellectual Responses to European Culture*. Madison: University of Wisconsin Press, 1972.

————, ed. *Imperialism*. New York: Harper and Row, 1971.

Danquah, J. B. *Self-help and Expansion*. Accra: Gold Coast Continuation Committee, Gold Coast Youth Conference, [1943].

Davenport, R. H. *The Beginnings of Urban Segregation in South Africa: The Natives (Urban Areas) Act of 1923 and Its Background*. Grahamstown: Institute of Social and Economic Research, Rhodes University, 1971.

Davis, J. Merle, ed. *Modern Industry and the African: An Enquiry into the Effect of the Copper Mines of Central Africa upon Native Society and the Work of the Christian Missions*. 2d. ed. London: Frank Cass, 1967.

de Courcel, Geoffroy. *L'Influence de la Conférence de Berlin de 1885 sur le droit colonial international*. Paris: Editions Internationales, 1935.

Denoon, Donald. *A Grand Illusion*. London: Longman, 1973.

————. "Participation in the 'Boer War,'" in Bethwell A. Ogot, ed. *War and Society in Africa: Ten Studies*. London: Frank Cass, 1972.

————. *Southern Africa since 1800*. London: Longman, 1972.

Deschamps, Hubert. "L'Afrique Occidentale, Centrale et du Nord-Est," in Jean Ganiage, Hubert Deschamps, and Odette Guitard. *L'Afrique au XXe Siècle*. Paris, Sirey, 1966.

————. "French Colonial Policy in Tropical Africa between Two World Wars," in Prosser Gifford and William Roger Louis, eds. *France and Britain in Africa: Imperial Rivalry and Colonial Rule*. New Haven: Yale University Press, 1971.

————, ed. *Histoire générale de l'Afrique noire, de Madagascar et des Archipels*, vol. 2, *De 1800 à nos jours*. Paris. Presses Universitaires de France, 1971.

————. *Les Méthodes et doctrines coloniales de la France*. Paris: Armand Colin, 1953.

de Villiers, René. "Afrikaner Nationalism," in Monica Wilson and Leonard Thompson, eds. *The Oxford History of South Africa*, vol. 2, *South Africa 1870-1966*. Oxford: Clarendon Press, 1971.

de Wet, C. R. *Three Years' War*. Westminster: Constable, 1902.

Dike, Kenneth O. *Trade and Politics in the Niger Delta*. London: Oxford University Press, 1950.

Dodson, Richard. "Congo-Léopoldville," in David G. Scanlon, ed. *Church, State and Education in Africa*. New York: Teachers College Press, Columbia University, 1966.

Douglas, Mary. *The Lele of the Kasai*. London: Oxford University Press, 1963.

————, and Phyllis M. Kaberry, eds. *Men in Africa*. London: Tavistock Publications, 1969.

Duffy, James. *Portuguese Africa*. Cambridge: Harvard University Press, 1959.

————. *A Question of Slavery*. Oxford: Clarendon Press, 1967.

Dyck, H. L., and H. P. Krosby, eds. *Empire and Nations*. Toronto: University of Toronto Press, 1969.

Ehrlich, Cyril. "The Uganda Economy, 1903-1945," in Vincent Harlow, E. M. Chilver, and Alison Smith, eds. *History of East Africa*. Vol. 2. Oxford: Clarendon Press, 1965.

Eliot, Sir Charles. "The East Africa Protectorate," in Charles S. Golden, ed. *The Empire and the Century*. London: John Murray, 1905.

Elliott, C. M. "Agriculture and Economic Development in Africa: Theory and Experience, 1880-1914," in E. L. Jones and S. J. Woolf, eds. *Agrarian Change and Economic Development*. London: Methuen University Paperback, 1974.

Emerson, Rupert. *Self-Determination Revisited in the Era of Decolonization*. Occasional Papers, no. 9. Cambridge: Center for International Affairs, Harvard University Press, 1964.

Ene, John C. *Insects and Man in West Africa*. Ibadan: Ibadan University Press, 1963.

Epstein, A. L. *Politics in an Urban African Community*. Manchester: Manchester University Press, 1958.

Evans, Maurice S. *Black and White in South East Africa*. London: Longmans, 1911.

———. *Black and White in the Southern States of America*. London: Longmans, 1915.

Evans-Pritchard, E. E. *The Nuer*. Oxford: Clarendon Press, 1940.

Fage, John, "British and German Colonial Rule: A Synthesis and Summary," in Prosser Gifford and William Roger Louis, eds. *Britain and Germany in Africa: Imperial Rivalry and Colonial Rule*. New Haven, Yale University Press, 1967.

Fearn, Hugh. *An African Economy: A Study of the Economic Development of Nyanza Province of Kenya*. Oxford: Oxford University Press, 1961.

Feis, Herbert. *Europe: The World's Banker, 1870-1914*. New Haven: Yale University Press, 1935.

Fernandez, James W. "Fang Representations under Acculturation," in Philip D. Curtin, ed. *Africa and the West: Intellectual Responses to European Culture*. Madison: University of Wisconsin Press, 1972.

Fieldhouse, D. K. *The Theory of Capitalist Imperialism*. London: Longmans, 1967.

First, Ruth. *The Barrel of a Gun*. London: Allen Lane, 1970.

Firth, Raymond. *Man and Culture: An Evaluation of the Work of Malinowski*. London: Routledge & Kegan Paul, 1957.

Flint, John E. "Britain and the Partition of West Africa," in John E. Flint and Glyndwr Williams, eds. *Perspectives of Empire*. London: Longmans, 1973.

———. *Sir George Goldie and the Making of Nigeria*. London: Oxford University Press, 1960.

———, and Glyndwr Williams, eds. *Perspectives of Empire*. London: Longmans, 1973.

Foot, Sir Hugh. *A Start in Freedom*. London: Hodder and Stoughton, 1964.

Ford, Richard B. "The Urban Trek: Some Comparisons of American and South African Mobility," in Heribert Adam, ed. *South Africa: Sociological Perspectives*. London: Oxford University Press, 1971.

Foster, Philip J. *Education and Social Change in Ghana*. London: Routledge & Kegan Paul, 1965.

Frankel, S. Herbert. *Capital Investment in Africa*. London: Oxford University Press, 1938.

Fyfe, Christopher. *Africanus Horton, 1835-1883: West African Scientist and Patriot*. New York: Oxford University Press, 1972.

———. *A History of Sierra Leone*. London: Oxford University Press, 1962.

———, ed. *Sierra Leone Inheritance*. London: Oxford University Press, 1964.

———, and Eldred Jones, eds. *Freetown: A Symposium*. Freetown: Sierra Leone University Press, 1968.

Galbraith, John S. *Mackinnon and East Africa*. Cambridge: Cambridge University Press, 1972.

———. *The Reluctant Empire: British Policy on the South African Frontier, 1834-1854.* Berkeley: University of California Press, 1963.

Ganiage, Jean. *L'Expansion coloniale de la France sous la Troisième République.* Paris: Payot, 1968.

———, Hubert Deschamps, and Odette Guitard. *L'Afrique au XXe Siècle.* Paris: Sirey, 1966.

Gann, Lewis H. *A History of Northern Rhodesia: Early Days to 1953.* London: Chatto and Windus, 1964.

———. *A History of Southern Rhodesia: Early Days to 1934.* London: Chatto and Windus, 1965.

———, and Peter Duignan, eds. *Colonialism in Africa, 1870-1960,* vol. 1, *The History and Politics of Colonialism, 1870-1914;* vol. 2, *The History and Politics of Colonialism, 1914-1960.* Cambridge: Cambridge University Press, 1969-70.

———, and Michael Gelfand. *Huggins of Rhodesia: The Man and His Country.* London: Allen and Unwin, 1964.

Gavin, R. J., and J. A. Betley, eds. *The Scramble for Africa: Documents on the Berlin West African Conference and Related Subjects, 1884-1885.* Ibadan: Ibadan University Press, 1973.

Geiss, Imanuel. *The Pan-African Movement.* London: Methuen, 1974.

Gifford, Prosser. "Indirect Rule: Touchstone or Tombstone for Colonial Policy?" in Prosser Gifford and William Roger Louis, eds. *Britain and Germany in Africa: Imperial Rivalry and Colonial Rule.* New Haven: Yale University Press, 1967.

———, and William Roger Louis, eds. *Britain and Germany in Africa: Imperial Rivalry and Colonial Rule.* New Haven: Yale University Press, 1967.

———, eds. *France and Britain in Africa: Imperial Rivalry and Colonial Rule.* New Haven: Yale University Press, 1971.

———, and Timothy C. Weiskel. "African Education in a Colonial Context," in Prosser Gifford and William Roger Louis, eds. *France and Britain in Africa: Imperial Rivalry and Colonial Rule.* New Haven: Yale University Press, 1971.

Gluckman, Max. *The Judicial Process among the Barotse.* Manchester: Manchester University Press, 1954.

Golden, Charles S., ed. *The Empire and the Century.* London: John Murray, 1905.

Good, Charles M., Jr. *Dimensions of East African Culture.* East Lansing: African Studies Center, Michigan State University, 1966.

Gourou, Pierre. *The Tropical World.* 4th ed. London: Longmans, 1966.

Graham, Gerald S. *Peculiar Interlude.* Sydney: University of Sydney Press, 1959.

Gray, Richard, and David Birmingham, eds. *Pre-Colonial African Trade: Essays on Trade in Central and Eastern Africa before 1900.* London: Oxford University Press, 1970.

Gray, Robert F. "Medical Research: Some Anthropological Aspects," in Robert A. Lystad, ed. *The African World.* London: Pall Mall Press, 1965.

Grimal, H. *La Décolonisation, 1919-1963.* Paris: Armand Colin, 1969.

Hailey, Lord. *An African Survey: A Study of Problems Arising in Africa South of the Sahara.* London: Oxford University Press, 1938.

———. *An African Survey Revised 1956.* London: Oxford University Press, 1957.

———. *Native Administration and Political Development in British Tropical Africa.* London: His Majesty's Stationery Office, 1942.

Hammond, Richard J. *Portugal and Africa, 1815-1910: A Study in Uneconomic Imperialism.* Stanford: Stanford University Press, 1966.

Hance, William A. *The Geography of Modern Africa.* New York: Columbia University Press, 1964.

Hancock, W. K. *Survey of British Commonwealth Affairs*, vol. 2, *Problems of Economic Policy*. London: Oxford University Press, 1942.

———. *Wealth of Colonies*. Cambridge: Cambridge University Press, 1950.

Hancock, W. P. *Smuts: The Fields of Force*. Cambridge: Cambridge University Press, 1968.

Hardy, Georges. *Une Conquête morale: L'Enseignement en Afrique Occidentale Française*. Paris: Armand Colin, 1917.

Hargreaves, John D. *Prelude to the Partition of West Africa*. London: Macmillan, 1963.

Harlow, Vincent, E. M. Chilver, and Alison Smith, eds. *History of East Africa*. Vol. 2. Oxford: Clarendon Press, 1965.

Heard, Kenneth A. *General Elections of South Africa, 1943-1970*. London: Oxford University Press, 1974.

Henderson, W. O. "German East Africa," in Vincent Harlow, E. M. Chilver, and Alison Smith, eds. *History of East Africa*. Vol. 2. Oxford: Clarendon Press, 1965.

Herskovits, Melville J. *The Human Factor in Changing Africa*. New York: Knopf, 1962.

———. "Peoples and Cultures in Sub-Saharan Africa." Reprinted in Peter J. M. McEwan and Robert B. Sutcliffe, eds. *The Study of Africa*. London: Methuen, 1965.

Hertslet, Sir Edward. *The Map of Africa by Treaty*. 3 vols. London: His Majesty's Stationery Office, 1909. Reprint 3d ed., Frank Cass, 1967.

Hill, Polly. *The Migrant Cocoa-Farmers of Southern Ghana*. Cambridge: Cambridge University Press, 1963.

Hinden, Rita. *Empire and After*. London: Essential Books, 1949.

Hinsley, F. H. *Sovereignty*. London: C. A. Watts, 1966.

———, ed. *New Cambridge Modern History*. Vol. 11. Cambridge: Cambridge University Press, 1962.

Hoagland, Jim. *South Africa: Civilizations in Conflict*. London: Allen and Unwin, 1973.

Hodgkin, Thomas. *Nationalism in Tropical Africa*. London: Muller, 1956.

Hooker, James R. *Black Revolutionary*. London: Pall Mall Press, 1967.

Hopkins, Anthony G. *An Economic History of West Africa*. London: Longman, 1973.

Hopkins, Elizabeth. "The International Boundary as a Factor in the Extension of Colonial Control," in Daniel F. McCall, Norman R. Bennett, and Jeffrey Butler, eds. *Boston University Papers on Africa*, vol. 2, *Eastern African History*. Boston: Boston University Press, 1962.

Hunter, Monica. *Reactions to Conquest*. 2d ed. London: Oxford University Press, 1961.

Hyam, Ronald. *Elgin and Churchill at the Colonial Office*. London: Macmillan, 1968.

———. *The Failure of South African Expansion, 1908-1948*. London: Macmillan, 1972.

Iliffe, John. "The Age of Improvement and Differentiation," in I. N. Kimambo and A. J. Temu, eds. *A History of Tanzania*. Nairobi: East African Publishing House, 1969.

———. *Tanganyika under German Rule, 1905-1912*. Cambridge: Cambridge University Press, 1969.

Ingham, K., ed. *Foreign Relations of African States*. London: Butterworths, 1974.

James, Wendy. "The Anthropologist as Reluctant Imperialist," in Talal Asad, ed. *Anthropology and the Colonial Encounter*. London: Ithaca Press, 1973.

Janssens, E. *J'étais le général Janssens*. Brussels: Charles Dessart, 1961.

Jeffries, Sir Charles J. *The Transfer of Power*. London: Pall Mall Press, 1960.

Johns, Sheridan W. III. "Trade Union, Political Pressure Group or Mass Movement? The Industrial and Commercial Workers' Union of South Africa," in Robert I. Rotberg and Ali. A. Mazrui, eds. *Protest and Power in Black Africa*. New York: Oxford University Press, 1970.

Johnson, G. Wesley, Jr. *The Emergence of Black Politics in Senegal*. Stanford: Stanford University Press, 1971.

Johnston, Sir Harry H. *The Negro in the New World*. London: Methuen, 1910.

Johnston, W. Ross. *Sovereignty and Protection: A Study of British Jurisdictional Imperialism in the Late Nineteenth Century*. Durham, N.C.: Duke University Press, 1973.

Jones, Abeudu Bowen. "The Republic of Liberia," in J. F. A. Ajayi and Michael Crowder, eds. *History of West Africa*. Vol. 2. London: Longman: 1974.

Jones, E. L. and S. J. Woolf, eds. *Agrarian Change and Economic Development*. London: Methuen University Paperbacks, 1974.

Jones, Stephen B. *Boundary-Making*. Washington, D. C.: Carnegie Endowment for International Peace, 1945.

Kadalie, Clements. *My Life and the ICU: The Autobiography of a Black Trade Unionist in South Africa*. Ed. Stanley Trapido. London: Frank Cass, 1970.

Kanya-Forstner, A. S. *The Conquest of the Western Sudan: A Study in French Military Imperialism*. Cambridge: Cambridge University Press, 1969.

Karis, Thomas, and Gwendolen M. Carter. *From Protest to Challenge*, vol. 2, *Hope and Challenge*. Stanford: Hoover Institution Press, 1973.

Katzenellenbogen, S. E. *Railways and the Copper Mines of Katanga*. London: Oxford University Press, 1973.

Kay, Geoffrey B., ed. *The Political Economy of Colonialism in Ghana: A Collection of Documents and Statistics, 1900-1960*. Cambridge: Cambridge University Press, 1972.

Kemp, Tom. *Economic Forces in French History*. London: Dobson, 1971.

Kiernan, Victor G. "The Old Alliance: England and Portugal," in Ralph Miliband and John Saville, eds. *The Socialist Register 1973*. London: Merlin Press, 1974.

Kilson, Martin. *Political Change in a West African State: A Study of the Modernization Process in Sierra Leone*. Cambridge: Harvard University Press, 1966.

Kimambo, I. N., and A. J. Temu, eds. *A History of Tanzania* Nairobi: East African Publishing House, 1969.

Kimble, David. *A Political History of Ghana, 1850-1928*. Oxford: Clarendon Press, 1963.

King, Kenneth J. *Pan-Africanism and Education: A Study of Race, Philanthropy and Education in the Southern States of America and East Africa*. Oxford: Clarendon Press, 1971.

Kirk-Greene, A. H. M., ed. *Lugard and the Amalgamation of Nigeria: A Documentary Record*. London: Frank Cass, 1968.

———. *The Principles of British Administration in Nigeria*. London: Oxford University Press, 1965.

Kirkman, W. P. *Unscrambling an Empire*. London: Chatto and Windus, 1966.

Klein, Martin A. *Islam and Imperialism in Senegal: Sine-Saloum, 1847-1914*. Edinburgh: Edinburgh University Press, 1968.

Kruger, D. W. *The Age of the Generals: A Short Political History of the Union of South Africa, 1910-1948*. Johannesburg: Dagbreek Book Store, 1958.

Kruger, Rayne. *Good-Bye Dolly Gray*. London: Cassell, 1961.

Kuhn, Thomas S. *The Structure of Scientific Revolutions*. Chicago: University of Chicago Press, 1962.

Kuper, Hilda. *The Uniform of Colour*. Johannesburg: Witwatersrand University Press, 1947.

———, ed. *Urbanization and Migration in West Africa*. Berkeley: University of California Press, 1965.

Lackner, Helen. "Social Anthropology and Indirect Rule: Eastern Nigeria 1920-1940," in Talal Asad, ed. *Anthropology and the Colonial Encounter*. London: Ithaca Press, 1973.

Lamb, Alastair. *Asian Frontiers*. London: Pall Mall Press, 1968.

Langley, J. Ayodele. *Pan-Africanism and Nationalism in West Africa, 1900-1945*. Oxford: Clarendon Press, 1973.

Last, Murray. *The Sokoto Caliphate*. London: Longmans, 1967.

Lee, J. M. *Colonial Development and Good Government*. Oxford: Clarendon Press, 1967.

Leftwich, Adrian. "The Constitution and Continuity of South African Inequality: Some Conceptual Questions," in Adrian Leftwich, ed. *South Africa: Economic Growth and Political Change*. London: Allison and Busby, 1974.

———, ed. *South Africa: Economic Growth and Political Change*. London: Allison and Busby, 1974.

Lewis, Roy. *Sierra Leone*. London: Her Majesty's Stationery Office, 1954.

Liebenow, J. Gus. *Liberia: The Evolution of Privilege*. Ithaca, N.Y.: Cornell University Press, 1970.

Lockhart, J. G., and C. M. Woodhouse. *Cecil Rhodes: The Colossus of Southern Africa*. New York: Macmillan, 1963.

Lofchie, Michael F., ed. *The State of the Nations*. Berkeley: University of California Press, 1971.

Lombard, Jacques. *Autorités traditionelles et pouvoirs européens en Afrique noire*. Paris: Armand Colin, 1967.

Louis, William Roger. "The Berlin Congo Conference," in Prosser Gifford and William Roger Louis, eds. *France and Britain in Africa: Imperial Rivalry and Colonial Rule*. New Haven: Yale University Press, 1971.

———. *Great Britain and Germany's Lost Colonies, 1914-1915*. Oxford: Clarendon Press, 1967.

Low, D. A. *Buganda in Modern History*. London: Weidenfeld and Nicholson, 1971.

———. *Lion Rampant*. London: Frank Cass, 1973.

———. "Uganda: The Establishment of the Protectorate, 1894-1919," in Vincent Harlow, E. M. Chilver, and Alison Smith, eds. *History of East Africa*. Vol. 2. Oxford: Clarendon Press, 1965.

———, and R. C. Pratt. *Buganda and British Overrule, 1900-1955*. London: Oxford University Press, 1960.

Lugard, Lady Flora. *A Tropical Dependency*. Facsimile of 1905 ed. London: Frank Cass, 1964.

Lugard, Sir Frederick D. *The Dual Mandate in British Tropical Africa*. Edinburgh, William Blackwood and Sons, 1922.

———. *Political Memoranda*. 1906. Reprint ed., London: Frank Cass, 1970.

Lystad, Robert A., ed. *The African World*. London: Pall Mall Press, 1965.

Mabogunje, A. L. *Yoruba Towns*. Ibadan: Ibadan University Press, 1962.

Mackenzie, W. J. M., and Kenneth Robinson, eds. *Five Elections in Africa*. Oxford: Clarendon Press, 1960.

Macmillan, W. M. "African Development," in C. K. Meek, W. M. Macmillan, and E. R. J. Hussey. *Europe and East Africa*. University of London Heath Clark Lectures, 1939. London: Oxford University Press, 1940.

———. *Bantu, Boer and Briton*. London: Faber and Faber, 1929.

———. *Complex South Africa*. London: Faber and Faber, 1930.

Maine, Henry. *International Law*. London, 1888.

Mair, Lucy. *Native Policies in Africa*. London: George Routledge, 1936.

Malinowski, Bronislaw. *The Dynamics of Culture Change*. New Haven: Yale University Press, 1945.

Maquet, Jacques. *Africanity*. London: Oxford University Press, 1972.

——. "The Cultural Units of Africa: A Classificatory Problem," in Mary Douglas and Phyllis M. Kaberry, eds. *Men in Africa*. London: Tavistock Publications, 1969.

Marais, J. S. *The Fall of Kruger's Republic*. Oxford: Clarendon Press, 1961.

Marks, Shula. *Reluctant Rebellion: The 1906-8 Disturbances in Natal*. Oxford: Clarendon Press, 1970.

Mason, Philip. *The Birth of a Dilemma*. London: Oxford University Press, 1958.

Mazrui, Ali A. *Cultural Engineering and Nation-Building in East Africa*. Evanston, Ill.: Northwestern University Press, 1972.

——. *Violence and Thought*. London: Longmans, 1969.

McCall, Daniel F., Norman R. Bennett, and Jeffrey Butler, eds. *Boston University Papers on Africa*, vol. 2, *Eastern African History*. Boston: Boston University Press, 1962.

McEwan, Peter J. M., and Robert B. Sutcliffe, eds. *The Study of Africa*. London: Methuen, 1965.

McIntyre, W. David. *The Imperial Frontier in the Tropics, 1865-1875*. New York: St. Martins Press, 1967.

Meek, C. K., W. M. Macmillan, and E. R. J. Hussey. *Europe and West Africa*. University of London Heath Clark Lectures, 1939. London: Oxford University Press, 1940.

Meillassoux, Claude, ed. *The Development of Indigenous Trade and Markets in West Africa*. London: Oxford University Press, 1971.

Middleton, John. "Kenya: Administration and Changes in African Life," in Vincent Harlow, E. M. Chilver, and Alison Smith, eds. *History of East Africa*. Vol. 2. Oxford: Clarendon Press, 1965.

Miers, Suzanne. "The Brussels Conference of 1889-1890: The Place of the Slave Trade in the Policies of Great Britain and Germany," in Prosser Gifford and William Roger Louis, eds. *Britain and Germany in Africa: Imperial Rivalry and Colonial Rule*. New Haven: Yale University Press, 1967.

Miliband, Ralph, and John Saville, eds. *The Socialist Register, 1973, 1974*. London: Merlin Press, 1974.

Miner, Horace. "Urban Influences on the Hausa," in Hilda Kuper, ed. *Urbanization and Migration in West Africa*. Berkeley: University of California Press, 1965.

Miracle, Marvin. *Agriculture in the Congo Basin*. Madison: University of Wisconsin Press, 1967.

Moore, Barrington, Jr. *Social Origins of Dictatorship and Democracy*. Harmondsworth: Penguin, 1966.

Morel, E. D. *Affairs of West Africa*. London: Heinemann, 1902.

——. *Nigeria: Its Peoples and Its Problems*. London: Smith Elder and Co., 1911.

Morgan, W. B., and J. C. Pugh. *West Africa*. London: Methuen, 1969.

Morris, H. F. "Protection or Annexation? Some Constitutional Anomalies of Colonial Rule," in H. F. Morris and James S. Read. *Indirect Rule and the Search for Justice: Essays in East African Legal History*. Oxford: Clarendon Press, 1972.

Mortimer, Edward. *France and the Africans, 1944-1960*. London: Faber and Faber, 1969.

Mottoulle, L. *Politique sociale de l'Union Minière du Haut-Katanga pour sa main d'oeuvre indigène*. Brussels: I. R. C. B., 1946.

Moukouri, Jacques Kuoh. *Doigts noirs: Je fus écrivain-interprète au Cameroun*. Montreal: Editions à la page, 1963.

Moyer, R. A. "Some Current Manifestations of Early Mfengu History," in *Collected Seminar Papers on the Societies of Southern Africa in the Nineteenth and Twentieth Centuries*. Vol 3. London: Institute of Commonwealth Studies, University of London, 1973.

Mungeam, G. H. *British Rule in Kenya, 1895-1912: The Establishment of Administration in the East African Protectorate*. Oxford: Clarendon Press, 1966.

Murdock, George P. *Africa: Its Peoples and Their Culture History*. New York: McGraw-Hill, 1959.

Murphy, Agnes. *The Ideology of French Imperialism*. Washington: Catholic University Press, 1948.

Murray, A. Victor. *The School in the Bush*. London: Frank Cass, 1967.

Mwase, Gideon Simeon, ed. *Strike a Blow and Die: A Narrative of Race Relations in Colonial Africa*. Cambridge: Harvard University Press, 1967.

N'Diaye, J. P. *La Jeunesse africaine face à l'impérialisme*. Paris: Maspero, 1971.

Newbury, C. W. "Partition, Development and Trusteeship," in Prosser Gifford and William Roger Louis, eds. *Britain and Germany in Africa: Imperial Rivalry and Colonial Rule*. New Haven: Yale University Press, 1967.

———. "The Tariff Factor in Anglo-French West African Partition," in Prosser Gifford and William Roger Louis, eds. *France and Britain in Africa: Imperial Rivalry and Colonial Rule*. New Haven: Yale University Press, 1971.

Nicolson, I. F. *The Administration of Nigeria, 1900-1960: Men, Methods, and Myths*. Oxford: Clarendon Press, 1969.

Nielson, W. A. *The Great Powers and Africa*. London: Pall Mall Press, 1969.

Nkrumah, Kwame. *Ghana: The Autobiography of Kwame Nkrumah*. Edinburgh: Thomas Nelson, 1959.

Nyerere, Julius K. *Freedom and Socialism*. London: Oxford University Press, 1965.

———. *Nyerere on Socialism*. Dar es Salaam: Oxford University Press, 1969.

O'Brien, Donal B. Cruise. *The Mourides of Senegal: The Political and Economic Organization of an Islamic Brotherhood*. Oxford: Clarendon Press, 1971.

O'Brien, Rita Cruise. *White Society in Black Africa: The French of Senegal*. London: Faber and Faber, 1972.

Ogot, Bethwell A. "Kenya under British Rule," in B. A. Ogot and J. A. Kieran, eds. *Zamani: A Survey of East African History*. Nairobi: East African Publishing House, 1968.

———, ed. *War and Society in Africa: Ten Studies*. London: Frank Cass, 1972.

———, and J. A. Kieran, eds. *Zamani: A Survey of East African History*. Nairobi: East African Publishing House, 1968.

Olusanyu, G. O. *The Second World War and Politics in Nigeria, 1939-1953*. London: Evans Bros., for the University of Lagos, 1973.;

Omer-Cooper, J. D. *The Zulu Aftermath: A Nineteenth Century Revolution in Bantu Africa*. London: Longmans, 1966.

Owen, Roger, and Bob Sutcliffe, eds. *Studies in the Theory of Imperialism*. London: Longmans, 1972.

Palley, Claire. *The Constitutional History and Law of Southern Rhodesia*. Oxford: Clarendon Press, 1966.

Panter-Brick, S. K., ed. *Nigerian Politics and Military Rule: Prelude to the Civil War*. London: Athlone Press, 1970.

Parrinder, Geoffrey. *Religion in Africa*. Harmondsworth: Penguin African Library, 1969.

Pasquier, Roger. "Mauritanie et Senegambie," in Hubert Deschamps. *Histoire générale de l'Afrique noire, de Madagascar et des Archipels*, vol. 2, *De 1800 à nos jours*. Paris: Presses Universitaires de France, 1971.

P'Bitek, Okot. "Indigenous Ills," in Lionel Cliffe and John S. Saul, eds. *Socialism in Tanzania*. Nairobi: East African Publishing House, 1972.

Peel, J. D. Y. *Aladura: A Religious Movement among the Yoruba*. London: Oxford University Press, 1968.

Perham, Margery. *The Colonial Reckoning*. London: Fontana, 1961.

————. *Colonial Sequence, 1930-1949: A Chronological Commentary upon British Colonial Policy Especially in Africa.* London: Methuen, 1967.

————. *Lugard,* vol. 2, *The Years of Authority.* London: Collins, 1960.

————. *Native Administration in Nigeria.* London: Oxford University Press, 1937.

Person, Yves. "Guinea-Samori," in Michael Crowder, ed. *West African Resistance: The Military Response to Colonial Occupation.* London: Hutchinson, 1971.

Peterson, John. *Province of Freedom: A History of Sierra Leone, 1787-1870.* London: Faber and Faber, 1969.

Pettigrew, Thomas Joseph. *Memoirs of the Life and Writings of the Late John Coakley Lettsom.* 3 vols. London, 1817.

Platt, D. C. M. *Finance, Trade, and Politics in British Foreign Policy, 1815-1914.* Oxford: Clarendon Press, 1968.

Post, Ken W. J. *The Nigerian Federal Election of 1959: Politics and Administration in a Developing Political System.* London: Oxford University Press, 1963.

————, and Michael Vickers. *Structure and Conflict in Nigeria, 1960-1966.* London: Heinemann, 1973.

Prescott, J. R. V. *The Geography of Frontiers and Boundaries.* London: Hutchinson, 1965.

Projet d'organisation de l'enseignement au Congo Belge avec le concours des sociétés des missions nationales. Brussels: Société Anonyme, 1925.

Randles, W. G. "L'Afrique du Sud et du Zambèze, 1800-1880," in Hubert Deschamps. *Histoire générale de l'Afrique noire, de Madagascar et des Archipels,* vol. 2, *De 1800 à nos jours.* Paris: Presses Universitaires de France, 1971.

Ranger, Terence O. "Missionary Adaptation of African Religious Institutions, the Masasi Case," in T. O. Ranger and Isaria Kimambo, eds. *The Historical Study of African Religion.* London: Heinemann, 1972.

————. "The Movement of Ideas," in I. N. Kimambo and A. J. Temu, eds. *A History of Tanzania.* Nairobi: East African Publishing House, 1969.

————. *Revolt in Southern Rhodesia, 1896-1897.* London: Heinemann, 1967.

————, ed. *Emerging Themes of African History.* Nairobi: East African Publishing House, 1968.

————, and Isaria Kimambo, eds. *The Historical Study of African Religion.* London: Heinemann, 1972.

Raum, Otto F. "The Demand for and Support of Education in African Tribal Society," in *Year Book of Education.* London: Evans Brothers, 1956.

Rex, John. *Race, Colonialism and the City.* London: Routledge & Kegan Paul, 1973.

————. *Race Relations in Sociological Theory.* London: Weidenfeld and Nicholson, 1970.

Roberts, Andrew, ed. *Tanzania before 1900.* Nairobi: East African Publishing House, 1968.

Robinson, Austin. *Fifty Years of Commonwealth Development.* Cambridge: Cambridge University Press, 1972.

Robinson, Kenneth, and Frederick Madden, eds. *Essays in Imperial Government.* Oxford: Basil Blackwell, 1963.

Robinson, Ronald E., and John Gallagher (with Alice Denny). *Africa and the Victorians: The Official Mind of Imperialism.* London: Macmillan, 1961.

————. "The Partition of Africa," in F. H. Hinsley, ed. *New Cambridge Modern History.* Vol. 11. Cambridge: Cambridge University Press, 1962.

Rodney, Walter. *How Europe Underdeveloped Africa.* London: Bougle-L'Ouverture, 1972.

Rosberg, Carl G., and John Nottingham. *The Myth of Mau Mau: Nationalism in Kenya.* New York: Praeger, 1966.

Rotberg, Robert I. *Christian Missionaries and the Creation of Northern Rhodesia, 1880-1929.* Princeton: Princeton University Press, 1965.

——. "Psychological Stress and the Question of Identity: Chilembwe's Revolt Reconsidered," in Robert I. Rotberg and Ali A. Mazrui, eds. *Protest and Power in Black Africa*. New York: Oxford University Press, 1970.

——. "Resistance and Rebellion in British Nyasaland and German East Africa, 1888-1915: A Tentative Comparison," in Prosser Gifford and William Roger Louis, eds. *Britain and Germany in Africa: Imperial Rivalry and Colonial Rule*. New Haven: Yale University Press, 1967.

——. *The Rise of Nationalism in Central Africa*. Cambridge: Harvard University Press, 1966.

——, ed. *Rebellion in Black Africa*. London: Oxford University Press, 1971.

——, and Ali A. Mazrui, eds. *Protest and Power in Black Africa*. New York, Oxford University Press, 1970.

Ruark, Robert. *Uhuru*. 1962. Reprint ed., London: Transworld Publishers, 1970.

Rubenson, Sven E. "Adwa in 1896: The Resounding Protest," in Robert I. Rotberg and Ali A. Mazrui, eds. *Protest and Power in Black Africa*. New York: Oxford University Press, 1970.

Rudin, Harry R. *Armistice, 1918*. New Haven: Yale University Press, 1944.

——. *Germans in the Cameroons*. New Haven: Yale University Press, 1938.

Salomon, Laurence. "The Economic Background of the Revival of Afrikaner Nationalism," in Jeffrey Butler, ed. *Boston University Papers in African History*. Vol. 1. Boston: Boston University Press, 1966.

Sarraut, Albert. *La Mise en valeur des colonies françaises*. Paris: Payot, 1923.

Saul, John S. "The State in Post-Colonial Societies: Tanzania," in Ralph Miliband and John Saville, eds. *The Socialist Register, 1974*. London: Merlin Press, 1974.

Saul, S. B. *The Myth of the Great Depression, 1873-1896*. London: Macmillan, 1969.

——. *Studies in British Overseas Trade, 1870-1914*. Liverpool: Liverpool University Press, 1960.

Saylor, Ralph G. *The Economic System of Sierra Leone*. Durham, N.C.: Duke University Press, 1967.

Scanlon, David G., ed. *Church, State and Education in Africa*. New York: Teachers College Press, Columbia University, 1966.

Schaffer, Bernard B. "The Concept of Preparation," in Bernard B. Schaffer. *The Administrative Factor*. London: Frank Cass, 1973.

Schapera, Isaac. *A Short History of the Bakgatla-bagaKgafela*. Cape Town: School of African Studies, University of Cape Town, 1942.

——. *Tribal Innovators: Tswana Chiefs and Social Change, 1795-1940*. London: University of London Press, 1970.

Schoffeleers, M. "The Resistance of the Nyau Societies to the Roman Catholic Missions in Colonial Malawi," in T. O. Ranger and Isaria Kimambo, eds. *The Historical Study of African Religion*. London: Heinemann, 1972.

Shafer, Boyd C. *Faces of Nationalism*. New York: Harcourt Brace Jovanovich, 1972 (and 1974).

Shepperson, George, and Thomas Price. *Independent African*. Edinburgh: Edinburgh University Press, 1958.

Shivji, I. A. "Tanzania: The Silent Class Struggle," in Lionel Cliffe and John S. Saul, eds. *Socialism in Tanzania*. Vol. 2. Nairobi: East African Publishing House, 1972.

Shorter, Aylward. *Chiefship in Western Tanzania: A Political History of the Kimbu*. Oxford: Clarendon Press, 1972.

——. "The Kimbu," in Andrew Roberts, ed. *Tanzania before 1900*. Nairobi: East African Publishing House, 1968.

Sillery, Anthony. *Botswana*. London: Methuen, 1974.

Simons, H. J., and R. E. Simons. *Class and Colour in South Africa, 1850-1950*. Harmondsworth: Penguin, 1969.

Skinner, Elliott P. *The Mossi of the Upper Volta*. Stanford: Stanford University Press, 1964.

———. "The Mossi under Colonial Rule," in Michael Crowder and Obaro Ikime, eds. *West African Chiefs*. New York: Africana Publishing Corp., 1970.

Slade, Ruth. *King Leopold's Congo*. London: Oxford University Press, 1962.

Smith, Alan. "The Trade of Delagoa Bay as a Factor in Nguni Politics, 1750-1835," in Leonard M. Thompson, ed. *African Societies in Southern Africa*. London: Heinemann, 1969.

Smith, John. "The Relationship of the British Political Officer to His Chief in Northern Nigeria," in Michael Crowder and Obaro Ikime, eds. *West African Chiefs*. New York: Africana Publishing Corp., 1970.

Smuts, Jan C. *Africa and Some World Problems*. Oxford: Clarendon Press, 1930.

Sorrenson, M. P. K. *Origins of European Settlement in Kenya*. Nairobi: Oxford University Press, 1968.

Southall, Aidan W. *Alur Society*. London: East African Institute of Social Research, 1956.

Stamp, L. D. *Africa: A Study in Tropical Development*. 2d ed. New York: John Wiley, 1964.

———, ed. *A History of Land Use in Arid Regions*. Paris: UNESCO, 1961.

Stengers, Jean. "King Leopold and Anglo-French Rivalry, 1882-1884," in Prosser Gifford and William Roger Louis, eds. *France and Britain in Africa: Imperial Rivalry and Colonial Rule*. New Haven: Yale University Press, 1971.

Stigand, C. H. *The Land of Zinj*. London: Thomas Nelson, 1913.

———, *Native Administration*. London: Constable, 1914.

Stocking, George W., Jr. *Race, Culture and Evolution*. New York: Free Press, 1968.

Stryker, Richard. "Developmental Strategy in the Ivory Coast," in Michael F. Lofchie, ed. *The State of the Nations*. Berkeley: University of California Press, 1971.

Stultz, Newell M. *Afrikaner Politics in South Africa*. Berkeley: University of California Press, 1974.

Sundkler, Bengt G. M. *Bantu Prophets in South Africa*. 2nd ed. London: Oxford University Press, 1961.

Suret-Canale, Jean. *Afrique noire occidentale et centrale: De la colonialism aux indépendance, 1945-1960*. Paris: Editions Sociales, 1972.

———. *French Colonialism in Tropical Africa, 1900-1945*. London: Hurst, 1971.

Swanson, Maynard W. "South West Africa in Trust," in Prosser Gifford and William Roger Louis, eds. *Britain and Germany in Africa: Imperial Rivalry and Colonial Rule*. New Haven: Yale University Press, 1967.

Sy, Cheikh Tidiane. *La Confrérie sénégalaise des Mourides*. Paris: Présence Africaine, 1969.

Symonds, Richard. *The British and Their Successors: A Study in the Development of Government Services in the New States*. London: Faber and Faber, 1966.

Talbot, William J. "Land Utilization in the Arid Regions of Southern Africa: Part 1, South Africa," in L. D. Stamp, ed. *A History of Land Use in Arid Regions*. Paris: UNESCO, 1961.

Taylor, Alan J. P. *Germany's First Bid for Colonies, 1884-1885*. Hamden, Conn.: Archon Books, 1967.

Temple, Charles L. *Native Races and Their Rulers*. Cape Town: Argus Publishing Co., 1918.

Thompson, Leonard M., ed. *African Societies in Southern Africa*. London: Heinemann, 1969.

———. "Co-operation and Conflict: The High Veld," in Monica Wilson and Leonard Thompson, eds. *The Oxford History of South Africa*, vol. 1, *South Africa to 1870*. Oxford: Clarendon Press, 1969.

———. "France and Britain in Africa: A Perspective," in Prosser Gifford and William Roger Louis, eds. *Britain and France in Africa: Imperial Rivalry and Colonial Rule*. New Haven: Yale University Press, 1971.

———. *The Unification of South Africa, 1902-1910*. Oxford: Clarendon Press, 1960.

Tordoff, William. *Ashanti under the Prempehs*. London: Oxford University Press, 1965.

Touval, Saadia. *The Boundary Politics of Independent Africa*. Cambridge: Harvard University Press, 1972.

Trapido, Stanley. "The South African Republic: Class Formation and the State, 1850-1900," in *Collected Seminar Papers on the Societies of South Africa in the Nineteenth and Twentieth Centuries*. Vol 3. London: Institute of Commonwealth Studies, University of London, 1973.

Trollope, Anthony. *South Africa*. 1878. Reprint ed., London: Dawson, 1968.

Turnbull, Colin. *The Forest People*. New York: Simon and Schuster, 1961.

———. *The Lonely African*. London: Chatto and Windus, 1963.

Turner, Henry A., Jr. "Bismarck's Imperialist Venture," in Prosser Gifford and William Roger Louis, eds. *Britain and Germany in Africa: Imperial Rivalry and Colonial Rule*. New Haven: Yale University Press, 1967.

Tylden, G. *The Rise of the Basuto*. Cape Town: Juta, 1950.

von Albertini, Rudolf. *Decolonization: The Administration and Future of the Colonies, 1919-1960*. New York: Doubleday, 1971.

Walker, Eric A. *The Great Trek*. London: A. and C. Black, 1934. Reprint 3d ed., London: Longmans, 1957.

———. *A History of Southern Africa*. London: Longmans, 1959.

Wallerstein, Immanuel. "The Range of Choice," in Michael F. Lofchie, ed. *The State of the Nations*. Berkeley: University of California Press, 1971.

Walshe, Peter. *The Rise of African Nationalism in South Africa: The A. N. C., 1912-1952*. London: Hurst, 1970.

Watson, Richard A. , and Patty Jo Watson. *Man and Nature: An Anthropological Essay in Human Ecology*. New York: Harcourt, Brace and World, 1969.

Webster, J. B. "Political Activity in British West Africa, 1900-1940," in J. F. A. Ajayi and Michael Crowder, eds. *History of West Africa*. Vol. 2. London: Longman, 1974.

———. "Tribalism, Nationalism and Patriotism in Nineteenth and Twentieth Century Africa," in H. L. Dyck and H. P. Krosby, eds. *Empire and Nations*. Toronto: University of Toronto Press, 1969.

———, A. A. Boahen, and H. O. Idowo. *The Growth of African Civilization: The Revolutionary Years—West Africa since 1800*. London: Longmans, 1967.

Wehler, Hans-Ulrich. "Industrial Growth and Early German Imperialism," in Roger Owen and Bob Sutcliffe, eds. *Studies in the Theory of Imperialism*. London: Longmans, 1972.

Welensky, Sir Roy. *Welensky's 4,000 Days*. London: Collins, 1964.

Welsh, David. "The Political Economy of Afrikaner Nationalism," in Adrian Leftwich, ed. *South Africa: Economic Growth and Political Change*. London: Allison and Busby, 1974.

Wheare, Joan. *The Nigerian Legislative Council*. London: Faber and Faber, 1950.

Whittesley, Derwent. *The Earth and the State*. 2d ed. New York: Henry Holt, 1944.

Widstrand, Carl G., ed. *African Boundary Problems*. Uppsala: Scandinavian Institute of African Studies, 1969.

Wilson, Ellen G. *The Loyal Blacks*. New York: G. P. Putnam's Sons, 1976.
———. *A West African Cook Book*. New York: M. Evans, 1971.
Wilson, Francis, and Dominique Perrot, eds. *Outlook on a Century, 1870-1970*. Braam-fontein: Lovedale Press, 1973.
Wilson, Henry S., ed. *Origins of West African Nationalism*. London: Macmillan, 1969.
Wilson, Monica. "The Nguni People," in Monica Wilson and Leonard Thompson, eds. *The Oxford History of South Africa*, vol. 1, *South Africa to 1870*; vol. 2, *South Africa 1870-1966*. Oxford: Clarendon Press, 1969, 1971.
Winch, Donald. *Economics and Policy: A Historical Survey*. London: Fontana, 1972.
Wolff, Richard D. *The Economics of Colonialism: Britain and Kenya, 1870-1930*. New Haven: Yale University Press, 1974.
Wright, Marcia. *German Missions in Tanganyika, 1891-1941: Lutherans and Moravians in the Southern Highlands*. Oxford: Clarendon Press, 1971.
Wrigley, C. G. *Crops and Wealth in Uganda*. East African Studies, no 12, Kampala: East African Institute of Social Research, 1959.
———. "Kenya: The Patterns of Economic Life, 1902-1945," in Vincent Harlow, E. M. Chilver, and Alison Smith, eds. *History of East Africa*. Vol. 2. Oxford: Clarendon Press, 1965.
Young, M. Crawford. "Decolonization in Africa," in L. H. Gann and Peter Duignan, eds. *Colonialism in Africa, 1870-1960*. Vol. 2. Cambridge: Cambridge University Press, 1970.
———. *Politics in the Congo*. Princeton: Princeton University Press, 1965.
———. "Rebellion and the Congo," in Robert I. Rotberg, ed. *Rebellion in Black Africa*. London: Oxford University Press, 1971.

ARTICLES

Abbott, George C. "A Re-examination of the 1929 Colonial Development Act." *Economic History Review* 24:68-81 (1971).
Afigbo, A. E. "West African Chiefs during Colonial Rule and After." *Odu* 5:99-110 (1971).
Ajayi, J. F. A. "The Place of African History and Culture in the Process of Nation-Building in Africa South of the Sahara." *Journal of Negro Education* 30:206-213 (1960).
Alpers, E. A. "Re-thinking African Economic History: A Contribution to the Discussion of the Roles of Underdevelopment." *Ufahamu* 3:97-129 (1973).
Amin, Samir "Underdevelopment and Dependence in Black Africa." *Journal of Modern African Studies* 10:503-524 (1972).
———. "Underdevelopment and Dependence in Black Africa: Historical Origins." *Journal of Peace Research* 2:106-119 (1970).
Amunemey, D. E. K. "German Administration in Southern Togo." *Journal of African History* 10:623-639 (1969).
Asika, Ukpabi. "The Uses of Literacy: Notes towards a Definition of the Nigerian Intellectual." *Nigerian Opinion* 3:154 (1967).
Atmore, Anthony, and Peter Sanders. "Sotho Arms and Amunition in the Nineteenth Century." *Journal of African History* 12:535-544 (1971).
———, and Nancy Westlake. "A Liberal Dilemma: A Critique of the Oxford History of South Africa." *Race* 14:107-136 (1972).
———, J. M. Chirenje, and S. I. Mudenge. "Firearms in South Central Africa." *Journal of African History* 12:545-556 (1971).
Balandier, Georges. "La Situation coloniale: Approche théorique." *Cahiers internationaux de sociologie* 11:44-79 (1951).

Basalla, George. "The Spread of Western Science." *Science* 156:611-622 (1967).

Berg, Elliot J. "Backward-Sloping Labor Supply Functions in Dual Economies—The African Case." *Quarterly Journal of Economics* 75:468-492 (1961).

———. "The Economic Basis of Political Choice in West Africa." *American Political Science Review* 44:391-405 (1960).

Bernard, Guy. "Perspectives pour une sociologie dialectique de la décolonisation du Congo." *Canadian Journal of African Studies* 6:33-43 (1971).

Bienen, Henry. "National Security in Tanganyika after the Mutiny." *Transition* 5:39-48 (1965).

Blainey, G. "Lost Causes of the Jameson Raid." *Economic History Review* 18:350-366 (1965).

Bouche, Denise. "Autrefois, notre pays s'appellait la Gaule . . . " *Cahiers d'études africaines* 8:110-122 (1968).

Brunschwig, Henri. "De la résistance africaine à l'impérialisme européen." *Journal of African History* 15:47-64 (1974).

———. "Politique et économie dans l'empire français d'Afrique noire." *Journal of African History* 11:401-417 (1970).

Bundy, Colin. "The Emergence and Decline of a South African Peasantry." *African Affairs* 71:369-388 (1972).

Cliffe, Lionel, Peter Lawrence, and Richard Moorsome. "Western Economic and Political Involvement in Portugal and the Colonies in the 1970s." *Ufahumu* 4:145-165 (1973).

Clignet, Remi. "Inadequacies of the Notion of Assimilation in African Education." *Journal of Modern African Studies* 8:425-444 (1970).

———, and Philip J. Foster. "French and British Colonial Education in Africa." *Comparative Education Review* 8:191-198 (1964).

Crouzet, F. "Commerce et empire: L'Expérience britannique du libre-échange à la première guerre mondiale." *Annales* 19:281-310 (1964).

Crowder, Michael. "Indirect Rule—French and British Style." *Africa* 34:197-205 (1964).

Curtin, Philip D. " 'Scientific Racism' and the British Theory of Empire." *Journal of the Historical Society of Nigeria* 2:40-51 (1960).

Dachs, Anthony J. "Missionary Imperialism—the Case of Bechuanaland." *Journal of African History* 13:647-658 (1972).

d'Azevedo, Warren L. "Some Historical Problems in the Delineation of a Central West Atlantic Region." *Annals of the New York Academy of Sciences* 96:512-538 (1962).

Deschamps, Hubert. "Et Maintenant Lord Lugard?" *Africa* 23:295-306 (1963).

———. "Les Frontières de la Senegambie." *Revue française d'études politiques africaines* 80:44-57 (1972).

Dorjahn, V. R., and Christopher Fyfe. "Landlord and Stranger: Change in Tenancy Relations in Sierra Leone." *Journal of African History* 3:391-417 (1962).

Ehrensaft, Philip. "The Political Economy of Informal Empire in Pre-colonial Nigeria, 1807-1884." *Canadian Journal of African Studies* 6:451-490 (1972).

Ferreira, A. Rita. "Labour Migration among the Mozambique Thonga." *Africa* 30:243-245 (1960).

First, Ruth. "Southern Africa after Spinola." *Ufahumu* 5:88-108 (1974).

Fisher, Humphrey J. "Conversion Reconsidered." *Africa* 63:27-40 (1973).

Furley, O. W., and T. Watson. "Education in Tanganyika between the Wars." *South Atlantic Quarterly* 65:471-490 (1966).

Goody, Jack, and Joan Buckley. "Inheritance and Women's Labour in Africa." *Africa* 43:108-121 (1973).

Green, R. H., and Stephen Hymer. "Cocoa in the Gold Coast: A Study in the Relations between African Farmers and Agricultural Experts." *Journal of Economic History* 36:299-319 (1966).

Hailey, Lord. "Nationalism in Africa." *African Affairs* 36:134-147 (1937).

Hair, P. E. H. "Africanism: The Freetown Contribution." *Journal of Modern African Studies* 5:521-539 (1967).

Harris, Marvin. "Labour Migration among the Mozambique Thonga: Cultural and Political Factors." *Africa* 29:50-66 (1959).

Henderson, Ian. "The Limits of Colonial Power: Race and Labour Problems in Colonial Zambia, 1900-1953." *Journal of Imperial and Commonwealth History* 2:294-307 (1974).

Herskovits, Melville J. "The Cattle Complex in East Africa." *American Anthropologist* n.s. 28:230-273, 361-388, 494-528, 633-664 (1926).

———. "A Preliminary Consideration of the Culture Areas of Africa." *American Anthropologist* n.s. 26:50-64 (1924).

Hillier, Alfred P. "The Native Races of South Africa." *Proceedings of the Royal Colonial Institute* 31:30-67 (1898-99).

Hopkins, Anthony G. "Economic Imperialism in West Africa." *Economic History Review* 21:580-600 (1968).

Horton, Robin. "African Conversion." *Africa* 61:85-108 (1971).

Hourani, Albert. "Independence and the Imperial Legacy." *Middle East Forum* 42:5-27 (1966).

Hyam, Ronald. "African Interests and the South Africa Act, 1908-1910." *Historical Journal* 13:85-105 (1970).

Idowu, H. O. "Café-au-lait: Senegal's Mulatto Community in the Nineteenth Century." *Journal of the Historical Society of Nigeria* 6:271-288 (1972).

Ikime, Obaro. "Colonial Conquest and Resistance in Southern Nigeria." *Journal of the Historical Society of Nigeria* 4:251-270 (1972).

Kiwanuka, M. Semakula. "Colonial Policies and Administrations in Africa: The Myths of the Contrasts." *African Historical Studies* 3:295-313 (1970).

Klein, Martin A. "Social and Economic Factors in the Muslim Revolution in Senegambia." *Journal of African History* 13:419-442 (1972).

———. "Traditional Political Institutions and Colonial Domination." *African Historical Studies* 4:659-668 (1971).

Koehl, Robert. "The Uses of the University. Past and Present in Nigerian Educational Culture." *Comparative Education Review* 15:116-131 (1971).

Korsah, K. A. "Indirect Rule—a Means to an End." *African Affairs* 43:177-182 (1944).

Linden, Jane, and Ian Linden. "John Chilembwe and the New Jerusalem." *Journal of African History* 12:629-651 (1971).

Lloyd, P. C. "Kings, Chiefs and Local Government." *West Africa*, January 31, 1953.

Lonsdale, J. M. "Some Origins of Nationalism in East Africa." *Journal of African History* 9:119-146 (1968).

Makinde, J. O. Oye. "West Africa between the World Wars: The Economics of the Colonial Impact." *Ghana Social Science Journal* 2:74-86 (1972).

Marder, Murrey. "Nixon Altered U.S. Policy in Southern Africa." *International Herald Tribune* (Paris), October 14, 1974.

Maxwell, Kenneth. "Portugal: A Neat Revolution." *New York Review of Books*, June 13, 1974, pp. 16-21.

Mboya, Tom. "This So-Called Elite." Interview, *Sunday Nation* (Nairobi), April 27, 1969.

McKay, Donald V. "Colonialism in the French Geographical Movement." *Geographical Review* 33:214-232 (1943).

Mitchell, Philip E. "The Anthropologist and the Practical Man: A Reply and a Question." *Africa* 3:217-223 (1930).

Mumford, W. Bryant. "Education and the Social Adjustment of Primitive Peoples of Africa to European Culture." *Africa* 2:138-159 (1929).

——. "Malangali School "*Africa* 3:265-290 (1930).

Newbury, C. W. "The Protectionist Revival in French Colonial Trade." *Economic History Review*, 2d ser. 21:337-348 (1968).

——, and A. S. Kanya-Forstner. "French Policy and the Origins of the Scramble for West Africa." *Journal of African History* 10:233-276 (1969).

Oloruntimehin, B. Olatunji. "Anti-French Coalition of African States and Groups in the Western Sudan, 1889-1893." *Odu* 3:3-21 (1970).

——. "Theories of 'Official Mind' and 'Military Imperialism' as Related to the French Conquest of the Western Sudan." *Journal of the Historical Society of Nigeria* 5:419-434 (1970).

Pallinder-Law, Agneta. "Aborted Modernization in West Africa? The Case of Abeokuta." *Journal of African History* 15:65-82 (1974).

Person, Yves. "L'Afrique noire et ses frontières." *Revue française d'études politiques africaines* 80:18-43 (1972).

Phillips, Earl. "The Egba at Abeokuta: Acculturation and Political Change, 1830-1870." *Journal of African History* 10:117-131 (1969).

Platt, D. C. M. "British Policy during the 'New Imperialism.'" *Past and Present* 39:120-138 (1968).

——. "The National Economy and British Imperial Expansion before 1914." *Journal of Imperial and Commonwealth History* 2:3-14 (1931).

Raum, Otto F. "Indirect Rule as a Political Education." *Internationale Zeitschrift für Erziehung* 5:97-107 (1936).

Robertson, H. M. "150 Years of Economic Contact between White and Black." *South African Journal of Economics* 2:403-425 (1934), 3:1-25 (1935).

Saul, S. B. "The Economic Significance of 'Constructive Imperialism.'" *Journal of Economic History* 17:173-192 (1957).

Schneider, Harold K. "The Subsistence Role of Cattle among the Pakot and in East Africa." *American Anthropologist* n.s. 59:278-301 (1957).

Shepperson, George. "Africa, the Victorians and Imperialism." *Revue belge de philologie et d'histoire* 40:1228-1238 (1962).

Spitzer, Leo, and La Ray Denzer, "I. T. A. Wallace-Johnson and the West African Youth League. Part II: The Sierra Leone Period, 1938-1945." *International Journal of African Historical Studies* 6:565-601 (1973).

Stengers, Jean. "The Partition of Africa. I. L'Impérialisme colonial de la fin du XIXe siècle: Mythe ou réalité." *Journal of African History* 3:469-491 (1962).

Stokes, Eric. "Late Nineteenth Century Colonial Expansion and the Attack on the Theory of Economic Imperialism: A Case of Mistaken Identity?" *Historical Journal* 12:285-301 (1969).

Thomas, Roger G. "Forced Labour in British West Africa: The Case of the Northern Territories of the Gold Coast, 1906-1927." *Journal of African History* 14:79-103 (1973).

Thorson, W. B. "Charles de Freycinet, French Empire-Builder." *Research Studies of the State College of Washington* 12:257-282 (1943).

Touval, Saadia. "Treaties, Borders, and the Partition of Africa." *Journal of African History* 7:279-292 (1966).

Trapido, Stanley. "The Origins of the Cape Franchise Qualifications of 1853." *Journal of African History* 5:37-54 (1964).

————. "South Africa in a Comparative Study of Industrialization." *Journal of Development Studies* 7:309-320 (1971).

von Strandmann, Harmut Pogge. "Germany's Colonial Expansion under Bismarck." *Past and Present* 42:140-159 (1969).

Wallerstein, Immanuel. "Africa in a Capitalist World." *Issue: A Quarterly Journal of Africanist Opinion* 3:1-11 (1973).

Wehler, Hans-Ulrich. "Bismarck's Imperialism, 1862-1890." *Past and Present* 45:119-155 (1970).

Willis, John Ralph. "Jihad fi Sabil Allah, Its Doctrinal Basis in Islam and Some Aspects of Its Evolution in Nineteenth Century West Africa." *Journal of African History* 8:395-415 (1967).

Wilson, Andrew. "Why the U.S. Tilted towards Vorster." *Observer* (London), January 5, 1975.

Yates, Barbara. "African Reaction to Education: The Congolese Case." *Comparative Education Review* 15:158-171 (1971).

UNPUBLISHED STUDIES

Barnes, Clive. "The Harlem Riot." Seminar paper, University of York, 1971.

Howard, Allen M. "Big Men, Traders and Chiefs: Power, Commerce and Spatial Change in the Sierra Leone-Guinea Plain, 1865-1895." Ph.D. thesis, University of Wisconsin, 1972.

Lonsdale, J. M. "A Political History of Nyanza, 1883-1945." Ph.D. thesis, Cambridge University, 1966 (to be published).

McCall, Malcolm. "Luawa under British Rule." Ph.D. thesis, University of York, 1974.

Selected Supplementary Reading

Works cited in the text usually have been commented upon in context. Many other works have enriched my understanding of colonization in Africa, however, and a selection of them is included in this bibliographical essay.

Bibliography. Peter Duignan and L. H. Gann, *Colonialism in Africa*, vol. 5, *A Bibliographical Guide to Colonialism in Sub-Saharan Africa* (Cambridge: Cambridge University Press, 1973), is the most comprehensive bibliography available. The bibliographical section in Catherine Coquery Vidrovitch and Henri Moniot's *L'Afrique noire*, pp. 18-86, listed in Works Cited, is also very useful.

Maps. The study of history often involves coping with many unfamiliar place names, so good maps are essential. A wall map is probably best, as, for example, the *African Relief of Land, Political and Communications*, scale 1:9,000,000, published by George Philip & Son, Ltd. John D. Fage, *An Atlas of African History* (London: Edward Arnold, 1958), is valuable, as is R. Van Chi, ed., *Grand Atlas du continent africain* (Paris: Jeune Afrique, 1973). There are also some good single-country atlases. For example, the series issued by the University of London are models of their kind: J. I. Clarke, ed., *Sierra Leone in Maps*, 1966; D. Hywel Davies, ed., *Zambia in Maps*, 1971; L. Berry, ed., *Tanzania in Maps*, 1971; Stefan von Gnielinski, ed., *Liberia in Maps*, 1972; Swanzie Agnew and Michael Stubbs, eds., *Malawi in Maps*, 1972.

General Histories. Beside the work by Catherine Coquery-Vidrovitch and Henri Moniot, and Hubert Deschamps, ed., *Histoire générale de l'Afrique noire*, both listed in Works Cited, I have found J. Ki-Zerbo, *Histoire de l'Afrique noire* (Paris: Hatier, 1972), and Basil Davidson, *Africa: History of a Continent* (London: Weidenfeld and Nicholson, 1966), especially stimulating.

Regional Histories. Histories of West Africa, edited by J. F. A. Ajayi and Michael Crowder, and of East Africa, by Vincent Harlow, E. M. Chilver, and Alison Smith, have been noted in Works Cited. J. D. Fage's *An Introduction to the History of West Africa* (Cambridge: Cambridge University Press, 1969), marshals a mass of material with great clarity. Terence O. Ranger, ed., *Aspects of Central African History* (London: Heinemann, 1968), is a sound introduction to recent research.

Anthropological Approaches. Ideas deriving from anthropology have become so woven into the general approach of modern scholarship that I have followed the usual practice of historians and cited works by anthropologists, such as M. G. Smith and Monica Wilson, together with the writings by historians on the same topics. Certain works, though, both epitomize the best anthropological insight and are somewhat difficult, for one reason or another, to classify with "straight" histories.

Some of the best of the writings by Georges Balandier have been translated into English and are especially useful to the historian of the "colonial situation"; for example, his *Ambiguous Africa* (New York: Pantheon Books, 1966), and *The Sociology of Black Africa* (London: Andre Deutsch, 1970). For the importance of Balandier in the development of ideas on Africa among the French intelligentsia, see the important article by J. Copans, "Pour une histoire et une sociologie des études africaines," *Cahiers d'études africaines,* 11:422-442 (1971).

Wyatt MacGaffey, *Custom and Government in the Lower Congo* (Berkeley: University of California Press, 1970), opens up new perspectives on the perception of African "customs" by colonial science. Jan Vansina, a prolific and penetrating writer, in his latest and best book, *The Tio Kingdom of the Middle Congo, 1880-1892* (London: Oxford University Press, 1973), makes original contributions to both anthropology and history.

European Expansion. Henri Brunschwig has supplemented his perspicacious study of *French Colonialism* (see Works Cited) with a brief work, *Le Partage de l'Afrique noire* (Paris: Flammarion, 1971), which includes a chronology as well as commentary on various historiographical controversies. Fresh light is thrown on Portuguese colonialism by Allen F. Isaacman in *Mozambique: The Africanization of a European Institution—the Zambesi Prazos, 1750-1902* (Madison: University of Wisconsin Press, 1972), and M. D. D. Newitt, *Portuguese Settlement on the Zambesi: Exploration, Land Tenure and Colonial Rule in East Africa* (London: Longman, 1973). The study of British expansion through chartered companies, first illuminated in John Flint's classic study, *Sir George Goldie and the Making of Nigeria,* has been extended by John S. Galbraith in *Mackinnon and East Africa* (both books listed in Works Cited). Clement F. Goodfellow's *Great Britain and South African Confederation, 1870-1881* (Cape Town: Oxford University Press, 1966), is enlightening on the motivation behind early British attempts to consolidate their position in the South.

African Resistance. Beside Terence Ranger's pioneering *Revolt in Southern Rhodesia,* listed in Works Cited, his "Connections between 'Primary Resistance' Movements and Modern Mass Nationalism in East and Central Africa," *Journal of African History,* 9:437-454 and 631-642 (1968), is seminal. John Hargreaves in "West African States and the European Conquest," in L. H. Gann and Peter Duignan, eds. *Colonialism in Africa, 1870-1960,* vol. 1 (see Works Cited), makes direct comparisons with Ranger's account. Yves Person's *Samori: Une Révolution dyula* (Dakar: IFAN, 1968), is superbly detailed. The succinct examination of African resistance to the Portuguese in Angola by Douglas C. Wheeler and C. Diane Christensen, "To Rise With One Mind: The Bailundu War of 1902," in Franz-Wilhelm Heimer, ed., *Social Change in Angola* (Munich: Weltforum Verlag, 1973), came to my attention after the manuscript of this book was completed.

The European Colonial Regimes. On the British in Africa, Kenneth Robinson's concise *The Dilemma of Trusteeship* (London: Oxford University Press, 1965), is very good on on colonial policy between the wars. Margery Perham's second *Colonial Sequence, 1949-1965* (London: Methuen, 1970), and Sir Charles Jeffries' *Whitehall and the Colonial Service: An Administrative Memoir, 1939-1956* (London: Athlone Press, 1972), also reveal the context in which policy was formulated.

The early development of a corps of Nigerian historians has led to detailed consideration of the colonial regime. In addition to the works cited in the text, I recommend A. E. Afigbo, *The Warrant Chiefs: Indirect Rule in Southeastern Nigeria* (London: Longmans, 1972), and various writings of Takena N. Tamuno, *Nigeria and Elective Representation, 1923-1947* (London: Heinemann, 1966); *The Police in Modern Nigeria, 1861-1965: Origins, Development and Role* (Ibadan: Ibadan University Press, 1970); and *The Evolution of the Nigerian State: The Southern Phase, 1898-1914* (London: Longman, 1972); all of which elucidate important aspects of the colonial period. Obaro Ikime, *Niger-Delta Rivalry: Itsekiri-Urhobo Relations and the European Presence, 1884-1936* (New York: Humanities Press, 1968), sheds light on the interplay among these groups.

Non-Nigerians also have made significant contributions. The anthropologist M. G. Smith's *Government in Zazzau, 1800-1950* (London: Oxford University Press, 1960), is a superb study of indirect rule, and Robert Heussler has followed up his earlier general study of the British colonial service, *Yesterday's Rulers* (Syracuse: Syracuse University Press, 1963), with a well-focused examination of *The British in Northern Nigeria* (London: Oxford University Press, 1968).

Although sizable schools of history have developed elsewhere in the Anglophone sphere, notably in East and Central Africa, where the influences of Bethwell Ogot and Terence Ranger have been very significant, they have shown less preoccupation with the framework of imperial rule. Several of the best works, such as D. A. Low's on Uganda, have been noted in the text. R. E. Wraith's *Guggisberg* (London: Oxford University Press, 1967), is a solid biography of one of the most important colonial governors. John Flint's *Nigeria and Ghana* (Englewood Cliffs, N.J.: Prentice-Hall, 1966), is a compact and learned analysis of the history of the two biggest Anglophone states in West Africa, which sets the colonial regime in historical sequence.

The key works of modern research on broader aspects of French imperialism in Africa, such as William Cohen's *Rulers of Empire* and those by Brunschwig and Suret-Canale, have been noted in the text. J. D. Hargreaves' *The Former French African States* (Englewood Cliffs, N.J.: Prentice-Hall, 1967), is comparable to Flint's study of Nigeria and Ghana. Brian Weinstein's *Eboué* (New York: Oxford University Press, 1972), explores the career of one of the most influential administrators.

On Belgian imperialism, first-rate works by Jean Stengers, other than that cited in the text, are *Combien le Congo a-t-il coûté à la Belgique?* (Brussels: Centre de Recherche et d'Information Socio-Politique, 1957), and *Belgique et le Congo: L'Elaboration de la Charte coloniale* (Brussels: Academie Royale des Sciences Coloniales, 1963).

Marvin Harris's "Portugal's Contribution to the Underdevelopment of Africa and Brazil," in Ronald H. Chilcote, ed., *Protest and Resistance in Angola and Brazil* (Berkeley: University of California Press, 1972), is brief and powerful. Among writers on the German empire, the best modern works by Wehler and von Strandmann on motivation and by Iliffe, Bley, and Chilver on the actualities of colonial rule are cited in the text.

Economics. Alpers' article, "Re-thinking African Economic History," listed in Works Cited, is a good critical analysis of current trends. Several of the important writers, such as Samir Amin, Catherine Coquery-Vidrovitch, Cyril Ehrlich, Polly Hill, Anthony Hopkins, and Christopher Wrigley have been noted in the text. Walter Elkan, *Migrants and Proletarians: Urban Labour in the Economic Development of Uganda* (London: Oxford University Press, 1960), is a careful, balanced treatment of this important theme. J. A. Hellen,

"Colonial Administrative Policies and Agricultural Problems in Tropical Africa," suggests some lines to approach to the history of farming in Africa in M. F. Thomas and G. W. Whittington, eds., *Environment and Land Use in Africa* (London: Methuen, 1969), as also does M. L. Chanock's brief, but very suggestive, "Development and Change in the History of Malawi," in B. Pachai, ed., *The Early History of Malawi* (Evanston, Ill.: Northwestern University Press, 1972). Thomas R. de Gregori's *Technology and the Economic Development of the Tropical African Frontier* (Cleveland: Case Western Reserve Press, 1969), contains a wealth of information as well as controversial views on African development.

Religion. Ranger and Kimambo, eds., *The Historical Study of African Religion*, which has been listed in Works Cited, provides a good survey of recent scholarly trends. Roland Oliver's important *The Missionary Factor in East Africa* (London: Longmans, 1952), pioneered the modern study of missions, which was then developed by some fine Nigerian scholars: J. F. A. Ajayi, *Christian Missions in Nigeria: The Making of a New Elite, 1841-1891* (London: Longmans, 1965); E. A. Ayandele, *The Missionary Impact on Modern Nigeria, 1842-1914: A Political and Social Analysis* (London: Longmans, 1966), and *Holy Johnson, Pioneer of African Nationalism, 1836-1917* (London: Frank Cass, 1970); and F. K. Ekechi, *Missionary Enterprise and Rivalry in Igboland, 1857-1914* (London: Frank Cass, 1972). James Bertin Webster, *The African Churches among the Yoruba, 1888-1922* (Oxford: Clarendon Press, 1964), analyzes the early development of West African separatism, while Harold W. Turner in *History of an African Independent Church* (Oxford: Clarendon Press, 1967), and Gordon M. Haliburton, *The Prophet Harris* (London: Longman, 1971), carry further the story of the "Africanization" of Christianity. Humphrey J. Fisher's *Ahmadiyyah: A Study in Contemporary Islam on the West African Coast* (London: Oxford University Press, 1963), is a perspicacious analysis of developments within African Islam.

The writings of John V. Taylor, *The Growth of the Church in Buganda* (London: SCM Press, 1958); (with Dorothea Lehman) *Christians of the Copperbelt* (London: SCM Press, 1961); and *The Primal Vision: Christian Presence amid African Religion* (London: SCM Press, 1963), are informative and scholarly on developments in East and Central Africa. Frederick B. Welbourn writes very perceptively in *East African Rebels* (London: SCM Press, 1961), and again, in fruitful collaboration with the senior East African historian, Bethwell A. Ogot, in *A Place to Feel at Home: A Study of Two Independent Churches in Western Kenya* (London: Oxford University Press, 1966).

For southern Africa, beside Dachs's short, penetrating article listed in Works Cited, there are now an outstanding study of missions by Claude Hélène Perrot, *Les Sotho et les missionaires européens au XIXeme siècle* (Abidjan: Annales de l'Université d'Abidjan, 1970), and Monica Wilson's study, from the standpoint of a committed Christian and anthropologist, *Religion and the Transformation of Society: A Study in Social Change in Africa* (New York: Cambridge University Press, 1971), which is full of keen insights.

Nationalism. There has been no comprehensive book on African nationalism since Thomas Hodgkin's pioneering study, *Nationalism in Colonial Africa* (London: Muller, 1956). The recent triumph of the African liberation movements in the Portuguese sphere suggests a reappraisal is due. Meanwhile, John Lonsdale's "The Emergence of African Nations: An Historiographical Analysis," *African Affairs*, 67:11-28 (1968), and Pierra Bonafé, *Le Nationalisme africain: Aperçus sur sa naissance et son developpement* (Paris: Foundation Nationale des Sciences Politiques, 1964), are essential reading. Ndabaningi Sithole's *African Nationalism*, 2d ed. (London: Oxford University Press, 1968), ranks with Nyerere's writings, listed in Works Cited, in the power of its exposition. Robert W. July's *The Origins of Modern African Thought: Its Development in West Africa during the Nineteenth and Twentieth Centuries* (London: Faber and Faber, 1968), and Immanuel Geiss, *The Pan-African Movement* (see Works Cited), are useful general surveys. Hollis R. Lynch, *Edward Wilmot Blyden: Pan-Negro Patriot, 1832-1912* (London: Oxford University Press, 1967), lucidly sets this major thinker in context. Ken W. J. Post and George D. Jenkins's biography of Alhaji Adelubu, the "Lion of the West," *The Price of Liberty: Personality and Politics in Colonial Nigeria* (Cambridge: Cambridge University Press, 1973), throws fascinating light on the process of decolonization in Nigeria. The cited studies by J. P. N'Diaye and G. W. Johnson on the Francophone area should be supplemented by Ruth Schacter-Morgenthau's significant work, *Political Parties in French-Speaking West Africa* (London: Oxford University Press, 1964). On Angola, John Marcum's *The Angolan Revolution* (Cambridge: Massachusetts Institute of Technology Press, 1969), is excellent.

Literature. African creative writing is a marvellous aid toward the imaginative leap necessary to comprehend the imperial experience in Africa. The African Writers Series put out by Heinemann's Educational Books covers virtually all the major Anglophone writers and many others from different language groups in translation. Its founding editor, Chinua Achebe, has provided perhaps the most brilliant account of the European impact yet in his trilogy: *Things Fall Apart* (1958; reprint ed., London: Heinemann, 1962); *No Longer at Ease* (London: Heinemann, 1960); and *The Arrow of God* (London: Heinemann, 1964). O. R. Dathorne, *The Black Mind: A History of African Literature* (Minneapolis: University of Minnesota Press, 1974), and Wilfred Cartey, *Whispers from a Continent* (New York: Random House, 1969), are good general surveys of black African writing. Among South African authors, the playright Athol Fugard, and the novelists, Alan Paton, Ezekiel Mphahlele, and Nadine Gordimer (in her later novels) add a fresh dimension to an understanding of their unique society.

Contemporary Developments. Ernest W. Lefever, *Spear and Scepter: Army, Police, and Politics in Tropical Africa* (Washington, D.C.: Brookings Institution, 1970), and Aristide R. Zolberg, *Creating Political Order: The Party-States of West Africa* (Chicago: Rand McNally, 1966), are sober assessments of current political trends. Finally, academic Africanists have learned much from Basil Davidson, a fine journalist and historian who demonstrates the difficult art of viewing contemporary events in historical perspective in *Can Africa Survive? Arguments against Growth without Development* (Boston: Little, Brown & Co., 1974).

Index

Index